Antonio de la Cierva y Lewita – Conde de Ballobar and Duque de Terranova – was born in Vienna in 1885 where his father was serving as Spanish military attaché. In 1911 Ballobar entered the Spanish consular service and in May 1913 Ballobar was appointed consul in Jerusalem. In 1920 he married Rafaela Osorio de Moscoso and the following year, Ballobar resigned his commission as consul and moved back to Spain where he served the Ministry of Foreign Affairs with different assignments. Between 1949 and 1952 he served again as consul in Jerusalem and until 1955, as director of the Obra Pia. Ballobar died in Madrid in 1971, aged 86.

Eduardo Manzano Moreno is a Research Professor at the Consejo Superior de Investigaciones Científicas (CSIC) and Director of its Centro de Ciencias Humans y Sociales (CCHS). His research has concentrated on the history of Muslim Spain and the political implications of historical memory. While studying at the School of Oriental and African Studies (SOAS), University of London, he came across references which led him to identify, locate, and publish in Spanish the Diaries of Conde de Ballobar. His recent publications include 'The Iberian Peninusla and North Africa', in *The New Cambridge History of Islam; Epocas Medievales* and *La gestion de la Memoria.*

Roberto Mazza is an Assistant Professor in the Department of History, Western Illinois University, Macomb, IL. He is also a Research Associate in the Department of History at the School of Oriental and African Studies (SOAS), University of London.

'[This is a] fascinating narrative of daily life in Jerusalem during the Great War as observed by the Spanish consul Ballobar – one of the few European diplomats who remained in the embattled city during the war. Roberto Mazza's erudite introduction – based largely on the underutilized Spanish and Italian archives – contextualizes the diary within the debate about the nature of Ottoman rule of Palestine at the turn of the century. Of particular importance, and originality, is the discussion about the diarist's close relationship with the controversial figure of Cemal Pasha, the Military Governor of Syria, and a leading figure of the Young Turks.' – **Dr. Salim Tamari, Director of the Institute for Palestine Studies, Editor of the** Jerusalem Quarterly, **Professor of Sociology at Birzeit University.**

'With this excellent translation of the Spanish consul Conde de Ballobar's diary, another invaluable historical record is added to our growing knowledge of the history of Jerusalem and its communities during the years of World War I. The diary offers a vivid and lively description of the city and enriches our understanding of the complex reality of this period, with the different agents acting within it: its residents from the various religious and national groups, the representatives of foreign powers as well as the Ottoman authorities. This translation will surely be used as a source for future studies of the city of Jerusalem during the fascinating times of World War I and the change of regimes.' – **Dr. Abigail Jacobson, author of From Empire to Empire: Jerusalem Between Ottoman and British Rule.**

'The Diary of the Spanish consul in Jerusalem, Conde de Ballobar, is a treasure for historians of World War I in Palestine. [Until now] it was a hidden treasure. This translation of the diary into English presents this treasure to the astonished public. From now on, this diary will be an indispensable tool for those who try to really understand the situation in this decisive period almost hundred years ago.' – **Dr. Norbert Schwake, author of Deutsche Soldatengräber in Israel.**

JERUSALEM IN WORLD WAR I

THE PALESTINE DIARY OF A EUROPEAN DIPLOMAT

CONDE DE BALLOBAR

Edited by
EDUARDO MANZANO MORENO
and
ROBERTO MAZZA

Edited by and with an introduction and notes by
ROBERTO MAZZA

New paperback edition published in 2015 by I.B.Tauris & Co. Ltd
London • New York
www.ibtauris.com

First published in hardback in 2011 by I.B.Tauris & Co. Ltd

Copyright original text © 1996 Maria Isabel de la Cierva
Copyright Introduction and notes © 2011, 2015 Roberto Mazza
Copyright Translation © 2011, 2015 Colleen Combs

The right of Roberto Mazza to be identified as the author of this work has been asserted by the author in accordance with the Copyright, Designs and Patents Act 1988.

All rights reserved. Except for brief quotations in a review, this book, or any part thereof, may not be reproduced, stored in or introduced into a retrieval system, or transmitted, in any form or by any means, electronic, mechanical, photocopying, recording or otherwise, without the prior written permission of the publisher.

Every attempt has been made to gain permission for the use of the images in this book. Any omissions will be rectified in future editions.

ISBN: 978 1 78453 066 2
eISBN: 978 0 85773 709 0

A full CIP record for this book is available from the British Library
A full CIP record is available from the Library of Congress

Library of Congress Catalog Card Number: available

To my Parents: Paolo and Carla

CONTENTS

List of Illustrations and Maps   ix

List of Abbreviations   xi

Acknowledgements   xiii

Preface   xv

Introduction   1

1914   27

1915   43

1916   85

1917   126

1918   194

1919   232

Notes   246

Bibliography   268

Glossary   274

Index   278

LIST OF ILLUSTRATIONS AND MAPS

Illustrations

1. Ballobar in his official uniform *(with permission of the family)*
2. Young Ballobar *(with permission of the family)*
3. Mayor of Jerusalem and Turkish Official, 1914-1917 *(Matson Photograph Collection, Library of Congress, 07438)*
4. Enver Paşa visiting the Dome of the Rock, 1916 *(Matson Photograph Collection, Library of Congress, 11599)*
5. Ballobar in the Gethsemane, 1913 *(with permission of the family)*
6. Mosque of Omar, northeast side *(Matson Photograph Collection, Library of Congress, 06628)*
7. Ceremony of the Holy Fire at the Holy Sepulchre *(Matson Photograph Collection, Library of Congress, 00873)*
8. Ballobar at the site of the Good Samaritan *(with permission of the family)*
9. Ballobar amongst local clergy *(with permission of the family)*
10. Ballobar and Casares *(with permission of the family)*
11. Jamal Pasha (Kutchuk) with Zaki Bey, former Military Governor of Jerusalem, St George's Cathedral 1917 *(Matson Photograph Collection, Library of Congress, 08126)*
12. Ballobar with Durieux, French Military Officer *(with permission of the family)*
13. Franciscan monk reading the proclamation in Italian, 1917 *(Matson Photograph Collection, Library of Congress, 00173)*

Maps

Map 1: Modern Jerusalem 1915.   25
Designed and edited by George Adam Smith and prepared under the direction of J.G. Bartholomew. London, Hodder and Stoughton [Public domain]
Map 2: Present Political Divisions 1915.   26
Designed and edited by George Adam Smith and prepared under the direction of J.G. Bartholomew. London, Hodder and Stoughton [Public domain]

LIST OF ABBREVIATIONS

ACTS	Archivio Custodia di Terra Santa
AMAE	Archivo Ministerio des Asuntos Exteriores
ASMAE	Archivio Storico Ministero degli Affari Esteri
ASV	Archivio Segreto Vaticano
LPL	Lambeth Palace Library
MAE	Ministère des Affaires Étrangères
NARA	National Archives and Record Administration
TNA	The National Archives

ACKNOWLEDGEMENTS

I began researching the life of Antonio de la Cierva, Conde de Ballobar, almost by accident. When I was working on my PhD I came across the diary of the Spanish consul, and it came to be one of my most important sources when attempting to discuss Jerusalem in the period of the First World War. I then realized that, because the diary was in Spanish, that the source was likely inaccessible to many working on Middle Eastern or transnational history. When presenting at conferences and talks, discussing Ballobar, his views of Jerusalem and its residents through his recollection of social events, such as dinners, parties and even pool games, I was often pushed to pursue the translation of the diary.

Reaching the end of this work of translation and contextualization, I am indebted to many people and institutions. First and foremost, I am indebted to Professor Eduardo Manzano Moreno, the editor of the Spanish edition of the diary. We first met in 2004 when while I was looking for researching the Spanish archives looking for evidence supporting the entries of the diary entries in the Spanish archives. His edition of the diary has been a useful source for my previous work and an inspiration for the English edition of the diary. Similarly, I must thank the family of the Conde de Ballobar. Not only did they allow me to translate the diary but also provided me with more personal information and invaluable pictures: Their kindness is inestimable.

In the summer of 2009 I left London for the unknown prairies of the American Midwest, moving from SOAS (School of Oriental and African Studies) to Western Illinois University. Here, the project of translation rapidly became a reality when I met Professor Colleen Combs. She was the Professor of Spanish language and literature at Western Illinois University, and she was about to retire when I asked her to translate the diary. She immediately loved the idea: One last goal to accomplish before leaving academia. I must say that she did an excellent job: Considering the way in which Ballobar structured his entries, and the massive use of jargon, it would have been very easy to miss what the consul wished to convey. It has been a pleasure working with her, and I hope Colleen and her husband enjoy their deserved retirement.

I would like to thank my friends and colleagues who read the diary in part or in full and offered valuable advice and were willing to share their sources and knowledge with me. Specifically, I must thank Abigail Jacobson, Issam Nassar, Norbert Schwake and Vivian Ibrahim. On several occasions I presented and published papers relating to Ballobar, and I want to thank everyone who provided useful feedback and contributed to ameliorating my research and writing. In particular I would like to thank Nelida Fuccaro and all my colleagues in the History Department at SOAS. I am also grateful to the staff of the Archives of the Spanish Foreign Office in Madrid, the Italian Foreign Office in Rome, the Archives in London and certainly, the staff of the Vatican Archives and of the Archives of the Custody of the Holy Land and Latin Patriarchate in Jerusalem: I am really grateful to Father Narcyz Klimas and Sister Marija Sijanec.

I would like also to express my gratitude and feelings of friendship with the people of the Kenyon Institute in Jerusalem, as most of the diary was edited while I was there working on my next project of research. I would also like to extend my gratitude to Joanna of I.B.Tauris for her constant support and to Cypriano Stephenson for his impeccable editing and Lily Blouin for her faultless proofreading of the paperback edition.

Finally, my greatest thanks go to Monica, my parents and my friends: Without them this book would not have seen the light of day in such a short amount of time.

PREFACE

The current edition of the diary is based on Professor Eduardo Manzano Moreno's 1996 publication of the original manuscript. The original was written by Antonio de la Cierva y Lewita and is composed of six books.[1] After perusing the manuscript, I decided to adopt the version edited by Manzano Moreno, omitting irrelevant descriptions and very personal issues; missing parts are identifiable by an ellipsis (...). Some modifications have been made to make the English text more readable. In the introduction, I have used the modern Turkish alphabet and spelling for Turkish names, and for Arabic, I followed the spelling of the *Encyclopaedia of Islam*; in the edition of the diary, however, I chose to follow Manzano Moreno's simplified transcription of names and places, adopting a more common spelling (Cemal in Turkish is rendered Djemal in the diary). Ballobar often referred to persons and places without providing much information; I have therefore written entries in the glossary and notes in order to provide more information on names which may be unfamiliar to the reader. Some names and dates were not entirely legible from the manuscript; to keep this edition more scientifically correct I tried to find the correct names and dates, but where this was not possible it has been recorded in the notes. I have anglicized nearly all places' names, and as mentioned above, tried to spell correctly most of the names mentioned in the diary; nevertheless, I was able to make corrections only when I was able to find sources: To this extent I benefited by the precious suggestions of Dr. Norbert Schwake. I added brief comments in the text always between squared parentheses [...] in order to give a full name or the exact geographical location of less known places.

It is difficult to know whether the Spanish diplomat planned to publish the diary at some stage in his life, but I suspect it was written more as a companion to record events and his impressions of war-time Jerusalem, and partly to overcome his immense sense of isolation and distance from Madrid. The language is colloquial, though emotions ranging from anger to excitement are well articulated and very clear. Despite the clear subjectivity of the diary, Ballobar changed his attitudes and opinions of people and philosophies throughout his account, making the diary a genuinely interesting historical source. Unlike some of his contemporaries, such as T.E. Lawrence and Ronald Storrs, Ballobar never had time to edit his own work, barring some annotations in the margins of the original manuscript itself. Ballobar was not interested in providing a unique perspective of Jerusalem and Palestine during the crucial age when the entire Middle East was re-designed by the winners of the First World War. He was merely recording his own thoughts for his own purposes.

One question, at least in my mind, remains unanswered throughout the diary: How did Ballobar develop his friendship with Cemal Paşa, and was it an authentic one, as it seems from the diary? In the unfolding of the diary it is clear the two men developed something more than a friendship of necessity; it was more than a 'simple acquaintance.' Nevertheless, as much as Cemal is mentioned before the arrival of the British, he vanishes from the diary after December 1917.[2] Perhaps Ballobar was concerned that his friendship with the Ottoman Paşa could become not only an obstacle to his career but also a threat to his life. The mystery remains, as there are no sources that have yet shed light on this relationship.

Ballobar's writings convey how deeply he suffered in Jerusalem, particuarly due to a feeling of complete isolation; much of what Ballobar wrote expresses the challenges he faced and how he dealt with them. The diary can be understood also as a confidant, a best friend in his isolation. Ballobar processed his experiences, difficulties and relationships, writing his understanding of these, while at the same time providing the reader with a vivid perspective of Jerusalem, Palestine and to an extent international politics from the point of view of a young Spanish man, resettled in the Ottoman Empire. The particular circumstances of the war, and the relatively marginal position of Ballobar in Jerusalem, have made the diary an invaluable source in highlighting the particular historical time and geographical space in which the Spanish consul acted as a historical agent whether he was aware of it or not.

INTRODUCTION

> His diary [Ballobar's], judging from other samples with which he occasionally favoured me, is, to my regret, not likely to be published *in extenso* during his lifetime.[1]
>
> - Ronald Storrs

Antonio de la Cierva y Lewita Conde de Ballobar 'set out the first time for the Holy Land on 26 July 1913 by train.'[2] The fate of the Ottoman Empire was not yet doomed; however, the empire in which the Spanish diplomat came to live was in its final stages of life. Ballobar arrived in Jerusalem in an extremely problematic period for the Ottomans, who were constantly assaulted by internal and external threats. In order to understand the contents of the diary, it is crucial to provide a general context into which the consul was placed. This introduction does not aim to be an exhaustive discussion of the late Ottoman Empire, or to provide a detailed discussion of Palestine and Jerusalem at the beginning of the twentieth century. The reader will be provided with a general overview of the late Ottoman era, particularly from the diplomatic point of view, and Ottoman entry into the First World War. Looking specifically at Palestine, late Ottoman Jerusalem, as well as the Spanish consular mission in the city and the region, will be under scrutiny to provide the historical context in which Ballobar came to act as an historical agent. Relying, then, on a variety of primary sources, I will provide a short biography of Ballobar, as well as a discussion of some of the major issues he had to deal with while staying in Jerusalem: The Custody of the Holy Land, the Zionist question and the living conditions of the city during the war. In the conclusion, a paragraph will be dedicated to the discussion of war-time Jerusalem as portrayed in other diaries and memoirs, in order to underline the relevance of Ballobar in the redefinition of the socio-political space of the city during a contested and often neglected historical period. To the non-scholarly reader this could be an interesting story; however, this publication also aims to provide a new historical source for scholars focusing on the late Ottoman history of Palestine. As such, before proceeding into the diary, I will briefly discuss sources available for further study.

Ballobar, as an historical agent, quickly disappeared from the stage of British-ruled Palestine, but for a short while he was both a witness and an active actor in the context of war-time Palestine and Jerusalem. Not much has been written about him; in fact, apart from the publication of his diary in 1996, and a number of publications in which he only tangentially appears – often misspelled – he clearly never stood center stage in professional historical research. Besides material available in the Spanish Archives of Madrid and Alcalá de Henares, the name of Ballobar appears in a plethora of archives, including the British National Archives and the Archives of the French Foreign Office. It is therefore surprising that Ballobar was not studied *per se*, nor included in works dealing with Palestine, Jerusalem and the holy places. Perhaps Ballobar as historical source and agent has been underestimated, a situation which I aim to rectify with this edition of the diary.

The Eastern Question and the late Ottoman era
Without getting into deep historiographical debates, such as the legacy of Muhammad 'Ali in Egypt and the paradigms of modernity and decline in the Ottoman Empire, it is important to understand the wider context into which Ballobar came to operate as an historical agent in the second decade of the twentieth century. In the nineteenth century, the Ottoman Empire, through Western eyes, was often referred to as the 'Sick Man of Europe.' Many scholars have argued that the process of disintegration of the Ottoman Empire began earlier, in the eighteenth century, with the signing of two treaties which marked a dramatic shift in Ottoman history. In 1699 the Ottomans signed the Treaty of Karlowitz with Austria, ceding Hungary to the Hapsburgs; in 1774 the Ottoman-Russian war, which had been launched by the Ottomans in 1768, ended with the Treaty of Küçük Kaynarca, among the most humiliating treaties signed by the Empire.[3] Not only did the Russians emerge as the main enemy of the Ottomans, but they also advocated the right of protection over the Greek Orthodox Church throughout Ottoman territories; although, this was more an interpretation of the treaty rather than a proper given right.[4] Thereafter, it was clear to the European powers that Ottoman military superiority was over and that the Empire was in a state of disarray, affected by political and economic disintegration. However, this is not to say the Ottomans were fundamentally incompetent, which was a common view, but it is indeed true that a number of causes, including the inability to face long-term challenges due to lack of human and physical resources, left the Ottomans unable to answer a number of internal and external threats.

The problems caused by the slow decay of the Ottoman Empire have been defined as the 'Eastern Question.' Though there is no easy definition of the 'Eastern Question,' the major issue centered on Russia and her desire to control the Ottoman's possessions in Europe, and above all, the

Straits, which were intended as the Russian gate to the Mediterranean basin. The Eastern Question centered also on the conflict between Ottoman rulers and Christian subjects, particularly in the European lands of the Empire.[5] Christians in the Balkans strongly advocated reform and autonomy, if not independence, requests the Ottomans resisted. Until 1878 (Treaty of San Stefano and Treaty of Berlin), European powers prevented Russia from reaching those goals, as it could have led to a major European conflict. The crisis of 1875-1878 marked the emergence of the Balkan states as independent entities, while at the same time making the Ottoman Empire mainly a Middle Eastern empire, with a Muslim majority. The 'Eastern Crisis' also altered the interests and behavior of the Great Powers: The policy of strict maintenance of the Ottoman Empire was abandoned in favor of the idea that sooner or later the empire would be dismembered and that the European powers could only delay this event to avert open war over the spoils of the empire itself. It must also be said that despite the perceived threat of a major conflict over the dismemberment of the Ottoman Empire, this potential event never turned into reality, as Europeans preferred to adjust their divergent interests through treaties and agreements. A good example of this is provided by the Crimean War (1853-1856), which could have turned into a major European conflict. A dispute over the control of the holy places in Palestine eventually brought Russia to occupy the principalities of Moldavia and Wallachia. Ironically, the British and French could not allow Russian interference in Ottoman sovereignty over its subjects and therefore attacked the Russians in Crimea, where a multinational coalition won over Russian forces.[6] It was only with the outbreak of the First World War in 1914 that, finally, the 'Eastern Question' was resolved, at least in the eyes of diplomats and politicians.[7]

Diplomacy and politics were crucial in drawing up the borders of the Ottoman Empire and the new states in the Balkans. The 'Eastern Question,' however, can also be discussed through the lenses of nationalism and economics. The emergence of Muhammad 'Ali as ruler of Egypt in 1805 and Syria beginning in the 1830s, Greek independence in 1830, and the capitulations, were not only the outcome of diplomatic 'games' amongst European chancelleries or the result of internal struggles.[8] Nationalism and economics went hand-in-hand, producing different results in different areas of the empire. In the Balkans, nationalist fervor spread not just as a result of strong nationalist feeling but also as a result of class and religious struggles. Christian peasants revolted against their Muslim landlords, asking for a change from subsistence to capitalist agriculture; similarly, Christian merchants increased their trade with Europe and they lobbied the Ottoman government, asking for more freedom and less taxes.[9] Rebellions eventually took on a nationalist character, though we should not underestimate European involvement in these events. Less noted is the fact that many rebellions were against an expanding Ottoman state that, from the early nineteenth century, was engaged in the re-establishment of central power through economic and administrative reforms.[10]

The economic aspect of the 'Eastern Question' was represented by the capitulations, whose abolition Ballobar witnessed in 1914. The capitulations were bilateral treaties between sovereign states, as well as unilateral concessions granted to groups of merchants which, in the Ottoman Empire, were first signed in 1536 with an agreement between the Sultan and the king of France, Francis I.[11] Known in Turkish as *ahdname* or *imtiyazat*, the capitulations had precursors in the early Muslim tradition to the Fatimid and Mamluk governments.[12] The first capitulations were mainly commercial agreements, which granted French citizens the right of residence and trade in the Ottoman Empire, allowing them to enjoy rights of extra-territorial jurisdiction in the Empire.[13]

After the French signed capitulary treaties, other European countries followed suit. In the sixteenth century, the Ottomans granted England and Holland capitulary rights; later, in the eighteenth century, capitulations were also granted to Austria, Sweden and the Kingdom of the Two Sicilies.[14] Initially, the capitulary regime favored the Ottomans, but this became increasingly disadvantageous as it was exploited by the European powers. Capitulations originally granted the Ottomans an opportunity to share the benefits of world trade, in the fifteenth and sixteenth centuries, with Florence, Genoa, Venice, Netherlands, France and England.[15] Meanwhile, they allowed European countries to maintain consular posts in Ottoman territories, but the same was not granted to the Ottomans, who started to establish representatives in Europe only at the end of the eighteenth century.[16] The capitulations became one of the most important instruments of economic and political penetration in the empire. Foreigners were granted a special status which eventually created social, political and economic divisions between Ottoman subjects and foreign residents. These divisions were particularly felt in Palestine, where the capitulations had a visible impact on the local indigenous population starting with the large presence of consulates whose primary purpose was to protect and promote their subjects' interests.

The Ottoman Empire lost its financial independence in 1881 when, following the unilateral decision on the part of the Ottoman government in 1875 to default on interest payments, the Decree of Muharram established the Public Debt Administration. This institution was composed of representatives of various creditors, mainly European governments and financial institutions, charged with collecting a variety of Ottoman revenues in order to pay the interest on the debts. As payments to reduce the debts were given priority, the Ottoman budget was largely reduced, causing a strong negative reaction amongst Ottoman subjects.[17]

Late Ottoman Jerusalem

Until recently, literature produced in relation to Ottoman Jerusalem has often portrayed the development of modernity in the city as the combination of European encroachment, Zionist immigration and British rule since 1918. I have argued elsewhere that this is a very limited perspective, which does not take into account the internal dynamics within the city.[18] The diary of Ballobar is clearly affected by a strong disapproval of the Ottoman regime, but at the same time, he (perhaps unconsciously) provides the reader with evidence of a genuine autochthonous development, even in times of war.

Late Ottoman Jerusalem was part of the *beylerbeylik* (region) of Damascus, which included Palestine, and it was assimilated into the administrative structure of the empire soon after the conquest of *Bilad al-Sham* (Greater Syria) in 1517. The Ottomans, however, established a form of indirect rule, relying on local notables whose importance continued until the establishment of the State of Israel in 1948.[19] The *beylerbeylik* of Damascus was composed of fifteen *sancaks*, a smaller administrative unit.[20] The *Sancak-i Kudüs-i Şerif* (Province of Jerusalem) was divided into a number of *nahiyes* (sub-districts) whose boundaries changed during Ottoman times.[21] Until the beginning of the nineteenth century, Jerusalem was a city with no particular economic or strategic value for the empire; nevertheless, with the Napoleonic invasion of Egypt in 1798, the question of the Holy Land and the holy places was revived. French rule was short lived, but the legacy of Napoleon was picked up by Muhammad 'Ali who eventually became the ruler of Egypt in 1805.[22] In 1831, Muhammad 'Ali and his son, Ibrahim, invaded *Bilad al-Sham*, which became part of Egypt, an event which was a turning point in the history of modern Jerusalem.

The city experienced two periods of administrative, political, social and economic change in the nineteenth century: First under the rule of Ibrahim Paşa, and then as a consequence of the *Tanzimat* reforms implemented by the Ottomans once they re-captured the city.[23] Muhammad 'Ali's dynasty in Jerusalem lasted only a decade (1831-1840), but its effects should not be underestimated; in fact, under Ibrahim Paşa's rulership, the local governors fell under the check of a council, the *meclis*, composed mainly of the Muslim elite, but it also included some of the most influential Christian and Jewish members of the community. Elements of representation and of checks and balances were introduced, while several consulates were opened: The British did so in 1838, and other European countries followed suit. European Powers promoted business, protected travelers, and supported the construction of hospitals and hospices for visitors and locals alike: The French, for instance, opened three hospices between 1851 and 1889.[24] The activism of the European powers reinvigorated pilgrimage and tourism. Moreover, Jerusalem's increased importance on the international stage coincided with the Crimean War (1854-1856), which brought the issue of control of the holy places to the forefront of intra-European politics. With the Ottoman restoration in 1841, the Ottomans established a municipality in Jerusalem which eventually became the most important local administrative body of the city.[25] The creation of this institution was part of a larger project of modernization which entailed the transformation of the traditional Ottoman administrative machine through the adoption of new legal and administrative tools.

The administrative organization of Palestine and Jerusalem was very much the by-product of the *Tanzimat* reforms; transformations were not carried out overnight, and should be understood within the larger context of the reorganization of the empire itself. In the summer of 1872 the *sancak* of Jerusalem was detached from the *vilayet* of Syria and made independent, under the direct control of Istanbul.[26] The *sancak* (or *mutasarrıflık*) of Jerusalem was ruled by a *Mutasarrıf* (governor). After the *sancak* was detached from the *vilayet* of Syria, the *Mutasarrıf* of Jerusalem became unique amongst the other governors throughout the Ottoman Empire, as he was directly appointed and therefore responsible to the central administration in Istanbul rather than the *Vali* of Syria.[27] In the late nineteenth century, during the reign of Abdülhamid II, governors were appointed from among the palace secretaries of the Sultan and, later, at the beginning of the twentieth century, by the Young Turks from among Turkish officials.[28] The *Mutassarıflık* was the largest and most important administrative unit of Ottoman Jerusalem, and the governor was the most important Ottoman official Ballobar dealt with during the war, barring Cemal Paşa.

Other administrative units were present in Jerusalem, such as the *Belediye* (municipality) - one of the first to be established in the Ottoman Empire - but during the war the municipality lost importance due to the effects of the military mobilization.[29] Jerusalem's administrative structure comprised three councils, which, by the time of mobilization in August 1914, were frozen and their activities suspended. The *Meclis-i Belediye* (Municipal Council) was responsible for providing services: Cleanliness of the town and the streets; maintenance of roads and water systems; supervision of public health, cafés and restaurants; commercial activities and so forth.[30] The municipality also controlled a local police force which supervised urban communities and the sanitation of the city. The *Meclis-i Umumi*, the general council of the *Vilayet*, met once a year for a period of no more than forty days. The general council had the power to review the draft budget for the province, as well as checking and supervising projects. The last council in Jerusalem was the *Meclis-i Idare*, the administrative council of the Jerusalem district, which was set up as a result of the issue of the *Vilayet* Law of 1864. The main purpose of the council was to deliberate on public works, police, land registry, agriculture, finance and tax collection.[31]

Besides the administrative structure controlled by the Ottomans, with the cooperation of local elites, a less formal structure existed, composed of local groups possessing, to different degrees, social and political influence.[32] These groups, who formed the backbone of local elites, were a class of notables who functioned as intermediaries between the population and the Ottoman administration. These *a'yan* (notables), whose political profile was rather complex, derived their power from economic wealth and from their religious legitimacy. It is with these members of Jerusalem's elites that Ballobar dealt with, providing a variety of opinions about them and an interesting perspective.

Attempts on the part of the Ottomans to develop a genuine and locally-based administrative structure were often challenged by Europeans. One of the major issues in late Ottoman Jerusalem, as well as in the whole of the Ottoman Empire, was the capitulary regime discussed earlier. From the mid-nineteenth century, as the Europeans renewed their interest in the Holy Land, the British government opened the first consulate in Jerusalem during the rule of Muhammad 'Ali. It was the beginning of the arrival of a considerable number of European and American citizens who earlier attempted, without major success, to settle in Palestine and particularly in Jaffa. They were not simply Christian pilgrims, they planned to settle in the city and start to work as physicians, teachers and businessmen.[33] Under the protection of the capitulations and the foreign consulates, European entrepreneurs and governments built educational and health institutions. The capitulations granted Europeans substantial reductions in tax and customs duties, and extraterritoriality rights.[34]

Capitulations were considered by local to be a restrictive measure and an interference with foreigners in several areas, while Ballobar believed them to be necessary to perform his duties. By late 1914, Jerusalem services like post offices and higher education were in the hands of the Europeans, who promoted their own interests. In the summer of that year, the Ottoman government used the outbreak of the war in Europe to abolish the capitulary system throughout the empire. In September, the Ministry of Foreign Affairs sent a note to the foreign embassies of Istanbul, stating that the capitulations would be abolished starting October 1; meanwhile in Jerusalem, Macid Şevket, the Governor of the city, wrote to the foreign consuls informing them of the closure of the foreign post offices, which was tantamount to the abolition of the most visible capitulary privileges.[35]

The imperial order which abolished the capitulations was read to the people of Jerusalem in an official ceremony held in the garden of the municipality. After the Governor read the document, Said al-Husayni, a local member of the Ottoman parliament, delivered a speech on the value of this measure, but also asked the crowd to show respect for the foreigners.[36] As elsewhere in the empire the abrogation of the capitulations was hailed as the beginning of a new era. Religious orders, foreign clergy and laity had to deal with this new situation without relying on any foreign help.[37] Foreign citizens were threatened with expulsion (and many indeed were), and Jews began a movement of Ottomanization: The adoption of Ottoman citizenship in order to avoid deportation.[38] Ballobar and Glazebrook, the American consul, remained, while all the other consuls left. Among Christians, panic spread rapidly as demonstrations against the Europeans started to be staged throughout the city, but, as Ballobar noted, in Jerusalem things did not turn as violent as in other parts of the empire.[39]

The First World War, the Ottoman Empire and Jerusalem

Ballobar often discussed in his diary the military aspects of the conflict he was witnessing, so it is important to briefly outline the situation on the battlefield and to discuss some events preceding the war itself. The outbreak of the First World War was not the first incident in which the Ottoman Empire was challenged both internally and externally. In 1908, the Young Turks overthrew the Sultan Abdülhamid II and re-instated the constitution, which had been suspended in 1876. The Empire was then attacked by the Italians in 1911, losing Libya. The following year, the outbreak of the Balkan wars further weakened the position of the Ottoman government.[40] Finally in 1913, the leadership of the Empire changed when a *coup d'état*, staged by the members of the Committee of Union and Progress (CUP) installed a military dictatorship.[41]

In the months preceding the beginning of the war in 1914, the Ottoman Empire was diplomatically isolated. Most of the European governments considered the Ottoman government to be on the brink of a collapse. Prior to 1914, Britain acted as an ally to the Ottoman Empire, primarily to defend the Dardanelles from Russia and to protect the imperial route to India. In June of the same year, the Anglo-Turkish convention regarding the Arabian Peninsula granted the Ottomans a little room to recover from the Balkan and Libyan wars.⁴² By the outbreak of the war in August 1914, the British were no longer interested in any alliance with the Ottomans, and British policies towards the Ottoman Empire changed radically.⁴³

Rough plans for the partition of the Ottoman Empire preceded the explosion of the war, and the conflict simply acted as a catalyst for the plans which had been drawn by Great Britain, France and Russia. They envisaged the complete and final downfall of the Ottoman Empire, finally solving the 'Eastern Question.'⁴⁴ It was taken for granted that, as a result of the war, the Ottoman Empire would be dismembered.

Prior to joining the Central Powers, the Ottoman Empire was in a state of ambivalent neutrality towards the warring parties.⁴⁵ This ambivalent neutrality was not meant to last, as the CUP was desperately looking for an ally in Europe. In the words of Erik Zürcher: 'they were prepared to accept any alliance rather than continued isolation.'⁴⁶ Isolation was not an option for the CUP. Slowly, a neutral stance became equally unacceptable for the Entente and for the Central Powers, as territories under Ottoman control were strategic for both alignments.⁴⁷ In the two years preceding the war, German-Ottoman relations were cold. Both the Young Turks and members of the CUP disliked Germany's support of the Hamidian regime.⁴⁸ Things, however, were to change. When the war began, the British government refused to deliver two warships - *Sultan Osman* and *Reşadiye* - commissioned by the Ottomans, which had been financed through a popular subscription. Although this caused a great deal of popular resentment, which was echoed in official circles, Great Britain was still considered the natural ally of the Ottoman Empire by many politicians, such as Cavid, the CUP Minister of Finance.⁴⁹ On 28 July 1914, the Minister of War, Enver Paşa, met German ambassador Wangenhaim in secret to discuss a defensive alliance with Germany while Cemal Paşa, Minister of the Navy, and well known for his sympathy with the French, continued to favor contacts with France.⁵⁰ In August, ideological, economic and geopolitical factors, and the personal pressure of the Kaiser Wilhelm II himself, brought together the Ottoman and German Empires with a secret agreement signed by the CUP triumvirate in power and German representatives.⁵¹

When Russia entered the war alongside the Entente, the *casus foeder* arose. The CUP, however, delayed the entry of the Ottoman Empire into the conflict for a number of reasons, including the fact that the government was in no condition to fight a war. Logistics was the main problem, as the government could not easily deploy the army through the empire's vast domains. Moreover, Ottoman involvement in war operations was dependent on supplies from their German and Austrian allies.⁵² On September 9, 1914, the Ottoman Empire unilaterally declared the abolition of the capitulations, finally regaining full sovereignty over its subjects. While the European powers involved in the war did not protest, neutral countries forwarded their complaints to the Ottoman government.

At the end of October 1914, Ottoman warships opened fire on a Russian naval base in the Black Sea, but it was only in November that the Ottomans officially entered the war. Nevertheless, the Ottoman army had already been mobilized earlier in August, and was comprised of four army corps whose effectiveness had yet to be tested. Ottoman officials hoped to increase military performance during the war thanks to German support. Palestine came under the military district of Syria, which included two army corps composed of two or three infantry divisions in each, plus one cavalry brigade, three howitzer batteries, a battalion of engineers and a company of telegraphers.[53] As soon as the fourth army was established in Damascus, it was sent to the Palestinian front under the direct command of Cemal Paşa.

For their part, since the outbreak of the war in 1914, the British government had focused on Egypt, which had been under British control since 1882. Although the war cabinet advocated the direct annexation of the country, it was instead declared a British protectorate in December 1914. British officials were concerned with the possibility of an attack against the Suez Canal, which was vital for British interests in the region and beyond. In the early stages of the war, Palestine was a secondary issue on the agenda of the British War Office, as military operations conducted on the Middle Eastern front were to serve the strategic necessities of the British Empire.

While Britain, France and Russia were discussing the future of the Middle East, on the Ottoman front Cemal Paşa was appointed Governor and Commander in Chief of Syria and Palestine, and would later become a good friend of Ballobar. He was assisted by General Friederich Kress von Kressenstein, the German Chief of Staff who played a key role on the Palestinian front. According to Bruce, the Germanization of the Ottoman army led to tensions between the officers of both armies.[54] These tensions were confirmed in the following years by many observers inside Jerusalem.[55] A surprise offensive against the Suez Canal was launched from Syria in early 1915 but failed, with heavy losses on the Ottoman-German side. Ottoman victories in Mesopotamia and at Çanakkale (Gallipoli), and the hope that a further attack on the canal would raise an anti-British rebellion in Egypt in the name of Islam, led the German and Ottoman commands to plan a second strike. By the beginning of the summer of 1916, troops were ready, but the British soon discovered the advance through aerial reconnaissance. By mid-August, the British outnumbered the German-Ottoman troops, ending *de facto* their Palestinian campaign.[56]

Palestine and Syria had remained virtually unscathed in relation to the direct conflict between the British and the Ottomans. In 1917, however, the British army, led by General Archibald Murray, commander of the Egyptian Expeditionary Force (EEF), moved from a defensive strategy to an offensive one. He twice attempted to take Gaza in the spring of 1917, but both campaigns failed. In London, the Military High Command and Prime Minister, David Lloyd George, viewed the inability to take Gaza as unacceptable. While the British army was advancing, the Ottoman and German commands established a new military unit called Yıldırım (Storm) under the command of General Erich von Falkenhayn.[57] The purpose was to launch a strike against the British forces in Southern Iraq using guerrilla tactics. Although this new corps was meant to be offensive, it turned out to be a defensive force. In view of the British advance towards Palestine, in 1917 Von Falkenhayn suggested that the Yıldırım should be sent to Palestine in order to defend the Gaza-Beersheba line rather than defending an indefensible Baghdad. It was, however, too late.[58] By 7 November 1917, the Ottoman-German troops were retreating from the Palestinian front, and the path for the British advance towards Jerusalem was opened. In June 1917, General Edmund Allenby assumed command of EEF, with instructions to prepare for an offensive campaign during the autumn and winter. He soon adopted new, and more hazardous, military strategies which allowed the British army to occupy Gaza trough Beersheba. Jerusalem was eventually taken from Gaza before Christmas, in fulfillment of Lloyd George's order to make Jerusalem a gift for the nation.[59]

Besides military action, the beginning of hostilities led to a greater deal of planning, and in 1915, Britain agreed to the Russian occupation of Istanbul and the straits while the French government began to claim Syria.[60] At the same time, Hebert Samuel, president of the local government board,[61] submitted a proposal to the British Foreign Office in order to create a Jewish national home in Palestine. In London, British officials wondered whether the acquisition of new territories in the Middle East would strengthen or weaken the global position of their empire.[62] As the idea of partition became increasingly prevalent, in 1915 the British government established the De Bunsen committee, which made a number of recommendations according to different scenarios that could occur at the end of the war. Regarding Palestine, and particularly Jerusalem, the committee recommended that the city and the holy places be internationalized.[63] Jerusalem and Palestine were also mentioned in the Husayn-McMahon correspondence of 1915 and in the Sykes-Picot agreement of 1916; however, the position of the city in the future arrangement of the Arab Middle East remained intentionally vague.[64]

It is important to underline the fact that, though not at the center of major battles, barring one in late 1917, Palestine and especially the civilian population, served as one of the 'home fronts' of the Ottoman Empire, and was still very much affected by the war. The presence of Ottoman and German forces contributed to radical changes in the local landscape, as did the sea blockade, which had grave consequences such as an increase in the price of basic resources, which created long-term famine and isolated Palestine from the outside world.[65]

Antonio de la Cierva y Lewita Conde de Ballobar

Antonio de la Cierva y Lewita, later Conde de Ballobar and Duque de Terranova, was born in Vienna in 1885. His mother was Austrian, of Jewish origin, but had converted to the Catholic faith. His father was a Spanish military attaché to the Spanish embassy in the Austrian capital.[66] Educated in Zaragoza, in 1911 Ballobar entered the Spanish consular service and was appointed vice-consul to Cuba. In May 1913 Ballobar was appointed consul in Jerusalem; according to his personnel file, he began at the consulate in August 1913, though he then traveled for several months before settling down in Jerusalem. He remained until the end of 1919.[67] When Ballobar reached Jerusalem his task was limited to the protection of Spanish interests, mainly religious in nature, and to re-establish 'diplomatic' and more friendly relations with the Custody of the Holy Land.[68] By the time the British occupied Jerusalem in December 1917, he found himself the only consul in the city, in charge of the protection of the interests of all countries involved in the war; Glazebrook remained in the city until the US joined the war against Germany in April 1917. Ballobar became a crucial personality but, as will be shown later, rapidly faded away.

In January 1920, Ballobar took charge of the Spanish consulate in Damascus; however, in November of the same year, he moved to Tangiers where he served for a few months.[69] In 1920, he married Rafaela Osorio de Moscoso, Duchess of Terranova. On June 24, 1921, Ballobar resigned his commission as consul and moved back to Spain.[70] Ballobar was commissioned to carry out a report on the Spanish convents and hospitals in Palestine in 1925 and then disappeared from the Spanish consular service. Until 1936 he took an extended leave of absence, which is reported in his file as 'excedente voluntario.' According to his family, Ballobar went back to Spain where he took care of the family business; his wife was not eager to raise their five children while traveling around the world. They mostly lived in Botorita, a small village in the outskirts of Zaragoza where Ballobar took care of his agricultural land, *Granja San Luis*.[71] Maria Isabel, Ballobar's daughter, recalled that in Botorita Ballobar grew an olive tree that was taken from the Garden of the Gethsemane.

In August 1936, Ballobar decided to publicly support Francisco Franco and his 'Junta de Denfensa Nacional de España' against the left-wing Popular Front, which won the election a few months earlier. Due to some anti-clerical violence against the Church, which took place after the elections, it is not surprising that the pious Ballobar supported Franco; nevertheless, Ballobar remained a strong supporter of the monarchy, and his support for the new regime was more of a convenience than belief. From August 1936, Ballobar was first appointed to the Diplomatic Cabinet of the 'Junta' and then as Secretary of External Relations for Franco's Foreign Office. During the interwar period, and in the 1940s, Ballobar mainly worked at the Spanish Foreign Office, with a particular interest in the relations with the Holy See.[72] During this time, Ballobar was offered important positions as consul around the world, including in Canada and the United States, but he did not accept these appointments. Ballobar's wife was not ready to move, and the education of their children was more important. Furthermore, he asked for short leaves of absence, which he alternated with short periods at the Spanish Foreign Office.[73] In January 1948 a terrorist attack carried out by the Haganah against the Semiramis Hotel in Jerusalem killed Manuel Allendesalazar, Spanish vice-consul in Jerusalem, who was the brother of Ballobar daughter's husband, José Allendesalazar. It is unclear if there is any connection, but a year later, in May 1949, Ballobar was appointed consul to Jerusalem; this time he accepted the appointment, and he served in Jerusalem until 1952.[74] He then moved back to Spain where he was appointed Director of the *Obra Pia* until he retired in 1955. Ballobar eventually died in Madrid in 1971, aged 86.[75]

The Custody of the Holy Land

Central to Ballobar's mission in Jerusalem was the protection and support of the Custody of the Holy Land and, in particular, its Spanish clergy and properties. Among the Christian institutions of Jerusalem, *Custodia Terrae Sanctae* (Custody of the Holy Land) had some of the deepest roots in the religious-social fabric of the city at the beginning of the twentieth century. The Custody belonged to the Franciscan order, founded as a Franciscan Province during the thirteenth century by St. Francis of Assisi.[76] Since its establishment, the highest authority of the Custody, the *Custos*, has always been an Italian subject. Membership of the council, which regulated the life of the Custody, was also based on nationality. In the period under discussion, the Custody was administered by a Discretory composed of the *Custos*, one French vicar, one Spanish procurator and six members: One Italian, one French, one Spanish, one German, and, after 1921, one British and one Arabic-speaking member.[77] The *Custos* had religious jurisdiction over the Catholics of Palestine, parts of Egypt, Jordan, Lebanon, Cyprus, and Rhodes, which meant a degree of competition with the Latin Patriarch of Jerusalem. The *Custos*, alongside the Greek Orthodox Patriarch and the Armenian Patriarch, became responsible for the enforcement of the *Status Quo* regarding the holy places.

The Custody had a complex relationship with the European governments. The balance in the ruling council of the Custody was quite fragile, as these governments attempted, through their members, to influence the institution. However, it was the very nature of the Custody, a transnational organization, which had protected its existence throughout the centuries. As an institution ruled by Ottoman law, the Custody was not allowed to own properties such as convents, schools and other buildings. Only individual clergy were allowed to own properties in their personal name, and the decision as to who should be entitled to ownership was taken by the Custody, according to nationality. The international character of the Custody meant that every decision was subject to international scrutiny; during the war, however, the Custody was left somewhat to its own devices, although the Spanish and Austrian consuls did intervene to support the Custody when it felt harassed by Ottoman authorities. During the war, Spain donated at least 60,000 French Francs to the Custody, while the Central Powers, and primarily Austria, supported the organization financially.[78]

When the conflict broke out, the Ottoman Army began to seize buildings and properties of the Custody that had been registered in the name of the clergy of Allied citizenship.[79] The Vatican, concerned with the future of the Holy Land, urged Cardinal Dolci to explain to the Ottoman authorities that an infringement upon property rights was to be considered an act of defiance against the Vatican State, which claimed ownership of these properties contrary to Ottoman terms.[80]

Because it was customary for the *Custos* to keep a diary of events, it is possible to study the Custody throughout the war in a way not available to historians of other institutions. Although the *Custos* left at the beginning of the hostilities, the diary was maintained by Fr. Eutimio Castellani, President of the Custody, between 1914 and 1918, written in the form of a chronicle, and includes notes updated on a daily basis.[81] Following the Ottoman government's entrance into the war, the Custody found itself isolated internationally; the functions of the Custody were then carried out only in Palestine and Jerusalem. The financial situation of the Custody began to worsen because its main sources of income, such as pilgrimages and agricultural production, were no longer available. Early in September 1914, the Custody reduced the activities of their workshops producing wheat, fabrics and other commodities, dropping the wages of their employees by fifteen percent.[82] In November of the same year, Ottoman authorities ordered religious congregations scattered around Jerusalem to gather in the city center. The Franciscans hosted the clergymen in the convent of St. Savior, and the clergywomen in the Casa Nova. A few days later, the police registered all names of the clergy living in the two houses.[83] Local police visiting the convents became a common event throughout the war, often for the purpose of seizing provisions and supplies: For instance, with winter approaching, the military requisitioned coal from the Custody, and their mill worked for five days in order to supply the Ottoman troops in Jerusalem with flour and bread.[84] The Ottoman military seized nearly all property including both buildings and supplies, *de facto* mobilizing for the war effort all human and material resources 'offered' by the Custody. Ottomans had seized schools, convents and hospitals as part of the process of mobilization, but Dolci obtained permission to reopen the convents in Jerusalem belonging to the Custody. However, the order emanating from Istanbul was not followed by prompt action on the part of the local authorities in Jerusalem, and most of the convents remained closed.[85]

When Italy joined the war alongside the Allies, the situation became worse still, as the Ottomans saw the Vatican as an ally of the Italian government. Furthermore, the Ottoman authorities ordered that all clerics of Italian nationality, primarily Franciscans, must leave Jerusalem.[86] The few British and French missionaries among the Franciscans had already been ordered to leave in 1914, though their departure was permanently delayed thanks to external intervention.[87] Similarly, thanks to the American and Spanish consuls, and decisive intervention by the Austrians, the Italian clergy were allowed to remain.[88] As a result, in 1915 the Franciscans living in the city comprised seventy-two Italians, thirty-one Spanish, seventeen Ottoman subjects, thirteen Germans, five Dutch, four Portuguese and three Americans.[89] Although the Ottoman order only related to males, it also stated that 'all nuns, the women who are not nuns and the male children below 18 years of age, who may desire, must also be sent out of the country.'[90]

In 1916, the Custody suffered a tremendous blow. In April, the pharmacy at St. Savior was looted and then closed down; then, in June, Ottoman troops occupied St. Savior and Casa Nova, which were subsequently converted into hospitals, leaving only ten rooms in the two convents for the use of friars and nuns.[91] Despite the precarious conditions, the Custody continued to run a soup kitchen for Jerusalemites. As the activities of the Custody were reduced drastically, the entries in the diary kept by the President of the Custody for 1917 also fell, mainly dealing with news coming from outside Jerusalem. Realizing that the British army was not far from the city after the evacuation of Jaffa in March 1917, they hoped that the British would free Jerusalem one day soon.

Spain and the Custody

The reasons behind Ballobar's central mission of aiding the Custody of the Holy Land can be found in the relationship between the Custody and Spain, which dates back to the thirteenth century when Spain was still divided into several kingdoms, and part of the Iberian Peninsula was still under Islamic rule. At this time, the Aragon dynasty re-established its control over territories previously controlled by the Muslims, and began to support Christianity in the Holy Land. Alfonse III of Aragon established a treaty of friendship with Al-Malik Al-Ashraf Khalil, the Mamluk Sultan of Egypt, in 1290. Due to this friendship, twelve Franciscans of Spanish origin were given the right to celebrate in the Holy Sepulcher and the Church of Nativity in Bethlehem, and took care of several sanctuaries.[92] In the fourteenth century, Peter of Aragon emerged as protector of the Franciscans in the Holy Land, and, ever since, all kings and queens of Spain have taken care of the Spanish Franciscans in the Holy Land.[93] In the eighteenth century, the relationship changed between the Custody of the Holy Land and the *Real Casa* of Spain. With the arrival of the Bourbons on the Spanish throne, donations to the religious institutions in the Holy Land grew, as did the power of Spanish friars. In 1746, Pope Benedict XIV defined some Spanish rights inside the Custody, deciding that, in six convents, the superior should be a Spanish national. It was also decided that the *Procutarore Generale* (the financial administrator) would be Spanish.[94]

A radical change in Spanish policy towards the Custody of the Holy Land took place in 1772, with Charles III. The Spanish king issued the *Real Cedula*, which, for the first time, not only regulated the relationships between the state and the Church but also had a large impact on the missionary activities of the Spanish abroad.[95] Charles III claimed to be a descendent of Robert of Anjou, *de facto* asserting the title of King of Jerusalem and protector of the holy places of Jerusalem; but the title disappeared in 1291 with the end of Crusader presence in the Middle East. Most importantly, Charles III gave himself the right to name missionaries and also the *Custos*, decisions usually taken by the Franciscan Order. In 1787, Charles III managed to have Pope Pious VI recognize his claims, but in 1794 the Pope revoked his earlier decree and practically reversed his previous decision.[96] While Charles III did not win this political battle, he did establish the *Obra Pia de Jerusalen*, tasked with collecting donations for Spanish clergy in the Holy Land. The money collected was then sent to the *Procuratore* (a Spanish subject), who managed both the Spanish money and the money collected around the world to support the Custody. This created major divisions within the Custody and, slowly, a number of convents became 'Spanish' as the majority of the clergy was of Spanish nationality. However, although the *Real Cedula* was effective, it was never recognised by either the Vatican or the Custody.[97]

A side effect of the *Real Cedula* was to create ambiguity and confusion over the concept of nationality in relation to the convents of the Holy Land. Clearly, convents were property of the Church and not of the states sponsoring them; nevertheless, Madrid claimed that, since in a number of convents it was customary to appoint Spanish friars, it was possible to define those convents as Spanish and belonging to the Spanish state. This was obviously a violation of the *Status Quo* of the holy places. It is also important to bear in mind that, according to Ottoman law, the convents belonged to the Sultan, and religious institutions only had the right to use them. The situation was further complicated with the re-opening of the Latin Patriarchate of Jerusalem in 1847, paving the way for a new conflict between the newly opened institution and the Custody.

In 1853 the Spanish government gave control of the *Obra Pia* to the Ministry of the Interior and, with the same decree, opened a consulate in Jerusalem with the purpose of defending Spanish interests in the region: The protection of the Spanish clergy and the effective distribution of the donations collected by the *Obra Pia* to the Spanish convents.[98] This consular mission was not at all concerned about diplomatic relations with the Ottomans, and even less so with local Ottoman authorities. The consul was charged with the distribution of financial aid received from Spain to the Spanish friars of the Custody, carefully avoiding any interference, particularly from the Latin Patriarch.[99] More broadly, Spain was challenging the Vatican over the privileges of the Spanish clergy, *de facto* attempting to renegotiate the relationships between the two. An agreement was only finally reached in 1980, when the Vatican recognized Spanish ownership of several properties, and the Spanish government abandoned claims of protection of the holy places.[100]

By the beginning of the twentieth century, the relationships between the Spanish clergy and other nationalities were poor and, at times, nonexistent. According to the *Custos*, Roberto Razzoli, the Custody was in a state of anarchy in 1906, as friars of different nationalities – presumably mainly Spanish - challenged the authority of the *Custos* through local consulates.[101] A report by Bernardino Klumper, who visited the Custody under the authority of the general of the Franciscan order in 1909, claimed that the largest internal conflict within the Custody was caused by a minority of Italian and Spanish friars who sought the control of relevant positions in order to have power over the Custody as a whole.[102] International scuffles were not the only issues revealed in the report: Budgetary anomalies were also discovered.

In 1913, relations between Spain and the Custody reached their lowest point. The newly-appointed *Custos*, Onorato Carcaterra, was given papal authority through the decree *Cum ad Nos* to reform the Custody and re-establish order within the Franciscan family. Following complaints from the Spanish government, the Vatican suspended the decree but could not stop the following events which brought the Custody to dire relations with Spain. When Carcaterra ordered a number of Spanish friars be redeployed, Spanish guards were posted at the Jerusalem train station to prevent the clergy from leaving. The clash then escalated as the *Custos* asked for the involvement of the Italian consul, Senni, while the Spanish consul, Casares, was already working to protect the Spanish clergy.[103] Interestingly, in a variety of available sources, the only missing voice is the Vatican, which was looking for a diplomatic solution. The *Custos* took the initiative and traveled to Italy, hoping for a meeting with the Pope and leaving the Custody under the protection of the Italian consulate. Carcaterra was stopped in Naples by the general of the Franciscan order, and the Vatican decided that national and political circumstances were more important than the stability of the Custody. Carcaterra, according to Daniela Fabrizio, was a zealous Christian, exasperated by the internal divisions of the Custody and the primacy of the so-called national privileges, and he did not hesitate to challenge papal decisions, albeit with very little success.[104] Galvanized by the Vatican decision to recognize some of the Spanish claims, the internal situation of the Custody in Jerusalem degenerated. In September 1913, Carcaterra was promoted to bishop of Ariano di Puglia, and Serafino Cimino was named the new *Custos*, but this change did not alter the tense diplomatic relations with Spain.[105]

A new Discretory was formed in 1914, but the death of Pious X in the summer of the same year, which meant the suspension of any activity, followed by the outbreak of war in Europe and the refusal by Ballobar, newly-appointed Spanish consul in Jerusalem, to recognize any change, meant the crystallization of relations within the Custody and between national governments involved, including the Vatican. Ballobar was sent to replace Casares and to soften the relationship between the Custody and Spain. This did not mean a radical change, however, as proved by the fact that, on 15 December 1914, Ballobar closed and sealed the *Procura* of the Custody, claiming the right of ownership for Spain.[106] The Italian consul, Senni, and the Latin Patriarch, Camassei, witnessed the opening of the door by the *Custos* on January 12. Ballobar claimed he was ordered the same day to remove the seal, but more relevant was the election of the new *Procuratore*.[107] Tension was at its highest point both in Jerusalem and between Spain and the Vatican. In Jerusalem, though, the war and the isolation of the city from the rest of the world brought some relief. Clearly, from the diary, Ballobar came to accept the status of the relationships within the Custody and between Spain and other international actors.

The election of the *Procuratore* remained a major issue of contention between Madrid, the Custody and the Vatican. Eventually, in May 1915, an agreement was reached between the Vatican and Spain, which granted Madrid a number of convents to be governed by Spanish clergy, and prohibited Spanish direct interference in the appointment of the *Procuratore* and members of the Discretory. Eventually, the war and the Ottoman occupation of many convents owned by the Custody reduced the polemics, but this did not mean the issues were resolved and completely forgotten.[108] With the British occupation of Jerusalem in December 1917, and later of Palestine, a new question arose between Spain, the Custody and the Vatican. Unlike the Ottomans, the British allowed religious orders to own their properties, initiating a complex procedure of cadastral registration.[109] The Franciscans provided the British authorities with a full list, including 26 houses in Jaffa whose ownership was claimed by the Spanish. Ballobar was not involved in this controversy, however, as he left Jerusalem in May 1919 and only in 1921 did this become a new conflict.[110]

Obviously, relations between the Custody, the Vatican and Spain were never easy. Ballobar played his role in this as Spanish emissary and, examined through Italian, Vatican and Franciscan sources, he appears to be a man whose only purpose was to protect Spanish interests and to expand them throughout the region; Spain was not really challenging the Vatican on religious issues, but rather was challenging Italy and France over the protection of Catholics in the Holy Land.

Ballobar, the Jews and Zionism

Given that Ballobar's mother was a converted Jew, and the particular region and period in which the diary unfolded, many may certainly wonder whether the Spanish consul was pro- or anti-Zionist. It is certainly a legitimate question, but one which has no clear answer. Ballobar first helped the Jews as needy citizens of war-time Jerusalem. He was then put in charge of distributing the financial help to the Jews, which mainly came from the United States once his American colleague, Glazebrook, left Jerusalem as a consequence of the breaking of diplomatic relations between the United States and the Ottoman Empire in the spring of 1917.[111] Nevertheless, neither in the diary nor in other sources is there any evidence of his position on Zionism.

It appears from some entries in the diary that he was afraid that Zionism could be an element of instability in the region.[112] On the other hand, the Spanish consul was very familiar with the Jewish colonies in Palestine, which he visited several times and of which he had varied opinions, while still respecting their achievements. Besides visiting colonies and administering aid to the Jewish residents of Jerusalem and Palestine, Ballobar became a historical agent and a crucial source in an event which, at the time of its unfolding, created great uproar in Europe and America, and it has been treated by some historians as proof of the anti-Semitism of the Ottoman leaders, and in particular, Cemal Paşa.

On 29 March 1917, Ballobar received a small group of Spaniards from Jaffa who informed him that while visiting Jaffa, two days earlier, the *mutasarrıf* of Jerusalem announced the order of evacuation of the city issued by Cemal Paşa. All inhabitants were covered, although German and Austrian subjects could remain at their own risk.[113] The principal reason for evacuation, according to the Ottoman authorities, was a possible attack against the city by the British. Many in German and Austrian circles thought this was a policy to force the Jews of Jaffa to leave. Jewish residents were very concerned, as German and Austrian Jews were invited to leave contrary to the order of evacuation which gave a choice to German and Austrian nationals.[114] Fear of pogroms spread amongst the Jews of Jaffa, but the much-feared massacres did not materialize. In April 1917, about 9,000 Jewish residents of Jaffa left, the majority heading to Petah Tikva, while others moved to the Jewish colonies in Northern Galilee, and a small group headed to Jerusalem. Ballobar visited Jaffa on 11 April and noted that not many Jews were left: Some watchmen and some farmers, but, in the words of the consul, the city was 'half dead.'[115]

Despite various interpretations of these events, what really matters is how the news of the evacuation of Jaffa reached Europe and America, and Ballobar's role in this. The British received news through Aaron Aaronsohn, a Jewish Ottoman agronomist who was in charge of a small network of spies in Palestine, that 'Tel-Aviv has been sacked. 10,000 Palestine Jews are now without home and food. [...] Jemal has publicly stated Armenian policy will now be applied to Jews.'[116] News that the Jewish community of Palestine was on the verge of annihilation quickly spread throughout the world. Comment and reportage in the Entente and neutral press, however, were less concerned with establishing the truth than with conveying the impression that Palestine had been devastated, the Jews being the sacrificial victims of the Ottomans. In Germany, too, concern grew and a press campaign was staged, trying to undo the damage caused; the Germans even called for the establishment of a commission of inquiry. Neutral countries like Spain and the Netherlands, where sympathies towards the Entente and the Central Powers were divided, were called to investigate the matter.

The commission did not materialize, but on June 11 Ballobar received a cable from the Spanish embassy in Istanbul asking him to be ready to investigate and write a report on the situation regarding the Jews in Palestine.[117] According to Friedman, the suggestion of a separate inquiry by the Spanish consul was shelved, but a partial view, in fact, a short report of Ballobar's, is available in the British archives:

> [...] It is not true that there have been massacres or persecutions of Jews such as in Syria and Palestine; but that the Jews have only shared the same lot as the Christians owing to the application of the measure taken by the military authorities with the regard to the evacuation of those districts.[118]

Interestingly, Glazebrook, too, was invited to write a report on the events of Jaffa, even though he left Jerusalem in late May 1917; he had previously stated that the 'acts of violence said to have been committed against the Jewish population of Jaffa are grossly exaggerated.'[119] Ballobar's small role in all of this –which could have become crucial – was almost entirely ignored. The press reported nothing of the report he produced, and, in subsequent years, his historical agency has almost completely disappeared.[120]

War-time Jerusalem redefined through diaries and memoirs

Given this context and the main themes of his journal, this diary and the historical agency of Ballobar could be instrumental in redefining war-time Jerusalem: A space where several conditions coexisted. Clearly, the war brought disruptions, and the mobilization of human, natural and other resources radically altered the urban-social life of the city. From August 1914, mobilization of material and ideological resources began to affect Jerusalem and Jerusalemites: Although the Ottoman Empire was not yet involved in the war, for example, the governor of the city, Macid Şevket, declared martial law.[121] Men born between 1872 and 1893 were conscripted, banks stopped providing credit and selling gold, food was rationed and requisitioned, buildings and open spaces were seized for military purposes: This is the city Ballobar found at his arrival in the summer of 1914.[122] Closure of foreign post offices and the imposition of strict censorship contributed to frustrations suffered by the Spanish diplomat who, from the early days of his mission in Jerusalem, complained about his isolation from the rest of the world: A feeling shared by other Jerusalemites.[123]

The Ottomans, aware of the consequences of mobilization, to an extent, attempted to create confidence amongst the local population with the abolition of the Capitulations. The Imperial order was hailed as the beginning of a new era.[124] Among the Christians, panic spread rapidly, above all amongst foreign subjects who were reassured by local authorities now claiming to be in charge of providing them safety. Nevertheless, many countries recommended that their citizens abandon Jerusalem and Palestine; many left even before the Ottoman Empire officially joined the war.[125] Although the abolition of the Capitulations meant the empire regained full sovereignty, local benefits did not materialize and it remained very much an act of propaganda which did not really affect the people of Jerusalem, despite complaints of many foreign citizens, including Ballobar, who believed the abolition could promote anti-Christian demonstrations and sentiments.[126]

The major concern for Ballobar at the beginning of the war was the status of the Catholic religious institutions in the city and the broader region. At the end of 1914, Ottoman authorities told religious orders to abandon their convents and gather in residences in Jerusalem. Ballobar carefully noted in his diary most of the events surrounding this. On November 22, the Mother Superior of the convent of the Assumptionist informed Ballobar of the impeding Ottoman occupation of their convent. The Spanish diplomat ran to see the local Ottoman military commander, Zaki Bey, to ask him to respect this convent, as well as the Sisters of Charity.[127] Ballobar was also concerned with the fate of the French and other clergy who were deported from Jerusalem to Syria or left for Egypt.[128] Despite these events, life went on, as Ballobar noted in 1915 when the Easter celebrations were performed as usual, although the absence of pilgrims meant less animation in the city.[129]

The city faced several challenges during the war, including an invasion of locusts. The plague began in Egypt and slowly spread to Palestine. Locusts destroyed whatever was in their path, as claimed by Ballobar when he witnessed the damage caused by the locusts in Jericho in March 1915.[130] When the locusts reached the city of Jerusalem, the municipality established a committee in order to coordinate the battle against these vicious insects. Residents were co-opted into collecting locust eggs to be brought to the nearest police station: Failure to comply was punished with a fine.[131] The damage caused by the locusts was instrumental in a further rise of the price of wheat, causing even more hardship for the inhabitants of Jerusalem and Palestine. Famine and the increase in prices were also caused by the sea blockade implemented by the British and French, as well as by the effective sealing of the internal borders implemented by the Ottomans.[132] Famine, to different degrees, hit everyone in the region, including Ballobar.

Despite being a city suffering great distress, a city of beggars, prostitutes and thieves, war-time Jerusalem was also a city which allowed, to an extent, the inhabitants to adapt to the new state of affairs. It was not an easy task, and only people with enough resources, like notables, foreigners and wealthy residents, found a way to deal with the brutal disruptions of the war. Still, life was not halted, and disruption did not mean annihilation, as proved by other diaries and memoirs available (and by the fact Jerusalem is still there).

To date, the diary of Ballobar is the only diary produced by a western resident of Jerusalem during the First World War. To keep record of events or secure memories for a later period was, and still is, a common habit amongst the consular community. Ballobar was no different, and his diary has become a very interesting source that sheds light on lesser-known aspects of the history of the city. Above all, if compared with other diaries and memoirs produced by local residents in the same period, the diary of Ballobar becomes crucial to fundamentally changing the picture of war-time Jerusalem provided by many accounts produced soon after the war, which affected later academic and informative narratives. This does not imply these narratives were all-wrong, but they were certainly filled with stereotypes and general opinions weakly supported by unverified evidence.

The diary of the Spanish consul, and the context in which it was written, have been the focus of the previous paragraphs; here, the focus will shift to two narratives produced by two Jerusalemites: Wasif Jawhariyyeh and Ihsan Tourjman.[133] The diary of Tourjman and the memoirs of Jawhariyyeh have been very much the focus of the work of scholars like Salim Tamari, Issam Nassar and Abigail Jacobson. Their work has challenged conventional narratives in relation to the modernization of Jerusalem and its socio-physical definition. The memoirs of Wasif Jawhariyyeh, who was a local young musician belonging to the Greek Orthodox Church by the time war broke in Jerusalem, sheds light on a community that disappeared after the arrival of the British in 1917, and certainly after the establishment of the State of Israel in 1948.[134] Through Wasif, as well as through other sources and, indirectly, also through Ballobar, the conventional spatial division of Jerusalem based on ethnic and religious lines is challenged, and clearly, the boundaries which were superimposed after the British occupation of the city were not necessarily defined by ethnicity or confession.[135] The *mahallat* (neighborhood) was the primary unit; therefore, communalism was the real marker: Shared festivities and ceremonies, as well as solidarity, undermined the static picture of a city divided along religious and ethnic lines. Solidarity and shared events are often reported by Ballobar, as well as by Bertha Vester Spafford of the American Colony, perhaps without a clear understanding.[136] In the popular memoirs of Spafford, though influenced by later events, we can see that Jerusalem was not a stagnant city divided into four quarters. If, as suggested earlier, Ballobar could not grasp the full complexity of Jerusalem, we can still see in his diary signs of a strong religious and cultural syncretism taking place in Jerusalem. Wasif experienced firsthand this syncretism, which meant that popular religious celebrations were shared: Wasif notes in his diary and memoirs the Jewish festivity of Purim also being celebrated by Christians and Muslims, while the Ramadan celebrations were very much an event involving all communities living in the city.[137]

The writings of Ihsan Tourjman, a recruit in the Ottoman army who served in the *manzil*, reveal the misery of Jerusalem during the war. Tourjman, not being part of the Jerusalem elites, and certainly not part of the consular environment, focused on daily life, taking a dimmer view of the Ottoman government. Unlike Ballobar, whose criticism was mainly influenced by his apparent and latent Orientalism, Tourjman criticized the Ottomans as part of the Ottoman collective.[138] It would be very interesting to compare the two diaries to see how they perceived common experiences in Jerusalem. Diaries are the conversion of intimate thoughts into written words, which can allow us to project personal experiences into a larger context while trying to understand and define that context, as well as answer crucial questions through the eyes of those writers.

The Palestine life of Ballobar was driven by his sense of duty and personality; passionate about his job, the diary reflects his practiced pessimism and, at the same time, his youthful confidence. In the end, his writings are the embodiment of one man's life and one city's history, which makes them unique and invaluable.

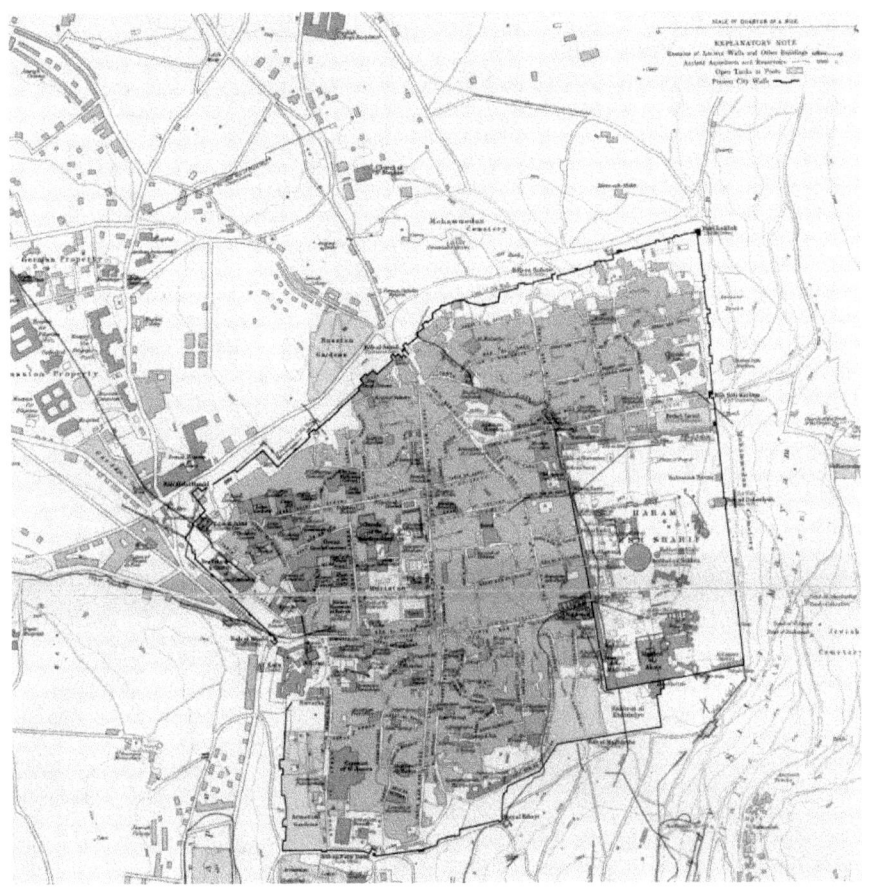

Map 1: Modern Jerusalem 1915.

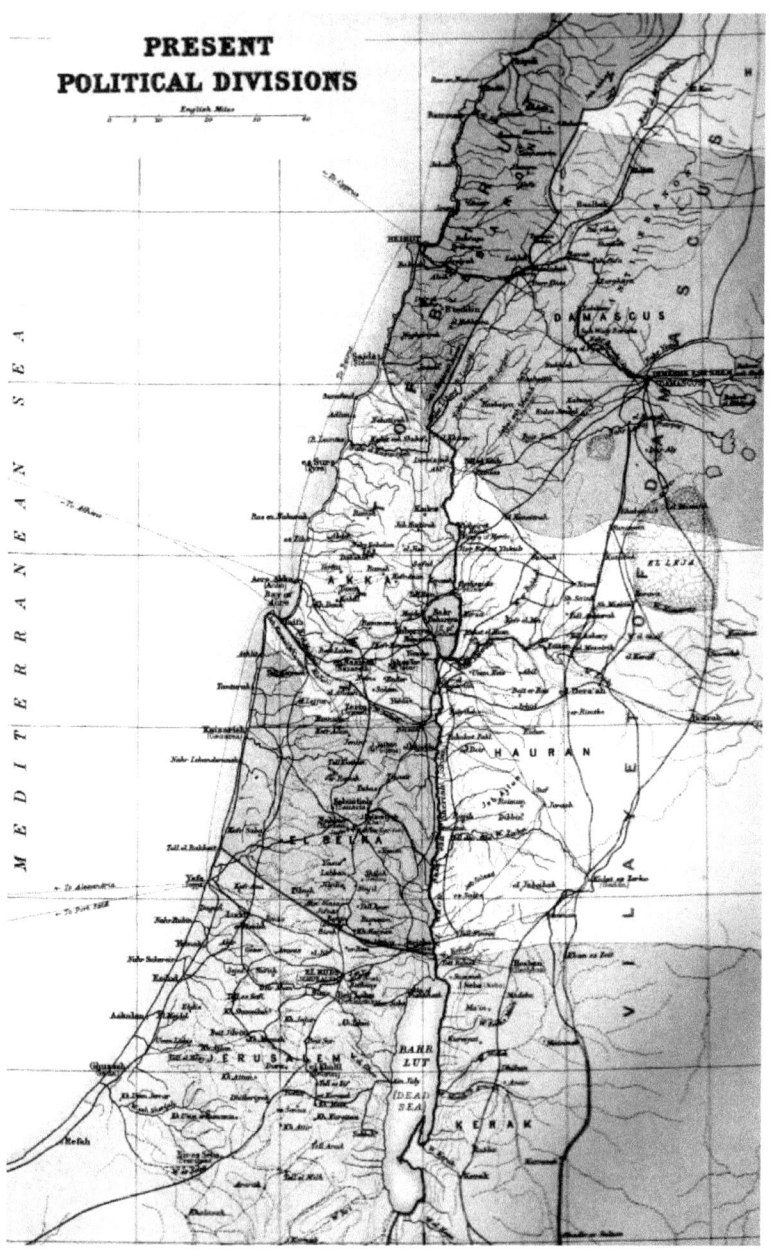

Map 2: Present Political Divisions 1915.

1914

Major Events[1]

I have to remember what happened on these dates that were, by the Spanish and all Europe's point of view, very important. On September 8 the Ottoman Grand Vizier communicated to all the foreign ambassadors that the Sultan had signed an *irade*, abolishing the Capitulations. The effect of such a notice can scarcely be described: Christians fell victim to a tremendous panic, given that demonstrations immediately began against the Europeans. In Jerusalem there was one that did not take on great importance, but it did have an official character. The governor of the city attended it and read out a telegram from the Minister of the Interior, confirming the news. The information I get from other zones is much more serious, as events have now a marked anti-Christian character.

20 October, 1914

Gueyrand (the French consul in Jerusalem)[2] came to the hotel this evening to tell me that he had a telegram from the French ambassador in Constantinople, Mr. Bompard, warning him of the possibility of a diplomatic break between France and Turkey because Russian ports have been bombed by the 'Goeben' and 'Breslau.'[3]

21 October, 1914

Gueyrand semiofficially handovered to me the French consulate in which I hoisted up the Spanish flag.

12 November, 1914

The local government sealed the rooms occupied by the former consulate of France. I found out in time by a warning from Count Senni, the Italian consul in Jerusalem, and taking his car I ran to get out money, objects of silver and papers before it was sealed.[4] The police, however, stopped me upon leaving in the carriage, and a great hullabaloo was on. I managed to get them to let me go after much shouting, and in a few days the Chief of Police of Jerusalem came to ask my pardon, which I granted without any trouble, but after warning him 'that it is the first and last time.'

16 November, 1914

Today I begin to write these lines, which will not be very literary but, nonetheless, should be interesting. Will I conclude these notes? Will the terrific announcements one can hear everywhere come to pass? I do not know, but in any case I am so alone, so isolated, that lacking a family to tell my life to, I'll tell it to my distant family, which surely must be worried about my fortune because I imagine that the newspapers of Europe are making things even uglier than they are in reality... which is bad enough. If I see my family again, as I hope, these lines will serve to awaken our memories, on the one hand indelible, and in the opposite case, I would like to think that these notebooks will get to their hands.

And let's begin. This afternoon, at 1:45 my good friends and colleagues, George Gueyrand, consul general of France, the chancellor of the consulate Mr. Clouet and the English consul W. Hugh, who gave us such good times interpreting the works of Mozart or Beethoven, left on the train for Jaffa. In the station there were a lot of people: Miguel Antonio Guerássimo, director of the Crédit Lyonnais in Jerusalem was going too, and the Barluzzi couple.[5] The impenetrable military governor of Jerusalem, Zaki Bey, sealed in front of me the safe-conducts given to the consuls by the civil governor, Madjid Bey. After farewell hugs, my French colleague recommended me to his good compatriots and obtained my promise to do everything possible so that nothing should happen to them. I returned later to my office with the firm conviction that very bitter days were awaiting me, that I would spend many sad days and sleepless nights over the 'little charge' of the protection of French interests in Palestine.

In the afternoon, I received a visit from Monsignor Camassei, Latin Patriarch of Jerusalem, and the (Franciscan) monks, Aquilino Llaneza and Carlos García Argüelles, Procurator General of the Custody and the Superior of the convent of Ramla, respectively. I then conferred in the home of Mr. [Dr.] Otis Glazebrook, the American consul with him and Count Senni.[6] We spoke about the proposition made to me by the governor's secretary, Barciara Effendi, which consisted of obtaining from Spain, Italy and the United States a declaration from the Entente powers not to bomb non-fortified Ottoman ports, in exchange for which the Turks would allow the subjects of the belligerent countries, whom they had as hostages, to leave. We also agreed to telegraph Constantinople asking our ambassadors to insist upon obtaining the freedom of the Russian consuls Krouglof and Razomowsky, who were still not being allowed to leave.

I returned afterwards to the Hotel Marcos to eat and say goodbye, since I have installed myself once and for all in Guerássimo's house, certainly in a delightful area and in my judgment the most comfortable and *chic* of the Holy City, always so sad, but most especially in these present circumstances.⁷ I am writing these memories comfortably installed in my new abode, but with a silence and solitude so great that I feel very much like leaving everything and marching off to my country or to Egypt. About both hypotheses I make a thousand combinations, but above all I'm worried about the possibility that the terrible, although nice, Hasan Bey, the military general of Jaffa, may oppose the departure of the consuls. My *dragoman* [translator] Rauf Lorenzo is accompanying them, and upon arriving in Jaffa will turn them over to the Italian consular agent there, Alonso Alonzo; may God protect him so they [Ottomans] don't play dirty tricks and let the consuls depart on the Italian vessel that is waiting for them. I will not be calm until tomorrow.

I think that tomorrow I also have to start sending dispatches and protests about the occupations ordered by the Turkish authorities of the convents of the Clarissas, St. Anne, St. Peter [of Ratisbonne] and Notre Dame de France. ⁸ I also should say something about the Hospital of St. Louis and the matter of the seals that I have put on the consulate of France. I'm frightened of the responsibility that weighs upon me.

17 November, 1914

I took my first meals in my new house. The truth is that I am magnificently lodged with splendid bedrooms, a dining room, bathroom, billiards room and even a gymnasium. Wonderful!

Rauf returned from Jaffa and told me that there was no difficulty about the loading: Only the evil state of the sea. In the afternoon I visited the Russian colleagues, Krouglof and Razomowsky, and, to my great surprise, the Janissary of theirs speaks to me in correct Spanish and turned out to have a Spanish passport. That old Cossack!

18 November, 1914

A great day for Jerusalem. By previous announcement and public proclamation, Muslims, and many people who are not, have gathered in the mosque of Umar to hear the declaration of Holy War against the Allies. ⁹ This thing is a little strange because, frankly, if the war is about religion, it should logically be against all Christians. Are not the Germans and Austrians Christian? This is easily explained, knowing that the Muslims have called the Kaiser 'Muhammad Guillaume', and it makes them believe that he is the protector of Islam and almost a convert.

After the parade of all the unarmed garrison forces in the city, they organized, at the exit of the mosque, a triumphal march of the consuls of Germany and Austria, Schmidt and Kraus, who paraded in their car preceded by the military band and followed by many people who applaud and cheer them. In the mosque was an atmosphere of temperance and moderation towards the Europeans, but what will happen if, as I believe likely, the Turks are overthrown?

I'm waiting for the reply from the Spanish government to the telegram I sent announcing the complete change of the Discretory and the manner in which it was done. The telegram said:

> The *Custos*, by order of the Franciscan General, dismissed the Discretory and obliged the Procurator to register his duty by that night without my being able to oppose it. I beg the urgent delivery of promised, but not received, instructions.[10]

The Spanish monks are so offended that, with very rare exceptions, they are disposed to depart for Spain if a satisfactory response does not come from the Minister of Foreign Affairs, the Marquis of Lema. These days I have issued certificates and passports to almost all of them.

19 November, 1914

I continue without receiving instructions and in the same amusing situation. The monks have shown their impatience (unjustified but very understandable) with the tardiness in receiving a reply from our government. The truth is that if the latter keeps on with their policy of allowing us to lose our rights little by little in such a manner that our grandchildren will see the end of those rights, I believe that we can expect little from the gentlemen of the ministry.

I am also sending a telegram about the possible pact of no bombing of the Turkish ports, previously approved by civil and military authorities. Upon speaking to the civil authority, the latter expressed to me his desire to see the subjects of belligerent nations out of here for many reasons, among them the coming scarcity of provisions and the possibility of aggression on the part of the people of the country.

And nothing more. Many things occurred to me to write down in a report to the government that cause fear, but on the one hand, the Turks do not allow me to telegraph in code, nor to write sealed letters, and, on the other, there is no boat other than the Italian one which leaves every two weeks, and no one to whom I can pass on a dispatch because if they catch him, they will shoot him. I wonder how things are in Constantinople and the rest of the Ottoman Empire. The situation has me extremely worried because I am completely isolated from the rest of the world. Without the Capitulations, without the *French protection* for the clerics, what to do?

20 November, 1914

The person who was sub-director of the Crédit Lyonnais communicated to me (. . .) that the ports of Egypt are full of English and French warships. There they are ignorant of the true situation and believe that there is only war between Russia and Turkey (. . .). In Constantinople, a bomb was thrown at Enver Pasha, who turned out to be hurt only slightly in one leg, but wounded some officers who accompanied him (. . .). In Jaffa, fear of a slaughter of Christians if some warship approaches with hostile intentions is constant.

Being a day of celebration for the Muslims, I cannot see the governor to speak with him about the School of the Brothers of Christian Schools, which it seems that the authorities are going to close. I write to Monsignor Camassei to ask him to tell Father Cimino, *Custos* of the Franciscans, not to oppose the departure of the Spanish clerics who want to do so and that, if he is not authorized for it, that he solicits the Father General of the Order by telegraph.[11]

21 November, 1914

The Latin Patriarch answered me in writing, and after, he repeated to me in person that Father Cimino refused to telegraph Rome and that he didn't want to telegraph propaganda either so they could transmit it to the Father General of the Franciscans.

In the morning, in my daily meeting with the civil governor, the latter announced to me that the Brothers of the Christian Doctrine can return to Europe but that their schools, like all religious teaching establishments, will be closed. The Superior did not hide his joy at being able to leave, but I think we'll have to apply the motto of 'seeing is believing.' The truth is that if they authorize the departure of the Brothers, why not authorize that of the other religious people, and, above all, the women?

22 November, 1914

In the morning, the Superior of the convent of Marie Reparatrice gave me a fright, writing to me announcing that troops are going to occupy her convent. Alarmed, I ran in search of Zaki Bey, who promised me he will respect that convent and that of the Sisters of Charity, as well as that of Notre Dame de France. In the latter they will only lodge some officials.[12]

Barciara Effendi let me know that a civil and military commission will examine the archives of the French consulate and asked me for the authorization to do it in the presence of the *dragoman*. I roundly denied permission, and considering the gravity of the act, I telegraphed the embassy asking for instructions.

23 November, 1914

Two lines. Orders have been received to close all the schools governed by subjects of the belligerent states as well as authorization to leave for the religious personnel who want to and are teachers at those schools. General rejoicing among the fortunate (…) and me, seeing that many apprehensions have been lifted from me. The governor of Damascus wants to close the (Franciscan) convent of that city, and I telegraphed asking him not to do it, being Spanish and belonging to an international religious order. Will my petition have effect? I don't think so.

25 November, 1914

Yesterday, much ceremony. The last bit of ceremony was the one I offered to the civil governor, Madjid Bey, and his secretary, whom I had eat lunch in my borrowed house, a succulent menu prepared by my Arab cook who delighted my fellow guests, especially with the stuffed marrows which, together with the coffee, are the only attractions the food here has for me.

Today was a very busy day. I had hassles by the dozens with all the superiors of the religious convents and with the director of the Rothschild Hospital. A Sephardic rabbi also came to see me together with other companions of his, who were very frightened because they had it announced to them that all the Jews protected by the belligerent states had to become Ottomans, or else they would be expelled from Turkey after their goods were confiscated. I sent Rauf to find out if this news is true, and the government answered affirmatively. Poor people!

The honorary Spanish vice consul in Jaffa, Kuebler, telegraphed me that the *kaymakam* (of this city) wants to occupy and confiscate the Franciscan convent given that, before, it was under the protection of France, and for that reason it should be considered French. I am fighting this absurd theory based on the fact that, from the moment Turkey does not accept French protection, it should consider this convent as Spanish or international, and in both cases it is neutral, and they should not occupy it. Will I obtain a victory this time? I have perhaps more chances of reaching it than in the case of the convent of Damascus.

27 November, 1914

It has begun under the worst impressions and ended under the best. The first, due to having received in the morning the visit of a religious from the Sacred Heart to tell me that the soldiers will occupy their convent in Bethlehem tomorrow. I am prepared to expose the governor, Madjid Bey, accusing him of not having kept his promises and threatening him with my resignation. Fortunately, the way out comes in the form of a telegram from our minister, ordering me to demand that they return to the Crédit Lyonnais everything that had been confiscated by the government. Besides that, the ambassador in Constantinople, Arroyo, telegraphed me approving completely my 'prudent' conduct concerning the taking possession of the General consulate of France and announcing that soon they will send me instructions from Madrid about the conduct I should continue. . . (*which, naturally, never arrived*).

28 November, 1914

The uninterrupted pilgrimage of monks and nuns continues. Father Lagrange the illustrious Dominican, in whose health the Minister of State and the ambassador Arroyo had taken interest, came to thank me and afterward told Father Colson, Superior of St. Peter of Ratisbonne, that the foreigners of the belligerent countries will be sent to an interior city to remain 'available.' I laughed trying to calm down the cleric, but in reality I felt differently inside.

I decided, finally, to send my official correspondence to Constantinople. Although I intended to send it in a sealed envelope, and hoped that they would authorize me to do so, I found that the letter I received from the Spanish ministry was already open. In what country are we living?

30 November, 1914

The previous day was spent in preparations for the departure to Europe of the religious teachers who should abandon the country according to the order from the civil governor. But today the military governor, Zaki Bey, said that he did not have orders to let them leave, and, naturally, they were stranded. Unquestionably, if I stay here many months, all of these worries are going to kill me.

Our vice consul in Jaffa, Kuebler, arrived in the afternoon unexpectedly and triumphantly brought a document he has found in the convent of that city, in virtue of which the monks of this convent are authorized by the Ottoman government to raise the Spanish flag. We are very happy with that document issued in Jerusalem more than a century ago, which I hope will have some effect on the governor so he will not occupy the convent.

Yesterday, Sunday, they woke me up at 7:00 A.M. with a telegram from Damascus where the governor of the city threatened to close the convent if they do not present, by today, a document that proves their ownership. I ran to the home of the German consul, Schmidt, and he telegraphed the consul in Damascus and the embassy of his country in Constantinople asking that they intervene on our behalf. In agreement with me, he proposed that the German consul would take charge of the defense of our interests in that city until a consul is named who will be recognized by the Ottoman government. [*Arroyo answered me later such a thing is not feasible, because it would offend the French government.*]¹³

3 December, 1914

Today I have acted as a politician, a diplomat and almost as a fraud. Last night I received a telegram from Mr. [Eletherios] Venizelos, Greek Prime Minister, in which he announced to me the arrival of Mr. Raphaël as Greek general consul in Jerusalem. You need a sense of humor to come to Jerusalem at this point! His arrival gladdens me very much because it relieves me of the protection of the Greek interests which, given the enmity the Turks profess for them, was an assignment of some concern.

I sent my *cavas*, Abed, to Jaffa to wait for the new colleague, and his visit was in the style of that famous villager who went out to 'kill two birds with one stone.' I don't know who the first bird would be, but the second turned out to be Umar Effendi Bittar, mayor of Jaffa, removed from office by the *kaymakam* of that city.

Dear Umar came here afterwards and did us the great service I am going to recount. Last night, at 11:00, I received a telegram from Kuebler informing me that the *kaymakam* had sent a communication to Father Mateo Hebreo, Superior of the convent (St. Peter's of Jaffa), announcing that if he did not evacuate it within twenty-four hours, he would occupy the convent by force. They handed me the telegram when I was already in bed, and between natural indignation at the arbitrary measure and a bad mood at having my sleep interrupted, I sent a telegram to Kuebler ordering him that in case this little chieftain refused to listen to his petition, to wait for the matter to be resolved in Constantinople, and he should raise the Spanish flag over the convent and seal the door with the consulate seal.¹⁴

This morning Umar arrived, and right away negotiations began that resulted in the following plan: I wrote a letter to the governor of Jerusalem begging him to write to the *kaymakam* of Jaffa so that he would suspend the execution of his threat, and Umar himself took the letter *with a little gift*. In view of this, His Excellency sent the requested telegram, also forbidding the closure of the Ramla school (of the St. Nicodemus convent) which was also threatened. After Umar came to let me know all about this, we agreed that he would see the governor again to see if he would consent to send in his official mail a 'coded' letter of mine directed to our ambassador in Constantinople, in which I would ask that they work on the removal of the *kaymakam* from Jaffa, with whom His Excellency the governor was also on bad terms. We said goodbye, and in a little while the governor's secretary came in to ask me to telegraph and write forcefully to

Constantinople against the *kaymakam* of Jaffa. I can scarcely relate the impression this offensive/defensive alliance with Madjid Bey made on me.

But, more important, was my victory yesterday. An aide of Zaki Bey's, named Nur al-Din Effendi [Chief of Police?], came to tell me that they were going to search the archives of the general French consulate. I immediately sent a very strong letter to Zaki himself, such that the military types began to doubt it was necessary to take such a serious step, especially when I told them that I would receive them with *gunfire* those who entered or tried to enter the consulate. I showed them a pistol (...) which naturally was not loaded since I didn't have any cartridges. In addition, I sent a message to the governor saying that he should turn over my passport if they were determined to jump on top of everything (that is to say, presenting my resignation as consul).

The news of my energetic attitude immediately ran through the city and was celebrated with an outburst of passion. Father Athanase contributed to this since he told everyone about it 'in all secrecy.' In short, the French archives are saved for the moment, and the telegram from the embassy charging me to energetically oppose the operation was satisfactorily fulfilled.

4 December, 1914

The commotion continues. Zaki Bey came to see me, furious with Count Senni whom he accused of being a conspirator. He assured me that, in the case of opening one of the archives, the first one he would search would be that of the Russian consul, who is under Italian protection.

At 12:00 the Greek consul arrived. In the station, Barciara, Dr. Mazaraky, the Archimandrite Jacques, the one from Acre and Rafael Lorenzo were waiting. We headed immediately for the hotel, where the Greek colleague told me that the Germans were defeated everywhere, that the English are in Basra, the Russians in Erzurum and that 75,000 Canadians are waiting for the Turkish attack in Egypt. I know nothing of the war because of my absolute isolation, but on the other hand the official telegrams from the German and Austrian embassies say just the opposite, and, according to the Ottoman news agency, the day the Germans take only 10,000 prisoners is almost a defeat. Everyday it's nearly 100,000!

I had lunch with Rauf and the ex-mayor of Jaffa, Umar. Afterwards, I went with the latter to see Madjid Bey, who was very frank with me and reiterated that I should write a letter to Constantinople by means of the German consulate or even a coded telegram complaining about the *kaymakam* of Jaffa. If I manage to bring him down it will be a coup, since I would have in my hand the military governor and the civil governor. The first for his enmity with Senni and the second for the recognition of getting the *kaymakam*, his nightmare and enemy, off his back. Madjid Bey also told me that Senni is plotting against me, which I already knew by the aggressive attitude of the Italians towards my person and administration.

In the evening, the Greek consul, Raphaël, dined with me, and his news was: The formation of the sultanate of Egypt under Hussein, uncle of the Khedive, the delivery of Turkey, the decision of Italy to fight against the Central Powers, the annexation of all the islands by Greece and many more curious and fantastic details. I, for my part, told him the picturesque plans of the Turkish military staff: To cross the Suez Canal by a bridge made of oil barrels, a battle in which an official and two English soldiers died, and the rest of the army fled, etc. . .

Since we were down this road, we talked about the news from the Ottoman agency and these people who believed things literally. One of the most extraordinary was that a whale had sunk two French cruisers. We also laughed a lot over the famous blunder of the canon: The Turks had heard that in an English Protestant cathedral there was a *canon* (as is natural) and entered the cathedral, knocking down the main altar looking for the cannons.

5 December, 1914

Few things: Official visits from the new Greek consul in the morning. The German colleague promised me to send a coded telegram asking his ambassador to tell the Spanish diplomatic representative that I consider the removal of the *kaymakam* of Jaffa very convenient to our interests.

10 December, 1914

Umar Effendi returned from Hebron and Gaza, where he went to do some propaganda in favor of Madjid Bey. The latter came out Sunday with the *astonishing* news that he had tendered his resignation, which produced real panic in the city. I campaigned in his favor, visiting the other consuls, who all telegraphed Constantinople asking that his resignation not be accepted. Even the four Patriarchs (the Latin, the Greek, the Armenian and the Coptic) sent a message too. The panic was due, above all, because it was rumored that his substitute would be the *kaymakam* of Jaffa. In short, up until today, Madjid continues in his post, which gives us some hope.

Barciara Effendi came in the morning to announce to me that they would send all the clerics of the belligerent countries to Urfa, which is to say two days' trip from Aleppo. Keep in mind that the Turkish telegrams said that the Russians were already at Lake Van. Are they going (and it is no joke, I'm in no mood for jokes now) to send them to the meeting with the Russians to threaten them with beheading the hostages if they advance? Or are they simply going to keep them there as hostages because they fear a near and rapid invasion of the Allied Forces from the Egyptian border or by means of a landing at Jaffa? *Chi lo sa?* [who knows?] In any case, the situation is beginning to get serious, and if the ambassadors don't get the belligerents authorized to leave, the matter will become alarming.[15]

I exchanged several telegrams with Arroyo and Kuebler about the (St. Peter) convent in Jaffa. The *kaymakam* is truly enraged against us, and should be, for my tenacious and desperate defense of the Spanish nature of the convent. For the one in Damascus, Arroyo has obtained an order from the Ottoman Minister of the Interior that it be respected, although I fear that the governor of that city will insist, like the one in Jaffa, on considering it French for having been under French protection… and they will probably stay with him. What patience… my God!

11 December, 1914

General revolution in the religious element. Instead of sending them to the interior, the Ottoman government decided to keep them here but gathered in two or three convents to have them better under watch. I think that this is a pretext so that the majority of the convents will be empty, and these will be occupied by the troops they say they are going to send from Damascus.

Along with the Patriarch, Monsignor Camassei and the bishop of Capernaum, Monsignor Piccardo, I presided over a meeting of the Superiors of all the French establishments. The *Custos*, Father Cimino, was also there, and I limited myself to greeting him, bowing my head. Now, because of his attitude, almost all the Spanish Franciscans had asked His Obedience to go back to Spain. In the meeting it was agreed that the convents designated to lodge the clerics would be Notre Dame de France, St. Steven and the Brothers of St. Lazarus, as well as another in Bethlehem for the clerics who were found in that population.[16]

I insisted that the duality of dispositions in Constantinople cease and that they decide to let all who wish to leave Turkey do so.

16 December, 1914

It's over. All the French clerics, with very few exceptions, have left for Damascus and Urfa. We will write a bit of history: On the 13th, significantly a Sunday, the exodus of all the clerics began; before I had made enormous efforts to impede their departure, but in view of a telegram from Arroyo saying that it was impossible to exempt the clerics from a measure taken by the commander of the Army Corps of Damascus, I could no longer insist. I decided to write to the governor declining all responsibility, and rather energetically.

Although the Turkish order was that they should leave on foot, including the elderly, all wound up going by car thanks to my exertions. The departure was at 7:30 in the evening in cold and rainy weather. Father Jaussen (Dominican, and one of the most illustrious professors of the École Biblique), part of the expedition, wrote me a heartfelt note of thanks from Ramla in the name of all.[17]

Before the caravan left I received particularly marked proof of the gratitude of the clerics, and at midday we met in the magnificent refectory of the Dominicans (from whose convent all the expeditions left); some fifty Franciscans, Dominicans, Brother of the Christian Doctrine, White Fathers, Brother of the Assumption, a brother of St. John of Tantur and even some English Protestant missionaries. As an exceedingly rare exception, reserved for the visits of princes and bishops, we spoke during the meal. During dessert, Father Crechet gave a heartfelt toast to thank me for what they called my infinite attentions, and I call my duty.

On the 14th, the second caravan departed, comprised almost entirely of the sick and elderly: In it were, among others, Father Lagrange and Father Athanase, the latter the Superior of Notre Dame de France.

On the 15th I rested from my hard assignment of working day and night for my protectorates, but you cannot call a rest the sorrow with which I had to go to the convent of San Savior to close and seal the Procurator Office of the Holy Land. Much, much grief it gave me to leave the Procurator Office alone and abandoned. The good Father Aquilino Llaneza could scarcely contain himself to keep a tear from escaping.[18]

The third and last expedition left on that date, various Franciscans and Benedictines forming part of it along with the pleasant Abbot Gariador, Superior of the latter, additionally Father Roux, with all the Trappists of Al-Atrun, and four lay people: Mr. De Pavie, director of the railroad to Jaffa, Mr. Saintperon, director of the French Mail, Mrs. De Pavie and a servant from Notre Dame de France.

Upon returning to the consulate they told me all kinds of details about the landing of 25,000 British in Ashkelon and the presence in Jaffa of 13 war ships of said nationality. It turned out that the only thing that happened was a cruiser in front of Jaffa yesterday, and another bombed a police position on the coast of Gaza.

19 December, 1914

A great and solemn reception was held for the troops that came from Damascus at the orders of Djemal Pasha. After much artistic preparation, arches of triumph etc., the troops made their triumphal entry, each soldier carried a handful of wild flowers. The so-vaunted army formed two battalions, looking not at all martial and not very brilliant. I believe these are fresh troops.

In the afternoon a rumor began to spread that all of the female clerics would be able to go also, which would make a frightful amount of work for me, arranging lists, passports, special trains, etc. Nevertheless, and after receiving a telegram announcing that the *kaymakam* of Jaffa did not oppose the departure, today came an order to the contrary and no one, absolutely no one can leave. But the order turned out to be even broader, since it considers us prisoners because it adds that no one can write or telegraph anywhere. (*This order was in effect for scarcely a day.*)[19]

I had tea in Glazebrook's house (…) with the Greek consul. We spoke about the news and the rumors going around, and especially about the real or supposed landing of the French in Alexandretta, of the cutting of the telegraph line to the north, and the Russian and English advance. Since there is no means of communication it is impossible to know a single bit of news. The local government's passive resistance to communicating in writing the orders received is highly suspicious and that, together with the reigning anarchy, put me in a devil of a mood.

21 December, 1914

Also a memorable date in these sad, very sad days. Since yesterday morning I started preparing passports, giving orders, receiving people: In short, a horror. Yesterday, Rauf communicated to me that the government had received an order to let everyone leave. Rauf himself brought a copy of the order, and it turned out to contain the following dispositions: 1) The clerics of the belligerent nations, including the women clerics, are obliged to be at the cited points (Jaffa, Haifa, Beirut, Mersin) before the 28th of this month and then leave Turkey. 2) The same disposition is applicable to the women and children under the age of 18 belonging to one of the four enemy nations. 3) Subjects of neutral nations can leave, under the same conditions and the indicated time frame, by sea.

From all of this, various thoughts can be deducted: First, the trip that the poor French clerics were obliged to make to Urfa had no purpose. Another thing: What will be the fate awaiting those who stay here, belligerent or neutral, after the indicated date? It is very likely that the neutrals can leave via Constantinople, but that is not just a little jaunt that is waiting for them. As far as the belligerents, they will undoubtedly be considered prisoners of war.

Yesterday, the banner of the Prophet Muhammad made its entrance, and I would have liked to attend it but I was so busy all morning that it was not possible. Some rain showers fell which were capable of dissolving the most enthusiastic demonstration, and they even increased in intensity throughout the night and during today, accompanied by a wind so strong it caused the failure of the projected send-off of the religious women, the few clerics that remained and the rest of the belligerents, since the boat that should have picked them up could not approach Jaffa because of the storm.

The Spanish clerics left in various trains, fed up with the tyranny of Father Serafino Cimino, *Custos* of the Holy Land (...). The following people, whose names I list here left without His Obedience: Father Aquilino Llaneza, Father Hilarión Bahamonde, Father Aquilino Alemos, Father Celestino Fraga, Brother Luis Pereiro, Father Andrés Morato, Father Pedro Sorazu, Father Ramón Toyg, Father Gabriel Rojo, Father Julio Alonso, Father Julio Alonso Lemos and Father Pacífico Sempere. Father Francisco Castro left the following day with His Obedience.

23 December, 1914

Yesterday there was another departure of religious women. This time it was the turn of the Sisters of Marie Reparatrice and the Carmelites. Among the first group there were four Spanish women who promised to write to my father from Egypt, telling him that I am well and happy... to a certain extent. I charge them to tell him not to believe anything that the newspapers say about Palestine, since, for example, *Il Corriere d'Italia* published that the killings were widespread and that there were 50,000 Kurds in Jerusalem. They told me in confidence that the Italians blame me for everything that happened in the Custody.

24 December, 1914

Merry Christmas. At 1:30 in the afternoon the Latin Patriarch made his solemn entry, all arranged by protocol, in the church of the Nativity of Bethlehem. No alterations in the *Status Quo* in the sanctuary were made. I had visited Barciara Effendi, secretary to the governor, about this matter yesterday, and he assured me that the authorities would change nothing in the ceremony.

In the afternoon I went to Bethlehem, after bidding farewell at the station to a rather large group of expelled religious women. The day was splendid, and in Bethlehem one breathed the animation belonging to the inhabitants who have a justified reputation of being happy and boisterous, while the sadly famous Jerusalem is an immense tomb.

I attended part of the religious function and returned to Jerusalem because of the announced arrival in Jaffa of the American battleship, 'Tennessee', given that I had asked my American colleague permission for the Spanish clerics to make the trip to Egypt on board this ship.

Around 10:00 P.M. Elias (one of my French *cavas*) came to tell me that the telegram I tried to send advising of my arrival in Jaffa could not go out, thanks to the admirable system of military censorship that they have here, and which consists of the interested party going in person in search of the military censor so that the latter can authorize the transmission of the dispatch. When the censor is not at the seat of the military governor office, you must follow his footsteps until you find him. This evening my *cavas* ran around to all the hotels in search of him and couldn't find him, so the telegram had to wait until tomorrow, if we find *Sir Censor* tomorrow. Keeping in mind that the reason for the existence of telegrams is the necessity of communicating rapidly, one will understand that with this system the matter gets to be the same as if they didn't permit the sending of dispatches at all.

30 December, 1914

On the 25th I left for Jaffa in the company of the last-expelled female clerics and some civilians who wanted to leave. The following day, and in view of the fact that the American battleship had not left, I decided to put all the Spanish clerics and my protectorates on board of the 'Firenze' without waiting for the arrival of the battleship. I installed myself from 8:00 A.M. in the Customs Office (to whose director I presented the warm letter of recommendation from Madjid Bey), and there I watched the loading all day. Really, this could not have been done in better conditions. Hasan Bey, the terrible and ferocious military commander, conducted himself admirably. For the Spanish monks, who boarded first, they did not search their luggage, save one suitcase and a box for mere form. (…)

Finally, I visited the ship with the Sisters, whose Superior, as well as Father Llaneza, gave me letters making it very clear how satisfied they were with the authorities of Jaffa. With these letters I gave a pleasant surprise to the famous Hasan Bey. To the latter I paid, in effect, a visit the following day, and he entertained himself with nothing less than showing me the working of various explosives and taking several shots with a gorgeous pistol, Colibrí brand, with which he killed no one by sheer miracle.

After having coffee, Hasan Bey insisted that I waited for the tea, which made its entrance at the same time as the commander of the 'Tennessee', Mr. Decker, who had just arrived and was coming on an official visit accompanied by his consul. Refining his friendliness, Hasan had me eat some candies and those masses of gum the Arabs call crystallized fruit and which are really dynamite. I had an official lunch afterwards in the Hotel Hardegg, my fellow guests being my colleague Glazebrook, his wife and Mr. Decker. Toasts in honor of the Sultan, our king and the president of the United States. The American commander told me that he fought against us in Cuba on board of the 'Indiana', and showed me the decorations earned.

In the afternoon I went by coach to Tel-Aviv and after I visited the battleship, where they did not honor me with cannon fire for fear that the people of the towns neighboring Jaffa would think it was a bombardment. On board I chatted a moment with the Superior of the Ladies of Zion, the only religious women embarked on the American boat. (…)

I had dinner with Rabl in the Kuebler's home: German dishes, wine from the Rhine, beer from Munich, singing from the Spring of the Valkyrie, German cigars, tales of Austrian victories: In short, pure Germanism.

Monday I returned to Jerusalem, and the following day the governor communicated to me the order of expulsion of the French Jews within three days if they don't want to become Ottoman citizens. Back to the start!

Zaki Bey, the former military governor, came dressed in civilian clothes to see me. I wonder why they would order him into the reserve. For the rest, Jerusalem is rapidly Germanizing: The new military governor is a German general that they call Bach Pasha. In addition, the Chief of the Military Staff, the Military Censor, etc. are German.

1915

5 January, 1915

To celebrate the New Year, I received a telegram from our ambassador in Constantinople asking what has been my conduct during the time that followed the naming of the new Discretory of the Custody of the Holy Land, and what has been the attitude of the Spanish clerics. I responded on the 2nd with an extremely long dispatch explaining what happened and submitting to the ambassador these three solutions: First, my resignation; second, a transfer; and third, my continuation here but with the firm and unconditional support of the government. Which one of them will the Marquis of Lema adopt?

Having obtained a period of one week for the evacuation of the Jews, the latter continue their slow departure, which was, in the first days, an avalanche. I don't remember having seen in my life such queues of people as those formed at customs during the departure of the French clerics, the Russians, etc. and in the consulate on the first day of the exodus of the Jews. The Chief Rabbi read in the synagogue of the Spaniards and the Algerians a very clear communication of mine about this departure, which was defined clearly as an act of expulsion.

Turkish troops keep marching in the direction of the Egyptian border in spite of the fact that, in Europe, according to a letter from my father, they think the Turks have already seized the Suez Canal. The canal continues as always, up to now, and it seems to me that it will be the canal that seizes the Turks. Several good battalions march by and about a hundred Negroes (…).

Today I received a very special visit of thanks from Monsignor Camassei and a visit from Lieutenant Colonel Von Laufer Bey, who brought me the greetings of the new military governor.

The troop occupied the convent of Artas; complaints from the chaplain, Salvador [Issa] Bandak, would have been avoided if the nuns (Italians, Argentineans and Uruguayans) had preferred the Spanish protection rather than the French. With it, the Turks would not have occupied the convent until the matter had been clarified.

And nothing more. Oh yes, I and the other consuls received a communiqué from Lieutenant Colonel Von Laufer permitting us to use Spanish in the official communications to the embassy, and he also said that our newspapers would not be censored. On the other hand, my friend, the director of Austrian mail, came to occupy the Turkish Post, and thanks to that the service is beginning to be more regular. As you see, everything is in the hands of the Austro-Germans, and I ask myself what is left for these poor Turks.

6 January, 1915

I leave for Tantur and Bethlehem with my *cavas*, Elias, who is of Lebanese origin. After a religious function in Bethlehem, which was extremely long, I went to visit the Carmelites to whom I gave instructions. It seemed like a harem, since with their faces covered and being in cloistered rooms, they looked like Turkish women. After, I returned to Tantur where I spent the night.

New parades of troops in Jerusalem. This time (and I call this time the last two weeks) they were already better: They brought some artillery and cavalry squadrons.

7 January, 1915

The governor, Madjid Bey, has resigned. Definitely, the thing is going to become ugly, because the only authority in whom we could have any hope to calm the population and counteract the excessive and unfriendly influence of the military is leaving us. I visited him in the afternoon, and he charged me to write a letter to Arroyo, that he himself will take, which explains what his work has been here and the reason for his departure.

9 January, 1915

The arrival of Djemal Pasha (the great), the Minister of the Navy and the Commander in Chief of the Army Corps of Damascus.[1] His entrance, in the middle of a phenomenal downpour, was of the most mundane style ever. By car!

The majority of the troops we have seen these days are leaving for the conquest of Egypt. I have witnessed the most comic scenes: For examples, a soldier pulling a little child's wagon, but full of tins of water. A few days ago, a cavalry officer was exercising jumping his horse over the tombs in a Turkish cemetery; someone asked him the reason for that exercise and he answered, 'so that the horse would be able to jump over the canal.' But the morale of the troops was defined by the phrase of a colonel who said in a circle of officers: 'You know Jesus Christ, right? He is a prophet. Moses was another prophet and Muhammad is ours. Well, none of them could cross the Suez Canal, not even the three of them together.' How about that?

The state of the soldiers who are leaving is truly painful. Many of them are barefoot. Some companies, never the less, go by singing very animatedly. The artillery doesn't seem bad and, although they are taking the cannon covered, I think they must be Austrian; but they will not cross the canal.

Djemal Pasha announced that today is the last day the Jews can embark. Nonetheless, at the sight of the considerable number that are still in Jaffa, whom the 'Tennessee' has still not been able to pick up because of the strong seas, the authorities agree to the petition of the interested consuls to prolong the period until they can be picked up.

11 January, 1915

Yesterday, with a previous official announcement, Djemal Pasha granted us an audience. The protocol of the visit was very original. After turning in our documents to an officer of the Navy, who was serving as an assistant, they had us pass through the salon where he received us in the following order: First the consuls from Germany and Austria (his allies), then the American and I (protectors of the enemies) and finally the *honorable*.[2] Today His Excellency acknowledged the visit, sending us a card. Perfect.

15 January, 1915

From the 13th my situation has become unpleasant. That day (although I am not superstitious I remember that on a 13th of November the Discretory was changed) I received a telegram from the Spanish Minister of Foreign Affairs, the Marquis of Lema, ordering me to lift the official seals that I myself had placed on the door of the office of the procurator, and that I maintain cordial relations with the *Custos*, Father Cimino. The minister added that I should take away the seals in case the *Custos* asked it, and said that he would judge that question in depth later when he was more familiar with it. My soul suffered a great deal, and I was left completely disheartened by the order to 'lift the seals and be judged later,' since they should have told me to explain the matter and then judge, so that if I were wrong they could have given the order to lift the seals.

Despite all of this, I was ready to fulfill the order, and I went to the Latin Patriarchate to say that I would not object to removing the seals, if Father Cimino would so request. The Patriarch was not there and in the afternoon I found out the following which is, frankly, a bit too much: The Italian consul had received a telegram from Sonnino, the Minister of Foreign Affairs of his country, ordering him to attend the opening of the office of the procurator as a witness in the company of the Patriarch. In view of the telegram, and without anyone warning me about it, the *Custos* Father Cimino forced the doors (spending about an hour and a half in the operation) and carried out that act in the manner ordered by the Honorable Sonnino. With what right?

Naturally, I wrote a telegram resigning and asking for telegraphic instructions to know to whom I should turn over the consulate. Rauf announced his firm proposal to leave with me. I hope the minister accepts my resignation and thus will put an end to the sad story of my work in defense of the interests of the Royal Spanish Patronage, a job that has cost me a great deal of vexation, falling out with notables and authorities and spending a lot money out of my own pocket. This last humiliation was the last straw.

Djemal Pasha created a *coup d'état* awarding the St. Anne sanctuary to the Greek Catholics. In my judgment, it is a very smart move to avoid having to cede it to the Muslims who have been vehemently requesting that sanctuary to turn it into a mosque. The Greek Catholics are disciples of the White Fathers, the original owners of the sanctuary; I believe it is in good hands. Nonetheless, the donation is void now that the sanctuary is not property of the ministry, and they cannot transfer what is not theirs.

18 January, 1915

I had lunch in Tantur and had to act as an interpreter between my American colleague who speaks only English and the Austrians and Brother Cirillo who speak Italian. Fortunately, an inhabitant of Bethlehem who speaks Spanish and English helped me with the assignment.[3]

Djemal Pasha left yesterday morning for the canal. To my friend, 'Abd al-Rahman Pasha, he wrote: 'See you soon, on the other side of the canal…or in heaven.' I think the latter is easier, unless they find themselves on the other side of the canal, but as prisoners.

22 January, 1915

Arroyo has telegraphed me, saying that the Marquis of Lema had communicated to him to order me not to abandon my post for any reason in the present circumstances. I answered that I would continue here for the necessary time but that my resignation was logical because of the intervention of the Italian consul on a matter that was absolutely none of his business.

Without a doubt, due to a bad interpretation, yesterday I received a new telegram saying that the Marquis of Lema was impatiently waiting for news about the incidents that occurred in the Custody during last October. I answered Arroyo, asking that he send to the ministry the text of the telegrams that I had directed to Constantinople the 14th and the 19th of the current month in which I explained what happened. We will see if, this time, the minister understands what I mean.

The troops keep marching by, and this time they are really good. Yesterday I witnessed the parade of an artillery battery but only four field guns. What I cannot explain to myself is that this army has almost no cavalry; at least you don't see them anywhere, but I have not detected more than two squadrons. Doubtless, they are going another way, or they are not counting on more than the irregular cavalry of the Bedouins. All in all, they have accumulated a real army now, for the number of those who have passed through the city is no less than 40,000 or 50,000. But the organization is admirable: They don't have anything to eat. The officers eat black bread and a thank you very much. (…)

23 January, 1915

The Chief of Police, Nur al-Din Bey, who is going away to Trabzon, came to say goodbye. I am very sorry because he has been extremely helpful. [4] On the 30th I went to Jaffa by train and made friends with a Circassian lieutenant colonel. Many more officers were going also, since it seems they were trying to defend themselves in Ramla and other positions between Jaffa and Jerusalem.

The object of my trip was to turn over to Hasan Bey the order I got from the military governor of Jerusalem, Bach Pasha, that the military should vacate our convent in Jaffa in such a manner that Hasan cannot avoid its completion. To this end I paid him a visit the next day. Instead of the military system, I employed the diplomatic one, telling him that I brought the order myself to avoid having it sent by mail, which would have caused everyone to find out about it. He thanked me for my visit and my delicacy, or at least pretended to do so, and after the customary compliments and congratulating him on Muhammad's birthday, I left to take a spin around town with Kuebler. In a little while they came to urgently warn us on behalf of Hasan Bey, and I feared it was some complication, but it turned out to be an invitation to watch a 'fantasy' by the Bedouins, commanded by my friend Arif Bey, second military commander of Jaffa, and the son of a tribal chieftain of the Bedouins. The fellows, who paraded, were really savage, and, although the horses were nothing to write home about, one of the famous riders nearly went rolling on the ground.

Today the Dutch priest who has remained in charge of the establishment of St. Anne has come to let me know of the inauguration of the Muslim school, Saladin, that has been established at that place. He also informs me of the Greek Catholic services in the church and sanctuary of the Nativity.

Various Spanish Benedictines who stayed in Abu Gosh are getting rather alarmed and, the truth is, rightly so. Edelman [Samuel], who arrived a few days ago, told me that the opinion in Egypt was the same as here, that is, in case of the Turks being defeated, we Christians would run great risk upon their return from the canal.

They keep sending troops, cannons pulled by oxen, and today several ships arrived with small-sized bombs. Do they want to intimidate the British on the Canal? In front of the consulate several hundred volunteers passed by with green banners and singing *la Allah ilá Allah wa Muhammad rasul Allah* (There is no god but Allah, and Muhammad is His prophet). This makes the matter uglier. On the other hand, Bach Pasha, Christian and German, attended the inauguration of the Muslim university [of Saladin].

The Greek consul, Raphaël, came by in the evening to tell me about the rumors circulating in the city: That the war on the Egyptian border had begun, that there are rumors that Rumania is involved in the conflict dragging in other Balkan nations, etc.[5] We also talked about what happened in Jaffa with the English cruiser that stopped a boat and by means of £5 got its crew to take charge of sharing among the population proclamations written in Arabic and Turkish inciting the Arabs to rise up against the Ottoman tyranny and put themselves at the orders of the new Sultan of Egypt, a famous piece of work of the English. Hasan Bey had the boat torn to bits and found the proclamations hidden in it. The crew, (three Muslims and three Christians) have been sent to Damascus, on foot, to be judged. The Christians had no part in it, but the Muslims want to publicize that they were accomplices.

The *Custos* Father Cimino 'educated' me with his Christian humility, refusing absolutely to give me the explanations in writing that the Spanish ministry announced to me. We shall see.

4 February, 1915

Late yesterday, the new civil governor made his entrance. Rauf went to wait for him, and he said he is nice and young, but in any case I will miss his predecessor Madjid Bey.

A new victory: The priest of Artas has come to tell me that, by order of Bach Pasha the Argentinean-Uruguayan convent has remained free. The same day I received a telegram from Kuebler announcing that the Jaffa convent is also empty, without soldiers. I communicated these two pieces of good news to Monsignor Camassei, and he answered me *la ringrazio e saluto* in a card. Always the same! I am becoming anticlerical in Jerusalem. This is really funny.

On the first of the month word was going around that the Turks had crossed the Suez Canal. With such auspicious cause the soldiers gave free rein to their enthusiasm, firing their guns in the air. Father Aracil tells me, nonetheless, that several bullets were found in the San Savior terrace. The people of the neighboring towns, especially those of Siloe and Mount of Olives, which from ancient times were famous for bandits, upon hearing the shots, they presented themselves in Jerusalem armed and ready to take part in the killing and sacking that they believed was taking place which, frankly, is not very reassuring.

There is someone who assured me that there was no such news of the crossing of the Canal and that what happened was that a Turkish regiment refused to advance and mutinied, killing one officer. To cover up the matter, they invented the news so that in the general rejoicing the people would not realize what was happening.

My great friend, Roshan Bey, advised everyone to 'save your bullets for the enemies of Turkey', but in any case a popular demonstration was organized by about a hundred savages with a boat occupied by drummers from Jaffa, who went by in front of the consulate shouting the greatest insult that an Arab can shout: *Russian son of a bitch*.

8 February, 1915

The day before yesterday the news about the crossing of the Canal went around again. That this news was telegraphic I know because my *cavas's* son is employed in the Telegraph Office. I asked the new civil governor, and he told me that the news was not official, but that unofficially it was known that the troops had crossed the Canal, having sunk two English warships, the rest fleeing. I stick to my guns, and I do not believe the crossing very probable unless it is an English stratagem, which does not seem very likely to me.

The first French *dragoman*, Jean Rahil, told me in order to *calm me down*, that the sailors that I saw go by the other day were bringing mines that they have deposited in the fortress of Mount Zion with the goal of blowing up the whole city if it is attacked by the English. I don't believe that either, and my opinion is confirmed by what I saw yesterday morning: When I was headed to Tantur, I found various coaches that were headed to the border loaded with boxes of dynamite, so the most likely thing is that those mines are for Egypt and not for Jerusalem.

I went to Tantur yesterday and, upon arriving at the road from which the Jewish colony of Montefiore leads to the station, I ran into Monsignor Fellinger, the rector of the Austrian hospice, who accompanied me in the car. At the left of the highway, in the improvised aviation field, there were quite a few soldiers doing field exercises and playing tag. Afterwards, and accompanied by Brother Damian, we went to the convent of Artas to attend the luncheon with which they were paying tribute to me for having managed to save the convent from military occupation. During the lunch we had the surprise of hearing the music of Spanish *zarzuelas*, which increased, if possible, my homesickness.

Once the lunch was finished, there was a little bit of the inevitable Arab music, national hymns, etc. Then I mounted a horse, and in the company of the chaplain and two Italian clerics, as well as two armed Algerians, just in case, we ascended the mountain situated to the south of the convent. It belongs to the convent and is a real balcony over the desert. From there I could contemplate St. Chariton, Teqo', the Mount of the Franks, St. Theodosius, almost all of the desert to the east of the Dead Sea, the mountains of Moab, Jerusalem and Bethlehem. (...)

9 February, 1915

I have witnessed another new demonstration to celebrate the taking of the Canal. From my balcony I saw the people gathered in front of the city hall. The police guards were going first on horseback, then the students of the Muslim university of Saladin (located, as you will remember, in the convent of the White Fathers), the infantry battalion and, finishing up the march, the band of the most fantastic music that I have seen up until now, with red and green banners, enormous drums, kettle drums, tam tams, etc. One of the demonstrators, who must have been the most eloquent, gave a speech on the little stairway of the city hall saying that, after the conquest of Egypt, the Turks would take over Tripolitania, Algiers, Tunisia, and Morocco. Imagine that!

Today I went with Dr. Glazebrook to show Bach Pasha the proclamation signed by 'Abd al-Aziz Urani, *mudhir* (director) of the Saladin school and famous Egyptian agitator. Bach Pasha has just assured me that the troops in Jerusalem are excellent and reliable. They came out of Asia Minor, and there are many Christians among them so that, in case of disorder, he would have them at hand. With respect to the proclamation, he promised us he would talk about it to the civil governor and take the appropriate measures.

10 February, 1915

Some say that instead of crossing the Canal, the Turks have suffered a tremendous defeat and that Djemal Pasha is returning without having accomplished his goal. None of these bits of news is confirmed, but I find them more believable than that of the crossing of the Canal.

12 February, 1915

Yesterday I had my first *business* meeting with Medyet Pasha, the new civil governor of Jerusalem, who had complained about the terms on which I had protested the occupation of the Notre Dame de France. We agreed that, in place of, 'I hold the governor responsible,' I would put, 'I decline all responsibility.' Naturally, this change was heavenly music. The governor assured me that the *mudhir*'s famous circular does not go against all Christians but only against the Allies. I asked him then: 'Who are the adorers of the Cross and the descendents of the Crusaders? Are they only the English and the French?' I don't like the new Pilate at all, but I trust that he will not simply wash his hands if it comes to a case of crucifying us.

When I asked Barciara Effendi if they had had official news about the battle for the Canal, he answered me that the victory had not been as brilliant as they had first believed. I have also been told that Bach Pasha will depart for Constantinople. For God's sake, I hope not.

13 February, 1915

I have seen a policeman on horseback, who was gathering all the cars of the Jews. I figured it would be to drive the wounded, and sure enough, a little later they left, headed for Hebron and Beersheba, loaded with beds. Poor people.

15 February, 1915

Yesterday was Sunday (…) we saw Bach Pasha leaving precipitously, and in a little while he appeared again to tell us all good-bye and went off to Damascus … or who knows where. It is a shame.

16 February, 1915

A day of big, fat lies. The tale of the Canal battle, according to a witness who was there: At 4:00 P.M. the first troops arrived some five kilometers from the Canal, and immediately the military leaders telegraphed Djemal Pasha, asking if they should attack and, as the response was negative, the action was put off until the following morning. The Arabs, the only ones who were sent ahead, advanced at 6:00 A.M., being greeted by a cannon shot a minute by an unseen enemy. The cannon fire diminished in intensity and, finally, ceased altogether. Then the advance was made with great speed, the troops arrived at the Canal (all this without seeing the enemy), and some 8,000 men crossed it, but then a rain of fire shot by artillery batteries, warships and fifty airplanes, completely destroyed the Turkish army. Nothing like this is remembered in history. As you see, the oriental fantasy is truly remarkable.[6]

My *cavas* Elias asserted that Count Senni has ordered, or at least advised, all his compatriots to leave Turkey and that the consulate will pay for the voyage for the poorest. I don't believe it, unless the insistent rumors of Italy next entering the war are confirmed.

Djemal Pasha is probably staying here for a while longer, since he has bought himself some 'souvenirs' of Jerusalem. He is living in the sanatorium of the Mount of Olives, and this I know thanks to my barber's son, who had the honor of trimming his beard.

The Arabs are angry against the Turks for having sent them to their death. But there is no single one who is capable of resisting the oppressors. These people have no consciousness of what nationalism is.

20 February, 1915

Frankly, the review of the Turkish army carried out the day before yesterday has been comical. Djemal Pasha, with his staff, situated himself in front of the consulate, and in front of him paraded about 4,000 infantry, who may be good troops but are little accustomed to military parades. The horses were disastrous. There was an officer whose horse did not obey him, and both of them, man and beast, tumbled down in front of the minister, who had to take a whip to the noble beast. The infantry went in the direction of Bethlehem, but before, I saw eight pieces of artillery, two squadrons and a half dozen *meharis* who were marching in the opposite direction. It seems they intend to renew the attack on Suez.[7]

23 February, 1915

A splendid day, spring-like. My Greek colleague came by in the afternoon, gave me a drubbing at billiards and then we went together to visit the new military governor, Ali Riza Bey. This nice man fought a long time in the Balkans and was named general (Pasha). When the constitutional regime was inaugurated he was dispossessed of his rank and sent as a business representative to Montenegro. Then he went back to the army, but with a rank of colonel (Bey). He made a good impression, and he has even told us news of the war. He talked to us about a new bombardment of the Dardanelles, carried out by the British squadron as well as about 65,000 Russian prisoners taken by the Germans, a figure that seems to me a bit exaggerated.

9 March, 1915

It has been quite some time since the previous date, but I have been able to do almost nothing because of an operation on my foot. The news that I have had during this time confirms that there really was a great slaughter at the Canal. They assured me that the attack was at 2:00 A.M., that the English let them approach the Canal and even that many soldiers crossed it. Perhaps it was then that they telegraphed Jerusalem that the army was on the other side, but then the English attacked in such a manner that in a few hours those who were on this side of the Canal began a disorderly retreat, abandoning their dead. It seems that, in Cairo, there was a parade of 5,000 prisoners in a really deplorable shape.

After the battle, an English airplane presented itself in al-'Arish, announcing that the British had in their power several thousands of wounded soldiers they were carefully looking after. The same proclamation begged the Turks to return to bury their dead, to avoid epidemics. There must have been, in fact, a great number of casualties in the retreat, since a real sanitary service did not exist, nor did they have even food or water. Proof of it is that one of my French *cavases*, Nagib, writes (and he didn't even get to the Canal) that he has had to spend 100 Francs out of his pocket in order to eat.

An Armenian told us that he didn't even shoot his rifle, since he did not know where he should shoot since he did not see a single Englishman. There were only warships, airplanes and heavy caliber batteries, and at a range much greater than their cannons. Is it going to turn out to be the truth what I, days ago, branded as lies?

I am not a military man, but it seems to me a mistake to have attacked the Canal, and instead I think it would have been more effective to have limited themselves to sustaining some forces that would have been a constant threat to the English. That would oblige them to always keep a strong army in Egypt not available for the European front. But, I repeat, I am not a military man.

It looks like the railroad from Hedjaz has been cut by the English and that the Yemeni tribes have risen up against the Turks, recognizing the new Sultan of Egypt. 'Abed confirms to me that the Bedouins have done nothing more than steal weapons and mounts from the Turkish army. It is 4:00 in the afternoon, and the artillery keeps on moving towards the Canal.

11 March, 1915

They told me that the railroad which I mentioned before was not cut by the English but rather by the Bedouins, naturally.

Since yesterday, I found myself in a state of re-concentrated anger that is truly unbearable. The cause? Simply, the absurd measure taken by the Turks of closing all the Franciscan convents. Who will have been the instigator of this measure? Undoubtedly, there is one, and I would like to know who he is. The result is that, yesterday, they closed Bethphage and today they have done the same with the Casa Nova of Bethlehem.

I sent Rauf to see the governor with the text of the note sent by Arroyo to the Grand Vizier and Minister of the Interior with respect to the property of the Spanish convents, but I don't know if the dear French protection has given scant service to the Holy Land this time. Naturally, this matter has Jerusalem stirred up, since half the city lives off the Franciscans.

12 March, 1915

From early on, a swarm of clerics came to see me. The Yankee consular agent, Mr. [George] Young, communicated to me that Father Gabino Martín Montoro, led away under escort, is a prisoner in Aleppo and that Fathers Adriano and Miguel Angel are still detained in Damascus. Hmmmm!

To my complaint, that the Custody communicated nothing to me with respect to the closing of Bethphage, Father Nicolini responded to me with what, in good Castilian, is called a 'blunder'.

13 March, 1915

Today I have had the real pleasure of giving a good lesson to the mayor of Jerusalem, Husayn Effendi.[8] For some time he has been bothering me with his fanaticism and incorrectness. Well: Today he announced to me that he wanted to enter the storerooms of Mrs. Bost's house to requisition some iron objects. I let him know that a representative of the consulate would attend, would make receipts and would open the door with the key that was in my hands. When my *cavas*, Elias, took him the message, he answered insolently, saying that he would not permit anyone to attend since the Capitulations no longer exist – what does one have to do with the other? – and finally declared he was inclined to knock down the doors.

In the afternoon, the mayor went to the storerooms with a police officer and Elias. The latter opened the door and Husayn immediately took charge of the key and dismissed my *cavas* in rather eloquent terms. I got very angry, and sent Rauf to see the governor, who got rather angry himself and launched a monumental tirade at the mayor by phone. Despite the mayor's invocation of the famous suppression of the Capitulations, the governor told him where to go, not to commit such barbarities, nor to enter where he was not invited. Next, the governor asked me in very courteous terms, and in an official manner, to open the storerooms with my *dragoman* in attendance under the terms outlined by law: That is, paying half the price at the time of the count and the other half with a receipt to collect after the war, which, naturally will be worthless, but the correct thing. Besides, he particularly charged Rauf to give me all sorts of explanations on his part, that he recognized that the mayor had skipped over me and that he would oblige him to return the key to me.

This morning I got up early, and I saw passing by nothing less than seven battalions of infantry with the corresponding supply of camels and some (very few) machine guns. A band of musicians from Smyrna was at the head; they were really good and would be even more so if their director was not mounted on horseback directing with a baton. The troops are composed almost entirely of Turkish elements, the same ones that sent the Arabs to their death and fought brilliantly...from the rearguard.

Details about this Turkish army: Upon entering Jerusalem almost all the soldiers, on the march, bought bread. Doubtless, they were starving; one of those who bought bread was a captain mounted on horseback. When he realized the presence of the Prince of Hohenlohe, whom he had to salute, he had no choice but to return the bread to the boy who sold it to him. But for that, it would have been a triumphal entry into Jerusalem with a little loaf of bread in one hand and a saber in the other! Another detail: While passing by my balcony, a trumpet boy made a mistake and played a wrong note. An officer shoved him back with his horse and I thought he was going to run him through with his sword. The poor soldier took such a fright that he couldn't play anything then. After the mentioned battalions, quite a few soldiers went by without weapons: They were Armenian troops whom the military leaders suspected of conspiring to provoke a military uprising.

17 March, 1915

Djemal Pasha published an official account of his expedition to Egypt and says that there are only 800 deaths to mourn.

20 March, 1915

One of my French *cavases*, Nagib, a soldier in the Turkish army and employed in the ambulances, arrived from the desert. He told me that there were soldiers who were so hungry that they got to the point of cutting off pieces of flesh from the camels they were riding. It seems to me a bit too much to swallow, but these exaggerations (assuming that they are) prove the military and patriotic spirit of this army.

23 March, 1915

Yesterday I marveled and was convinced of how small we are despite our pretensions. I made this reflection while contemplating the passing of a cloud of locusts. I was in my office when I was surprised by the strange color of the sky, with a light similar to that of a solar eclipse.[9] Upon peeking out from the balcony I saw that an immense cloud had completely obscured the light of the sun. The ground, the balconies, the roofs, the entire city and then the countryside, everything was covered by these wretched little animals. At least it lasted less than an hour, but the unfortunate fields of Jericho, from whence the plague proceeded, must have been left without a blade of grass. As a consequence of all of this, the price of wheat has risen enormously. Just what we needed.

With all of this, the soldiers returned and occupied Jerusalem, Bethlehem, and the surroundings. They celebrated another demonstration similar to the one that took place at the 'taking of the Canal,' but this time to celebrate that the Turks have sunk four warships.

26 March, 1915

With perseverance worthy of a better cause, the Turks succeeded in their wish to occupy in part the Franciscan convent of Jaffa; what is certain is that they have only closed a few empty rooms.

Today the famous pilgrimage of Nebi Musa has left. [10] The green banners went by, Djemal Pasha, the governor, the *Mufti* and a few dozen pilgrims excited by the shouts and song of the Muslim women who occupied the terraces. From the Austrian hospice, from where I witnessed the procession, I went to the hospice of St. Paul to visit General Bruno Traugott Trommer and from there to Notre Dame de France, where I managed to confirm the ravages caused by the Turks. (…)

It seems to be confirmed that, a few days ago, a bombardment took place in Haifa. 'Abed tells me that the Bedouins from Shatt al-Arab (in southern Iraq) have risen up against the Turks.

28 March, 1915

Yesterday my visit was returned by General Trommer, who turned out to be very nice and not at all fanatical concerning the successes of his compatriots. He commands the 8th and 10th divisions of the Ottoman army, which are from Rodosto [Terkidağ] and Smyrna.

Locusts have appeared again, although this time of lesser importance. I did not even see them.

The Greek consul, Raphaël, let me know what happened in Greece lately. The Prime Minister, Venizelos, wanted to take the country to war following the pretensions of France and Great Britain, both of which need a Greek army of 120,000 men to attack the Dardanelles by land.[11] King Constantine was not of this opinion, since such a decision would leave Greece exposed to an attack by the Bulgarians. The matter was getting so tense that Raphaël received a coded communication from his ministry giving him instructions so he could turn over the Greek interests to me in case hostilities break out with Turkey.

30 March, 1915

I am frankly impressed, because last night near my house they hanged two poor devils accused of espionage. One of the sentenced men was a Christian from Gaza, and the other a Muslim from Sudan. The execution took place near the Jaffa gate. The matter, keeping in mind the extremely grave times we are going through, did not make me stop worrying. On the one side, the possibility that the Allies will take over Constantinople (although, as far as I can see, they are taking it calmly) and will want to finish Turkey once and for all, and on the other hand the ominous omens from the *Young Turks* and the publications from Jaffa and 'Abd al-'Aziz Urani are not likely to calm anyone. I confess what most disconcerts me is the cynicism with which the Turks take control of all the property of the belligerents, without any care, and even that of their own allies (who, for their part, are already fed up). Do you suppose they think they are going to come out as winners? Are they sure of their ruin and just want to ruin everyone else beforehand? Will this desperation come to cutting our throats? *Voilá l'affaire*.

In the police station that is next to the Jaffa gate, 'Abed found a black man who had been a doorman in our convent in that city. It seems that the poor man had been detained as a suspect (of espionage) and has suffered a nervous attack, since to show him what awaited him they made him witness the hanging of the two unfortunates. It seems that the rope to hang the Christian broke twice and then the poor man said to his executioners: 'God doesn't want you to kill me.' But they replied: 'God may not want it, but we do.'

They say that desertions among Arabs are extremely numerous because they don't give them food. Nonetheless, General Trommer assured me that the soldiers' rations here are double what they give German soldiers. But then, what is it that the Germans eat?

6 April, 1915

The Holy Week has ended, and I have attended the services of all the Christian denominations in Jerusalem. The Abyssinians, especially, are so extraordinarily strange that I would willingly have spent hours listening to their monotonous psalms and observing their colorful fellows, with crowns of tinplate, red mantles and other extravagant colors that would have been the dream of any chorus girl in 'La Africana.' It was all a real comedy.

The Greeks were very, very friendly, so as soon as they saw me they arranged to make way for me among the people and place me in the same gate as the Holy Sepulcher, facing the Orthodox Patriarch Damianos. The *Greek Fire* is an impressive show, and not at all Christian.[12] This year, however, it was not as animated as in others for the lack of pilgrims. Next to me there were the authorities, and among them Mehmet Djemal, who is chief of the army operations in this part of Turkey. As a good Muslim, he must not have formed a very good impression of the Greeks.

Later I had a visit from the Greek Patriarch Damianos and the archbishop of Jordan, Monsignor Meletios, who came accompanied by another Greek priest who, to my great surprise, began speaking to me in Spanish, turning out to be a converted Jew. The truth is that one finds these Sephardic Jews everywhere.

7 April, 1915

Since we all live on memories, I'm going to stop writing current impressions to recall something of my trip to Jerusalem. I set out for the first time for the Holy Land on July 26, 1913 by train. I arrived in Marseilles in the evening, and I got up early the following day. I remember spending the time thinking of the marvelous legends of the Orient, where my destiny was leading me. (…)

The first of August we visited the low and sandy coast of Damietta (in Egypt), our ship 'paraded' before the great dredges that work ceaselessly to impede the sediment of the Nile from overwhelming the Suez Canal. With the usual formalities completed, we advanced to the very beautiful Port Said. On board, I waited for a little calm in the infernal hubbub that is always raised in the East by the line boys, the drummers and vendors with such shouts and such pressuring that you have to reject them almost with shoves.

I decided to take a small boat and landed in front of Customs. After I began to contemplate the unique attraction Port Said has, which consists in sitting in one of those European style cafes, tasting the delicious Turkish coffee and dedicating oneself to observing how sorts from all countries and all tastes go by: Arabs, Europeans, Bedouins, Jews, Japanese, Chinese, Indians, Persians…it's the limit. One has to recognize that the most interesting types are the Bedouins, arrogant and with a majestic walk, since the custom of carrying great weights on their heads makes them have movements of surprising dignity.

A little later (and after having installed myself in Jerusalem) I obtained a license to return to Spain, owing to the fact that I found myself recovering, or rather, I was still sick with malaria. When I arrived in Jaffa to board I found out that there were some cases of the bubonic plague. Fortunately, I managed to free myself from the order that prohibited passengers from that city from embarking; I boarded a merchant ship, the 'Olympus' of the German Line of the Levant which took me as far as Haifa. In this city I boarded the steamship 'Minieh' in which I went as far as Beirut. The boat was pretty bad and dirty, but, at least, I managed to make the trip.

Beirut has no charm as a city, since it has not the typical population of the East, nor it is a good European city. Nevertheless, it is pleasant to spend a few days in it, and above all, the view from the sea, having as a background the marvelous mountains of Lebanon, is an incomparable grandeur.

There, the Parodi's couple, Arturo de Luciano and Gómez Muros from Granada, attached to the Spanish consulate, lavished much attention on me. I took the ideal excursion: I went by train to the first foothills of Mount Lebanon, where Father Victoriano Argote, Gómez Muros and Father Salvador Frasquet were waiting to take me by car as far as Haris. As we went up in elevation, the temperature cooled. In the middle of our trip we made a stop at the palace of the Maronite Patriarch, and taking advantage of the circumstance of his retirement, I paid him a visit. He showed himself to be extremely friendly with me, and more deferential one could not be.

We continued our way through the middle of pines and oaks, not to mention some fields of mulberry trees (extensively cultivated in Lebanon), and thus we reached the peak. The view that they have from the Franciscan convent of Haris – one of the oldest of the Order in the area –is really extraordinary. At the foot of the mountain is the beautiful bay of Yunie, at the southwest a whole series of little towns and white and merry country homes, populated in the great majority by people who have made their fortune in America and speak Spanish, and there in the background, Beirut, so picturesquely situated. In the middle of that beautiful nature, Father Victoriano Argote has a life that I envy, although naturally I refer to the summer, since in the winter the snow and the cold do not make living there very tempting. Father Victoriano, raised in Turkey, speaks Arabic marvelously.

The following day, I got up very early and heard a Maronite mass, very curious for us Europeans since it is celebrated in Arabic. After giving my thanks to Father Victoriano, we began our return journey to Beirut, enjoying the truly unsurpassable landscapes, above all the Nahr al-Kalb.

That same day I set off for Alexandria in the 'Ernest Simmons' of the Maritime Messengers, an old and run-down boat that moves like a swing and does not much honor that company. The only sociable people on board: The wife of the director of the German mail in Jerusalem and a traveling German (. . .). At quite a distance from the port, a haughty police motorboat boarded us. The truth is that the first thing that occurs to one is to think that the English parcel out riches and comfort everywhere, although they are the ones who enjoy it mainly.

As we were coming from a place suspected of the plague of which I spoke, they kept us in the outer harbor until very late. Only when it got dark did they let us enter the port. (…)

[In the company of the Spanish ambassador, Cristóbal Fernánadez Vallín], I got into one of the trains that circulate between Alexandria and Cairo. The *Jamsin*, or desert wind, had blown the day before with such force that when we were anchored in the outer harbor we couldn't see the city. (…)

From the marvelous station of Cairo, Rosario and Carmen Vallín took me to visit the Egyptian Museum. Later, we made the obligatory visit to the pyramids.

Another excursion that has left me unforgettable memories is the one I made at the beginning of 1914 to Damascus. The Italian consul in that city, Vivaldi, had behaved so inappropriately with our monks that, by order of the Marquis of Lema, I had to go there to intervene in the matter.

The trip from Jaffa to Haifa was made on board the ship 'Anfitrite.' At dawn we arrived in Lebanon, admiring the beautiful spectacle of the bay of St. John of Acre with the grandiose shape of the Mount Carmel (it is the unsurpassable charm of this 'country of names'). Through whatever part one travels, one finds and sees the most famous cities, mountains, ports and places in the world. At first, one feels disillusion, but I think I will end up feeling the most irresistible nostalgia for the land of Jesus, of the Crusades, of the Prophets: For the land where the most interesting human history has developed.

In Haifa we disembarked on the iron pier, and right away went to Mount Carmel where the fathers, extremely friendly, showed me the church, the 'grotto of Elijah' and the entire convent. I spent a long while on the terrace, contemplating the marvelous view that one can appreciate from up there.

The following day I took the train to Damascus. Accustomed to the inconveniences of the Jerusalem-Jaffa railway, I found the car of this new line to be splendid. The Plain of Esdraelon made me sad, for in a country of that agricultural wealth it was completely barren and unproductive.

We continued the trip, and the view of the mountains of Lebanon covered with snow entertained me and made the time shorter for me until my arrival in Damascus in the afternoon. The surroundings, neatly cared for and cultivated, the modern roadside stations and the Damascus station itself made me fear a new disillusion. Nonetheless, it was not so; upon asking who had been the architect who had designed the station they told me its author was the engineer, Aranda, a fellow from Madrid who is also our honorary vice consul in Damascus.

26 April, 1915

Since April 7th I have suspended these notes to let these memories I have just impressed on paper to pass by. A neighboring person from Haifa told me that up until now, and despite what has been said, this city has not been bombarded and that there were only a few cannon shots against Mount Carmel. What did seem certain is that the Allied ships entertained themselves by tossing bottles in the water containing papers in various languages that tell of the British plan to set the Arabs against the Turks so as to 'divide and conquer.'

I have taken an excursion to Jericho in the company of Rafael Lorenzo and Father Van der Vliet, a Dutchman. It was pouring down rain when we descended the slope that leads from the Josafat Hill to Gethsemane, from where we went up to the Mount of Olives. After crossing in front of Talia we contemplated a castle built by the Templars, of which only a few stones remain that serve as housing to various Bedouins. Upon arriving at Wadi al-Qalt, from the edge of a giant canyon I contemplated an immense desert and a frightening precipice on whose side, just in a depression, one finds the Greek convent of St. George. In a place so wild you don't hear even a fly, nor do you see the smallest sign of human life, excepting the convent with the goat trail that leads to it and some Bedouin tents in the distance.

From there, the road no longer merits such a name since it is a very pronounced hillside and is so neglected that we prefer to go down by foot. (...) We descended to the Plain of Jericho and, relentlessly pursued by the quite unpleasant flies, we crossed the new bridge over the little stream until we stopped at the Hotel Bellevue. (...) From there it's no more than a step to find ancient Jericho. The impression one experiences seeing that confused mound of houses and rooms so narrow and squeezed together is that you cannot conceive how those people could live.

Crossing a little part of the desert I arrived on foot at the famous mountain of the 'forty days.'[13] No one could form an idea of the hugeness of the place until arriving at the site in which the rise of the path begins, narrow and slippery, which leads to the Greek convent located there. Gigantic rocks, a solemn silence, eagles and sparrow hawks gliding over our heads by the dozens. About two-thirds of the way up the mountain I arrived at the convent, perched on the rocks, sunk among them on the brink of the abyss. You need to be clear-headed and tough to peek out over the balcony that surrounds the convent, and that is basically hanging by a thread over a precipice at least one hundred meters in height.

The monks of the convent welcomed us nicely when they found out who I was. They had us take a seat on the sofa for the compulsory, and traditional, coffee. Then, one of them accompanied us to the top of the mountain where they are building a church, and from which there is a marvelous view over the valley of the Jordan, Moab, Ammon and the Mount of Olives. (…)

4 May, 1915

When I least expected it, here I made another expedition to Jericho, at least a very interesting one. Let's consider a little history. On the anniversary of the advent of the current Ottoman Sultan they gave me an invitation from Djemal Pasha to a party that he was giving that same day at Notre Dame de France.

In the company of Raphaël I headed for the German Sanatorium of the Mount of Olives, where His Excellency received us accompanied by all his staff. Acting as a chronicler of society I will say that Mehmet Pasha, General Trommer with his wife, the Prince of Hohenlohe, Barciara Effendi, Antebi, Dr. Fotios with his wife, several officers and some Jews attended it too. Around 10:00 P.M. General Trommer came to look for me to tell me, on behalf of *el Generalisimo*, that he was waiting to have a glass of champagne with me. The glass converted into several glasses and, with warmth of the conversation, my colleagues from Italy and Greece proposed to His Excellency that he makes a trip to Jericho. The idea seemed fine to Djemal Pasha and, the following day, we began the preparations for the expedition.

On the first of May we set off. Djemal Pasha went with his two assistants, the four consuls (Italian, Greek, American, and me), and an officer with a section of cavalry and scouts. We stopped at the Caravanserai of the Good Samaritan to have a sandwich and a glass of beer. Once we arrived at the Mount of the Forty Days we mounted horses to go up to the garden situated at the foot of the mountain and which is the property of the Greek convent. I was riding a splendid four-year-old horse of pure Arab bloodlines, property of Djemal Pasha, and the latter was on another magnificent horse, a gift from the Sultan.

As soon as we appeared in view of the convent, bells began to greet *el Generalisimo*, and with this music we entered the garden, which was adorned with Turkish flags. There, we had a splendid lunch offered by the Greek Patriarch Damianos.

The meal lasted more than three hours, and then we made a triumphal entry into Jericho, where the entire neighborhood was peeking out the doors and windows, greeting the victor of the battle of the Canal with the greatest respect (!).

We rested peacefully in the Hotel Bellevue. A splendid dinner – always at the expense of the Greek Patriarch – and we went to bed. The following day we left at dawn for the Dead Sea. A delightful ride, because it is always really pleasant to trot on a magnificent horse on flat terrain.

We went then to the Jordan River, and on the same place where, according to the tradition, Our Lord was baptized, we watched the construction of a bridge by Ottoman bridge builders. There was, however, a small inconvenience in these practices: There was not a sufficient number of pontoons, for which reason they could not conclude the bridge which was reduced to two pieces, one on each side. But, after all, these are details. . .

I'm going to recall a bit of the great deal that the good Djemal Pasha told us. Above all, he said that he was thinking of writing the history of his expedition to Egypt and publishing it after the war. He stated that his army was 40,000 men, and he attacked the Suez Canal at five distinct points. He attributed his failure to the insufficiency of the means of transportation and of resources. He had counted on 15,000 camels and the water necessary for the whole army had to be transported. All this without counting the munitions, supplies, camping equipment, etc. It was an exploit almost impossible to achieve.[14]

The Pasha told me that he approached the Canal at night, and that he initiated the attack before dawn, directing it from a small height where the English bullets greeted him but, nonetheless, did not reach him. The troops managed to cross the Canal in part, but, attacked by the warships and the British army (which he considered to be quite superior to his own), had to withdraw. He gave the following numbers of casualties: 200 dead, 300 injured and 450 prisoners. These figures seem very modest to me. They retreated some seven kilometers during the night through the desert and thus continued with night marches until they crossed it on the road back.

The minister assured us that the efforts made to drag the cannons to the Canal were worthy of an epic: Each one of them was pulled not only by oxen and buffalos, but also by dozens of soldiers who performed truly heroic deeds. He had expressions of scorn for the Egyptians, who did nothing to help, nor did they revolt as they had promised.

He was very intrigued when Glazebrook spoke to him about the 'White Book' published by the British government about the war with Turkey. He confirmed part of what was attributed to him in it and confirmed the determined proposal of his country to appropriate once again the Greek islands, which naturally caused great uneasiness for my Greek colleague, Raphaël. He denied that it was true what the 'White Book' affirms in the sense that it was the Germans who caused the war: According to him, the Turkish fleet was attacked by the Russians.

After the war he plans to publish a reply to this 'White Book.' I asked him the reason for not doing it before, since it would have much more effect on the public now than after the war, when nobody would read it. In answering me that he could not do it now, he did not add any reason whatsoever.

The *Generalísimo* praised himself and his generosity, saying that he had respected the Christian churches. In spite of the determination shown by the Muslims to convert the sanctuary of the Nativity of the Virgin to a mosque, he had not consented to such an act, limiting himself to transforming part of the convent of the White Fathers to a school. This is true, and in these disjointed notes I have made clear my impression that this had been a cleverness of Djemal Pasha's.

How to reconcile the demonstrations of admiration and sympathy he manifested towards the French with the persecution of them now that gives him so many worries? He talked in detail about his visit to Paris, the reception that they gave him on the Elysium on July 14, and the shouts of 'long live Djemal Pasha' with which the people received him at the same time as the shouts of 'long live Poincaré.'

Dealing with a Turk one had to ask him, naturally, about his medals. He actually has some very important ones since, besides the two from Turkey, he wears the Great Cross of the Legion of Honor, the Red Eagle of Prussia, and the Iron Cross. But the picturesque part is that the Sultan has given him a special medal for the 'Campaign of the Canal.' In addition, the Sultan has promised him the title of *Gazi* or conqueror, if he continues to overpower Egypt, and His Excellency told me that he proposes to do so. For that he is counting on the new railroad that runs from Aleppo to Lydda and from there to Beersheba. This last part, however, has not even been begun. From Beersheba to the Canal, one must only cross...The Sinai desert, that is, the principal difficulty which Djemal now knows by experience. It seems to me rather difficult for him to gain the title of 'conqueror.'

He did not speak at all about the Crusades, and that is strange because he has a real mania about believing that Christians are always thinking about the arrival of the new Godfrey. Because of that he made them take down the flag of the Custody and of the Patriarchate, because it was the banner of the Crusades.

26 May, 1915

The sensational news that Italy has entered the war is received with emotion. This has been whispered for some time. So convinced was I that our 'Latin sister' would make one of her entries that I had bet with the Greek consul, Raphaël, that the entry would take place before the month ended.[15] Now we see that I was completely right, in spite of the denials from Senni and my German and Austrian colleagues. In the visit I made yesterday morning, Djemal Pasha assured me war now existed. In the evening, during the dinner we had in the Hotel Marcos, the same Djemal confirmed that the squadron of Austrian airplanes had begun the attack of the Italian coast near Venice.

The dinner to which I made reference had its touches of an incident. The American consul, Glazebrook, was giving it in honor of Djemal Pasha, and we were all invited: My German, Austrian, Greek and Italian colleagues. Logically, and in view of the news about the war, the Italian should have been the first to excuse himself, but it wasn't like that. The two allied consuls, the German Schmidt and the Austrian Kraus, were the first ones to decline the honor. The American thought that they would be resentful towards him, but I took charge of dissipating that error, making a visit to Kraus, who told me that he had excused himself so as not to find himself with the representative of a nation 'that did nothing but threaten his country and behaved so. . .' (here you put in all the epithets that occur to you).

In short, the banquet moved along in lively fashion, now that none of the new belligerents was there. Djemal Pasha spoke to us at great length about the offer made by Lord Kitchener of £20,000 to whoever would assassinate Talat Bey, the heart of the current situation. A Constantinople newspaper published today the proof of this accusation. Djemal Pasha had asked Enver and Talat if they had proof since, if not, it was a foolish thing to launch such an accusation against no less a person than Lord Kitchener. To that question his government friends told him to have patience, that all would come out in the press. They also shined up the time-worn phrase that is circulating everywhere, saying that a triumvirate governs Turkey: Talat Bey [Pasha] is the Father, Djemal Pasha is the son and Enver Pasha the Holy Ghost, but Djemal is also the All Powerful.

It was my Greek colleague Raphaël's turn to be surprised when His Excellency told him that, during his time as governor of Constantinople, he organized the police in such a way that he got to the point of having bought the employee who coded the dispatches of the Greek embassy, and therefore he was up to date with all the projects of that country. This seems to me an absurdity from His Excellency, with all due respect.

After having hurried through a regular supply of champagne, we all went to the cinema to the great function organized for the benefit of the Jews. There were applause and hymns to the 'all powerful' upon entering the area, ice cream, candies, flowers, etc. I had to congratulate the great Antebi, who was the organizer and was in his glory.

29 May, 1915

Such have been the irritations of the stifling heat that we have suffered in the last few days that I have not even had the strength to write.

My Austrian colleague told me that our representatives in Italy have taken charge of the protection of the interests of Austria. I wonder who will look after the Italians in Austria.

Last night the son of Sharif of Mecca, who is no less than the descendent of Muhammad, made his entrance into Jerusalem. Under the circumstances, I'm not happy about his visit, and much less so knowing that Djemal Pasha has brought as a personal guard the most fervent and fanatical Muslims he could find in all the *vilayet*.

Zaki Bey (who has not been expelled as people say) showed me a sketch by which I saw that the Allies have not advanced any great amount, occupying a straight line that divides the peninsula of Gallipoli (in the Dardanelles) in two. The Allied ships are in a frontal bay, but they have not been able to advance. What one truly has to admire is the success of the Turkish censorship, since no one, absolutely no one, knows a word about what is going on in the Dardanelles and in Europe. With no communications with our governments, we have to content ourselves with the news the Turks and Germans give us, and God knows if it's true.

After the first excursion that we carried out with Djemal Pasha, a series of them began: Lunch in Gethsemane, *idem* in Tantur, a meal in the German Sanatorium (a name with which the true character of the palace is disguised), etc. At all these excursions champagne is and, as a logical consequence, a good mood. Raphaël always amused us with his stories, for example the one about his interview with a cannibal who told him that what he liked was not the flesh of sailors but that of plump English missionaries, etc. Salient features of these excursions also included the lecture Djemal Pasha gave us in Tantur about Turkish women, the discussion about Darwinian theories, and the more or less serious polemics between His Excellency and Raphaël about the Aegean islands. (. . .)

Unpleasant memories from that time were the expulsion of the nice Dr. Mancini with his wife, the order to expel Father Doumeth (of the École Biblique) and the sending of Madjid Bey to Damascus.

30 May, 1915

I was in the American Colony.[16] I am very intrigued by this institution, which possesses a perfect organization. Which religion do its members profess? I don't think anyone knows with absolute certainty: They talk about colossal orgies, women being common-law wives to the whole society…who knows what. But all that seems to be slander from the many in this country who are rising up against everyone. According to the 'Guide to Palestine' they are Adventists. The case is that they are a common organization whose base is work and each one of them chooses his religion with absolute freedom. Men, women and children, numbering around a hundred, take all their meals together in a refectory that features a painting of the Last Supper of Our Lord. They hold everything in common, even a magnificent collection of stamps. They possess a model farm, photography and cabinetmaker's workshops, a museum of natural history with collections of biblical plants, some interesting amphorae, lamps and little Canaanite statues and, from other epochs, a jar of the famous collections of sands of various colors made by the Bedouins from around Petra, a manufacturing center of preserves, painting workshops (one of the ladies showed me a superb collection of watercolors made by her, in which are represented wild flowers of Palestine that will be the basis of a book for tourists) and even the installation of a dentist. In short, a real beehive. As good Americans as they are (although there are all nationalities, and especially Swedes and Norwegians), they have a tennis court and as soon as they finish their household tasks they amuse themselves there a while.

31 May, 1915

The month is ending, but not the more or less naughty comments being made about the projected wedding of Djemal Pasha with a beautiful Jewish lady named Leah Tennebaum. The news seemed so unlikely to me that I gave it the least importance, but it persists, and there is no one in the city who is not commenting on it.

June 1915

Locusts! As I'm reading the Bible it serves as an illustration to see the millions and millions of little locusts that one sees everywhere in the country and in the city, and that will wind up leaving not a blade of grass in this country. The olive trees, the vineyards, the sown fields and orchards, they have eaten everything and I ask myself what we will be able to eat this summer. The defense that the members of the American Colony and of the U.S. consulate have made of their gardens has been truly heroic and I do not plan to forget the system employed in case sometime – God forbid – this terrible plague visits my farms.

Kuebler officially communicated to me that a great French cruiser of unknown name and with six chimneys appeared before Jaffa and, after having raised the red flag, was bombing the depository of municipal petroleum and the 'Vacuum Oil' [American], both situated in the south of the city. The cruiser fired twenty cannon shots, but the destruction has been insignificant since, luckily for the city, the 200 containers of petroleum stored there did not explode. After the bombardment the cruiser went off towards the north and began to patrol in front of Jaffa again.

9 June, 1915

Kuebler told me that Haifa has also been bombarded by a French cruiser. The ship sent a warning that, after one hour, it would begin to bombard the vice consulate of Germany. It gave as a pretext that the monument and sepulcher of the soldiers of Napoleon's army, which is located on Mount Carmel, had been violated at the instigation of the German vice consul. At the indicated hour it began to hurl grenades and, within a little while, not a stone of the building was standing. I don't know the name of the ship, but it seems that it was the 'Destrées,' which carried out the same operation on the German consulate of Alexandretta.

The French tactic seems perfectly stupid to me, and counterproductive. It would seem that Djemal Pasha has ordered that the prisoners who were in Damascus be sent to Urfa, which must be as a consequence of this blustering. It would be better if they behaved better in the Dardanelles![17]

15 June, 1915

I went to Jaffa by carriage and, in the company of Kuebler, on the 11th left Jerusalem with lovely weather and the illusion of enjoying the trip, but quickly I began to see the immense masses of locusts that infested everything and my enthusiasm cooled before such a spectacle. Upon arriving at the colony [Tel Aviv], one could no longer see the track of the main road for the thick layer of locusts that covered it. The olive trees had their trunks and leaves yellow; the fig trees had been lost some time ago, and some of them even the bark. The pines and cypresses, harder to chew, were now beginning to suffer attacks. Only by seeing it can one believe the ravages these little creatures have done.

The highway is very near the old church of Abu Gosh, and, from there, one can admire the beautiful (and justly famous) Plain of Sharon. From this point on the descent begins until, in Bab al-Wadi [the Valley Port] the plain properly begins. In this picturesque spot we stopped for more than half an hour and had breakfast with Mehmet Pasha and his party.

We continued the trip following the general's car, and in a little while two automobiles occupied by Djemal Pasha and his military entourage passed us at full speed. Near the Ramla station, His Excellency invited me to write a paragraph under some beautiful eucalyptus trees and watch the parade of the forces he was going to review there. I could see the military 'pose' of the German officials and their mathematical rigidity in saluting the *Generalísimo* and even in answering him. Look at this example: Djemal Pasha: 'Are you happy?' The officer: 'Yes, Excellency.' Djemal Pasha:

'Have you been here a while?' The officer: 'Not long, Excellency. From here I will go to Nazareth, from there to Jerusalem, from there to X, etc., etc.' A whole itinerary that mattered very little to the minister.

The *Pasha*, with the greatest kindness, introduced me to all the officers and encouraged me to make observations and ask them questions. It surprised me very much to see a young boy, about 18 years old, introduced to me as the leader of a regiment. They explained to me that, in Turkey, every German official occupies a position immediately above the corresponding one in Germany.

At 11:00 A.M. Djemal Pasha embarked with all his entourage in a special train and left for Damascus. Now one can make the trip directly by the railroad: The only advantage we have gotten out of the war. Within a short time we'll be able to go from Jerusalem, when they finish the work, to Ramla.

In the convent [of St. Nicodemus] of Ramla the Superior, Father Gregorio Ocio, Father Bernardino Fraga, Father Mateo Hebreo and Brother Ramón Sánchez were waiting for us. After greeting Baroness Freytag [Auguste von Freytag-Loringhoven], an Austrian who is actually at the service of the Red Crescent, we had lunch. At 4:00 P.M. we continued towards Jaffa. During this trip I saw the open trenches for the soldiers who were in Ramla. I could also admire once again the difference in the manner of cultivating the soil on the part of the people of this country and the German and Jewish colonies. What would become of this plain if it were all in the hands of the latter?

In Jaffa I visited the new *kaymakam*, Asad Bey, and I discussed with him the possibility of putting a special sign on our convent due to the likely case of new bombardments. He told me that the installation of that sign would be done by orders from Constantinople and in accordance with what was arranged through the Hague Conventions.

I then went to Tel-Aviv, where I visited the petroleum deposits that had been bombed by the French cruiser, which turned out to be the 'Ernest Renan.' Fortunately it did not present itself again to bombard the German vice consulate, as was announced, and thus I managed to dine peacefully.

While returning, a French hydroplane followed us for some time from the air. It flew very high and the soldiers stationed on the ground did not shoot at it. It is understood that they are convinced that it is useless to do so, since on previous occasions that it had shown itself they fired cannons and rifles.

On the way back to Jerusalem, there was sensational news. Senni came to see me and showed me a telegram from his ambassador, the Marquis Garroni, asking him to deliver the consulate and go straight away to Constantinople. On the other hand, the American consul Glazebrook received a few days ago a warning from the commander of a cruiser, the 'Desmoines' saying that, if the Italian consul wanted to leave, he would take him on his ship. So the situation between Italy and Turkey cannot be more tense, and we will see, in the case war is declared, if Djemal Pasha will authorize Senni's trip.

18 June, 1915

Today, Senni left. According to what he told me he is going first to Beirut, where he will board the cruiser 'Tennessee.'

22 June, 1915

Alonzo has also left, leaving the weight of the French interests to our vice consul in Jaffa, but without wanting to turn over the archives to him.

The German officials who were in the Sinai desert are all back here. The day before yesterday, Von Rabbios (the chief of the forces who were in Ramla)[18] asked me for the photographs I took when I was with Djemal Pasha there. Today I went for a walk with him and with Von Laufer. The latter has been in the desert for four months and detests the heat – which, on occasions, got to 50°C in the shade – the Turks and the lack of water there. He told me that the Turks have withdrawn all their forces, hoping for a better time in the future to attack the Canal. In view of this, the English forces that were in Egypt have been sent to the Dardanelles. According to Von Laufer, the brilliant defense of these straits was owed to the fact that the officers, the cannons and some of the soldiers (including 2,000 sailors) were German.

'Abed announced to me that a party of 'Young Arabs' has been formed, and that soon, they will assassinate Djemal Pasha, etc. I believe that this is all just talk and that the Arabs will never be capable of doing anything.[19]

6 July, 1915

Yesterday Raphaël and I visited the new mayor of Jerusalem, Mr. Ertogrul, who showed us, with an air of triumph, the plans for a new road stretching from the Jaffa gate to el Haram al-Sharif, from the park next to the walls of Mount Zion, and for the asphalting of Jaffa road. The good man told us that he now has 2,000 Turkish Pounds to begin. But what idea must this man have of what it takes to do works like that? The road alone will cost more than three million Pesetas. It could be, however, that the mayor is right if the Turkish system of not paying the expropriations, nor the workers, nor anything at all, continues. So, if you have to knock down a house? Well, knock it down and don't pay a cent to the owners. (*Naturally, nothing was done about these projects.*)[20]

From the Dardanelles, not a word. Through the *Sunday Reader* that came to my hands by chance I find out about the bombing of Dunkirk with howitzers from the 'insignificant' distance of 22 kilometers. It's the last straw. But I ask myself, why wouldn't the Allies occupy Syria and Palestine?

16 July, 1915

Time keeps going by with crushing monotony. What am I going to say in these brief notes? Nothing that is worth the effort. Almost every day I have an excellent beer from Berlin with the Austrian consul, Kraus, or with my friend Kittani in Faig's house. We watch the people go by, we eat some toasted almonds, and that's it. One cannot conceive of a life as stupid as this, or I, at least, cannot conceive it.

There was a function on the 11th in the Guirich movie theater. Medyet Bey, that useless creature we have as a governor, Djamil Bey, director of the Saladin school, Zaki Bey, Raphaël, Sa'dullah Bey, the illustrious Ertogrul and I have places reserved. (...) There were also movies with war scenes that couldn't be more interesting. (...) We left at 2:00 A.M. as if it were the latest at the Apollo. There was also a little bit of gymnastics on the part of the Jews and speeches in Arabic and in Hebrew.

We passionately discussed what is said to be a project of the Allies to get to Constantinople without going through the Dardanelles, building a canal to the east of Gallipoli; a project that to me, seems similar to that of Mr. Ertogrul.

Ramadan began with its great fast, and it seems to me that with the scarcity of provisions that we have, we will all wind up doing Ramadan.

21 July, 1915

Absolutely no news of the war. The hydroplane that visited Jaffa constantly tossed out newspapers and proclamations announcing that the Allies have taken control of Gallipoli and, in a short while, they will be in Constantinople. I am so accustomed to the lies that I don't believe this news, nor the news Kraus gave me yesterday: According to him, in the latest and terrible battle in the Dardanelles, the Allies had 10,000 casualties and the Turks another enormous amount (nonetheless, there must be something wrong).

The *shayj* al-Muigar preaches holy war again in the mosque of 'Umar. It will be a miracle if I am safe and sound at the end of the war.

23 July, 1915

It is the eighth anniversary of the Ottoman constitution. As a matter of form, I'm going to congratulate the governor and Mehmet Pasha, together with my Greek colleague. To my great surprise I saw that once again the consuls were received with the same honors that were granted to them before the proclamation of the constitution. I wonder what this means. In the Seray (the former convent of the Dominicans) the police in dress uniform presented arms at our approach. In the interior of the garden, a company of infantry was charged with rendering us honors.

We then went to visit Djemal Pasha in the Russian compound, and a company gave us the same honors with a musical band. All this change in the attitude of the authorities made me suspect that what was said in the flyers that the aviator threw out over Jaffa could be true: That the Russians are on the south of Lake Van, that the Allies will be in Constantinople within a month or two, that in Mesopotamia the English are advancing victoriously... Nevertheless, I am such a pessimist.

Saleh announced that an aviator threw a bomb in Nablus, where there were four dead, and another in Sabastiya where, as the Turks say, two *martyrs* perished.

8 August, 1915

During the last few weeks I was absent in Jaffa. The American ambassador in Constantinople, Morgenthau, had announced to Glazebrook that a cruiser, the 'Chester' would arrive on the third of August in Jaffa to take on board the Jews belonging to the belligerent countries, expelled by the government, as well as neutrals of all nationalities who wanted to leave Turkey.[21] As the cruiser was supposed to also take on board ten boxes of objects of worship I was sending to the Ministry, I decided to make the trip to take care of the frequent questions and difficulties I figured would turn up.

I left, then, on July 31 with wonderful weather. It had already completely changed the aspect of the country. Despite the locusts, the trees with deciduous leaves, like almonds and apricots, had recovered their strength and lushness, while the others were now budding out.

For the four days I spent in Jaffa I did nothing but sweat buckets and visit the *kaymakam* and Hasan Bey for the objective that brought me there. The first day I got the permission of Djemal Pasha for the departure of the neutrals. When the boarding was prepared, it turned out the commander of the ship didn't want to take them. Then, an order from the U.S. embassy, stating that they should board, arrived. In short, the usual: Orders and counter orders during this war, capable of making a saint lose his patience.

We had one sad note, and another rather artistic one. The first was the death of the second commander of Jaffa, 'Arif Effendi, 'the circumflex accent', as we used to call him. He died pursuing some deserters. They resisted and left him dead from a single shot. A police officer and a deserter died too. The other deserter was taken prisoner and, as is the custom in this country, was marched through the streets of Jaffa covered in horns [the sign of the horns is a gesture made with the hands], tripe from the butchers, old shoes and other elegant things of the sort. And the Turks still want to prove to us that they can live without the Capitulations!

I greatly regretted the death of 'Arif, who had always treated us very well: At the beginning of the war he gathered the soldiers and announced to them that if anyone entered the Spanish convent he would shoot them immediately in front of the Father Superior and the vice consul of Spain. I presided at the burial with the authorities, and it was the first time that I attended a Muslim ceremony of this kind.

I was in the famous vineyards of Sarona. [22] The wine cellar is good but for its urban development nor for the quality of its wines is it anything really notable: A deception. In the convent of Casa Nova, splendid hospitality as always. Brother Emilio Dubois, as a good Alsatian, was very worried by the course of the war.

A French ship with three chimneys made various visits, coming and going quietly without anyone taking much notice of it, now that the people are accustomed to its presence. A few days before my arrival it had fired 114 cannon shots at a Turkish sailing ship; a thing that seemed to me to be either throwing away gunpowder or really bad aiming.

On August 6, in view of the fact that the cruiser had not yet arrived, I went to Rishon LeZion with my friend, Feani. There, I was really surprised: 600 hectares of ground in cultivation, with all the modern advancements. Of them, no less than 400 are dedicated to grape vines, as well as a little forest of eucalyptus, plantations of almond, orange and palm trees surrounding a real town of 1,500 inhabitants, installed in modern and comfortable houses, all separated and fenced with flowers and trees. There was a magnificent synagogue, a party room, but, in short, those admirable wine cellars were the object of my visit. I did not expect to find so much. Baron Rothschild spent four million Pesetas on these cellars. I think that is a rather eloquent fact. The cellars constitute a magnificent building, with the wine in subterranean compartments, cement storehouses, cold-water refrigeration to avoid excessive fermentation and apparatus for pasteurization. There were also outbuildings, machine rooms (all electric, including the lighting of the wine cellars), workshops for making barrels, forging, hardware, etc.

Nor was there lacking in these cellars a very complete laboratory, in charge of which is a chemist who told me that he would soon make a trip to Spain. At the time of the visit he was doing studies about the nutritive value of a sesame paste that he planned to use as food. Most of the wines produced are the Alicante, Malaga or Oporto types.

In the magnificent office of the administrative head, Mr. Meerowich (an extremely intelligent leader), I tasted varieties of his wines with the necessary circumspection. I had lunch, splendidly, in the hotel of the colony with these gentlemen, other top officials and Ben Zion Ouziel, the Great Rabbi of Jaffa. The latter gentleman, and his lovely daughter as well, speak a fairly acceptable Spanish.

In the afternoon I took a good walk through the colony and vineyards accompanied by Mr. Brill, Rothschild's representative, and his daughter [Brill's]. Various 'Spanish' families greeted me. Among them are Catzler, Tratztenberg, Benjamín and Goldenberg, very Spanish names, as you can see. After dining I said goodbye, giving thanks to the nice administrator who writes a lot in the press under the name 'Abu Ihalim' and who published memorable articles when the proclamation of the Constitution made us hope for better times.

On the border of the farm a Turkish regiment and two battalions, commanded by my friend Von Rabbios, were camped. The officers, not content with permitting the soldiers to take whatever came their way in property and doing a lot of damage, announced to the colonists a few days ago that, if a French or English person came ashore in Jaffa, they would immediately bomb the colony. What heroism!

Upon arriving in Jerusalem I found the city decked in Turkish, German, and Austrian flags. I figured out right away what it was about: The taking of Warsaw and Ivangorsk.

13 August, 1915

Yesterday, the end of Ramadan was celebrated with great animation and the beating of drums in the City Hall. I did not attend, since it is customary that only the *dragomans* go.

They have confirmed the bombardment of the Wagner factory in Jaffa. The French cruiser 'Joan of Arc' launched six grenades that fell on the factory, without going off course or doing any harm to the German consulate in that city, nor to any of the neighboring houses. Truly, this honors the artillery men of this ship and justifies the disbelief with which one reads news of the following tenor published by the Turkish press: 'Yesterday the enemy launched 150 bombs on a single point of our positions, and we had only one injury.'

20 August, 1915

I have been very busy trying to save the generator that the Sisters of the Charity have in the asylum. I asked Roshan Bey to visit this place with me; he was moved to see the 250 sick and elderly, crazy and retarded, etc. who are sheltered there. Tears came to dear Roshan Bey, and he decided to go with me to see the governor and made him revoke the order that he had given to take away the generator, which would mean closing the asylum. I did manage to get the order revoked.

26 August, 1915

New adventures of our unfortunate convent in Jaffa. The *kaymakam*, Asad Bey, ordered the Italian clerics, lay people and Jews to be installed there. I tried to convince the governor, Medyet Bey, of the legitimacy of our claims, but all is useless now that the Sublime Porte considered those convents as property of the Ottoman government for having been under French protection. Kuebler returned to Jaffa by my order to try to take care of the matter but also because Dr. Prüfer who, with his harmless appearance is nothing less than a secret agent of the German government, secretary of the embassy and in possession of an extraordinary talent, had indicated something that we feared: That the imprudence of the Italians could bring some serious problems due to the hate that exists against them here.[23] There is a lot of talk, in fact, that there are Italian warships in Jaffa. I don't believe it, but Prüfer and Kuebler fear something.

Eleven people have been hanged in Beirut by order of the authorities. According to the manifest that Djemal Pasha has published in the press, the cause was that the executed belonged to a 'Decentralizing Committee,' whose goal is none other than to free Syria, Palestine and Iraq from Turkey, making them autonomous and under the protection of England. For that they planned to commit a series of assassinations that would provoke a European intervention. The Beirut daily paper also published the names of the people compromised.

I have taken steps so that an extraordinary journey of 'Villanueva' will take place, whose arrival was already announced by the Transatlantic Company, but the leader of the military staff, Sadullah Bey, cut me off, announcing that, as of noon yesterday, the Allies had established a blockade of the whole coast. So, we can't even think of such a trip now that, henceforth no neutral ship would be able to approach Turkish waters. The news discouraged me completely since it was an excellent occasion for our commercial interests.

Yesterday Hasan Bey visited me and let me understand his 'good intentions' towards the Italians; he then told me that, in case of a bombardment of Jaffa, for each Turkish dead there would be two Italians dead. Not bad!

The day before yesterday, the police believed they saw a man on the terrace of my house and undertook a search on this pretext; I believe they suspected the complicity of Jorge, one the *cavases* of the bank, a Montenegrin, and a good person. I don't know the real motives for the search, but I figured they are probably not what the police said.

The French 'Joan of Arc' was the one that announced the blockade to the military commander of Jaffa and to the German consul there. Very correctly, he did no more than cite the article through which the French vice admiralty was establishing the blockade. So, if I am careless, the sanctuary strongboxes will stay on land, since the trip of the 'Chester' will be the last one; that is, the American government gets the Allies to allow the cruiser to come through again to pick up the Italian clerics, and women and children, as well as the Jewish belligerents who remain. I doubt very much that they can do it, since the English continue to prevent their Allies from landing in Egypt.

4 September, 1915

The day before yesterday I visited Djemal Pasha, who had arrived the night before from Lebanon. His assistant, Abd al-Rahim Bey, told me that they had made an eight day trip on horseback, of which reason the nice *sailor* [Djemal Pasha] was so proud, ready to obtain a rank as a cavalry officer.

The minister didn't tell me much in particular. I extended to him the greetings of our ambassador in Constantinople, Arroyo, who charged me with asking him when he planned to return to Constantinople. To this he responded: 'Greet your leader affectionately in my name, and tell him I will not return to Constantinople if it is not victorious.' (…)

According to my calculations, the trip of the 'Villaverde' would have propitiated to the company a shipment of at least 110,000 Francs, counting the stops in Jaffa, Beirut, Latakia and Tripoli. As the charge was 60,000 Francs, that left 50,000 in net profit. What a shame! Oh well, perhaps another time. The *Beirut Daily* keeps on publishing compromising documents about the 'Decentralizing Committee.' The unrest is general.

7 September, 1915

Yesterday afternoon, when I was working in the consulate without collar or cufflinks and practically in short sleeves, Djemal Pasha presented himself for a visit. Hurriedly, I had coffee prepared, a sign of Turkish hospitality. After a brief visit, His Excellency left, leaving me in charge of locating the Greek consul, Raphaël, whom Djemal wanted us to visit together. Raphaël had gone to the German Sanatorium on the Mount of Olives to ask the minister if the news of a declaration of war between Greece and Bulgaria was true. When I finally found him, I told him to expect our visit.

A little while later, the minister arrived at my house again with scouts, assistants and bodyguards. I got in his car and, as soon as we arrived at the Greek consulate, Djemal began his accustomed jokes to my Greek colleague about the question of the Aegean islands, Macedonia, etc.; he brought everything up again. Djemal insisted that Greece shouldn't fear anything from England, since neither England nor France are capable of doing anything: The proof was in the Dardanelles where, besides having suffered great losses of ships, the English had had 70,000 dead and the French, 20,000: Figures that the minister assured us were accurate.

As always, the interview was long. Our conversation lasted more than an hour, and I took advantage of it to give him the Austrian *Red Book* about the *casus belli* with Italy, which he should read.

His Excellency told us something that I had read in *The Debate*: Five Turkish officers who were sailing to Tripoli were captured by an enemy ship. They were carrying arms and munitions and letters from Enver Pasha and Djemal Pasha for al-Sanusi.[24] According to Djemal, in them they advised him not to war with the Italians but rather attack Egypt. Commenting on this, he insisted on his enmity towards the Italians and that the latter had not said that they had seized said correspondence but only one from the Sultan of Turkey. This had been the pretext that the Italians had used to declare war against Turkey.

Djemal Pasha also told me: 'Do you know that I have married an Austrian Jewess?' Naturally, I supposed he was dealing with the bombshell news dropped before his departure from Jerusalem, to which I have referred previously. The most curious thing is that, not only did all of Syria already know the news, but it was published in a French newspaper (*Le Temps*), where they said that the *Pasha* was spending his time amusing himself in 'Ayn Sufar, without worrying at all about the army.

12 September, 1915

Yesterday a monstrous big gathering took place in the Food Rationing Inspectorate (situated in Notre Dame de Sion) for the benefit of the Red Crescent. I say 'monstrous' because having begun at 8:30 in the evening, I returned home at 3:00 in the morning, and it had not yet ended. I was at the side of Mehmet Djemal, who never ceased cracking jokes about the daily reports about me that the police were giving him, which always referred to the same subject. (…)

Today I visited Mehmet Djemal to congratulate him on having received the Iron Cross, and, afterwards, I had a few serious words with his Chief of Staff and Sharif Effendi. Sadullah Bey told me that the highway from al-Salt, the extension of the one to Jericho, was almost finished and that within a month the railroad to Beersheba would be ready. Because of this we talked at length about the difficulties of the expedition to Egypt because of the lack of water and sand storms that rendered useless all work done in the desert. There is a German engineer who is in charge of the construction of artesian wells, but up until now it seems there have been no great results. (...)

It seems that the Ottoman Bank has opened a line of credit of 100,000 Turkish Pounds to again begin the Canal campaign. There is no chance of having a good idea about the movement of troops, because this is done during the night. Unfortunately for me, there goes my dream.

25 September, 1915

During the last few days there has been unpleasant news in Jaffa. Hasan Bey, giving free rein at last to his spirit of vengeance against the clerics, whom he cannot tolerate, obtained from my friend, Djemal Pasha, the order to close the convent of St. Peter, throwing out the monks and occupying the building for military reasons that I cannot grasp. Without going into further detail, a German official assured me that the defense of Jaffa does not enter into war plans, nor logically should it, since it is an open city without any more fortifications than the ridiculous trenches that its ridiculous military commander improvised some time ago. There does not exist even a single cannon in that city, whose garrison is composed of a half dozen soldiers and some policemen. In short, Hasan Bey has gotten his way, but I hope to oblige him to free the convent soon.

2 October, 1915

The Sublime Porte ordered by telegraph that the Jaffa convent be evacuated and that the Franciscans occupy it again. Although the *mutasarrif* of Jerusalem has already received this order, he does not dare fulfill it for fear of Djemal Pasha, who is a high-ranking dictator.

18 October, 1915

In spite of the Sublime Porte having repeated the order of the re-opening of the convent, this has not taken place. I will await the results of the new petitions of Ambassador Arroyo, which I am almost certain will be negative.

30 October, 1915

(...) We have had a series of meals, one offered by Brode, another by Pözel, the Hungarian vice consul, and the latest I attended with Djemal

Pasha's current Chief of Staff, Baron Von Kressenstein. In spite of the fact that Muslims are not supposed to drink, one of my fellow guests, Zaki Bey, began to dance happily after the meal, to the hilarity of the passers-by.

5 November, 1915

This morning Father José Novoa passed away. He was a very good man and, although he was not recognized by our government in his role as member of Discretory, I held him in great esteem. (…)

On my last visit to Von Kressenstein, he announced to me that, on the first of the month, Djemal Pasha and all his staff will go to Aleppo. He also spoke to me about the projected second Canal expedition. It seems that the English fortifications are formidable, but because of the conformation of the land, they are forced to always fire indirect shots, which makes the enterprise feasible. He told me details of the construction of the rail road from Beersheba, from where they advance two kilometers a day by means of a veritable army of workers, and this thanks to the energy and talent of Meissner Pasha, the technical director general. One has to see the difficulties of the construction, without materials of any kind, making the trains run on wood because there is no coal and thanks to the thousands of workers gathered from everywhere and who work for free.

I've been three months without the slightest news from Spain.

7 November, 1915

After a very long time I have had some news from Spain: Two letters from the Marquis of Lema and one from my friend, Casares, who is now posted to the Political Section of the Ministry.

Yesterday I attended the burial of Father Novoa. Father Castellani, the President of the Custody, greeted me very cordially, much more so than his compatriots. What's more, I received a communication from the Patriarch, accompanied by another from the Custody, signed by the Custodial President himself, giving me very warm thanks for what I have done for them.[25]

The first drops of the rainy season are falling, which here lasts a few months, and the rest of the year disappears altogether. Hohenlohe is ready to leave for the desert, and promised me a great dinner on the condition of my standing as a neutral, if he manages to sink the French ship that is in the Canal.

18 November, 1915

Yesterday afternoon a man presented himself in the consulate whose card said 'Rafael de Nogales Méndez (Venezuela).' Believing that it would be a

Jew of Spanish origin, when he entered I was greatly surprised to see that Nogales was a captain of the Military Staff of the Turkish army, 'Spanish, ex-officer of the Mobilized Volunteers' and a member of the German military mission in Turkey.

The Venezuelan came from no less than the Caucasus. By all indications he is a worthy heir of conquerors and adventurers. My astonishment was not diminished when hearing him speak of the tremendous killings of Armenians that the Turks have done in the Van region. Nogales was there as Chief of Staff of the division of Kiazim Pasha and was the only *European* who attended the operations. He said he is a correspondent for the *Vanguard* of Barcelona and for various American newspapers. His conversation turned out to be highly interesting. I plan to see him again and to speak at length of his story, taking advantage of his role in the Turkish army for my own ends.

That same day I made a wonderful excursion to Emmaus. (...) Today, this is an insignificant town but with two magnificent buildings: The Franciscan convent and the hospice of the German Catholic Society of Palestine at whose head is Father Müller, a brother of St. Lazarus (caretaker of lepers).

The garden that surrounds the hospice is an example of what this country would be in other hands. The German priests, with limitless patience, have transformed the terraces of rock and sand into a series of little forests of pines and cypresses, little orchards, fruit trees, flowering bushes and fields of vegetables. Almost leaning against the building were some benches with marvelous views. Nevertheless, for one of those infinite questions of rivalry between the religious orders (which damages them so in public opinion) the German Fathers have not been able to acquire the next mountain, which very much dominates the view. The little bit purchased by the Franciscans has cost them as dearly as the whole mountain offered to the Germans.

Some Trappists who were lodged there, and who had come from Jerusalem, spoke to us about the great event of the day: A Greek schismatic friar said he had seen the Virgin of Calvary weep. Said Virgin is situated on an altar of the Holy Sepulcher, belonging to the Catholics. The news flew like the wind, and the influx of Christians of all denominations and Muslims was such that they had to close the Holy Sepulcher to avoid disorder.

24 November, 1915

The day before yesterday the great Nogales had lunch with me. He told me that Djemal Pasha is excessively sharp (I know that for sure) and that he is not getting along at all well with Enver. It is for that reason we fear that, when it is least expected, he will surprise us and 'change sides' in favor of France, in contrast to the Germanism of Enver. I do not continue because these simple notes are becoming excessively dangerous.

It seems that Kiazim Pasha, the chief under whose orders Nogales serves, has been captured by the Armenians, who have cut off his hands (and something else), causing, naturally, his death. According to Nogales, the Armenians are formidably armed with *Mauser* pistols, bombs and good rifles, constituting a nation in arms. Sacking and burning are, or at least have been, the order of the day. Almost no house is left standing because the Armenians have burned the properties of the Kurds, and the latter, those of the Armenians. (…)

30 November, 1915

The Turks gave orders that seem more like those of children. By order of the Chief of Police of Jerusalem all the doors of the houses have been painted gray and red: Those of the warehouses and stores, as well as the signs, white and red, which are the colors of the constitution. All the carriages have to carry a listing of prices, but they put it in front of the coachman's seat so no one can read it. The mayors of Jaffa and Jerusalem keep talking about the construction of great avenues in both cities, and as I have already commented, they are not paying a cent for the expropriations. They knock things down but they are not building anything.

9 December, 1915

This morning a tragicomic incident occurred. While in conversation with my *dragomans*, a noise like a bullet made us get up in alarm. It turned out that a window situated right by my head showed a round hole like a bullet hole, and in view of the fact that we couldn't find the supposed bullet in my office, I sent for the police. Right away two officers showed up, and the police chief himself, Nur al-Din Bey, in the company of the second-in-command. The matter took on proportions that I would never have wanted. They searched the entire room without finding anything, and finally one of the policemen, with the help of a magnifying glass, discovered little bits of sand among the glass, which made him suppose that the projectile had been a stone. Meanwhile, the police who had begun the investigation returned with a little boy of about twelve years, armed with a slingshot and who was, perhaps, the one who threw the stone, if the whole crime was not invented. Tears from the author, traditional coffee for the police, and that was that. The windows that leapt out fell in my face but did not produce a single scratch. If the stone had been off a little bit, it would have hit me in the head.

Yesterday, the day of the Immaculate Conception, I attended a solemn mass in the Calvary, which nearly gave rise to an incident.[26] Fortunately, in these times of war, no one worries about protocol or anything like it. The mass was a great affair, and I attended it face to face with the *Dolorosa*, with a 'prie-dieu,' and being sprinkled with incense by Brother Enrique. These honors are traditionally reserved *only and exclusively* for the consuls of France, the protecting nation, and they are done only when in uniform. As if that weren't enough, at my arrival I was received with the royal march. If the consul of France had been there he would have raised a real stink.

The day before yesterday, in the evening, Nogales Bey went to Baghdad, called by the German General Von der Goltz Pasha as he was attached to his staff. Things must really be serious there, judging by what the newspapers said (although, naturally, they said that the English have been defeated) and by what Saura of Damascus tells me: According to him, he has not been able to hand over my letter to Dominique Bourel because he was not able to communicate with Urfa. He added that when he knows where the French hostages are (whose whereabouts is not known because of the latest events) he will let me know. Hummm, hmmmm.

News of the war: It seems that Djemal Pasha is not returning. In his place, Von Kressenstein will lead the expedition against Egypt. Roshan Bey told me that 80,000 men are coming for that purpose. The enteritis and the recurrent fevers are up to their usual tricks among the troops from Jerusalem and Jericho. They assured me that there was a landing and combat without importance on al-'Arish, the English withdrawing again to their ships. Six or seven warships frequently passed by Jaffa.

Kuebler came to see me on the way back from Damascus, charmed with the new president of the Holy Land [the Damascus branch], Father Fuertes, who is such a good friend with the *wali* that, on the day of the Immaculate the latter went to have tea with the friars. It's a bit of an advantage that Father Fuertes speaks Turkish.

I'm waiting this afternoon for the visit of the Spanish engineer Mustafa Ibrahim. We'll see how it goes.

Yesterday they hanged a Bedouin next to my house.

Mehmet Pasha told me that it's no trouble to open the Jaffa convent for Christmas. The *mutasarrif* was not so pleasant and only promised me to telegraph Djemal Pasha. I don't have them all on my side.

19 December, 1915

Roshan Bey has been promoted to the rank of colonel. When I went to congratulate him he announced that the news was now official and that Djemal Pasha has been named the division general. I telegraphed him in

Constantinople, and they answered that he has already left, but they didn't tell me where he is.

Local news: Bombing of a German factory in Haifa by a French warship.

20 December, 1915

I finally managed to get the Jaffa convent reoccupied by our clerics. Hasan Bey promised me that from now on he won't bother them anymore.

23 December, 1915

It's been said that Von Mackensen would come to attack the Canal, but I don't believe it, unless they give him several German divisions. It does not seem likely that Germany will compromise the reputation of that field marshal on such a doubtful expedition unless it's done under the proper conditions. They also say that it will be the Austrian Von Koewer, when he arrives, but I insist on believing that Djemal Pasha will not be removed from his position. It seems there are a lot of troops prepared in Aleppo. There have been several cases of cholera and many of typhus (200 dead a day).

The Circassian, Hallet Bey Mertchen, commander of the 2nd Squadron of the Desert *Meharistas*, had lunch with me today. Very well educated, he studied in France and is an excellent horseman. Naturally, he rides 25 kilometers an hour by dromedary. He told me some details of life in the desert: The fear that a non-commissioned officer, a French pilot, had fallen into the hands of the Arabs who had taken him prisoner until my dinner guest freed him from the threats of the Bedouins. Today he will return to the desert to try to report on the fortifications of the Canal. According to him, the English don't have more than 10,000 men there and, among them, many Muslims who will go over to the Turks for religious sympathies.

26 December, 1915

(…) The night before last I didn't sleep at all because of Christmas. This was celebrated with the accustomed solemnity in Bethlehem. I arrived on the afternoon of the 24th, the moment the first procession of the Holy Grotto was ending. The Superior of the convent, although Italian, was obliged (no doubt) by the Custodial President [Father Castellani], to entertain me and have me share a little snack: Definitely, either the Custodial President is an impartial person who wants to be pleasant, or the Custody needs money, and the only country that can give it to them is Spain. It seems to me there may be some truth in both theories.

After a brief visit to the Grotto, I went to Tantur, where I ate with the people from St. John of God, and I then returned to Bethlehem in the company of various members of the Red Crescent. The religious function had already begun and Mehmet Djemal was attending it with his full staff, and Zaki Bey. All of them Muslims, a thing that they would surely not imagine in Europe.

The religious ceremony was extremely solemn, with the Patriarch celebrating it, accompanied by the bishop of Capernaum, Monsignor Picardo, and the rector of the Austrian hospice. With the mass ended, the procession was organized to lead the Baby Jesus to the Grotto and celebrate the services there. The bishop read the Gospel of St. Luke and, as he was doing so, he was putting into practice what the Gospel describes took place twenty centuries ago. One could not even move because of the enormous number of people who were squeezing to enter the Grotto. There was no lack of Protestants at the mass, and even a dervish. All in all, I went back to Jerusalem at dawn.

The novelty of the last few days is the presence in Jaffa of a German submarine. Its commander came ashore, and went to Sarona in the company of Hasan Bey to get provisions of gasoline. (…) The Allied warships that have been wandering around these coasts are probably not very calm.

1916

2 January, 1916

New Year, new life. That's the refrain, and, to a certain point, I'm beginning to fulfill it. I am prepared to reorganize the services of the consulate as if I were a first class Spanish general manager; the Turkish monetary system changed (naturally to the detriment of the public who always catches the worst of it); I'm also changing my ideas in favor of Turkey and the Turks; I opened an era of friendship with the Custody; I once again have my former cook; and in short, I'm making some changes to my ideas.

The Anglo-French forces have been thrown out from Anaforta and Aribouran [in the Dardanelles]: They only remain in Sedd al-Bahir. The truth is, these gentlemen have made a mess of it unless the expedition had some goals I don't know about.

I waited for the New Year in the Austrian consulate. A splendid dinner and as guests of Dr. Prüfer, were Commander Tiller, a German captain and Raphaël. According to the German captain, the government has occupied the Hotel Victoria of Damascus, and Saura has marched to Beirut. Everyone congratulated me on the reopening of the Jaffa convent. Certainly, Hasan Bey said that it was his duty to reinstate the friars into their convent because he should respect their religion as much as that of the prophet Muhammad. Thus, we see that there is new life. (…)

3 January, 1916

Since New Year's Day I've been receiving congratulatory visits, and among them is that of Giorgio Golubovich, who told me his traveling story. For having spoken with the Jewish doctor Cohen, who is suspected of espionage, he was detained in Nablus, packed up in a coach and, what's worse, tied with his hands behind his back. He had to spend the night in Jerusalem seated, on a hard floor and without food. The following day, he managed to get a special favor in that they permitted him to go out for a moment to take the customary cup of tea, thanks to which he could warn the Patriarchate and the Austrian consulate, to whose nationality he belongs. Thanks to this he was freed since in reality, there really was nothing against him, but it is hard to think that for simple suspicion the poor man has gone through such bad treatment and the resulting fright.

This morning, a great parade of *meharis*, with new uniforms, who are going to war. After, an enormous number of camels came loaded to the limit, also going to the desert.

13 January, 1916

In these days I have learned something about the war, sufficient to somewhat calm my anxiety about news. I visited Van Kressenstein in the German hospice of St. Paul, where he found himself lodged along with his military staff. To my questions he responded that he is no longer the Chief of Staff of Djemal Pasha but, rather, the commander of the expedition against the Canal. In fact, he is thus independent and has maximum authority. His guard (an interesting detail) is composed of *dervishes*.

The night before last I had a long visit with Prüfer, with whom I spoke at length about the war, who should know it very well considering his special mission. He said that it will not conclude for a long time: That the French will not lose any of their territory, but that the Germans will keep part of Belgium, while Poland will no longer belong to the Russians. Italy, they would not even try to occupy. The German submarine, to which I have made reference before, has come again to Jaffa and is the same one that sank the 'Ancona.'

Haifa and Jaffa have been bombarded in the last few days. I don't know anything about the first, but of the second I have been able to find out that it was the 'Joan of Arc' and that it has done considerable damage to some of the houses that are near the Wagner factory but without having destroyed the latter. Apparently a part of the German consulate also suffered the consequences of the bombing.

The preparations for the Canal are moving fast. Within a short while German troops will arrive; German cannons and some Austrian big calibers are also going to be sent there, as well as aviators with their machines.

They have celebrated with all solemnity the withdrawal of the Allies from the Dardanelles. The general who commanded the Turkish forces in Anaforta is my friend, 'Ali Riza Pasha. The victory celebration consisted of a type of civic procession formed by Jewish and Muslim schools, with music, speeches and other 'excesses.'

Some interesting details about the manner in which they do requisitions: In the Saladin School (formerly St. Anne), the Muslims have taken over for their use, among other books, the work *The Progress of the Soul in Spiritual Life*. Another example: While doing the inventory of Notre Dame de France, they included the Pontifical Library of the Jesuit Father Mallon in the following form: 2.5 cubic meters of books.

24 January, 1916

Cold, wind, rain and snow. My Austrian colleague, Kraus, has lunch every day in my house because his cook has typhus, which causes me a certain amount of panic. Let's hope there is no contagion.

Raphaël is worried about how things look in Greece. It seems to me that I will once again have to take charge of the consulate general of said country.

I attended a lunch that the members of the Red Crescent gave to my Austrian colleague, Kraus, and me. It took place in the former English hospital, outfitted now for infectious diseases (during the lunch one of the sick died). Sulayman Bey showed off his architectural knowledge, and I showed off my invented knowledge of Arabism and Orientalism, so to save the magnificent library of St. Steven I said that, by order of the Royal Geographical Society, I was busy writing a book about the geography and history of the East, for which I had purchased from the professors of the Biblical School of the Dominicans the majority of their notes and manuscripts about the matter. Given the object of the lie, I don't think I will have to confess it.

28 January, 1916

Yesterday, the anniversary of the birth of the Kaiser, I visited the German consul and some of his compatriots who are good friends of mine. They should have thanked me for the visit, because it was no time for joking around. For four days we have had a snow storm and wind that is rarely seen in Jerusalem. The thermometer went below zero; the stoves are consuming a quantity of firewood that is really something, and I fuming at the war, the weather and everything else in this miserable world.

There are rumors of peace so strong that it makes me think there is something true to them, but since the newspapers of the different countries talk about very different combinations, I don't know if such a beautiful thing could be true.

The Ottoman press agency said that, by the instigation of French representatives, a general revolution has broken out in Barcelona. (According to this agency) the French have expressed the desire to recruit workers trained in metalworking for the French factories. Fantasies!

3 February, 1916

Sensational news: The crown prince 'Izzet al-Din has committed suicide, according to what my Greek colleague assured me. The natural commentary is that something serious must have happened in Constantinople. Nonetheless, there are so many rumors that spread, so many news items that turn out to be false, that I don't know what to think.

Hasan Bey has come to deal with his projected appointment as commander of a zone of the desert, but this commission has turned out not to be decided, I do not know for what reason. Von Kressenstein told me that Hasan Bey himself had asked for it. However, they said that it has to do with a bit of vengeance from Von Kressenstein, because Hasan told him in Jaffa that the Turks were the ones who were doing everything in the war, and the Germans were not moving from Jerusalem.

8 February, 1916

The news of the suicide has been confirmed, or at least, that the crown prince had cut the veins of his left arm. The dismissal of Barciara Effendi (as the secretary of the governor) is also confirmed for his fraud during the time of Madyid Bey, the ex-governor of this city.

15 February, 1916

I have returned from a hunting excursion to Jericho, where I went with the Dutch priest Van der Vliet. On the road back we met two battalions of Turkish infantry, and, frankly, the military spirit and physical resistance of the troops were noticeable just for their absence. Behind each battalion we found many, very many straggling, sick soldiers, leaning on a cane to walk or sitting at the side of the road. It was pitiful to see them. A curious detail: Some Turkish officials have paraded through Jericho...singing the *Marseillaise*. I don't know if they have learned it in the trenches of the Dardanelles and if they feel sorry when they sing it. (...)

On Saturday, a great excursion to the Jordan. Truly I do not understand how there are people who can risk going through these dunes of the Jordan valley in the middle of June considering that, in the middle of February, I am congested. The ground, without the smallest plant, was full of sulfur and gypsum, and really looked like the moon. Not a bush, nor a bird; the ground full of dead and half buried locusts... an ideal landscape as you can see, but which also has its attractions for those who love the desert. Finally we got to the plain and there, at least, one could breathe, although it was rather hot.

We took the road towards 'Ayn Hidjla (Spring of the Partridges) without finding either partridges or any other game, but between the coolness of the water and the shade of the planting of palm trees that constitute this oasis, as well as the breeze from the Dead Sea one feels there, we had a very fine lunch, enjoying the hospitality of the famous Greek monk, Serapion. This cleric is one of the most intelligent of those of his order (and there are some very intelligent ones). He has purchased and put into cultivation great extensions of land. Within a few years the dates alone, which have the reputation of being the best in the region, will be worth a fortune. He is also the head of the *Laura*, or colony of monks who live there. Each one of them has an extremely poor hut crowned with a cross, which reminds me a lot in their appearance of the famous *barracas de Valencia*.[1] The huts have been built by their owners, who spend their whole existence in them, and within very little time they are as wild, or more so, than the land in which they live. The year before, one of them was murdered by the Bedouins, and who knows how many dramas must have taken place in those places.

It seems that, in the last two weeks, eight battalions have passed through Jericho. Are they really serious about this Canal business?

A detail typical of the Turkish administration: In Jericho there is a young dentist from Beirut; since he has such a diploma they have named him 'veterinarian for camels,' and there is a man taking care of their animals, about whose illnesses he knows as much as I do, according to the confession of the interested party. I figured he will take them to bathe in the Dead Sea, where sometimes their injuries are cured.

Turkish friendliness with me. I had asked Roshan Bey for two horses requisitioned by the army with the object of going to Jericho in a coach they granted me. It was enough to say it to my friend for them to put at my disposition horses for riding, for hunting, camels, coaches and everything I could have wanted. You have to recognize that when the Turks want to be friendly, they really are.

Yesterday I went to say goodbye to Von Kressenstein who is departing... where to?

A serious incident that, at first, worried me quite a bit seems to be on the road to resolution. Some time ago I received an urgent report from Kuebler letting me know that he had observed from our convent, or in a nearby house, that they were signaling the enemy warships that frequently go by Jaffa. I took charge of alerting P[rüfer] in order to try to entrust it to German hands.[2] Kuebler also begged me to work for a change in the posting of the priest of Jaffa, Father Lazzaro, an Arab of the Convent of the Holy Land of Jaffa who views us with great suspicion and is capable of making us the victims of slander, since Kuebler was sure that our friars were completely innocent.

I saw P[rüfer], who told me he was already updated on the matter, since an agent of his in Jaffa had spoken to him about it and that there really were signals made with white and red lights, as if with flashlights. 'It just so happened' that these lights were seen only on nights when the sea was rough and there were warships on the high seas. The lights were not coming from our convent but rather from a house near it.

Nonetheless, I insisted that Father Lazzaro be taken out of Jaffa, since he was extremely suspicious 'of committing acts that could be interpreted as posing a threat to the city of Jaffa.' I put a written denunciation before Colonel Von Kressenstein. He spoke with the canon of the Patriarchate threatening him with denouncing the case before Djemal Pasha if he didn't take the priest out of Jaffa. It looks like the Patriarchate will do it, and that Father Lazzaro will come to Jerusalem or another city of the interior.

20 February, 1916

The intrigue has had results. The President of the Custody has telegraphed the Jaffa priest. (...)

The next arrival of Enver Pasha is officially confirmed (although we still don't know the day). I very much want to meet the ruler of Turkey.

The new Austrian vice consul, De Marquet, arrived (some would say he is French) and also the captain of the Austrian cavalry, Baron Latscher. De Marquet told me that in Smyrna, where he has spent two years, a barrel of oil has risen to cost seven Turkish Pounds (!!!), that is 320.60 Francs cash. So we should congratulate ourselves that here it only costs 120 Francs.

26 February, 1916

Yesterday, the most sensational event since I've been here in Jerusalem, above all from the point of view of the rabble. Enver Pasha, Vice *Generalísimo* of the Army, Minister of War and the son-in-law of the Sultan, made his solemn entry to the Holy City. From the morning on, there was an extraordinary influx of people in the streets, a splendid sun; the cafes were full like a day of bullfights in Spain. The only thing that made you understand that this was not a bullfight were the triumphal arches erected by the different religious faiths. At the entry of the city near the Jaffa road, there were two tents where Enver, my friend, Djemal Pasha, and the rest of the leaders were received.

Following a suggestion from a German colleague, I sent my *dragoman*. The German, Austrian, Norwegian and American *dragomans* also went with the same objective. Well, not the slightest bit of attention was paid to them, and they didn't even have a place to sit, for which reason they returned to the city without having even been presented. Doubtless, the suppression of the Capitulations...

After a brief rest and the obligatory cup of coffee, the general headed for Jaffa road to the Hotel Kaminitz. From there they went to the sanatorium of the Mount of Olives. The students of the schools of the Alliance Israélite Universelle offered them and the members of the German Colony flowers. The people didn't seem to me as enthusiastic as one might expect from their southern character. Nonetheless, the triumvirate of Enver Pasha, Talat Pasha and Djemal Pasha did more for Turkey than any of their predecessors, and if Turkey is an important factor in this war, it is due to them.

Djemal Pasha greeted us very affectionately while passing by my house. The procession consisted of a half dozen automobiles, in which the German and Austrian military attachés from Constantinople rode, as well as the leaders of the military staff.

This morning the official reception took place in the sanatorium. It began with the consuls; the governor presented us one by one. Enver was very attentive with me. His questions, naturally, were the customary: 'How long have you been here? Do you have news from your country? etc.' He told me: 'I already know you, since Djemal Pasha has spoken about you a great deal.'

Today they spent the rest of the day in meals, visits to the Holy Sepulcher, the Mosque of 'Umar, Mount Zion, etc., but I did not attend any of these events. The following day they all left for Beersheba.

7 March, 1916

This morning Prüfer updated me on the situation regarding the very serious problem of the churches and religious objects, something that I already knew about because of certain indications and the confidences of a certain agent of the authorities. It seems that the elaborate plan by Enver Pasha is to definitively take over all the establishments belonging to the belligerent countries, destroy, or at least remove from them, the symbols of our faith, and occupy the churches.

Prüfer laid out the same consideration on this matter that I had. This is not an issue of a religious war, as in the Middle Ages, as the Turks are allied with Christians, among them the Austrians who are, for the vast majority, Catholic. These measures would alienate from the Turks the European sympathies and would give rise to grave consequences.

14 March, 1916

I went to Jericho again on a hunting trip. (...) We arrived at the Jordan, and there we took a car, crossing the famous bridge and following the al-Salt highway. While returning to Jerusalem we met two infantry battalions who were doing exercises, and I noticed in them the hands of the Germans, since they were well trained and equipped. Deployed as guerillas, they were dragging themselves along the ground and covering themselves with bits and pieces of the landscape. The uniforms were indistinguishable from the soil, but the backpacks could be seen more than they should.

According to Nogales Bey, who has just arrived again, the situation in Armenia and Iraq is the following: the Russians have crossed Trebizond, Erzurum, Mus, Bitlis and, they also say, Siirt.[3] In that case they can easily cut off the withdrawal of the Turks who are in Mesopotamia, even more so given how much the Bedouins are against the Turks. In Mesopotamia the English, after having taken Ctesiphon [some 25 miles south of Baghdad], have had to retreat to Kut al-Amara, where they were surrounded by Turks.[4] Nonetheless, the 'siege' didn't seem very dangerous for the English. Persia is largely occupied by the Russians and the English.

28 March, 1916

The heat is beginning to return to its old tricks, although there is a certain panic about the fevers so prevalent here during this period. However, the cisterns of Jerusalem are all full, and we will not need the great rains that have lately returned to visit us.

I have dedicated the morning to a sad duty; since yesterday my good German colleague, Dr. E. Schmidt, died of an attack of apoplexy. After eating lunch, the poor man suffered an attack, and, without ever regaining consciousness or being able to move his paralyzed limbs, he passed away yesterday at dawn. His love for this country, in which he had 25 years of service, and his excellent character have made us all feel bad about it. The funeral services in the Protestant church of the Redeemer were very well attended. The funeral procession was preceded and followed by infantry and marine forces and had at its head the excellent band of the 8th Army Corps.

The most pessimistic rumors have been circulating in the city these last few days. Diyarbakir is in the hands of the Russians, and the people are beginning to retreat in something only slightly less than complete disorder. They told me of horrors committed by the Russians in Armenia, in response to those committed by the Turks against the Christians. They exaggerate and lie so much in this country that now I don't believe anything.

The problems of the money exchange and of 'costly and bad bread' keep right on as usual, but with the indifference and fatalism of these people, both have now become endemic. The people don't resist them anymore and die peacefully of hunger without protesting or doing anything.[5] (…)

Commander Tiller told me that the reason for the relieving of Zaki Bey was that when Von Kressenstein came here for the first time, he asked him about the road to Beersheba and about the state of the highway construction works. The Turk answered him that he did not know, and when the German indicated the necessity of doing a reconnaissance in that part of the country, Zaki answered that 'it was very hot.' To that end, Tiller told me that, when he was the head of a battalion in Lebanon, he ordered some military exercises and found out upon taking command of the forces that the officers did not usually run any sort of exercises. He ordered them to do so henceforth, and the first day, he was surprised to see that the officers came to the terrain where the maneuvers were taking place…by car.

6 April, 1916

I have spent a few very pleasant days of rest in Jaffa. In this season the oranges and other fruit trees are in bloom, the sea is like glass and the sky is that shade characteristic of the East, which is unique, and one can never tire of admiring.

The highway from Ramla is excellent and well cared for. The edge of town is embellished with a new avenue (it is true that there were arbitrary acts committed in the making of these improvements). Demolitions made in the square of the Seray are countless. To top it off, luck would have it that not a single warship has presented itself to take away our tranquility, not even the 'Ernest Renan,' which I really want to see, since that's the one that launched the missile that fell in the bed I should have been occupying in the convent.

I was very honored. On one of the last few days, I made a visit to Hasan Bey, which had to be quite long since oriental hospitality demands the offer of coffee, bananas, sweets, rose water and even smoking *narguilé* with flowers.

13 April, 1916

The Turkish government continues with its policy of humiliating us all, it has been ordered that from now on correspondence cannot be written in Spanish. We can only write in our language [Turkish] to the embassy.

The 1st division of German airplanes is now in Damascus. A biplane that landed in Jerusalem the past few days seems to belong to it.

14 April, 1916

A procession took place from Nebi Musa in extremely bad weather. Wind and rain are a rare things in the early part of the year.

The same squeeze as always for the poor people who try to change a bank note in the 'Deutsche' or the 'Ottoman Bank'. This question of the bills threatens to end in catastrophe.

15 April, 1916

The search of the archives of the Consulate General of France in Beirut has been confirmed, with disastrous consequences that I have been able to avoid here by not consenting to the search of the consulate in my charge. A man, Joseph Hani, together with several others, had, in 1913, written a petition to the French consul there, asking for the occupation of Syria by France, the complete independence of the *Vilayet* from Beirut with French protection, and other things that would very much please France but that unfortunately for this gentleman, have now come to light. This has cost him his life, since he was hanged on the 5th of the month.

24 April, 1916

Gómez Muros has been here, and he is returning today to Damascus and Beirut to continue from there on his way home to Spain. He is carrying many material and affectionate souvenirs, and, for my part, I'm taking advantage of the occasion to send a big package of dispatches directed to the Legation and the Ministry that I hope will not fall into the hands of strangers. I paid for the trip out of my pocket, as well as that of Father Miguel Angel, considering it an embarrassment for our country that a cleric remains here, stranded, believing that Spain does not remember her subjects. This is one of the embarrassments that I have had to suffer seeing the stinginess of our governments for certain things.

The holidays of the Holy Week have gone by with a notable lack of enthusiasm. Even for the *Holy Fire* there was very little activity. In spite of the order from the Vatican that from now on we Catholics should not attend this celebration, the Custodial President, in a good decision and with prudent judgment, suspended for this year the execution of the order. The Abyssinians, as usual, constitute the great attraction of the holidays. During them I did not tire of admiring the very curious and singular coexistence of so many religions and nationalities (the primary attraction that I find in Jerusalem, but not to say the only one).[6]

Today, they have communicated to me the death of General Von der Goltz as a result of typhus. He passed away in Damascus, and, really, typhus causes more havoc than the war. The sanitary situation is frankly alarming. Not only in this city, but also in Syria and Palestine, the hospitals are full of sick people. The day before yesterday, the Superior of the Sisters of St. Joseph of the Apparition died too, the victim of her self-denial. Dr. Fotios and other people I know also have the same sickness. I pray God that this war ends soon and that I can 'verbally' tell all these things in Spain.[7]

Friar Bonifacio told me his tribulations, because the majority of the German and Austrian soldiers that come here are accompanied by the members of the German Colony [Protestant Order], who entertain them with [secular] excursions instead of letting them visit the Holy Places. It seems that the 'Templars' are not baptized as children but rather wait until their youngsters are older and have sufficient discernment to choose a religion. Otherwise, they are excellent people.

I found myself in full season of visits and congratulations from the different sects because of Easter, which this year falls at the same time for all of them. Monsignor Damianos (Orthodox), Camassei (Latin) and Ormanian (Armenian) were my principal visitors. The very rich Greek received me like a prince, and he is not as rich as the famous Eutimios, Superior of the Holy Sepulcher. The Muslims also wished me well, among them the great *Shayj* of the Mosque of 'Umar.

20 April, 1916 (This entry is posted after the 24)

Yesterday was the anniversary of the coronation of the Sultan, Mehmet V. There was an official reception in the Seray, and we visited Mehmet Djemal, who received us very well and honored us with a good concert by the band of the 8th Army Corps. The general told me about a battle that he says took place recently near the Canal, some 48 kilometers from al-Qantara. It seems that the English have suffered a thousand dead and quite a few prisoners, among them a colonel.

From time to time the city becomes livelier with the horns of the automobiles of the German Red Cross and trucks. Jerusalem, Jerusalem!

30 April, 1916

We are in full holiday because of the news that arrived yesterday of the surrender of Kut al-Amara. According to the Turkish telegrams, they have taken 10,000 English prisoners. It seems the Turks fight well, and, the truth is, they work miracles.

I also found out that in that combat, the nice Caucasian Hallet Bey Mertchen died and also, at his side, the extremely nice Manduh Bey. I am very sorry about them. In total, it seems that ten Turkish officers have fallen.

4 May, 1916

(...) I received a telegram announcing that the authorities of Ramla had presented themselves in the convent [of San Nicodemo] of the city saying that it must be evacuated that same afternoon to be converted into a hospital. I put into action all I have to prevent it.

The burial of the poor Dr. Fotios Euclides was truly a demonstration of sorrow. The doctor is not the only one who has died of typhus. Even young people of 20 years of age have passed away. The really bad thing of it is that there is no defense whatsoever, and the only thing that one can hope for is that the sick person's heart is strong enough to withstand it. Right now Alonzo (the director of the Crédit Lyonnais of Jaffa) and many others have typhus.

8 May, 1916

Finally, we began to see something that reminds us of Europe. A few days ago the English prisoners taken by the Turks in the battle of Katia were led to this city: 21 officers and about 130 soldiers. Among the prisoners, a colonel and a commander. I confess frankly that the Turks, at least in appearance, have behaved very well with them. In the first carriage that entered Jerusalem came the first commander of the fortress and, to his right the English colonel; in the second coach Kamal Bey and to his right, the English commander; in the remaining coaches the officers who were left, and then, in columns of two, the English soldiers, flanked by squads of Turkish infantry with fixed bayonets. It seems they are all from a cavalry regiment, but among the soldiers there were various Hindus. They ate very well, and the following day, left on the Damascus train.

For tomorrow, we are waiting for the formal entrance of 400 Austrian soldiers who come *as pilgrims* with their military band in front. Within two weeks some other Hungarian soldiers will come with an orchestra of *tziganes*. As you see it is all very European and pleasant.

16 May, 1916

Yesterday, the 'great week' of Jerusalem ended. The Austrian mountain division howitzer artillery von Marno left, and everything returned to the peace and quiet of the Holy City. Celebrations were composed of concerts, gymnastic exercises, dance and even cinema in Notre Dame de France, with scenes of the campaign in the Tirol, submarine maneuvers and descriptions of the tactical movements of the principal battles of the current war.

We continue with the typhus. The architect Pascal Serafini has died, as have a Greek doctor, Friar Enrique (Franciscan), Hanna Batato and many poor people of different faiths. In a single day there were 97 cases. Alonzo, the director of Crédit Lyonnais of Jaffa, has been saved. As if that weren't enough, there are some cases of cholera in Damascus and Aleppo, so it is not necessary to say that panic exists in the city.

19 May, 1916

At the present time there are 1,250 cases of typhus in Jerusalem. Yesterday the cashier of the public debt, my neighbor, was buried. This thing is getting closer.

Today Djemal Pasha is supposed to arrive. According to the public rumor, he is coming to crush Jerusalem, as he has done in Beirut and Damascus: The so-called 'decentralizing movement.' Recently he hanged 21 people in both cities, among them a senator and a member of the Ottoman parliament.

Fortunately today the desert wind (the *Jamsin*), which has been terrible, has stopped. Early in the morning it was 30°C in my room, but in the desert it got to 52°C in the shade.

20 May, 1916

Last night I got word that the Turkish authorities have taken possession of the Ramla convent. I immediately telegraphed ambassador Arroyo, but I have almost no hope of the success of our actions.

Yesterday evening Djemal Pasha arrived. This evening I am invited by the *mutasarrif* to a great dinner in his honor. I'm all for banquets!

21 May, 1916

Last night the *mutasarrif* received us in 'his house', that is, in the former Italian consulate. In the garden there were little tables where my colleagues and I had some appetizers while waiting for the arrival of Djemal Pasha. When he appeared, he greeted us, had a moment with his subordinates and right away sat down at our table with Heinrich Brode – the new German consul – Kraus, Raphaël, Glazebrook, a German captain and me. It was my turn to bear the burden of the conversation, and Djemal announced, joking, that he had it in mind to hang me, publishing 'compromising documents' that he had about my conduct and that, of course, did not refer to my lack of neutrality.

26 May, 1916

A young aviator, lieutenant Von Hesler, has come to see me; he could scarcely enter the office door since he measures more than 1.90 meters in height, for which reason he attracts a lot of attention here. He is an excellent artist and played an interesting program of Italian and German music on the piano. His companion is Von Bülow, belonging to the famous German family. They showed me very interesting photos of Jerusalem, taken on the last flight they organized.

Commander Witzleben, ex-director of the 'Deutsche Orient Bank' of Constantinople, left the day before yesterday for Beersheba.

The typhus is diminishing quite a bit in intensity and, above all in severity, so much so that now there are no more than 2% fatalities. On the other hand, they say that in Bethlehem there has been a case of cholera, which would not be fun at all.

Hasan Bey has definitely been sent to Der'a. With this in mind, the mayor of Jaffa, presiding over a committee, came to see me because he considered me 'the most influential person with Djemal Pasha' to get him to keep his commander in Jaffa. Fortunately, the General had left for the desert.

27 May, 1916

The remaining Austrian officers and soldiers arrived. Their arrival was less solemn than the previous one. Kraus and De Marquet attended the parade from my balcony. (…) The same military music accompanied them as for the others; and in the smallest details one could appreciate the Austrian correctness. They paraded very well, wearing the summer uniform of khaki green with the colonial helmet of the same color.

31 May, 1916

An airplane appeared over Jerusalem again. Flying at a height of 1,500 meters, it almost stopped with surprising precision over the Hotel Fast and dropped a German flag. At the end of the flag there was a sack containing a letter from Prüfer to his consul, announcing that he would arrive by evening and that he should prepare him a good dinner. According to what Prüfer told me later, upon finding out that the plane in question was going to do reconnaissance over Jaffa he charged him to 'get to Jerusalem' and turn over the letter to the German consul. Mission completed, the plane disappeared in the direction of Beersheba.

Prüfer has told me that Von Bülow had gotten the necessary permission from the captain of the aviation company to give me the interesting photography of Jerusalem from the air which, to a certain extent, was secret. We agreed that one of these days I will go to Beersheba to see the defense guns against airplanes. I will also examine the camp and the flights of the Fokker machines. The only news that cooled my enthusiasm was that there seems to be some cholera there. However, the camp was isolated and had as its cook no less than the chef of Shepherd's Hotel of Cairo, which is a guarantee against cholera. By the way, yesterday in Bethlehem there were 15 or 17 cases and one of the sick died in just a few hours.

2 June, 1916

The *dragoman* of the German general consulate, Rahil, came to tell me on behalf of his boss that, east of Denmark, a great naval battle has taken place in which five English battleships were sunk, as well as a great number of destroyers and one submarine. The news has produced a sensation, naturally.[8]

Today I had lunch with Mustafa Bey, who is leaving tomorrow for al-Hafir. He explained to me his ideas that Spain should take advantage of the war and ask for a rectification of the limits of the Franco-Spanish zone in Morocco, leaving our country with the entire Warza valley and having as the lower border the Sebu. But will Spain be listened to by the belligerents?

This morning Father Pablo Ibañez died of typhus. In Jerusalem we have five cases of cholera and 60 daily in Damascus. I decided to get vaccinated against the terrible epidemic. Tomorrow I will have the injection, due to a special favor from Talat Bey, in the former French hospital of St. Louis.

Kaminitz told me that the cigarettes he had bought for me in Damascus were stolen by a Turkish official. The guilty party has been discovered and will suffer the appropriate punishment, but the details are not really clear.

14 June, 1916

On the 10th, after receiving and answering all the congratulations for my name day, I finally undertook the trip to the desert. My German and Austrian colleagues, De Marquet, various German officers and I left in a German Red Cross vehicle. The car was rather comfortable since it served to transport the wounded, and it moved rather slowly thanks to which I could contemplate the countryside at my leisure.

In Hebron it was a surprise for me to see the pleasant appearance of its surroundings: Hills covered with vineyards, fruit trees and some little houses of a rather European style. Naturally all the houses belonging to the belligerents had been occupied as hospitals and, above them, waved the flag of the Red Crescent. Before arriving at the city we saw a construction that serves to protect a great fountain that has been used to bring water to Jerusalem for the last two years.

In Hebron we picked up a Tunisian doctor, whom I figured would go to visit those affected by some of the 'elegant' illnesses to which I have alluded. (…) Without further incident we arrived at Beersheba, where the headquarter camp is located. There, the military men got out, and only we consuls were left, covered in dust and rather tired; we went to the aviators' camp, where Von Kressenstein was waiting for us. We ate dinner and, of course, at the center of the table, in a place of honor, was the flag of Spain. Lacking an orchestra, a terrific gramophone made the succulent meal still more agreeable. A lieutenant aviator accompanied the choral pieces very well on the violin.

I slept very poorly because of the incredible cold that there is in the desert at night. This abrupt change in temperature had some rather unpleasant consequences for my health.

On Sunday morning I was in one of the hangars looking at three combat biplanes, and, although I sat down in the cockpit and in the observer's spot, I had no desire to fly, nor did I fly. I didn't see the famous Fokkers, but it is known that they have some manufacturing secrets. In the photography workshop, they showed me very interesting views of the Canal. In one of the photos one makes out an English camp above the Canal, where one sees soldiers in front of the tents shooting at the airplane. In another of them one can see the warships anchored in their special harbor, and one can even appreciate their guns.

At midday someone came to look for me in a truck, in which I was transported to the headquarters where there was a banquet of some fifty persons. At the main table, besides the consuls, were Van Marno, commander of Hungarian artillery, Baron Latschen, captain of the military staff, Kadri Bey, chief of the military staff of Von Kressenstein, Rifa' at Bey, commander of the Nazareth division, and various German leaders. (...)

After lunch, I returned to the aviators' camp and had a troubled nap, since at every instant I awoke because of the sand hitting against the canvas of my tent, despite it being installed in a trench underground. The heat was suffocating. The illumination was electric.

Then, [Adolf] Von Arnim came, and we undertook the trip towards Asludj by a highway built during the war, which is not bad at all, and follows near the railroad line that has also been built there now.

The desert there has the characteristics of the steppes, and, in some places, corn is cultivated there of a greenness that could do no less than surprise me. Upon arriving at Asludj we stopped to rest and contemplate what has been done in just a few months. In 1915 there was absolutely nothing there, and now, in little time, they have drilled five wells that give extremely abundant and clear water. A motor maintains the water supply and takes it through various little cement canals to the installations of the commander and officers of the post, the pharmacy, sickbay for horses and camels, and the camp of the *meharis* who form the garrison of the post. We had the traditional coffee in a pretty tent with the Turks, and admired in that desert an orchard and garden with abundant vegetables, eucalyptus and bananas.

We went back to Beersheba very slowly, having found on the road an endless number of loaded camels that formed convoys. The camels were frightened by our automobile, and one of them fell on its side, with all its load. A Turkish soldier who protested to us must have regretted it, since Von Arnim administered a real walloping to him. I confess that I really didn't like it much. We also came across a battery of anti-aircraft cannons pulled by oxen.

This time it was the Austrians' turn to honor me, who had given me an almost unreal meal in that place, since there was even lobster with mayonnaise. During the dinner, the band of Austrian music played and then, after them, the *tziganes* until midnight. Kieselbach showed me by star-light the eight 10 cm howitzers (Skoda) which form the ten batteries. The howitzers were bronze and have a range of six kilometers. Each piece needs three carts.

The following day I saw two planes going up that were going towards al-'Arish. Afterwards, I observed the bomb depots for the planes: There are ones that weigh from half a kilo to twenty kilos, and I confess I couldn't quite get over it, thinking that that depot could fly. The propeller with which each bomb is provided is designed to prevent it from exploding and destroying its own plane instead of the enemy's.

In Beersheba, as in Hebron, there are quite a few cases of cholera. In Asludj a case of cholera appeared that very day, and one can suppose that I was not very calm, even less so when they recommended that I not brush my teeth because of the cholera.

To sum up: The Austrian-German forces that are in Beersheba have in their charge the campaign howitzers, anti-aircraft cannons, wireless telegraph, trucks, *idem* for the Red Cross, Austrian-German sanitary system, airplanes and other technical services. There are Turkish soldiers only for guard-duty chores.

21 June, 1916

Incredible heat in this city. (…) Djemal Pasha arrived, and I went to visit him. The general assured me that there is no hope of any peace for now.

I have been to the hospital to see Von Bülow who is injured, although, fortunately, not seriously. In a fight against an English plane in al-'Arish he was hit by machinegun fire, but thanks to a cushion that his 'lady friend' had given him, which attenuated the blow, it saved him from certain death. The advantages of 'lady friends.'

It seems that the 8th Army Corps will soon go to the desert (Lord, what heat!) to assist in an attack against the Canal which will take place shortly.

9 July, 1916

On June 29 I received a notice from the Djemal Pasha's adjutant, telling me that he would come to see me that afternoon. He presented himself at my home with adjutant and escort, as promised. After the first greetings he said to me, dryly: 'Do you have complaints against the local authorities?' He assured me that he was asking this question because the censor had brought him the telegram that I had sent the day before to the embassy in which I said, 'I beg the Ministry to send me a telegraphic reply relating to my resignation, since my situation is intolerable.' The minister supposed that my resolution was due to friction with the local authorities and thus his question.

I explained then in detail the mistaken attitude of the governor, what had happened with the Spanish convents and other things. His Excellency promised to take care of those matters for me and asked me to withdraw my resignation, charging me to tell my government that Djemal Pasha had asked me to do so. He actually told me that he could not allow the *enfant gâtè* (spoiled boy) to leave Jerusalem.

We drank some beers, we called Raphaël to make the conversation more agreeable with his bright ideas, and, all in all, the visit lasted two hours. It goes without saying that the public stationed in front of my house had quite a commentary about such a long interview. There were rumors of the intervention of Spain and Greece in the war, a chance of peace: In short, there was something for all tastes. They were very far from knowing that, in reality, we did nothing more than chat in friendly fashion.

The minister told me of his plan to improve the city, building a park on Mount Zion, tearing down the houses facing mine and making an avenue from the Franciscan School to the Damascus Gate. The future Djemal Pasha Park, after so much work and so many lies, has come to nothing, and His Excellency told me that he was thinking of ceding it to the Armenians once again.

On Friday, in spite of it being a holiday for the Muslims, I made a visit of an hour and a quarter to the minister, and this is the summary of the interesting conversation we had and which was, for me, very satisfactory. With respect to my vindication over the Spanish convents, he assured me that two officers of his entourage will go to San John and to Ramla to see that the clerics are installed in the best rooms of both convents, leaving the rest for the officers and soldiers.[9] The *mutasarrif* will send me a communication telling me that the occupation is merely provisional and without any relationship to their political nature or property. The authors of the offense against the consulate over the question of the *Werko* will be punished (one was thrown out and two remained on half salary for some time). He promised me that none of the sanctuaries of the Franciscans would be touched, a promise I took advantage of to ask, 'Well, leave the sanctuary of the Visitation free,' which he immediately agreed to do.

One detail: Regarding the Visitation, he told me to *order* Mehmet Djemal Pasha to leave it free. Of course, I doubted I would do this task with anyone other than this general. However, since the minister ordered it, that's what I did, and Mehmet Djemal gave me an order directed to the military commander of San John, charging him to turn over the keys of the sanctuary to the Franciscans and to let them go there everyday, instead of the two days a week as the governor had decreed.

We talked about many other things: The Armenian question, religious fanaticism, his plans for after the war… The Armenian Patriarch, Ormanian, had gone to see him complaining that, in Der'a, the authorities obliged the Armenian refugees there to convert to the religion of Muhammad. The minister told him that, from the investigations made, it turned out that what happened was that some Muslim religious leaders, knowing the state of poverty of the refugees, took advantage of it by offering land, houses, or cash on condition of converting to Islam. His Excellency commented that it was propaganda, identical to what the Christian missionaries do, and putting his finger on the sore spot, he asked the Patriarch: 'What would you do if I were to ask you to baptize me, knowing, your most excellent Reverend, that he who makes a Muslim change his religion is punished by the death penalty in the Ottoman Empire? Would you baptize him or not?' The Patriarch, after reflecting a moment, answered no. 'Then,' the minister replied sharply, 'You are no Christian, you do not comply with the doctrine of Jesus Christ.'

I saw on Djemal Pasha's table the book by Dr. Ruppin about Syria. I spoke with His Excellency about this book, and referring to the author he said: 'What a swine.'[10]

On the 6th of the month, the minister came to eat at my house. Although I had set the time for the dinner at 8:00 P.M., he arrived much sooner, when I was in the full fever of the table placements and other details. The object of coming sooner was to introduce me to his two older sons (he has four boys and a girl) who had just arrived from Germany. The visit of the two young men was brief, and right away, the guests and I sat down at the table. I presided with the minister, and the rest of the places were occupied by the general of the 8th Army Corps, Djemal's assistant and my colleagues from Germany, Austria and Greece, as well as the indispensable Zaki Bey.

It was not a war-time menu, since it was composed of Turkish soup, fish in mayonnaise sauce, garden-style filets, Spanish cookies and stuffed turkey. For desserts, vanilla ice cream, frozen pineapple and fruit. As for the drinks, the wine cellar of the director of the Crédit Lyonnais provided them, and they consisted of St. Julien, Rhin (Sauternes Chateau La Tour Blanche) and Atler champaign. The meal went by in very animated fashion, above all with jokes as always about our Greek colleague. As if that weren't enough, the cigars were first rate and, after getting some fresh air on the balcony, we played a poker game that lasted until 1:00 in the morning.

News of the war: A few days ago a German telegram arrived, which was published in a local newspaper. Although the authorities gathered up the edition it was already too late, since we knew from said telegram that along the whole French-English front [in Europe] a generalized offensive had been undertaken. They said that never in history has a battle like it been seen. During one week the French employed all their heavy and light artillery. One could hear the noise of the cannons all the way to London, and the losses are enormous. The Germans have advanced their first line of defense, spreading out over ten kilometers. The German telegram added that this battle may decide the peace.

The Convent of St. John, just as they promised me, has been evacuated by the troops that occupied it, leaving only four cholera victims for a few more days. The Visitation will also be free within a few days.

The preparations continue for the new expedition against the Canal. I have seen various battalions of infantry go by, three campaign batteries and an endless number of camel caravans and wagons with provisions and munitions. The Red Crescent is already sending materials. Mehmet Djemal leaves on Sunday and has promised to install himself in Ramla, throwing the current occupants out of the convent [*a promise he did not keep*].

According to the *Berliner Tageblatt,* the invasion of Palestine by the 300,000 English who occupy Egypt is imminent. I still don't believe it.

The sister of Mr. Farhi, of the Alliance Israélite, celebrated her wedding. At De Marquet's insistence we both went in tuxedos (a sensation!). The ceremony, which I did not attend, took place in the afternoon, then the banquet and later still, in the evening, the dance, which I did attend. The curious thing is that the newly-weds stayed there, receiving congratulations and chatter until the wee hours of the morning, demonstrating a patience never seen before. They were seated under a canopy and on a type of great throne, like a campaign tent covered by rugs with emblems and Talmudic allegories. It is the custom to congratulate and spend a little time with the new couple, and thus I did so. The dance was nothing special, nor was the orchestra very good. Besides, there was such a mix of people of all classes and social categories that the groom installed those of my group in a salon apart.

(…) Yesterday I received a visit from the director of the Austrian military hospital of Ratisbonne, who asked me to transfer the convent of St. John to him for his convalescents.

26 July, 1916

I have spent five days in Emmaus. For one who is accustomed to the sadness and aridness of the environs of Jerusalem it is a pleasant surprise, for Father Müller, a German Lazarist, has converted the 'Sterile Mountain' – a name the indigenous people gave to the location of the current hospice – to a forest. How? Well, by working, that is, doing what the indigenous (and certainly not by their fault) do not do.

(…) Without ending the week of rest, I had to return to Jerusalem because Father García Pardoa sent me to Father Rosa with a *cavas* to forewarn me of the attempt of the governor and the Chief of Police, Djalal

Bey, to transform the St. Vincent de Paul hospice into a great orphanage for Christian, Muslim and Jewish children. Kraus stayed out of the matter, and I came with the best intentions. I think I have had partial success... [*In the end the Turks got their way*].

Djemal Pasha left yesterday for a few days, without saying where. The people believe it's Damascus or Medina. Others are sure it's to support the operations of the new Sharif of Mecca, named by the (Ottoman) Sultan to replace the one who rebelled against the Turks.[11] Nobody knows the truth, and although I had been having tea with Djemal Pasha himself and Zaki Bey on the Mount of Olives, there was no way to verify anything for sure. We spoke, as always, about the fairer sex and their weaknesses. The minister had on his table a whole collection of gold and silver watches that he gave as gifts to the Bedouin leaders who had come to shake hands with him. He gave me a letter for Roshan Bey ordering him to turn over to me a crate of oil, an almost unheard of luxury, since a crate costs 14 Pounds in this city. He excused himself for not having accepted until now my invitation to have lunch in Artas because we are in the month of Ramadan, and my *cavases* are Muslim and would be scandalized... and all the while we were having tea with lots of company.

2 August, 1916

The second anniversary of the declaration of the European war. We've gotten this far, but we'll see if we get to the third.

It is fully confirmed that the day Djemal Pasha left for Der'a, where he has provisionally installed his headquarters, two planes dropped four bombs on the railroad track, barely ten minutes after the general had gone by on the train. There were four people injured. As this is quite a coincidence, the authorities suspect there is a wonderful network of espionage in Jerusalem. I don't know if it is true, but a German colleague also told me about it, and he implicated Zaki Bey. It could be, but it is a very risky thing.

I have raised the flag for three days in honor of Muhammad and of Qurban Bayram.

The Germans gave me press cuts from many countries with abundant news from Spain to read confidentially, but I have my doubts.

Father Pardoa gave me 52 cartridges as a gift. I could put in a whole paragraph here to expose the penury of all types that one feels, including in ammunition.

Once again the question of the Sisters of Charity is confused. The Turkish government is definitely continuing its policy of fanaticism.

It seems that the Turkish troops are withdrawing again and desisting from a more or less serious attack on the Canal.

An English prisoner, who was here recently, managed to speak to a friend of mine, and, according to what he declared, the English will be in Jerusalem within a month. This agrees with what was announced in the *Mukhattar* [newspaper] of Cairo, according to which the English are coming to liberate Jerusalem and its sanctuaries held by Muslims to put them in the hands of the Arabs, as they have already done in Mecca (according to public rumor). I have my doubts and don't believe that they are landing right now.

6 August, 1916

A commander and a certain number of Arab troops have gone over to the English. In view of this, Von Kressenstein telegraphed Djemal Pasha, asking him to send Turkish troops and to transfer the Arabs to another front of the war. Djemal Pasha answered that he could not, for the simple reason he himself could not send Arab soldiers against those of the desert who have rebelled. He insisted that, on that side, the English and Sharif of Mecca are making great progress, and in 15 days they will arrive in Kerak. A Turkish division has been sent there recently.

Beersheba has been attacked by 50 English airplanes that set the wheat depots on fire. For this reason all the available stores of this grain have been sent to Jerusalem: Yesterday, nevertheless, the population was without bread. As I have an arrangement with the German baker, Frank, I have been able to eat, but many cannot say the same. As I believe this will be a long-term problem, I am buying coal, firewood and sugar for a year. Of course the budget is enormous, since the bank bills of one Pound are worth 50 and even 45 Piasters in the city. In relation to the articles of primary necessity, here is a short list:

	Before the war	War-Time
3 kilos of wheat	1 Franc	3 Francs (and you can't find it)
3 kilos of bread	0.80 Francs	3 Francs
Sugar	1.50 Francs	70.20 Francs
Rice	1.50 Francs	8.50 Francs
Petroleum (barrel)	8 Francs	250 Francs
3 kilos of lentils	0.45 Francs	2 Francs
Lard	6.50 Francs	18 Francs
Oil (cooking)	3 Francs	12.60 Francs
Potatoes	0.55 Francs	5 Francs
Onions	0.40 Francs	4 Francs
Country cheese	2.22 Francs	8.35 Francs
Candles	0.60 Francs	4 Francs

[*Woven goods, etc…increase of 400-500%. How about that?*]

8 August, 1916

Once again the question of Artas is brought up for discussion. The governor was there three days ago with Djamil Bey, the *mudhir* of the *waqf*. It seems that he is trying to send the orphan girls to the 'Ottoman asylum' of St. Vincent de Paul (the Sisters of Charity) and transform Artas into a hospital for convalescents. Grounds for that? The eternal question of the famous list of French establishments presented (in their day) by France to the Sublime Porte, and on which this convent was included.

10 August, 1916

The possibilities of a landing are increasing. Two French torpedo boats showed up in Jaffa (this was the official version) and turned over a letter to the *kaymakam* announcing that they will bomb without further warnings. The message added that the *konak* and the military government will be bombed. (...) Kuebler, who had lunch with me today, told me that he knows from a very good source that a landing is more likely. Will the Turks and the Germans, who also believe that, get their own way? Evidently I was mistaken... and it will not be the first time nor, I expect, the last.

12 August, 1916

Prüfer and Mustafa Bey have arrived. The latter has the job of chief engineer of desert construction and spoke with enthusiasm of how much they can do there while looking for subterranean water. He also told me where he has his office, in al-Hafir; it's not as hot as in Jerusalem, despite being desert. Prüfer gives me details of the latest battles: Today he received a telegram from Von Kressenstein, announcing that he is returning to al-'Arish. To sum up, they have been in Katia less than a month, have done some damage to the English railroad and were pushed back by an attack by the forces of Albion, while the latter have also been pushed back in their counterattack against the Turks.

My friend Von Bülow shot down an English airplane at an altitude of 3,000 meters, and, of course, there was not much left of the aviator. Prüfer bombed the English positions of Muhammadiyya and al-Rumani several times... and nothing more. To sum up, the bluff was called. Should Von Kressenstein return, considering a possible English landing? I'm inclined to believe that the Allies will send the famous torpedo boat to Jaffa to produce panic and that Von Kressenstein will withdraw, leaving them [British] quite calm.

13 August, 1916

In view of a possible landing in Jaffa, the Austrians and Germans are asking me to have our vice consul there taking charge of their interests.

The press published an official communication about the revolution organized by Husayn, the emir of Mecca. According to this information, for some time now the emir has been working against the Turkish government. Once, he had his own people steal 20,000 Turkish Pounds and the emir took charge of getting them to Yemen. Won over [later] by English gold, he tried to form a division of 'defenders of the faith,' composed, in reality, of his partisans in the campaign for Egypt. One of his sons was supposed to command that division and go over to the enemy at an opportune moment. The Turkish government, which was supposed to pay the expenses of that division, did not fall into the trap, and, seeing himself discovered, the emir decided to take off his mask. While the English ships were bombarding Jeddah, he telegraphed the Turkish government, which was urgently awaiting an imperial *firman* that would make Mecca an hereditary emirate in his family. Husayn knew in advance that the Turkish government would refuse, so without waiting for answers the forces commanded by his son attacked Medina while tribes of Bedouins won over by English gold advanced against the Hedjaz line. The Turkish garrisons of Mecca and Djedda defended themselves well but had to surrender when they ran out of water and munitions. The attacks against Medina and the railroad were easily pushed back, and the Taif detachment is still fighting (since July 27) against the rebels.

A new emir named by the Turks, 'Ali Haidar Pasha, is en route to Mecca with Turkish reinforcements. Besides, the imam Yahya and Ibn al-Rashid, the most influential people of Yemen and of the Nedjed, do not agree with Husayn, who has had to take refuge in Djedda.

Up to here is the official version. But in Jerusalem they insisted that things are going well for Husayn. He has been recognized by the Sultan of Egypt and by the Algerians and the Moroccans as Caliph. What's more, according to a certain version, 'Abd al-Malik, son of El Kader (the famous Algerian), is with the *sharif* and has brought many of his compatriots to fight against the Turks. The reason for the intervention of the latter is that Djemal Pasha hanged his brother, who lived in Damascus. According to some rumors, my friend, 'Abd Allah, brother of the afore-mentioned, has been expelled. I wonder who is right?

A telegraphic communication from Colonel Von Kressenstein to the General German consulate in Jerusalem: 'The attacks against the enemy near al-Rumani were stopped in spite of the satisfactory advances because our left flank was threatened by forces proceeding from al-Qantar. On August 5, the strong English attacks against our Katia front were repulsed with great losses for them. The losses of the German and Austrian formations have been minimal; one German officer has fallen.'[12]

20 August, 1916

The inauguration of the Austrian hospital of St. Peter of Ratisbonne took place on the 18th. To be precise, it was the day of the party of the emperor and the king. In the morning there was an 'unofficial' reception in the consulate, which was very well attended, with a concert by the Austrian artillery band, and, lacking champagne (which can no longer be found in the city), they honored us with sandwiches and white wine. The inauguration of the hospital was in the afternoon, with a speech by the Austrian consul, Kraus, during which the German, Austrian and Turkish flags were raised. I visited the establishment, which is nicely built with material brought from Austria.

The *Custos* and various other Italians must have been on tenterhooks and *idem de idem* as we were in charge of the French interests. And haven't those interests turned out fine! (...)

According to some German officials, the famous attack against the Canal has been a disaster, and three drummers were taken prisoners. There are some who interpret this as a result of the Turco-German discord.

Kraus came to ask me to take charge of the Austrian interests in case of a landing in Jaffa. He had to answer a telegram from his embassy, in which they asked him why he preferred that it be the consul of Spain, and not the one from the United States, charged with such matters. I do not know the answer of my colleague.

8 September, 1916

Since the previous date, there has been the declaration of war by Romania. In addition, there is certainty of the intervention of Greece in the conflict.

As I am tired of so much hassle and worry, I spent one day hunting at the Marrun house, in Abu Gosh. Between killing partridges and eating well I have rapidly revived.

9 September, 1916

Raphaël, Kraus and I have been in the Artas convent, invited by the governor. Then other guests arrived, and when Djemal Pasha came we sat beneath a stately walnut tree to have an aperitif. The minister entertained us with his pleasant conversation, but there was a dangerous moment given the probability that Greece would soon enter the war: Besides the jokes as always, Djemal Pasha began to attack the Greek consul and said that he was going to produce three documents related to the revolutionary operations of the Greeks in Turkey, which would oblige him to take vigorous measures of security. He even spoke of sending to Mesopotamia the three million Greeks that live in Turkey. Then, 'Ali Fuad Bey, the terrible Chief of Staff, added: 'We will treat them worse than the Armenians.' There is no need to explain the effect on the guests of the confession, and threat, from the mouth of the Chief of Staff in the presence of his general. The enormous number of Greeks who live in the Ottoman Empire is one of the principal reasons that they opposed the intervention of Greece in the war. Raphaël said that they, in their turn, had 300,000 Muslim Turks in Greece, and Djemal replied to him: 'And we have three million Greeks in Turkey.'

There were almost thirty fellow guests, the most distinguished being: Roshan Bey, Nihat Bey, Behçet Bey (the desert commander) and Djamil Bey. While chatting with some of them, they praised the activity of René Masié, who is making great plantations in the desert and is now occupied with one of 100,000 trees: The eucalyptus. If they turn out the same as those I have seen in Beersheba, I think no one will sit in their shade. Behçet Bey invited me to visit him in the desert, but, as there is a lot of cholera, frankly I'm not thrilled about making this visit.

23 September, 1916

This morning Prüfer departed for Germany. I had him over for lunch in the company of Brach. The former promised to send me gunpowder from Constantinople. (...)

I attended the burial of the wife of the director of the Austrian hospital, Mrs. Schrötter. Her husband is desperate, poor man, since they got married just four months ago, and he was hoping for children. (...) A cardiac embolism put an end to all their plans in half an hour.

24 September, 1916

I have been hunting for a few days and, this time, lodged in the house of the clerics of Ratisbonne. Brother Andrés and Brother Jorge gave us the warmest hospitality. We hunters were Rauf, Aisha and I. We devoured as many provisions as we brought, those we bought in town and those the clerics offered us. We passed the time hunting and sleeping, and my companions sang some of the monotonous and erotic Arabic songs that, famous as they are, I found an annoyance and besides, rather repugnantly off-color.

On this hunting trip I brought 'Rosa,' Dr. Morniellus' dog. This little animal is almost historic since her owner picked her up in the Dardanelles, where she belonged to a French officer and then was in the desert front. Certainly, her current boss is the only member of the 39th regiment who has not been taken prisoner by the English in the last battle of Romania.

This regiment behaved very well, so much so that their flag has been decorated, but now it has gone over completely, flag and all, to the enemy, and Enver Pasha has erased it from the list of imperial regiments. The curious thing of the case is that, last year, the guilt for the failure of the attack on the Canal was laid on the Arabs, partisans of the English, but now it is the Turks who are imitating them.

We don't have any more news of the war at home. By high-ranking order, the telegrams that, until now, were distributed at home are only put up on the bulletin board in front of the consulate. For what reason? If they don't want us to know the news then don't publish it anywhere; but to suppress it at home and authorize it for the bulletin board makes no sense.

1 October, 1916

The day before yesterday all the information sheets that were missing were suddenly published, and according to what one can get out of them (if they are telling the truth), the Allied countries have gotten some advantages, but without real importance, so we will still spend this winter at war. In view of this, like the ants, I am stocking provisions for quite a while.

Mr. Levi, the director of the Anglo-Palestinian Bank, Antebi and the governor Medyet Bey are making preparations for their departure from the city. The first is being expelled as Zionist and the other two as thieves. What I mean is that, according to the *vox populi*, these two have pocketed a good quantity of money that the Wheat Union had at its disposition, making fraudulent speculations. The governor, who at his arrival in Jerusalem seemed to be an honest person, must have been corrupted by Antebi and the sweetheart the latter provided for him, Fanny Kepot. Be that as it may, I think the population is sympathetic to the downfall of both people, who were nice to no one: The first for his fanaticism and little education, and the other for this latter reason and the fragility of his political options.

These last three days I have made countless visits because of the beginning of the Jewish New Year, which is no less than 5667, or 1334 of the Hijra.

For the hundredth time the rumor is going around that Turkey has requested a separate peace, but I grant it the same credit as the previous rumors. (…)

13 October, 1916

The vice consul of Jaffa had telegraphed me saying that my presence there was urgent and absolutely necessary. I left by night and dragged my bones (or better said, the horses dragged them) along the highway to this city. I had to excuse myself with Mehmet Djemal, who was leaving definitely for Damascus, and with Kaminitz, who had invited me to his daughter's wedding. I made the trip with the greatest concern, wondering what could be the cause of a call so unexpected. Providence protected me and we avoided killing ourselves (my *cavas* 'Abed, the coachman and I) when we got to a site bordered by a precipice where the horses took fright at a hyena that was peacefully eating a camel in the middle of the road.

Upon arriving at Jaffa, Father Mateo Hebreo informed me of the incident to which I owed the telegram, and which resulted in my presence there being as necessary, as that of an archbishop at a dance. They had told the German consul [in Jaffa], Schabinger [Karl Emil], that Father Hebreo had advised the girls of the Franciscan School not to learn German nor to attend the German school. The consul was so indignant that he announced to Kuebler that he was going to telegraph about the deed to Constantinople, granting a reprieve of 24 hours. For that reason our vice consul sent me the telegram.

I confess I really dressed down Kuebler and got very indignant over the scant seriousness of all those who intervened in the matter, since by the time I arrived Father Hebreo had denied such calumny and the whole thing had been taken care of. At first I was really annoyed, but then I slept tranquilly. The following day, I was awakened by a cannon shot from a merchant ship that did no more than that and disappeared right away directed to the north.

I took advantage of the trip to visit the new *kaymakam*, Amir Fuad Bey. A surprise: While discussing the matter of which I spoke before, Schabinger told me: 'I have a lot of sympathy for Father Hebreo, as I do for the Catholic religion although I am Protestant.' This phrase from the German consul shocked me, although, later, I found out he was thinking of converting to Catholicism before leaving Jaffa, and if he did not do it now it was in consideration of the German colony, the majority of whom are Protestant and very fanatic on this point.

(…) Let's move to a happier note about my stay in Artas with some companions. We were lodged for three days in the convent and Salvador Bandak treated us like kings with his usual splendor. The famous expediter told me that, when Djemal Pasha was in the convent, he served him a trifling six bottles of champagne. What would Muhammad say about that? Perhaps he would deal with the wine of Ishmit, which according to the Prophet is the only one that Muslims can drink. It is clear that the harvest of this site is insignificant but, with the pretext that it comes from there, they all drink any wine that looks like it.

(…) Salim Ayyub, honorary vice consul of Persia and Sweden and director of the Commercial Bank of Palestine, was called to Damascus by order of Djemal Pasha. Upon arriving there he found out that the minister was not in the city, and he quietly came back to Jerusalem. But he did not count on the hostelry, or more accurately the guests, who in the form of police officers and soldiers presented themselves at his house, conducted him to the station and from there to Damascus again. We will see what the end will be of this interesting story. It will be probably also maneuvered by Ayyub in the Wheat Union.

22 October, 1916

They assured me that the English are found in Bir al-Mazar, less than 40 kilometers from al-'Arish. According to Kraus they only occupied Bir al-'Abd.[13] What is certain is that the German aviators were in Beersheba, that few people remain in al-'Arish and that, since yesterday, the Austrian batteries are installed in Bethlehem (convents of the Salesians and the Carmelites).

29 October, 1916

I have made a short excursion to Bayt Tul, a town situated on a mountain near the Jaffa highway. We arrived after a long day of fatigue and heat that I don't know how I managed to bear. The town is perched on the mountain and surrounded by a beautiful olive grove. As soon as we arrived they received us in the plaza – let's call it that – where they receive strangers and guests. This plaza is bounded by the *wali* of some Muslim big shot, a series of great stones serving as sitting places and various tombs.

Slowly, slowly, the few Arab men who remained in the place came to greet us, and it's a sure thing they were deserters. Naturally I couldn't understand a bit of the conversation that, after the infinite greetings and phrases of welcome typical of the country, drifted towards the famous Canal expedition.[14] One of the men of the town was part of the Austrian troops and, being the exception, was not a deserter. He was on leave and assured us that there were French troops with the English and that the Austrians lost the majority of their horses and oxen, barely saving the cannons. (…)

3 November, 1916

Last night we had the first rain of the season, with some lightening that was really frightening.

Yesterday morning a ceremony took place in the square at the entrance to the Holy Sepulcher. As it was the Day of Remembrance, the Austrians organized a requiem mass for the fallen during the war. In the square, two Austrian batteries formed up, very officially. The Patriarch, Camassei, and the President of the Custody, Father Castellani, attended. The mass was officiated by the chaplain of Ratisbonne. The altar was a splendid piece of solid silver from Peru, a gift from Spain, a detail I hastened to communicate to my Austrian colleague. The chaplain gave two speeches, one in German and the other in Hungarian, about which I was well informed. One detail: In the minaret of the mosque which is across from the Holy Sepulcher there were two Franciscans, various Armenians and two Jews. One does not see this anywhere but in Jerusalem. Certainly, some Arabs ordered the Jewish women to stop when they tried to enter the square, which was forbidden, in spite of being accompanied by a Turkish officer.

It is curious what the state police of Constantinople have resolved and communicated to their section offices, as well as to the *imams* and neighborhood leaders of this city. First, it is prohibited for women to use cloth that is clear enough to allow under garments to be seen; second, coats must prevent the distinction of bare arms underneath; third, the length of dresses must descend to the ankle; fourth, their hair must be covered.

Commentaries: It is known that by custom, Turkish women have to hide their face and show their hair, arms and legs. It is logical. Besides, this edict seems counterproductive to me since to oppose women seems dangerous to me. In short, that's up to them!

7 November, 1916

The news of Salim Ayyub's bankruptcy fell like a bombshell. I feel bad about it because I take no pleasure in anyone's misfortune, but, really, he richly deserved it if my information is correct.

Finally, the matter of the protection of the Austrian interests has been taken care of, since Kraus brought me the coded telegram from his embassy in which Arroyo authorized me to take charge of them in case of the invasion of this territory. By another telegram I have also received the order to authorize the Austrian consulate so that the hospital of its nation occupies the St. John Convent 'respecting the property rights of Spain.' And, sure enough, today Father Aracil came to tell me on behalf of Father Trigo that the Turks want to occupy the St. John convent to convert it into a school for telegraph operators. I'm closing these notes to go to the Austrian consulate to discuss this matter.

9 November, 1916

Last night I visited Kraus and Schrötter, the director of the Ratisbonne hospital, about the St. John matter. A simple visit to Nihat Bey and it looks like the thing is on the way to being arranged.

17 November, 1916

Von Kressenstein has introduced me to a German princess from Reuss (Brigitte Reuß) who lives in the Hotel and is taking care of the organization of the Soldier's Home in a small hotel nearby. Truly the contrast is notable in this Austrian-German-Turkish entente. The Teutons and Austrians live the life of princes: Sanatoriums, hospitals magnificently equipped, automobiles, economical restaurants, great free warehouses, very well stocked, while the Turks do not even have shoes, eat almost nothing and are lodged and cared for any old way. I understand a lot of things.

20 November, 1916

The night before last, Djemal Pasha arrived by automobile. The same day, in the afternoon, he had put together a commission in Constantinople which, like all the commissions and visits of *effendis*, I fear will bring us nothing good. Djemal Pasha's adjutant asked for me in the name of his boss, with Zaki answering that I had not gone to see him because I was off hunting. In fact, I did spend that day with the shotgun… In all these excursions I used the coach that I bought from the governor, a marvelous victory. I paid 3000 Pounds on paper for the coach, horses and harnesses, and I am delighted with my acquisition.

22 November, 1916

Hohenlohe has just told me that, yesterday, someone set fire to a wagon loaded with mines in the Samakh station. Fourteen Germans dead and fifteen wounded this joke has cost.

It seems that the commission of Constantinople, among which can be found various representatives who are in Palestine doing their studies, is very honored by Djemal Pasha. Yesterday there was a review in their honor. In Jaffa they opened a press and for a few days published a newspaper to make people see the country's progress. For the rest, the commission was dedicated to playing poker. The day before yesterday they announced their visit with Djemal Pasha to Bethlehem, which caused those of the garrison there to organize a banquet. First they announced that they would arrive late and later… they didn't go.

23 November, 1916

They put the flags at half mast in the War Information Office situated across from my house, and I found out that it is because of the death of Franz Joseph, Emperor of Austria and Hungary. Naturally, I paid my condolences right away to my Austrian colleague.

As news from Madrid came in, it seems the Count of Romanones, Prime Minister, has declared that he will never abandon his policy of neutrality, which means that I must continue here.

Today the mass in the Patriarchate has been in accordance with the Maronite rite. As it is usually in accordance with the Latin rite I was very surprised that the priest crossed himself each moment and read the Gospel or the Epistles (since it was in Arabic, I'm not sure) facing the faithful and with some of the acolytes stretched out on the ground.

The Patriarch explained to me that the ceremony which took place two weeks ago in the mass, and which I had not understood, had also been a wedding in the Maronite rite between two Bedouins; he is a schismatic and she is Catholic. The groom vowed that he would not go to the schismatic Church to revalidate the oath, that he would not bother his bride about changing religion, and that their children would be educated in the Catholic faith. Since they were from families of wealthy Bedouins from Madaba [in Jordan], the ceremony was quite ostentatious. (…) The outfits of the guests were splendid.

3 December, 1916, Sunday

Important events this week. On Wednesday, a solemn funeral took place in the Holy Sepulcher for the soul of the Emperor Franz Joseph. The Patriarch officiated with three Franciscans. It produced no incidents, in spite of the ceremony being celebrated without arranging the details of the times under French protection, but this is not the time for fussiness and no one protested or complained. At the exit of the religious function, Von Kressenstein and Roshan Bey communicated to me that, within three or four weeks, a Spanish ship with 2,000 tons of wheat would come to Beirut and Jaffa. This is the first news I have heard of it.

The day before yesterday I reached the advanced age of 31 years old, and, with such auspicious motive I received countless visits. (…)

Monday I was in St. John, and Father Trigo told me that after I had gotten the telegraph operators to leave the convent alone, Turkish troops turned up again on two occasions with all kinds of demands to let them install themselves there. To put an end once and for all to so much cynicism and drama I decided that the Germans should move into the free part of the convent. In it they will install a sort of 'casino' for conferences and readings. That should clear up the matter.

8 December 1916, Day of the Immaculate Conception

Seeing that they were decking out the War Information Office, I supposed that Bucharest had fallen into the hands of the Allies (Austro-Germans). Roshan Bey sent me a Jewish messenger to express his condolences to me as the one charged with the Romanian interests. This joke cost him a little, since, to pay him back, I went to his office pretending that I was crying and told him I would not be consoled until I heard the order to turn over five hundred cigarettes to me, an unheard luxury. And he did it, causing the desperation of the *mudhir* of the Regie.

The Great Rabbi Nissin Danon came to see me to expose the sad situation of the Sephardim. The Sephardim, who have a minority representation in the American Aid Committees, are literally dying of hunger.[15] They have told me that there are now fifteen who have suffered such a sad fortune. I sent a telegram (which the censor had refused to accept from the Rabbi) to the embassy begging that they make some millionaire Jews of the United States aware of this circumstance in the most opportune manner.[16]

The news of the landing of an English plane in Lydda, near Ramla, has been confirmed, but it was not the German aviator who obliged him to do it, but rather the fire from the defense cannons and machineguns.

13 December, 1916

A day I will never forget! Let's go in sections. Yesterday I went in my coach to Bethlehem, stopping for a moment at the home of Salomon Jazir. I then continued along a truly infamous road through the olive forests, arriving in a little while at Bayt Jala. Before getting to the town we passed near a hangar where the Turks have improvised a garage: Three trucks and a tourist coach were there under repair. In the town, the Turkish troops have occupied the Patriarchate and the Russian religious establishments. There, the Germans explain to their allies the use of the telegraph.

A German Salesian was waiting for me near the Russian church, and I went with him to the farm of said order, called 'Cremisan'. A little before, we passed by the 'Hantas' farm of the German Benedictines and also by a field where some German soldiers were entertaining themselves with some shooting exercises, certainly with great success.

The field house of 'Cremisan' is as sad as all the convents. Surrounding the building are seventy hectares of farmland, olive trees and vineyards, a beautiful orchard and various pine trees. I slept in the convent, and today there was a surprise waiting for me: A magnificent luncheon with Spanish stew, sweet peppers and macaroni, that is, a sort of Italian-Spanish alliance. Father Sacchetti, Superior of Bayt Jala, did the honors. On the table was a sign "long live the consul" made with bread rolls and therefore quite appetizing.

While returning, close to Bethlehem, I met other Salesians who brought me the news that the chancellor of the German empire has declared that his government, by means of neutral countries, has turned over a note to the enemy powers inviting them to enter into negotiations for peace. I have no words to express the emotion with which I returned to Jerusalem.

26 December, 1916

Yesterday, Christmas, I had a first class gift, receiving a letter from my father, from whom I have not had news for a very long time. The country has had another gift, the beginning of the rains, which we've been waiting for quite a while this year. We hope the harvest will be abundant this year for, if it is not, I don't know where it's going to stop. Last year there was an excellent harvest and we could not even have wheat thanks to the 'fine Turkish administrative system.' Thus, if in the coming year the harvest is bad we will die of hunger, unless the war ends. But by all the signs this will not happen; since my last note there has been no new notice of communication about the matter. It seems the Allies have not yet replied. Whatever their answer might be, it will be heard. (...)

In this theater of war (not bad, a theater!) there has been important news. In a 70 person banquet that took place yesterday in the German military 'casino', Von Kressenstein declared that al-'Arish has fallen into the hands of the British. They have threatened up to Magdaba [in Egypt] and have withdrawn again to al-'Arish. Since I don't understand German I could not follow his speech, as well as the few Turkish officers (three from the headquarters of Von Kressenstein) who attended the banquet.[17] The thing must have been really curious, since the colonel alluded to the desertion of various Turkish and Arab forces that went over to the enemy in Magdaba. Among these forces there was an artillery battery. I commented on this with a German and an Austrian, who indicated that the matter was explained perfectly because the Turkish soldiers had nothing whatsoever to eat.

Von Kressenstein added that once the Christmas holidays were over and the Allied formations rested, the Germans and Austrians would go to the Sinai desert to complete their duty. This was, in summary, Von Kressenstein's speech, which ended with the obligatory *Hoch* in honor of the Kaiser.

At this meal I was the only neutral who attended. I was placed between the military doctor Dr. Vogel, who speaks Spanish very well, and the director of the Ratisbonne hospital, Dr. Schötter.

(...) I went on an unforgettable excursion before Christmas to Jericho, invited by that nice Wolff, captain of the engineering division and director of an important German enterprise of public works. We went in an automotive truck, certainly rather uncomfortable, and in the company of a respectable quantity of boxes, trunks and suitcases. On the road another lighter truck passed us that was also going, like many others these days, towards Jericho, transporting materials to the place where the ancient bridge over the Jordan is located. Wolff is rebuilding it with two objectives: To facilitate communication with al-Salt, Amman and the Hidjaz railroad (and consequently, with the army that operates against the *Sharif* Husayn) and to assure the retreat in case of an attack by the English. Besides, it guarantees the provisioning of the military posts that the Turks have established on the Jerusalem-Amman highway. They are constructing the bridge with iron and wood, and according to Wolff, it will serve the traffic for ten years.

The day of our arrival (in Jericho) we spent in dining. (…) During the meal they mentioned that, not long ago, a group of Bedouins appeared in Jericho who, without any warning, took control of as many horses as there were, including those of the Turkish soldiers. To avoid the repetition of similar deeds, a few days before our arrival they sent a battalion that camped between the Wadi al-Qalt and the fountain of Elishah. But since the Turks are so short of troops, these troops had to leave during our stay to reinforce those that are opposing the English advance in the desert. The really funny part is what happened in a nearby town (I'm not sure if it was in al-Salt or in Amman) where, before the installation of a military post there, the Bedouins also took control of all the horses and left a receipt telling them to discount the amount of requisitions that the government had arranged for them.

On the 16th we visited the site of the new bridge next to the ancient one. We ate lunch like the German soldiers, standing and with tin plates. At the beginning of the meal the famous Nogales Bey appeared on horseback and joined us. Accompanied by him we went to the Greek convent of St. John the Baptist, on the shores of the Jordan. Wolff and I went on horseback. We should never have done it, since we went astray and arrived at the convent at the same time as our companions who went on foot. The reality is that we had gotten lost, but this had its fortunate side as it convinced us of the truth of those stories about travelers who talk about the immensity of the desert, its aridness, the similarity of its dunes and the danger of not finding the road before nightfall. (…)

The convent of St. John (Mar Hannan) is truly a fortress in the middle of the desert, and they really need their loopholes and sackcloth since, in such a place, all precautions are futile, keeping in mind what I said before about the Bedouins. We returned in the afternoon, but not without having promised to the nice Father Panaretos, Superior of the convent, that we would come back there the next night, which we did. The silence and the solitude of that place are enough to impress anyone. Father Panaretos opened the solid door that gives access to the patio of the convent and, a little before sunset, let two wild dogs enter that come every day and have a meal there: Said animals are like almost all those of their kind that I have seen in this country: Not very big but very strong, and they are accustomed to eating dead camels that the Turkish lack of foresight leaves by the thousands on the plains of the Jordan.

(…) They gave us magnificent beds with the bedspread in the style of this country, folded in two, before going to bed. Father Panaretos made an inspection of my room before me and even looked under my bed. For the rest, my room had enormous bars on every window and was at a respectable height above the ground. I spent part of the night awake and without going to bed, not from some fear but because I could not tire of contemplating the fantastic and mysterious aspect of the desert by the light of the moon, watching hyenas and jackals go by. For noise, one heard no more than the barking of the wild dogs. Fortunately they did not howl, a habit that makes me very nervous and has often tempted me to scare them with a few shots.

(…) We took a new and delightful excursion to the mouth of the Jordan at the Dead Sea. We went by horse to the site where pilgrims always go. There had never been more than a miserable little shanty town there, in which were kept the remains of a motor boat that worked some time back in the Dead Sea and was destroyed. What a surprise to find myself amidst the installation of a real port, like a toy in its importance, but nonetheless useful. They are building a two-storey house for the main installation, and there were also a certain number of campaign tents and huts to have a cover for a motor boat under repair, as well as rooms for the 'navy commander' and soldiers. Also, there were storehouses of provisions and material, with a small but well-stocked snack bar. I could admire in the fresh air a huge, magnificent launch that they have brought from Constantinople. They have also built a little dock with a kind of sentry hut for the navy officer who watches the traffic, rather like a flagpole with a beacon. Altogether it was nice, but it looked more like a facility to amuse children rather than something for war.

The way things are, thanks to this installation I managed to take trips that tourists and pilgrims very rarely do for lack of means to do so. Provided with an order from the commander in Jericho, we presented ourselves to a lower rank official who was conversing with an interpreter. The latter, seeing my imposing aspect on horseback, and followed by an officer and two soldiers, answered the question I asked about if we had a boat available with: 'Yes, General.' I nearly fell off my horse laughing. It turned out that the interpreter was Jewish, and when he recognized me, he spoke to me in Spanish, giving us right away one of the boats from Jaffa that serve the lake and a little launch to be able to disembark more easily. (…)

Wednesday we went back to the Dead Sea. The night before, the nice 'captain of the Dead Sea,' who is a corvette captain, gave us a written order to requisition anything we might desire: Boats, launches, soldiers, etc. In spite of it two soldiers who occupied a launch refused to turn it over to us (long live discipline!), doubtless because we were European. Then Wolff employed the only system that one can when soldiers discuss the orders of their leaders and resist obeying them: He pointed his pistol at the chest of the soldiers who, before such eloquent resistance, threw themselves out of the boat, leaving it free.

On board the big motor boat, and followed by the launch, we began to appreciate the inconveniences of navigation by sail when there is no wind, particularly with sailors with little experience like us. It cost us more than four hours for the trip to the mouth of the Arnon by force of oars. There were three sailors from Jaffa, with a bandit style typical of these boaters, the reason for which I did not lose sight of my loaded rifle the whole time the expedition lasted. Seeing that one of them was very cantankerous, Wolff resorted to a heroic measure to make him work: He made him get in the launch and cut it adrift. Of course, to follow us the sailor was obliged to row with all his strength. One time it occurred to him to stop, separating considerably from our boat, but he never would have done it, for my companion sent him a shot from the Maüser, although of course he aimed well over his head. This affectionate warning produced the desired effect.

(...) This coast appeared to our view to be formed by mountains of rather difficult ascension, without being cut off at the peaks. From time to time we would see some gully or ravine, full of vegetation at the bottom, although generally we noted no trees of any kind. The mountain only gets green a little near the mouth of the famous river that separated the country of the Moabites from that of the Ammonites.

We arrived there at midday, and the boat was moored right at the shore, there being enough depth for it; my face was shining in the handling of the rudder. (...) Some little piles of ashes gave evidence that Bedouins had camped there not long ago. We advanced among the rock outcroppings in search of a site to have lunch, and suddenly we discovered the mouth of the Arnon, the wildest and most beautiful place I have seen in Palestine.

(...) We had continued all afternoon in the contemplation of that tranquil and solitary place of wildlife, but the continued lack of wind obliged us to take to the boat again. Once again our rowers, *lashed to the hard bench of a Turkish galley*, began to display an athleticism I could not have managed for five minutes. (...)

It was fully night by now and certainly a very dark night. Guided by the beacon of the little port of which I spoke before, I kept the direction well enough, and at 7:00 P.M. we landed. The hard work of the day was nothing compared to what waited for us to cross the distance that separated us from Jericho. We had to do it in a covered wagon of the type the Turks use for the transportation of munitions. What a prosaic end! (…)

The evening of that day there was a great dinner in honor of Burkhan al-Din Bey, Inspector General of Roads and Canals, a very nice Turk who had been carrying out this duty for a trifling fourteen years.

The following day I returned to Jerusalem in a tremendous heat, at the end of December!

29 December, 1916

A reliable person told me that the English have occupied al-'Arish without a fight, since the Turks had retreated, destroying beforehand as many buildings and wells as they had established there. The garrison of Magdaba, composed of some 2000 men with four old cannons and six modern machine guns, was attacked by enemy aviators who dropped more than 90 bombs. Afterwards, it was surrounded by numerous forces of cavalry, artillery, automobiles with machine guns, and *meharis* with two men per camel. The Turks could not resist and surrendered, my friend 'Izzet Bey, their commander, being taken prisoner. This man, who is an Arab, has done honors at the front of the company when I went on official visits. So, those troops did not go over to the enemy, as I heard by the Germans, but rather were cornered.

Did the English go back to al-'Arish, as they are trying to make us believe? There is someone who asserted that he has seen in the night the reflectors of a column that was headed to the northeast of Magdaba along a ravine towards the Turkish railroad between Beersheba and al-Hafir, with the obvious intention of cutting off the latter and leaving the population there isolated. Even if they do it, I do not think they will take many prisoners, because all the forces and workers who were in Al Qusayma, Bir Rafa and many from al-Hafir are now found in Beersheba. The Austrians and Germans have left, headed towards that population (according to the declaration of the interested parties). I think it is time they did so because, according to the person to whom I owe these reports, the English offensive looks serious this time. At the same time as Magdaba, Bir Rafa has also been attacked by airplanes. Between the workers and the soldiers, it seems there have been quite a few wounded.

The machine guns of the airplanes fired, so they say, with an astonishing precision, and it's natural because the aviators knew that they have nothing to fear from the anti-aircraft defense… for the simple reason that there isn't any. There was a witness who told me that a plane passed by just five meters above the site where he was hidden, and that he still had in his ears the infernal roar of the engine of the machine.

A detail: From Bir Rafa people saw the enormous column of dense, black smoke raised by the explosion of various warehouses, which made the commander of Magdaba, a brave Sudanese officer, jump to see the English this close.

Of the three famous railroads made, according to the *vox populi*, by the English there is no more than one whose existence is not in doubt, and it is the one on the coast, which arrived some days ago at al-'Arish and is a double line.

I do not believe the English have ventured so far from the base of provisions without being in great number, so we must have in front of us an army that, divided into various columns, occupied almost all the desert (of Sinai). So the Turco-Germans are fighting on their own territory and on the defensive. Whether the English will advance or not towards Jerusalem is a question impossible to clarify, since those of us who are here know nothing. Unless we are enlightened about it by the *Desert Daily* which is published here now, but, naturally, I don't believe anything it says. It talked about the electric trolley in Beersheba and the movie theater where the troops enjoy their free time. That's for the movies, all right!

A young engineer used to say: 'The Turks always think very well, but they always think... after.' I think he is not far off. Look at what happened recently: The Turks had built a narrow gauge railroad track between al-'Arish and Magdaba that provided very good service. The day before the taking of Magdaba a telegram ordered them to destroy part of the line leaving it unusable. A little later they received the order to rebuild what was destroyed, and a few hours later the English arrived and took advantage of everything that was in very good condition.

I don't know if these things are due to deficiencies in the information service or other lacks. Someone told me that the German planes executed their service at too great a velocity and without slowing down enough to do a proper reconnaissance, a thing the enemy planes do to perfection. These last few days the Turks have been complaining bitterly about not seeing the German planes when they are needed to fight against the enemy, but I think this complaint is baseless because they would be wiped out by the immense numerical superiority of their adversaries.

30 December, 1916

There is little left before this year ends and my goodness, it is ending well, since last night an epoch-making storm let loose, with an abundant display of lightening.

Today I have had in my home Dr. Schrötter and the Hungarian chaplain from the Ratisbonne hospital. The latter is from an illustrious family and, as with all Hungarian names, has a last name that is impossible to retain. I gave up trying to remember it. For the rest, he is a great guy, very nice and liberal. Schrötter, a geologist and a fan of all kinds of artistic things, spoke to me as always of his sympathies for Spain. (…) He also told me that a navigation company for the Orient had been formed, news which I see confirmed in the telegrams that said:

> Madrid. A great company of Spanish steamships has been established and will be called the 'Transmediterranean,' dedicated above all to serve the ports of the Orient to help develop commerce between Spain and Turkey.

This news put me in a good mood and made me enjoy even more the *Trips through Spain* by Pedro Antonio de Alarcón. His visit to the monastery of Yuste taught me a lot of things. [Among them] that we Spaniards cannot know the world very well and discharge the role in it we should if we do not first know our own country and history. At least for me, a very modest representative of Spain, this is true, and I don't think it is too extreme to affirm that almost the totality of my professional colleagues and the representatives of His Catholic Majesty find themselves in the same boat. For my part, I will try to mend my ways as much as possible by reading on the first occasion I find the *History of Spain* by Lafuente or that of Father Mariana. (…)

They have renewed the 'fantasy' that the Turks for every notable anniversary or for every notice, more or less truthful, make celebrations as for a victory obtained. A procession was formed by four guards, the normal school (or abnormal, since their foundation and installation in buildings that do not belong to them is not in the least bit normal) formed by some dozens of little boys dressed in khaki shirts, white pants and red ties (the colors of the Constitution, white and red) and, finishing up the march, the *hudyas* or Muslim seminarians of St. Anne, today Saladin, with white and red turbans and black tunics.

In all these ceremonies, which I know by heart, they arrived by Jaffa road with a little music in the front, they arranged themselves in several rows leaving a big space free in front of the municipal building, and for the following act an orator delivered a harangue, more or less long, more or less applauded and more or less a bore. It is directed generally at the man who is behind and carries a portrait of the Sultan (which is forbidden by their religion) or of one of the more famous Ottoman Sultans.

This time it was the anniversary of the formation of the Turkish Empire and before the portrait of reference there marched an individual with a big false mustache that threatened to fall off at every moment, to the desperation of the aforementioned soul. This good man was dressed as a janissary with a turban (white and red, for a change) half a meter wide and… with bare legs. This last detail made me sympathize with him, for with the cold, the wind, and the humidity there is today, he will surely catch pneumonia. But there was one thing that intrigued me; did the janissaries go bare-legged? If they didn't, I don't understand how Djamil Bey, who is a man of good taste, permitted such a carnival procession. Today the speech was short, no doubt because of the cold, which also influenced the fact that there were not very abundant demonstrations of enthusiasm and adherence to the constitution.

31 December, 1916

And I'm ending these slovenly notes in the current year of grace (damn little grace it has had) of 1916 with several sketches of the impressions that I have had during the year.

Next to Tantur, the Turks are constructing trenches to defend themselves from a likely English attack. When I saw them, the soldiers were strolling peacefully, keeping watch on the work that was being carried out by women and children armed with pickaxes, shovels and hoes. The women were working feverishly, and a soldier was watching them… while knitting. This detail has its humorous side, if only to paint the Muhammedan character.

A second sketch: Comparisons between the Austrians and the Germans. An Austrian said to me: 'I admire their sovereign; he is a gentleman king, like our King Franz Joseph, but not like other sovereigns.' The allusion could not be more direct.

Another detail: In front of a stranger who does not know German but rather French, the Germans speak German and the Austrians, French. They all know this language well. I've had good proof of it in my conversations.

About the Turkish army: They said that 'Izzet Bey, when about to be taken prisoner in Magdaba, told his soldiers: 'Tell Djemal Pasha to follow you handing out bread and *lentil soup* and not to order you to fight in this state.' After saying this he took out his sword and kept on fighting until he was taken prisoner.

Situation of the Turkish Treasury: Today, the last day of 1916, the Turkish Pound, which is nominally worth 100 Piasters, is quoted in the market of this city at 35, that is, a depreciation of 65%.

May the new era of peace longed for by all, begin tomorrow. Amen.

1917

3 January, 1917

The year didn't start out very quietly, at least in this atmosphere, because of an endless amount of lightening striking for days. The bad weather began on Christmas and, up to this moment, has not ceased raining, hailing, thundering, lightening and blowing a gale that would make the *Cierzo* itself envious if it happened to come by here to visit colleagues in the desert.[1] I caught a terrific cold and I've been at home the whole time.

On the first of the month I had countless number of visits from all castes, classes and religions. That day cost me a mere 100 Francs in *baksheesh*. I would really have liked to suppress or diminish them, but we are in the country of the *baksheesh*, and everything is anticipated and regulated.

No news of the war, or rather of the peace. A person told me the day before: 'Until the British take control of this country they will not make peace, because they need it for the defense of the Suez Canal. But they had better hurry, since the Amanus tunnels will be finished in a few months, and then it will be easy to bring in various German divisions.' Since the question of Syria and Palestine is the most essential for Britain, according to the person with whom I was speaking, will Turkey be sacrificed if they do peace negotiations now, and will they be able to compensate it in some way? That is the question.[2]

6 January (Day of the Magi Kings), 1917

This is a bad time for it, but I have to attend the solemnities of the day in Bethlehem. On the other hand, I don't think anything will happen, for the Greeks are more than satisfied with the blunder the Austrians made on Christmas and thus will not bother with us. The gaffe was the following: The Austrians who were lodged in Bethlehem tried to force the Christmas festivities to be celebrated in the Basilica, which is forbidden to the *heathens*.[3] It would have been a great victory for the Catholics since it would have remained set for every year. But the telegraph and money functioned efficiently, and the Orthodox won, getting an order from the Turkish authorities so that nothing would alter the ceremony from previous years.

Yesterday I began my *tournée* of New Year's visits. One of them was to Von Kressenstein, with whom I had a good chat. The good colonel told me that, because of the terrible rain storms, a train that was coming from Rayaq to Damascus derailed due to slipping on a very steep incline, and there were no fewer than 100 dead and 100 injured, many of them women and children. He also told me that, because of the storm, communications with the desert were cut off.

In Jericho, the floods have caused great damage. In a telegram received this morning, they tell me that 'all the houses, except that of the Spanish consul, have collapsed.' I think one will have to take that news with several grains of salt; it is probably not true that 73 people drowned, neither is it true that the house saved is mine, since it does not belong to me but rather to my *dragoman*. (Confirming this impression, the following day I received information saying there were no collapsed houses, nor any drowned victims. As always, the imagination of the Orientals…)

10 January, 1917

It looks like this is going fast now. My German colleague, Brode, told me that in his judgment the British will not get to Jerusalem and that they still have not moved from the line at al-'Arish. But… various German officials assured a good friend of mine that the British army, 50,000 men strong, is advancing a lot, and they may easily take control of Jerusalem within a couple of weeks. With all this Brode has asked me to move into the amazing building of the German consulate in case of a British invasion, and Hohenlohe has also asked me to guard his rugs. The matter is getting ugly… although for the majority it will be better.

11 January, 1917

It is 5:00 in the afternoon and, at this moment five German trucks are leaving for the desert, driving a company of Turkish machine gunners. The cars arrived across from my house at 11:00 this morning and, up until now, have been detained; I don't know the reason why. Poor guys! All of this under a constant rain that must have cooled what little enthusiasm they had for the war. They hardly had anything with which to cover themselves, and, at the moment of departure, they were given 'to warm them up' a miserable little bread roll for each one. What a roll!

For a long while I have contemplated these young men, 22-24 years old, who watched with hungry eyes the distribution of the bread, and I have also seen a girl who was selling them more bread. Without a doubt, they are convinced of the near and miserable ill fortune that awaits them and have decided to spend the little money they still have on something to eat. They assured me that their ration is a quarter of a kilo of bread a day and the famous 'lentil water'. Even so, the government must not have sufficient bread for them since the Food Rationing Inspectorate has borrowed wheat from the Greek convent, the Franciscans and whoever may have some grain to spare. It is no wonder that these soldiers go over to the enemy if they can, particularly [keeping in mind] that there are among them Arabs, Armenians, Jews, etc., who have no concept of country, because they don't have one. (...)

Little news, but bad. The telegrams said that the Count of Romanones has asserted that it is still not the opportune time to talk about the intervention of the neutrals in favor of peace.

From the desert: An airplane appeared the day before yesterday over Beersheba and dropped a communiqué for the military commander charging him to have the town evacuated of civilians, since there would soon be a bombing. He has done so. Also, the town records have been brought to Jerusalem.

This afternoon the new *mutasarrif* [of Jerusalem], Munir Bey, is received; I hope that he will confirm the impression he has made on everyone.

13 January, 1917

Really, Munir Bey is at least very polite, but we will see how he does. So far he is frank, since when Fr. Mateo, the Dominican father, tried to get the government to pay the indispensable costs of repairs after the big rainy season we just went through, he told him the government has no money and, as a consequence, cannot do it. You can't get any more frank than that.

In the official visit that [the *mutassarif* himself] made to me, he came accompanied by Isma'il Haqqi, no less than the director of the Office of Litigation and the legal advisor of Palestine. This man replaced, more or less honorably, the no less illustrious ex-director of political affairs, Barciara Effendi, a millionaire according to what is said, and decorated with more than 30 national and foreign orders.

Von Kressenstein has returned bringing, according to what they said, good impressions, the same that Von Arnim gave me, although the latter told me that the Turks have had 'a small catastrophe,' without pinpointing when or where.

15 January, 1917

Yesterday was the Greek New Year's Day. With such a plausible reason I had to make an endless number of visits. In the morning, to the Greek Patriarchate, and in the afternoon, to Kevalkian (director of the Ottoman Bank), Spiros Marry, Nikos Mariano, Dr. Pascal and Dr. Mazaraky. The Armenians also celebrated the beginning of the year that day. The last visit, and the most well attended, was to the home of Shaykh Asiri, where at my arrival I met with Raphaël, the Greek consul; Dick, the American vice consul, and the following *remarquées* people: Nissim and Jacob Valero, with their respective wives, Mrs. Alexix Frey (widow), Miss Clementine Bagary, Mrs. and Miss Massié (fortunately neither Mr. Massié), Mrs. Simone Huilsasmi, Mr. and Mrs. Rabinowitz, Miss Julia Mani, Nur al-Din Bey, Isma'il Bey al-Husayni, Mashar Bey, William Yale, etc. In short, the posh crowd and everyone who wants to be, but thanks to which I have not yet gone completely crazy.

It has been claimed that a company of machine gunners (No. 504, if my memory is not failing me) surrendered to the British in one of the last battles, there being some 15 Germans who were with them, taken prisoner. They also said that Beersheba has been attacked by a squadron of planes. What is positive is that von Kressenstein has told the Franciscan that he himself went up in a plane to do a reconnaissance, and he managed to verify the presence of French troops among the British, which confirms what was said by one of those who escaped from Magdaba and claimed to have seen Muslim soldiers (probably Moroccan or Algerian) who were speaking Arabic.

15 January, 1917[4]

It has been announced that a great person is going to arrive – they said it is the Minister of *Awqaf* - and that the town *is obliged* to prepare for him a brilliant reception and to close the doors of all businesses. As you see, the brilliant reception will be one of extraordinary spontaneity and enthusiasm.

They kept bringing an infinite number of things from Beersheba. Now it's the beds' turn. They have notified the Dominicans that they must abandon their current residence, since they are going to install in it 8,000 beds that are coming from the desert.

18 January, 1917

On the day announced for the arrival of the Minister of *Awqaf* I went to wait for him in my coach, but he didn't come nor do I think he will come now because, according to what the Muslims told me, his object was to go to Medina and withdraw from there the treasures of that city to take them to Constantinople. It is known that things are boiling there. In a tent there were some civilians and, in carriages, the representatives of the different faiths that were waiting for the minister. An exceptional note was the presence of numerous Muslim women who, in spite of what was ordered, did not cover their faces.

Yesterday, at dawn near my house, they hanged 'Arif, the disgraced *mufti* from Gaza and another individual. At the same time, the soldiers shot some other unfortunates, among them the son of the aforementioned.

The impression was unimaginable, since the *mufti* is for the Muslims like a patriarch or bishop for us. Besides, the deceased had enormous influence among the Arabs, especially the Bedouins. He was very splendid and had a proud coach with very good horses. The measure seems counterproductive to me, but we respect the lofty designs of the Turkish policy; to my poor understanding, it owes its existence to the 'Medina Front.'

Reinforcements for the desert are beginning to arrive. Yesterday, three squadrons of lancers went by, and this morning a campaign battery that was headed there but which precisely as it got to my house, received orders to retreat. For what purpose I do not know.

Truthful-sounding news: Not long ago there was a battle in Bir Rafa, and the result was similar to that of Magdaba: That is, all soldiers to be found there were taken prisoner. Of the battle of Khan Yunis nothing is known for sure; they pretended that the British retreated, but there is someone who said that they 'evacuated' that site, which is not exactly the same. According to aerial observations, in al-'Arish there are two army corps [British] and the troop landings continue. The German airplanes generally made these reconnaissance runs by night. To prove to the British that they are not sleepy either, they made several visits to the Turks in Beersheba. One of these visits cost the life of a dozen workers, among them an American. And it was certainly in curious circumstances. The aviator fell, probably by mechanical failure, at the station of Beersheba. Another aviator protected him with machine gun fire until he could get up again and drop new bombs that produced those deaths.

Until now, the British system is to threaten the flank of the Turkish provinces. Look at the map, and you will observe that the occupation of only al-'Arish has resulted in the evacuation of Bir Hasana, Qusayma and al-Hafri. If the British get to Gaza, I think Beersheba will be evacuated, unless they change the system.

Today the Egyptian engineer, A. R. Bey, came to see me. This dark-skinned man was part of a committee that was established not many years ago to try to prove to the civilized world that the Egyptians could govern themselves, without the need of British tutelage. During the discussion about whether they should extend or not the concession of the Suez Canal, one of the members of that committee assassinated Prime Minister Butrus Pasha, a partisan of the extension. Was this crime agreed to by the committee or was it the purely the personal work of its executor? According to A. R. Bey, in reality it was the latter. In any case, they made inquiries and detained a lot of the members of the committee but set them free. The person with whom I was speaking, who was in M. with W. managed to quietly return to Egypt without being bothered. But in case the British come here now, we will see if they again bring this up for discussion.[5]

This afternoon, Christmas for the Armenians, I took Mr. and Mrs. Pascal to Bethlehem in my coach. A magnificent afternoon. The curious thing about the ceremonies of the Armenian mass is that the songs quickly seemed rather inappropriate (there is a lot of Andalusian music in them), like the poetic orations of the *muezzin* atop the minaret. I listened to preaching in Armenian, naturally without understanding a word; I saw a prayer book of Mrs. Pascal in that same curious language, and I posed as a scholar, talking with her husband about the Lion King of Armenia. I ended the afternoon with a visit to the president of the Greek convent, Archimandrite Dositeos. This man led us to the terrace, from where one notes a marvelous panorama and can contemplate the cross shape of the famous church which is so abandoned. The Archimandrite showed us wonderful 12th century embroidery, a gift from a prince of the Caucuses, all embroidered in gold and silk. A truly precious thing.

Upon the return from Bethlehem we saw new Turkish reinforcements: Three mountain cannons with enough mules loaded with munitions and some machine guns, if I'm not mistaken. (…)

And nothing more. Oh yes: The bank bill is worth 28 piasters today, and some say it is at 25; that's a quarter of its nominal value.

21 January, 1917

The lovely weather we have had for a while has ceased, and now it's raining a lot… The day before yesterday three enemy airplanes went by at an enormous altitude, according to those who could see them with binoculars. From the desert (which is now rather well populated), nothing in particular. Yesterday two artillery batteries and numerous carts of munitions went by here. The people affirm that soon great reinforcements of Austrian and Bulgarian troops will arrive. But it seems to me that is the *popular* opinion. According to the calculations made by the German pilots counting the number of tents belonging to the British component that can be seen in a big photograph taken by them, there is an army of 100,000 men in al-'Arish.

In Jerusalem today bread costs 10 piasters… one loaf of bread!, which produces a general unease. We are in the most amusing of situations: A *rotal* of meat costs 36 piaster, compared to the 18 it used to cost in peace time.[6] They need 500 Pounds of gold a day to assure the bread for Jerusalem, and as the Bedouins do not accept paper, and it is impossible to find gold, the result is, as affirms the president himself of the Union or Bread Commission, Zaki Bey, within a very little while there will not be much to give the population, and then what will we do?

We have to believe that within a short while there will be armed robberies and disorders that are perfectly explainable and even justified. As in all matters in Turkey, some folks blame what happens on the others, and in the meanwhile, nothing changes. Zaki Bey came unglued with accusations against the former governor and Antebi, whom he affirmed have ruined the country. On the other hand, he said that the military will not let him use the camels necessary to bring the wheat. In short, if the war lasts a year, not even the rats will be left in Jerusalem.

As if the scarcity of food were not enough, the typhus is up to its old tricks and has not disappeared, nor anything like it. In the last few days I have found two lice in my clothing, so I am likely to contract it, since these sweet little creatures are the ones that transmit the microbes of the epidemic.

4 February, 1917

(…) Yesterday new troops went by, headed for Beersheba: A regiment (four squadrons) of lancers, a battalion of infantry and service corps. Not much. For the rest, it seems the British have made no new attacks, although they keep building their famous railroad.

7 February, 1917

Still more troops for the desert. Outside are two battalions of infantry. The thing is really getting serious. But still more serious is the intervention of America in the worldwide conflict. According to the Ottoman information agency, two nights ago the notice of the breaking of diplomatic relations arrived in the American embassy of Berlin. The Ambassador Gerard asked for his passport and closed the embassy, turning over the interests of the country to Spain. Good! Let's hope it won't be my turn to take care of everything for the foreign representatives.

Other news: The Grand Vizier of Turkey, Prince Sa'id Halim, has presented his resignation for health reasons, with Talat Bey replacing him while continuing as Minister of the Interior, and provisionally, of Finance (all little duties in Turkey!). Musa Khazim Effendi, *Shaykh al-Islam* and *Awqaf*; Nissim Bey, Minister of State; Khalil Bey, Minister of Justice and president of the State Cabinet; Enver Pasha, Minister of War; Djemal Pasha, Minister of the Navy; Salmuri Bey, Minister of Public Education and provisionally, Communication; Sharif Bey, Commerce and Agriculture; 'Ali Munif Bey, Public Works. Well, now I know who the new Ottoman ministers are. I don't even know who the Spanish ones are. That's the way things are going.

In Germany, Prüfer got me a subscription to *ABC* (newspaper), but I have not received a single issue. To blazes with everyone! This sort of exclamation will prove to those who have the patience to read or listen to me that I am very nervous. And how could I not be? I'm going on two and half years with no more news from my country than the fantasies that the Turkish agencies tell. I don't know if Spain will enter the war. I don't know anything about anything.

9 February, 1917

On the 8th my American colleague, Glazebrook, a friendly Protestant pastor and a good friend of mine, confessed to me to be absolutely unaware of news about the war between his country and Germany. He begged me that in case of the breaking of diplomatic relations with Turkey I take charge of protecting the American interests and of saving all the things found in storage in his consulate.

13 February, 1917

I am still sick, although I have no illness other than a nervous excitement that, nevertheless, will end up finishing me off. Thanks to a strong dose of bromide and some very hot baths I managed to sleep well the night before last after twelve nights of scarcely closing my eyes. But last night, in spite of having applied the same remedy, I didn't get anywhere, and couldn't sleep a minute. Is it possible to keep on living like this?

The causes of this insomnia are as easy to guess as difficult to cure. For starters, I have not received a newspaper from Spain for two years. Secondly, the authorities treat us consuls with such indifference and animosity that it seems like we are more of an enemy than the Allies themselves. Thirdly, here everybody looks out for himself. The police do whatever they feel like and the military authorities, ditto. The Turkish paper money is valued at 26 or 27 piasters to a Pound, and the Turks, to take care of it, forbid the circulation of gold, without which the currency will not rise, but rather only the gold. Third [sic]: The military service. Now they are calling up the Turks who have bought their redemption in cash (some of them several times). My *dragoman* Rauf, who has been declared useless for military service by the director of the Red Crescent, by the one from Ratisbonne, and by two more doctors, is declared apt for 'unarmed service' by a fifth doctor, Christian by all signs. This doctor is still boasting of his deed. Fine, but this matter is still not ended: In spite of this medical recognition, and even with the order from Constantinople that the personnel of the consulates will remain free from doing this service for five months, Rauf has to go to Damascus to be recognized, which is a very fatiguing journey. There are people who have taken fourteen days by train! I will spend a fair portion of Pesetas and all for a whim. What's more, a circular from the government to clinch the suppression of the Capitulations said that, from now on, it will not recognize either the functions or the name of *dragoman*, nor that of *cavas*. They will be called secretaries and servants respectively. I imagine they will soon suppress the *cavas* uniform and will oblige us to write in Turkish to the authorities (there is already talk of it). And since this is a never-ending story, I'll end this little tale of woe here.

Nogales paraded yesterday in front of the consulate, at the head of three weaponless companies of infantry he was supposed to lead to Gaza. They are Arabs, and are going guarded by some armed Turks.

The orange harvest from Jaffa is rotting for lack of wagons to transport it. (...) So the only wealth of the country that also serves as food for the army is allowed to be lost.

The British are not moving from al-'Arish. For the moment it seems to me as if their intention was just to create a diversion to draw troops to this area and in the meanwhile, give the Turks a beating in Mesopotamia. It must be so, for the official Ottoman telegrams confessing that, on the Tigris front, the enemy managed to overpower their first and second lines of defense... So if these people, who have not spoken of the thrashing of Madaba, confess this (...)

14 February, 1917

By a letter received from one of my friends, I know that Medina has fallen in the hands of Sharif [Husayn] of Mecca and that, among the Turkish prisoners, is Fakhri Pasha. But since the person from whom I received the letter is an Arab, I don't know if this is true.[7]

I found out that the nice 'Izzet Bey is a prisoner in Alexandria and is in good health, for which I am very glad.

Upon entering the consulate this morning I received some good news (it's about time): The ambassador telegraphed me announcing that the military service of my ex-*dragoman* and now secretary, Rauf Lorenzo, has been suspended from now on. Bravo for Mr. Arroyo.

I have been delivered two sealed letters from the Legation: In one of them there is 51,000 Marks for the Franciscans and, in the other, 10,000 and change for the purchase of sanctuaries. I also get a little bit, some 1,300 Pesetas... but all of it, unfortunately, in bank bills. Naturally, my share at least will be rejected by this priest and I will ask that it be paid to my father or that it be left to my disposition in the Hutch House, because I do not feel like losing three quarters of that sum [*I accepted it and lent it to the Patriarchate*].

16 February, 1917

February in this country is as crazy (*madjnun* in Arabic) as in Spain. To revive my spirits a little yesterday, I decided to do something a little crazy too, and in the home of my friends Mr. and Mrs. Mani I dressed as a *hanum* or Turkish lady, with such propriety that everyone took me for the daughter of the governor, Munir Bey. As this gentleman and his daughter know a little Spanish, the guests were not at all shocked that I spoke with Margot Massié and Julia Mani in our language. The comedy went on for half an hour and all the female visitors, married ladies and single, spoke about me in front of me and, strangely enough, they did not say anything bad, avoiding talking about me behind my back. The only thing that they said (in English, thinking that I did not understand them) was that it was a shame that I wasn't there at the consulate, because I would have enjoyed seeing the 'Turkish lady' even if at a distance. There was even a girl who told me I had pretty eyes!

17 February, 1917

My Austrian colleague read me a letter from De Marquet, announcing the next arrival of cigars, cigarettes, ties and collars, all things that one cannot find around here, or if you find them they are so bad it's not worth the trouble to buy them.

Prüfer must be in Constantinople by now. Having a good friend in the [German] embassy, I've got it made. From the war theater: The British airplanes amuse themselves by bothering the Turks in Beersheba. The other day, with Von Kressenstein there, eighteen of them showed up in the following battle order: Six at great height to really dominate the terrain and direct the fire; another six, lower, to drop plenty of bombs and another six at only 50 meters (absolutely true) to fire with machineguns and bombs. They dropped a total of 140 bombs, and there were no more injuries than a wounded horse, but on the other hand, great material damage. Five planes bombed Ramla recently without any damage to complain of.

4 March, 1917

I am back from Jaffa and its surroundings. I will not easily forget that trip, and I think that, even if I didn't write these notes, I will remember Jaffa and the 25th of February all my life.

To rest a little I decided to go to the sea and breathe fresh air and the aroma of the orange trees. I arrived in Ramla the 24th. I greeted Charles Ayyub (son of the banker and Persian consul, Salim Ayyub) who told me that enemy aviators were coming quite frequently but that, up until now, they had not managed to do any damage of some importance, not even destroy the wireless telegraph station that had been installed in the town square. One only knew the effect of the planes by the big holes that remained in the ground, as a result of the explosion of the bombs. It seems to me that the aviators are either very innocent or they are allowing themselves to be deceived, since they always drop bombs on top of a camp…

simulated, installed by the Germans near the railroad station, and as a consequence have destroyed neither that nor the wireless telegraph which are the bases of that military installation. Without being a military man, I understood at great distance that that camp was a fake and that it was composed only of little tents about a meter high and uninhabited... And the good thing is that the people have gotten used to the bombing and don't care a hoot about the presence of the aviators. (...)

I arrived at Jaffa, and after a look at the public works extending Djemal Pasha Boulevard and a walk through Tel-Aviv, I went to the movie theater with the governor of Jerusalem, Munir Bey, the *mudhir of Waqf* Djamil Bey, and Mr. Brill, the representative of Baron Rothschild. Who could have told me that this show in a cinema would save my life? Don't smile at this pathetic phrase, for now you will hear the story.

The last time I was in Jaffa I had stayed at Kuebler's house, that is, our vice consul. Now, Mr. Kuebler had the intention of inviting me also, but since he only found out about my arrival in the evening, he did not invite me to the theater for not having anything prepared yet, deciding to leave the invitation until the following day. That being the case, I was awoken at 7:00 in the morning of this infamous day, the 25th, by a tremendous boom. I flew out of bed thinking that a bomb had fallen on the Hotel Hardegg where I was staying. I got dressed in a moment and went up to the terrace of the hotel. Meanwhile, by the noise of the flags being raised (the hotel is the honorary consulate of the United States) and by the racing around that I heard in the corridor that were signs of the march precipitated by the governor and by Djamil Bey, I understood that we were dealing with a bombardment from some enemy cruiser and not from an airplane. On the terrace of the hotel the animation was great and the consul of Germany, the director of the Ottoman Bank, the mayor of Tel-Aviv and various Germans and Greeks were there. Four kilometers from the beach, a French cruiser was entertaining itself by firing at the city, with the feared red flag hoisted. On the stern of the ship (whose name none of us knows) we saw a hunt for a torpedo boat, and surrounding the first was a flotilla of fishing boats keeping watch over the sea to prevent a submarine attack.

For an hour the dear little boat lobbed a number of cannon shots, impossible to calculate. At first they did it with large caliber guns, I supposed 240mm., but then it continued with other smaller ones, including rapid fire. It was firing in such excess that it was impossible to count the shots. The fire was completely ineffective at first, and almost all the projectiles were going to fall on the Wagner factory. But little by little the aim was corrected, and they began to fall on the surroundings of the factory.

I should point out that, before beginning the bombardment, a hydroplane was situated just above the factory and dropped a rocket that subdivided into three other rockets. At this signal the bombing followed a few minutes later. The show was imposing. From then on, the blast of the cannon fire was so great that the houses shook, glass broke, and people ran, victims of panic. Each explosion was followed by a tremendous column of black smoke which rose up from the site that had been impacted. When we were dealing with the smaller cannon shots, apart from the fact the noise was much less, the column of smoke was whitish.

The noise was heard perfectly from Jerusalem and Jericho. There were broken windows in abundance, even in the Jewish colonies at great distance from Jaffa. Almost the whole time this spectacle lasted, two hydroplanes at great height were watching its effect. Lastly, the cruiser (afterwards they told me it was the *Requin*), after a few broadsides, turned its bow to the high seas, lowered the red flag, changing with the French flag and left as if it had never so much as broken a dish... or a window. The destroyer and the fishing boats followed it. Then, everyone rushed to the street to see the effects of the bombing. I went with the German consul to his consulate, which was still intact in spite of having flown the German flag all the while. A policeman told us that the vice consulate of Spain had been hit, and we began to run, fearing for the life of poor Kuebler.

The building, property of the director of the Austrian Post, was hit by two rockets, which opened up a larger than usual number of breaches. One of the missiles fell on top of the bedroom that *I was supposed to occupy* and completely destroyed all the furniture including the bed. The other missile made a mess of part of the furniture of the second bedroom that was the one Kuebler should have occupied. A fire broke out immediately, which was easily suffocated by various Jews and the police, but between the projectiles, the fire and the water they poured on to put it out, that exceedingly cute little house, which I liked so much and was so prettily furnished, was reduced to a sifting in which one saw bits of broken mirrors, destroyed furniture, clothing full of smoke, debris and water. Indescribable! Amidst all this, Kuebler and I congratulated each other and received congratulations from people for not having been in the house.

After receiving an infinite number of congratulatory visits, we both went to have breakfast at the home of Mrs. Strass. There, Kuebler told me that he owed his life to Mrs. Strass and me, since, if he got up early despite it being Sunday, it was because I had announced to him my proposition of going to the 9:00 A.M. mass of the Franciscans, and he wanted to accompany me in spite of being Protestant. As he was already shaving when the first cannon shot was fired, he decided to leave his home and went to Tel-Aviv to console Mrs. Strass, who was extremely frightened.

A curious thing: The only two rooms that remained intact in the house were the chancellery and the kitchen, so the money, the deposits and the documentation were saved, all so very important. Kuebler was now installed in the best house of Tel-Aviv, wonderfully furnished and very modern: Property of the Levantine family.

The same Sunday afternoon, I telegraphed Rauf to calm the personnel of the consulate, since I supposed it may have been said in Jerusalem that Kuebler and I were among the dead. And they did say so! I also telegraphed in code, by means of the German consulate, to alert our minister in Constantinople about what happened.

Some commentaries: Such a bombardment seems a barbarity to me. Look at the results: One woman and two children dead, five or six wounded, 23 houses more or less made a mess by the projectiles (six of them destroyed), the workshop of Wagner's cabinetmaker destroyed... which does not prevent the factory from functioning as if nothing had happened. One more thing: The vice consulate of Spain and Sweden, charged with the French interests, is seriously damaged. On top of everything else there is a great panic among the population, which is now changing its sympathies to against the French and their boats.

I figured the commander of the boat is probably not very pleased to know that he has bombed the vice consulate charged with the interests of his country. For all this we calculate that the cruiser fired 160 cannon shots. Was he trying to destroy only the German factory or the consulate too? Or, on the other hand, was it his goal to bomb the German colony of Wilhelma? In the first case, one has to say that their artillery did not exactly distinguish themselves, and in the second case it seems a bit savage. The German consul was of this opinion and has telegraphed it to his government. I do not want to get into such depths. (...)[8]

I forgot to mention that the hydroplanes that we had seen had previously bombed the Ramla installations quite freely, without major results. A little after the bombing of Jaffa a German biplane appeared over the city, but, one can say, 'too little, too late.'

The following day I visited the Tel-Aviv School. This establishment has all the defects that mixed education has for both sexes: At the age of 12, the young boys and girls are already falling in love. To heck with them! At least the locations are great, really airy and the teachers seem intelligent. The establishment possesses beautiful patios, collections of minerals, plants, etc. It cost 500,000 Francs.[9]

In the afternoon I visited the *kaymakam* (who was busy presiding over the Administrative Council, but in spite of that, he had the kindness to come out to receive me) and the Military Commander, Urfari Bey. In the evening, dinner at the German consulate. (...) Before, I had been at the Mikveh-Israel farm, the lovely foundation of Karl Netter, entrusted nowadays to the direction of Dr. Kraus.

On Tuesday I began to visit the Jewish colonies. I started with Rishon LeZion, where I arrived after an hour of travel on a decent road. I saw the nurseries installed by René Massié for the desert plantings, where they grow the trees that are to be planted by orders of Djemal Pasha, my very dear friend. Up to now Massié has planted 80,000 plants, balancing them, from among the different nurseries of Nahi Rubi, Rishon, Rehobot and Petah-Tiqwa.

After having lunch and a nap in the administrative house, I dedicated myself for a good long while to visiting the beautiful Plain of Sharon and to thinking that the Promised Land was not, as is thought, a bluff, but rather a reality that the Zionists count on resuscitating again.

That night I slept very well, a thing that has not happened to me for quite some time. Maybe the bombardment calmed my nerves. Before going to bed I had to attend a banquet that the 'Spanish colony' of Rishon gave, also attended by Mr. Merkovitz, Loubman, president of the Rishon Society, etc. Some curious details to judge what the Turkish government favors in agricultural enterprises: Rishon, which has 700 hectares, pays 24,000 Francs a year for 'security.' It also has to pay for schools, pharmacies, doctors, etc., that is, what in other countries would be supported, at least in part, by the state. But there is another picturesque detail. Lately the government has decided, as a money-saving measure, to found a national bank that will be called (if they will ever name it) Ottoman National Credit. Well fine, the system to buy shares is *voluntary*: They grab a citizen on the street and make him pay for the shares that the government has decided to *offer* him. If he refuses, they sweetly take him to the nearest police station. It is no exaggeration, for the latter has happened to my *dragoman*, Rauf, whom the police drove to the *karakol* for not having in his pocket the 30 Pounds that they demanded of him on the street. Well, returning to my story, I will say that between Petah Tiqwa, Rishon, Rehovot and Wadi Hatime they must pay as subscriptions to this bank no less than 5,000 Pounds (113,685 Francs). In short, thank heavens that only the Ottomans can participate in this bank, for otherwise they would have obliged the foreigners to take shares by force. Tell this to the consul of Persia, whose protégés have lately been recruited, to general surprise, as Turkish soldiers.

But let's cease these digressions, and let's leave Wednesday by coach with my friend Rene Massié and Ada Rabinowitz for Rehovot, on a splendid morning, traversing little forests of eucalyptus trees, plantations of almonds and apricots in bloom, precious olive trees and magnificent vineyards... All this, of course, while we crossed the Jewish colonies, since as soon as one leaves them, one no longer admires anything but the Bedouin tents, camels, vultures, little lagoons, focal points of fevers and reeds: That is to say, what is typical of the East, but not the cultivated part of the East.[10]

After crossing an extensive valley, the road for Rehovot that we kept following was excellently made, naturally, by the Jewish colonies, and is not finished. For what reason? Well, because the commander of Jaffa, my old and famous friend, Hasan Bey, without any formalities took control of the stone and materials that the Jews had prepared and safely used for the construction of a rather famous mosque.

Rehovot seemed to me very sad, and I would not want to stay there for very much time. There was also here the corresponding visit and party in the home of my 'subject' Levi and his obese wife. There were many dinner guests, but as the majority spoke nothing but Hebrew and German, I was reduced to conversation with Mrs. Jacobian (née Rabinowitz) and Mrs. Meerkawitz (née Strauss).

I was lodged in the town hotel, in a very clean room with a good bed, a sink... even a *water-closet*. For the food, all my praise would be too little: Vegetables and greens in profusion, chickens, eggs, delicious milk, fresh cheese, the famous yogurt, comparable to the finest cream, jams, in short, why go on?

From that colony I went to Ramla by a very sandy road that justifies the local name for it (in Arabic, 'sand'). We went through the town with the natural worry that it might occur that the English airplanes would make a visit coinciding with ours, and we continued down our way by an abandoned road and full of mud that meant my coachman could not contain a veritable litany of curses, with which the Arabic language is so rich. We successively passed by a very old bridge over a ravine, in which Dr. Moskowitz drowned last year, then Lydda and, further along, a beautiful prairie with hardly any cultivation and covered only with weeds and red, white and violet anemones. This prairie precedes the German agricultural colony of Wilhelma, where I proposed to reside for several days, but fortunately I only passed by it. That colony is more of a livestock operation, and its construction is beautiful, even better than the Jewish colonies. It has a curious American system of apiary, magnificent cattle, and good work horses, although, the cultivation did not seem very well perfected to me. The grape vines were very badly planted and cared for: The feet of the trees some 20 centimeters from the vines. As far as the roads, frankly these are poorly arranged. To sum it up: Nothing really caught my attention. The Ramla station picks up and exports its products, but since there is no war material, in the end the exportation is minimal.

Then we were in Petah-Tiqwa, a word that in Hebrew means 'Gate of Hope.' It is a magnificent property of 6,000 hectares situated some ten kilometers from the sea on a lightly undulating plain and formed almost in its entirety of sandy soil.[11] On this plain, whose current valuation is at about 60 million Francs, there are beautiful plantations of orange, lemon and almond trees, vineyards and fruit trees of a surprising wealth. The necessary water is provided by an installation formed by two powerful German engines. This installation raises the water from the Nahr al-'Awdja, and that enormous mass of water is distributed by means of a complicated and perfect system, up to a distance of three kilometers. The plantations of orange trees are irrigated twice a month during the dry period. The irrigation comes to about 300 Francs a year in the lands farthest from the river. The hectare produces 1,400 boxes of oranges that contain 144 pieces of fruit each and were sold before the war for between 15 and 18 Francs a box. The production of almonds was sent to England and the United States.

With the facts cited, one will understand that, in peace time, this farm was an excellent business for the stockholders of the society, all of them Jews, who earned good interest on the 10,000 Francs that each stock was worth. The losses experienced because of the war are impossible to describe.

One of the curious things about this colony is the test garden of Baron Edmond Rothschild. There they do studies of the different varieties of fruit trees, especially oranges and grapefruits, as well as plantings of thornless prickly pears, a very important resource for the livestock of the dry land farms. A hectare planted with them is enough to feed 25 cows. Moreover, the fruit doesn't have the very disagreeable seed that it does in our country. I observed with natural satisfaction that the best varieties of oranges were the ones that had the sign 'From Valencia.' As far as the almonds, the best is the one from a California variety called 'Non Plus Ultra,' as big as one of the fattest I know.

Alongside test plots there extends a marsh of 200 hectares, completely uncultivated, and a focal point for malaria and other such fevers. The Jews solicited the government, to whom it belongs, to permit them to clean it out, avoiding those diseases and planting it with eucalyptus and oranges, promising to pay the state one third of the produce. The state did not accept.

The houses of the colonies are not exactly distinguished for their beauty, but there are some very acceptable ones, such as the Cohen family's, where we had a *soirée*. The working neighborhood, dark and dirty, in the middle of a beautiful natural area, made a very bad impression on me. In contrast, I loved the hotel, big and comfortable, surrounded by a real garden and with an extremely pleasant avenue of cypresses and a rustic fountain. (…)

I received the friendly visits of the doctor, the president of the colony and my Spanish and Romanian protégés. The only thing I was not very happy about was the tea of Petah-Tiqwa, which is made of figs! This beverage has a certain similarity to real tea, such as real coffee has to the mixture of barley they are accustomed to serving me in Jerusalem since the war began.

A concert in the School of Music of Tel-Aviv had been organized in my honor, but I had to leave precipitously for Jerusalem since, according to German reports, the advance of the British towards Jaffa was imminent. Up to now this is not certain and seems to be limited to the evacuation of Gaza, which they assured has taken place, or soon will. Enver Pasha and Djemal Pasha have been with their military staff in Beersheba, and, according to one opinion that I believe is worthy of credit, the only thing going on at the moment is the evacuation of some Turkish positions in the hope of reducing the so-called 'Sinai front.'

The Ottoman agencies said that, according to the *Le Petit Parisien*, King Alfonso XIII insists on the maintenance of the neutrality of Spain and on inviting the belligerents to a peace conference that will take place in Madrid as soon as possible. They added the information that a commission representing all the municipal governments of Spain had gone to the palace to beg the king to use the Great Cross of Beneficence for the great services he had rendered during the war. The sovereign responded: 'Our country represents in the European conflict the humanitarian ideal. Therefore, I have always worked in a manner that recognizes this humanitarian sentiment in my people. I am not the one who should wear the insignias of the Great Cross of Beneficence, but rather all of Spain on her glorious flag. I will place the insignias on the standard of the regiment that bears my name, and thus the names of Spain and Alfonso XIII will remain linked in your memory.' My commentary to this, as you will understand, is 'Long live the King.'

17 March, 1917

There have been no sensational occurrences other than the march of the new Turkish recruits. These have now twice paid their *bedel*, that is, the extension of military service. Now they are obliged to be on active duty without having finished the period of the second *bedel*, unless they pay a certain quantity of grain valued at about 160 Pounds gold, or some 10,000 Francs. Doubtless to force those who would not have done so voluntarily, they created the following system: When the recruits were well accustomed to going every day to their respective commission to report in, one day several soldiers with fixed bayonets appeared, surrounded them, and prevented them from returning home. Next act, they were locked up in a little room with the poor recruits and in the friendly company of the lice, transmitters of typhus. They did not have any place to lie down or even to sit, seeing themselves reduced to standing, pressed against each other and trying to get near the windows to breathe the outside air. In short, to avoid this torture all those who had the money decided to pay the 10,000 Francs and the rest were packed off in uncovered wagons, to suffer the cold, and sent to Damascus. As you see, the system of Turks is to stimulate the love of country, and you should hear the descriptions, perhaps exaggerated, that the interested parties tell. (…)

From the Sinai front, two British aviators have been taken prisoner by the Turks. The latter have evacuated the convent of Ramla, being substituted by the Germans. Contrasting this news with what the Turks gave, according to them Djemal Pasha has founded a school of arts and trades in Beersheba, having contracted specialized professors, trusting the direction of the school to the Military Administration of the Desert: Well, what's left of the Desert Turks. Courses in Turkish, Arabic, music, drawing and other subjects will be imparted there, so that they will learn music accompanied by the professor on piano and by the British airplanes. It's all music… What is not music is that yesterday I turned over 51,000 Pesetas for expenses to the custodial president of the Holy Land, Father Eutimio Castellani.

19 March, 1917

Little by little, the 'known' families that remained are parading out of Jerusalem; the expulsion of David Yellin, Jewish town councilor, whose house I have taken, has been followed by that of Jacob Rabinowitz, whose order has been given probably at the request of… Yesterday the governor communicated the order to them and told them he could not explain the reasons for which they were being expelled. And it seems there will be other expulsions. They are talking about Massié and Mazaraky. The first result of that order has been that the few families that were still receiving have decided to suspend their receptions.

From Russia there is so much contradictory news that one doesn't know what to believe. They said that the Grand Duke Michael has been named as regent, but I repeat that we know nothing for sure.[12]

27 March, 1917

The heat is beginning in earnest, and I suppose that, like every year, we will then have the *Jamsin* and later the invariable and lovely weather that characterizes this country and which will continue until the first rains. After six years of tropical countries and the Orient, the cold is not a welcome guest for me. That's without considering that, if the war lasts any longer, I won't have a place to stay next year.

After these small weather considerations, let's go to those of a different genre. A few days back I found out about something that does not leave the correctness of the Turkish police in a good light. In short, Djalal Bey, their chief, believes that the private affairs of the consuls should be watched, as well as some people I hold in especially high regard... And this will end badly because, one day, I will give a piece of my mind in no uncertain terms to the chief or whoever keeps meddling in my affairs... of which I do not care to give any more details, because they are nobody's business.

To erase my bad mood a little, the same day that I became aware of what is happening I decided to visit the Red Crescent hospital, which occupies the location of the former British hospital. Dr. Akif Bey accompanied me with Nur al-Din Bey and the two brothers from St. Peter of Ratisbonne, Brother Victor and Brother Enrique, both of them in the service of the Red Crescent. I visited the operating room (pretty good) and the kitchen... which was absolutely shining clean. The cook was once in the service of Enver Pasha, and this is another detail. The presence of several German sisters of the Order of St. Charles who work there probably contributes a great deal to this cleanliness. The food was not bad, above all if you keep in mind the type of food to which the Turks are accustomed. (Lately, the soldier's food has been sensibly improved, and they say that it is due to the visit of the two Pashas to whom I referred before. They also say that certain changes in the *Manzil* are due to that.) After, I saw it distributed to the sick, and I observed that they gave them soup, *bugonal* and *laban*. *Bugonal* is a type of crushed wheat, very nutritious, which I know from personal experience, is worthwhile. *Laban*, or prepared milk, is a special ferment, which is repulsive to foreigners the first time and winds up being preferred above all beverages and foods when it is hot. At least, that is what happened to me.

Then it was my turn to visit the room of the injured men, where there were no more than half a dozen injured in work accidents. I examined the feet of one of them, which were infected with gangrene and horribly swollen. I won't go into more detail.

But the specialty of the hospital is the treatment of typhus. We spoke about it, and Dr. Akif concluded by proposing that I visit the sick, to which I acceded although not without a certain amount of panic. The room they occupied is immense, admirably ventilated and very clean. In it, and other smaller rooms, there were 110 sick men. Firstly, upon receiving a sick patient at the hospital he is given a bath (perhaps the first of their life, for some), and they are shaved completely to avoid lice. Afterwards, they go to these rooms surrounded by all kinds of care in hopes that they will go through a few days of high fever, for once passed, the sick are out of danger.

I examined some sick men, on whom one could see perfectly the rash, red spots that disappear when touched with the finger but reappear right away. The eruption is quite violent and covers the whole body. In general, this year the typhus is not of such a severe nature as the year before, since they have only had about seven percent fatalities. I saw only one who was hopeless, with a skeletal thinness and his cranium already had the appearance of a skeleton. Here is a small digression: How terrible it must be for the sick to see the removal of the cadaver of a companion who has just died of the same illness. A curious case I saw is that of a boy who had been paralyzed on the left side of his body but was now out of danger, thanks to the resistance of his heart, and could move his arm and leg with relative freedom.

In a separate room, and guarded by a sentinel with rifle and fixed bayonet, was a young Dutch Jew from Jaffa, who had been taken prisoner for having received Zionist brochures from abroad. In jail he caught typhus, but I think, according to what the doctors tell me, he will recover well from the illness. [*Later I found out that he actually did get well and free also.*]

Dr. Akif invited me to witness a 'pretty' operation (as Dr. Jörns says), such as, cutting off a leg or something similar, and the strange thing is, I have almost decided to attend. Assuredly, everything is evolving and changing in this world: Before, I wasn't capable of seeing a mouse die, and now, I not only watch typhus victims dying but can hear all about it almost with indifference and even feel like seeing an operation. Am I becoming a fatalist? Probably: It is the influence of the East. *Allah karim*, God is good, the Arabs say to console themselves when something bad happens. *Allah karim*.

Let's leave these sad things and go breathe some pure air, contemplate nature and life to forget death. That's what I thought and that's what I did, leaving the following day (March 23) for Jericho. I was remembering a lot about the quail that the Jews hunt in the desert, since as soon as I arrived it was clear they were waiting for me, and some went into my game bag. The tranquility did not last long, for moments later a sergeant presented himself to inform me with the highest possible quantity of vulgarity that they were going to requisition my coach and horses. I had to visit the military commander, who immediately gave me all kinds of excuses, saying that if he had known I was the owner he would have come himself to beg me to leave him the coach to go look for the Inspector of the Food Rationing (Rifa 'at Bey) and the *wali* of Damascus (Tahsin Bey) who were in the Dead Sea without so much as a miserable covered wagon to transport them to Jerusalem. In short, I sent my carriage to both gentlemen, with a card offering it to them. After eating, I went to wait for them, and both of the men, as well as Khadri Bey (the former Chief of Staff of Von Kressenstein), Ibrahim Bey (ex-president of the military justice tribunal of Jerusalem), an infirmary official and I enjoyed each other's company until midnight. (…)

29 March, 1917

Finally, there has been a serious battle near the city. I have here the text, quite simple to be sure, of the official telegram:

> Telegram of the Commander in Chief of the 1st Expedition Corps. March 27, 1917. After a fierce battle that has lasted two days, the English have been driven back near Gaza. They have suffered very heavy losses.[13]

Now some details, the few I know. It seems that, in fact, the British were pushed back, but the fatalities of the Turks and their allies must not have been light either. Up to now I know that a captain who commanded one of the Austrian batteries died. As far as the Germans, they are talking about a dozen officers and non-commissioned men. An Austrian official, whose name I don't remember, has been wounded and taken prisoner. The British warships helped their companions on land but had to withdraw under the Turkish fire. It seems there are 300 British prisoners, although it is compensated by the number of Turks fallen into British hands.

(…) Today we are hoping for the arrival of Djemal Pasha and Mehmet Pasha. They are also expecting many wounded of which I have seen only very light ones this morning.

(It is still March 29.) A commission of the Spanish colony of Jaffa has just arrived to tell me that the *mutasarrif* of Jerusalem went to Jaffa to communicate the order of Djemal Pasha to evacuate the city in a period of twelve days: Ottomans as well as neutrals. Only the German, Austrian and Bulgarian subjects will be able to remain, but under their responsibility. Very funny. So I figured that soon it will be our turn to evacuate Jerusalem, and if they leave me there, because of the Austro-German interests, I will have the right to choose between receiving a barrel of grenades on the head or being murdered or ruined if they send us to Homs or farther. Confirming these impressions, a German colleague told me in all confidence that they expect a combined attack by land and sea against Jaffa.

30 March, 1917 (9:00 A.M.)

We are learning something about the combat of the 26th and 27th. The German vice consul, Ziemke, told me that the British mounted a furious attack on Gaza and that, in the streets, there developed a very bloody battle in which Tiller showed great valor and military capability. The Austrian battery was, four times, at the point of falling into British hands: the Austrians defending themselves heroically hand-to-hand. On one of these occasions the captain fell with a gunshot to the chest. In the meanwhile, Von Kressenstein came with reinforcements, and the Turks managed to save the battery, charging impetuously against the British who at last saw themselves obliged to withdraw, leaving the 300 prisoners I spoke of before, various automobiles and a considerable loot. The number of British dead is 2000. Just on the front, occupied by the Arab companies, there were 700 British dead.

Ziemke also communicated to me a telegram from Kuebler about the evacuation of Jaffa, in which he asked me to get Djemal Pasha to let him and the Spaniards remain in the city.

30 March, 1917 (2:00 P.M.)

I am going to report my visit this morning to Djemal Pasha. I was... unfortunately with my Greek colleague, who is more doddering every day and has the least possible amount of diplomacy. His Excellency received us with his accustomed friendliness. After talking about many things and asking the Greek for news of his country 'if it does exist,' we spoke of Jaffa and the projected evacuation. His Excellency quickly relieved us of all doubt, explaining to us that his plan consists of making all the inhabitants leave, both Ottoman and neutrals, that they will leave by railroad at government expense and will be sent to Hama, Homs and other populations of the district between Baalbek and Aleppo. The class of travelers will be maintained by the government, but those who do not want to go to these points can head for wherever it seems more convenient to them, without having the right in that case to the pension the state will pay them. The German and Austrian subjects will be able to stay in the German colonies of the surroundings. I got the Minister to permit the Spanish clerics to come to Jerusalem, an order I appreciated very much. As far as the consuls, they will be 'invited' to come here.

I tried to get from His Excellency the order for the Spaniards to remain in Jaffa at their own risk, but he refused. I attacked the question saying to him: 'The intention of the government being to avoid the death of foreigners in case of bombing, if they renounce all rights of reclamation against the government...' But he cut me off saying, 'That is not our objective but rather to defend ourselves in the city as we have done in Gaza, and how do you want us to defend ourselves between the screams and wailing of women and children?' I had to capitulate unwillingly.

Another friend of mine is dead of typhus: 'Ali Galib Bey.

And I close the notes of today almost disposed to prepare the luggage, since Djemal Pasha at the last moment has refused to permit the Spanish to come to Jerusalem because 'why come now and have to leave later?' Decidedly, life is smiling at us or laughing at us.

2 April, 1917

Change of plan. Now as many people from Jaffa can come to Jerusalem, and, furthermore, all the farmers, owners and workers from the orange orchards and the plantations of the Plain of Sharon can stay there and in the Jewish colonies. It was confirmed to me yesterday by Djemal Pasha, whom I visited again in the afternoon in the company of two colleagues.

He first received the German, whom he was in such a hurry to see that he sent his own car for him. The object of the conversation was a complaint by the Pasha about the conduct of Schabinger, the German consul in Jaffa, who seems to have been a little exaggerated or violent in his language criticizing the evacuation of Jaffa. When Brode left the minister's office he indicated something about this to me, and I believed that the latter would not speak to me about this matter. After the greetings the General explained to me the new measures that he had adopted that really moderate the severity of the first ones: I asked him, 'And our vice consul? When should he leave?' To which he answered, 'I had given a period of only three days to all the consuls, but that was because, this morning, I was very nervous and agitated about the German consul in Jaffa. Now I have increased the grace period.' He was so angry that he wanted to have him judged by a military court.

I later spoke to the Pasha about the news service founded by our monarch, and he assured me that the military censors would offer no difficulty in letting it pass. Lastly, I asked him for authorization to telegraph to the Legation the measures taken for Jaffa, and this he refused, as I figured.

There has been a recent modification that has produced quite a commotion among the Jews; the evacuation order referred to all those who profess that religion, whether they are German or Austrians, so the Christian allies have the right to stay while the Jews do not. This confirmed my opinion that this is not only a military measure, but also an anti-Zionist one. Of course, I respect the point of view of the Ottoman government. Another reason has been, and is, that espionage must exist on a grand scale; look at the following example: When Enver Pasha announced his second trip to this region, a British airplane followed the train in which the Minister of War was supposed to come, and if it did not drop any bombs on it, it was because the minister delayed the trip one day, precisely for his security.

In the headquarters I asked the cause of the expulsion of the Rabinowitz family, and I was answered (and I quote): 'Because we received a complaint that a lot of officers met in their house.' The same person assured that neither Mazaraky nor any others who were told they were going to be expelled will leave Jerusalem. Not bad!

Yesterday I saw some sixty British prisoners enter. Palm Sunday entering in Jerusalem! One must hope they will not be crucified.

In one of my ordinary walks to the outskirts of the Jewish asylum, by Jaffa road, I had to fight against an unbearable wind and the quantity of accumulated dust on that road. Every time an automobile passed by (scarcely a dozen) we were covered in a layer of dust of a thickness variable according to the size of the car. Along the road I only saw women now that the men are all soldiers. The women for the most part were selling oranges to the soldiers. You should see the shouting and oaths to Allah that haggling over a single orange occasioned! At least after the three and a half years I've been here, I know the blood will not reach the river.

5 April, 1917

I have had several meals with Djemal Pasha. In one of them the conversation turned almost exclusively to the war and the diverse stories my Greek colleague told. The Pasha told me how the commander of the 534th Division, which was in Ramla, was taken prisoner when he decided to do a reconnaissance towards Gaza, which he supposed was attacked only from the south. He was calmly going along without worrying about anything when his subordinate shouted at him, 'Here come the British!' The chief paid no attention and even was irritated with his subordinate, hitting him because he thought he was afraid. And thus he stepped into the jaws of the wolf. A commentary of mine: A leader should not and cannot ever be wrong. No one is going to believe that the leader of the division was a first class general, because he was a simple colonel. Very simple. Since the Pasha usually fantasizes quite a bit I did not believe the news, and later I found out that, really, it had not happened quite that way.

6 April, 1917 (Good Friday)

Early this morning the famous Eutimio, Greek president of the Holy Sepulcher, and one of the richest inhabitants of Jerusalem, died. According to what they say, he was the instigator of the bloody conflicts between Franciscans and Greeks in the Holy Sepulcher when they tried to sweep the famous exterior stairway of the Basilica.[14]

I'm waiting for the arrival of the archival records of the vice consulate in Jaffa and those of the convents of our religious men and women. For it I have sent a truck that the Germans have left me and for which I am extremely grateful to them for there is no other means of transport other than camels or one's own feet. There is not a single coach left, for they have all been requisitioned by the authorities.

It seems to me that we will soon have to evacuate Jerusalem; at least, a German person was telling me the night before last that, 'The site is magnificent for defending, and if they destroy the Holy Sepulcher... what do we care!'

11 April, 1917

Novelties of the war: Declaration of war between America and Germany and between the latter and Cuba.

I was in Jaffa on Saturday (the 7th). I went by automobile with Brode and Kraus, and the beating I received can scarcely be described, since the highway has been made such a pitiful thing with the incessant movement of cars for the evacuation of the city. Since the truck was running empty we were bouncing around like lobsters in the cooking pot. In Ramla we stopped for a half hour, and the colleagues who accompanied me visited the convent where the aviators are lodged, and in which they have installed an American bar. Our clerics have been reduced to the Casa-Nova, and I advised them to transfer to Jerusalem as soon as possible, turning the keys over to the aviators.

Even before arriving in Jaffa we were breathing the delicious aroma of the blooms of the orange trees, but we went from the impression of nature in springtime to one of death in the city: We had been preparing ourselves for this transition by meeting the automobiles that were transporting the wealthy from Jaffa and carts that were taking the less wealthy. All of that completely filled the highway and you had to hear that hubbub of shouts, sticks, dust, smoke, the smell of gasoline, people on foot, orange vendors, etc.

The entry to Jaffa did not cause me any great sensation, because there were a lot of people (almost all Muslims) in the cafés, and one could almost believe it was a normal day. But upon arriving at the city center and seeing all the German [cafés] closed up like their houses and not a single woman on the street, it gave my heart quite a shock. I spent the whole day in business conversations with Kuebler, my colleagues from Jaffa and Father Mateo.

In Tel-Aviv I counted half a dozen people in the streets. On the highway there were a few more, but when I left the hotel in the evening to go to the German consulate, I saw no more than a single light among all the houses situated across from the hotel. To flee… to flee at all costs from that half-dead city was my most vehement wish. The following day in the morning I almost got into a good mood just seeing some distance from that city that once was so cheerful and nice.

The Jews have departed, for the most part, to the Jewish colonies of Galilee; the Christians and Muslims to God knows where, and very few people have gone to Jerusalem. The farm workers are staying in the city and the colonies until new orders from the government, in hopes of doing the harvest, but their wives and children have to leave.

Djemal Pasha told the consuls in Jaffa when he visited the city recently: 'You can stay here if you want until I warn you, but I think it is best if you send your respective records to Jerusalem.' It is clear that it's better not to wait for the warning from His Excellency, because one can suppose that when it comes there will not be a single automobile or other means of locomotion. So Kuebler will soon be coming here. (…)

17 April, 1917

Bad mood. Visit to the American consul to arrange details in case of a break in diplomatic relations of his country with Turkey. Arrival of a new Turkish general, 'Abd al-Karim Pasha, leader of the 2nd Army Corps that we have here now. I also see Meissner Pasha.

20 April, 1917

I have developed the habit of getting up early and working from 7:00 in the morning. Thus, with the windows opened one does not breathe dust in place of air, as happens a little later when the movement of the trucks begins. There are more than 200 of them here now. They have completely destroyed the paving stones (where there are some) and the highways. Going out to the street in the afternoon and converting into an imitator of the famous Don Tancredo is one and the same.

Yesterday morning, a vigorous shelling was heard in the city. On a walk in the afternoon I went to the Holy Cross convent; I also heard cannon shots that seemed to be coming from the city of Jaffa or from some place between that city and Gaza. They must have been large caliber weapons.

About a hundred wounded British prisoners who were in the St. Louis hospital have left Jerusalem now. A few days ago the wife of the *mutasarrif* visited them, accompanied by other Turkish ladies, sharing cigarettes and oranges with them. It was quite a surprise for the prisoners. So much so that one of them said to the doctor who was attending them: 'Is this a story from the *1001 Nights*? To receive the visit of fifteen Turkish ladies with covered faces. I would never have believed it!'

For the rest, little news. Very hot and absolute drought, because of which the wheat harvest will be bad. Yesterday Captain Axster, leader of the automobile drivers and director of a bank in Berlin, had lunch with me. Djemal Pasha told him that the latest telegrams he has had about the recent battle in Gaza were from 10:00 A.M., and, according to them, the British have been pushed back.

21 April, 1917

I have been warned that Djemal Pasha urgently wanted to see me. I figured out right away what it was about because I've been suspicious for days. My colleagues (with whom the general is also meeting) confirmed my belief, and I was not at all surprised that after having received the American consul (practically an enemy now) His Excellency would meet with his two allies and me. After a brief preamble, he communicated to us right away the possible evacuation of Jerusalem. Above all, he told us (and I quote): 'Yesterday was a day of victory for us. The enemy was attacking us from 5:00 A.M. to 8:00 P.M. and was driven back three times with great losses, ours being so small I can scarcely believe it. We have not lost even a single one of our positions, since the only one that we lost, situated very near the coast and exposed to the fire of English war ships, was retaken by bayonet in the evening. In spite of this we cannot know what the war is holding for us, and it is possible that I may see myself obliged to defend Jerusalem. To avoid a precipitous evacuation, when there are no railroads, coaches or other means of transportation, recommend to your respective compatriots that they begin now to get away from the city, since I would not accept any reclamations or protests if it is not done. Given the special nature of Jerusalem, it is necessary to guard the sanctuaries, churches, synagogues, etc. so the clerics strictly necessary for such service can stay here, as well as those for the hospitals and asylums. The nuns will also stay. You will give me the lists of your compatriots that want to take advantage of this offer of mine, and when a thousand people are gathered I will give them a train to take them. As for you, who are my personal friends, you are authorized near my person, and I will give you all possible facilities, including trucks. Your fellow citizens are free to leave for wherever they wish as long as it is towards Damascus and they do not settle in any point along the coast. They can go to the capital, to Spain. (...)'

Thus ended our interview. Immediately, the General got up and headed for the Sinai front amongst the clouds of dust and gases of automobiles.

22 April, 1917

Holiday: It's Sunday. May God spare us from such a good holiday! From 8:00 in the morning I have not stopped receiving visits related to the projected evacuation. The attitude of the interested parties is not exactly excited. The Germans, above all, distinguished themselves by the agitation that reigns among them. A commission from the Jewish Spanish colony asked me not to put the evacuation in effect. As if I had ordered it!

I tried to see Djemal Pasha for all the details of the evacuation, but he had left for Jaffa. I had a cup of Turkish coffee in Captain Moro's room, and he told us, as the only news, about the rupture of diplomatic relations between Turkey and the United States.[15]

They assured me that Gaza is in the hands of the British, but I don't believe it.[16] Who knows?

This morning 96 British prisoners marched in front of the consulate, the majority of them very young; also, some wounded, and one of them was carrying his shoes in his hand and was limping pitifully. On the other hand, the official parties kept talking about daily battles.

25 April, 1917

I have received a telegram from the Legation authorizing me to take charge of the protection of the Italian and Montenegrin interests, so I have the exceedingly high honor of representing King Nikita. Poor Otis Glazebrook will see himself in a very uncomfortable position if he wants to execute to the letter the orders sent to him by his ambassador (who certainly has typhus), and which consist of the following partition of interests within the Turkish Empire:

Spain: Italians, Romanians and Montenegrins.
Holland: Russians, English and French (except in Jerusalem).
Sweden: Americans and Serbian.

Telegrams from Sinai:

April 21, 1917.[17] After the battle near Gaza, which ended in complete success for us, the enemy retired to their former positions, having suffered harsh losses. Our losses were minimal in this battle. One of our aviators shot down an enemy plane, which went down in flames between the two lines. Another piece of enemy equipment was forced by our defense forces to land near Tel Abu Hurayra. The pilot was taken prisoner. In the course of the aerial combat, our aviators have the advantage every day. Another of our pilots dropped 300 kilograms of bombs on the encampments and enemy reserve troops. The enemy intentionally directed their fire towards the mosque of Gaza, which was destroyed.

April 23, 1917. The enemy, defeated in Gaza, has withdrawn its right flank towards the rear guard, where they are fortifying their defenses. To protect their right flank they have erected new defense fortifications. I must inform you also that a hundred of the enemies were taken prisoner near Gaza. This relatively small number is explained by the savageness with which both sides fought. Many automatic rifles were captured. We have also destroyed three of the armored vehicles that the enemy used in the fight.

I have protested that the mechanics of the German cars have charged our clerics no less than 40 Pounds to bring them from Jaffa. Von Kressenstein has taken it seriously and has ordered the proper investigations. The military is not dealing with 'little girls'.

27 April, 1917

The administrative disorder continues. My North American colleague brought me a telegram from his ambassador, Abraham Elkus [ordering him] to entrust me with the English and Russian interests.[18] Nonetheless, I have no official notice of it, and, of course, I cannot accept it more than informally. In addition, he put me in charge of giving instructions about great sums of money to pay to the Mission in charge of protecting American interests. And which is this Mission? Glazebrook received the order to entrust the Bulgarian and Serbian interests to the representative of Sweden, to which he has answered that there is no such representative here: According to the *vox populi*, Djemal Pasha has sent an order to the civil government and to the tribunal not to recognize Salim Ayyub as the consul of Persia, Sweden and Denmark.

Many of the lay Italians were sent to Damascus today, but I must make it clear that the order to send them was given before I was in charge of them. I helped them as much as I could at the moment.

A military holiday today, certainly abominably organized, in the Holy Sepulcher for the name day of Empress Zita of Bourbon. I attended in uniform, and from there I went to greet Djemal Pasha for the anniversary of the coronation of Sultan Mehmet V. His Excellency spent almost the whole time talking with the Greek and me. He told me, among other things: 'Now I know you are a universal consul. Your American colleague has informed me that you will be installed in his consulate. For the rest you will have little work, since you see that I'm expelling the belligerents that remained, with few exceptions. As far as the Russian women (about 800), I am in charge of protecting them, and I have even given them food.' (This is true, as is also the fact that they were so grateful that they bowed down before him).

To poor Marx, the director of the German Bank of Palestine and the honorary consul of Norway, he made so many allusions about his possible expulsion because of a matter of bank bills, that he and the German consul, Brode, were extremely angry. The Pasha told us that the director of the bank in Beirut had asked him by telegraph the motive for his expulsion, and he answered: 'For being a banker.' I thought it was necessary to comment on it, saying that being a banker was a bad job.

It seems that the Pasha will expel ten people every week chosen by lottery from a list that has been formed of 'personalities' of Jerusalem. He wants to see if, in this way, the price of bank bills comes to be the equal of gold. Perhaps he'll accomplish something, but as for even with gold, I think he'll be disappointed.

Of the war, His Excellency told us nothing important.

The telegrams say the following:

Sinai front. Afternoon of April 23, 1917. Cannon fire with intermittent violence near Gaza. During the morning it was weaker. The 23rd goes by in relative calm. On the 20th an enemy cruiser accompanied by a gunboat and a transport ship appears in front of 'Aqaba. After a violent bombardment, in which among other things they delivered asphyxiating gas, the British, numbering about 2,000 men, tried in vain to land. The 'Aqaba mosque was destroyed by enemy fire. Our losses were no more than seven dead.

29 April, 1917

Last night, Zaki Bey came to invite me on Djemal Pasha's behalf to have tea this afternoon in his home. I'm afraid this will include a poker game afterwards.

Today, for the first time, the Spanish flag has been hoisted at the American consulate, changed in Spanish by the consent of Djemal Pasha. His Excellency has behaved very well with Glazebrook and, the day before yesterday, told him to go congratulate him personally in the afternoon, on the holiday of the Sultan, since he could not do it officially. He also told him he would give him all the facilities for his journey. (…)

My old friend the 'Ernest Simmons' was sunk on April 3 as it was sailing from Marseille to Egypt.

4 May, 1917

Brode has told me that the evacuation of Jerusalem will not take place, news that produced in me real satisfaction, and which must be true since he gave me the news in Zaki Bey's house. In a little while, Djemal Pasha came so we could play our accustomed poker game.

There is quite a bit of typhus and not only here, since the German consul in Damascus and the American ambassador [in Constantinople] have it too. Coudsi has passed away, the unfortunate manager of our consulate in Damascus. The poor man suffered a lot during the war, much more than I, although I complain nonetheless.

The Legation authorized me to provisionally take charge of the American interests, but not of the English and Russian ones for lack of a request from them.

10 May, 1917

I am happy because Djemal Pasha has authorized me today to tell my American colleague that he can leave with his wife, Dick [vice consul] and the rest of the consulate personnel. Dick's wife (Eli Nikola, or Helle Spyridon) will leave too: The spirited vice consul began a relationship with her a week ago, is getting married on Sunday and is leaving on Monday. Those Americans!

Brode announced to me that I will finally receive the *ABC*.

Sad news: A few days ago a wedding was celebrated in the evening in Ramla. A British airplane must have thought it was dealing with Turkish troops and dropped two bombs that caused the death of 48 people and wounded many others. The Turks considered this a sign of barbarity, but I don't know if by night and from a plane one can distinguish whether one is dealing with soldiers or a civilian population.

20 May, 1917

Last Tuesday, Glazebrook left. On the list of his companions there was a very sensitive reduction: That of Mrs. Eli Nikola who was not able to get married. How did the break-up occur? For a very simple reason: Because the wedding would have had to have been celebrated before the consul of the United States and with the prior permission of the Secretary of State. To make a long story short, because of the speed of Dick and his future bride, the latter will remain 'future' until after the war.

At the station, the Jewish population was there in full. They very soon arrived at Damascus. Aranda, the manager of our consulate in the city, telegraphed to tell me to take steps in the station here to find the luggage they had lost. Here they told me that it had gone on the same train as the American personnel. Naturally, everything was in Damascus, and you can see how the organization of the service is just perfect.

Finally, I have a telegram from Arroyo begging me to assume the protection of the British and Russian interests. For that I will have to get in touch with the embassy of the Netherlands and not with our Legation.

The 17th, the birthday of our king, was celebrated happily in the midst of an abundance of champagne and sandwiches that was highly distressing to my wallet. But nothing can be done about it. The Patriarch came to see me, as did all my colleagues, Zaki Bey, Commander Mayer, Dr. Schrötter, Captain Wolff, Captain Axster, Lt. Bindernagel; friars of all nationalities (except the Italians of the Custody), commissions from the Spanish colony, etc.

There was one bit of foolishness on the part of the interim governor, Djamil Bey, who sent me a message saying that since I had not gone to visit him on the Sultan's day, neither would he come on my sovereign's day. He's not even right, nor does this incident matter to me, especially after the gentleman stole the portrait of His Majesty that was in the Artas convent, for which the authorities have no right to any attention on my part. Amen.

26 May, 1917

It is 11:30 P.M., and I have just returned from a party given by the German car drivers in honor of General Von Falkenhayn, the famous German ex-Chief of Staff, ex-Minister of War, and conqueror of Romania. This gentleman arrived yesterday and will leave tomorrow morning on his way back to Constantinople. As soon as Djemal Pasha saw me [at the party] he told me: 'I was very sorry not to be able to come to your house on your sovereign's day, but I'm inviting myself to come to your house another time to chat a while. Tell me what day I can come.' As is logical, I put myself at His Excellency's disposition, and we agreed on next Wednesday.

I also spoke a long while with Von Falkenhayn, as well as with Von Lossow. The former talked to me about Spain's attitude, told me that it was a delicate question, and that he understood perfectly the difficulties of our situation. He made a few comments about how everything is blamed on the Germans, and then we spoke about inconsequential things with Djemal Pasha.

The general fixed a date with me for Tuesday, at the Mount of Olives, where he wanted to ask me to refute the news about attempts against the sanctuaries, killings, etc. that were going around abroad. He had also received a telegram from Ramla, which I suppose referred to the case of the photographs of the king and queen. I promised to bring him a note about it all on Tuesday.

Continuing the jokes with which he always teased Raphaël - that he would hang him across from the Holy Sepulcher if his country entered the war - he told us: 'Before long I'll have to hang Ballobar instead of you. Fortunately, Romanones is no longer the Prime Minister.' So if it's true what the general and my Greek colleague have told me, the matter was touch and go... and it is still not settled. The Greek told me that he has heard an important person (I suppose Djemal Pasha) affirming that they are really afraid that Spain will enter the war. So, I decided to begin certain measures for departure and to take some precautions with the records. And the strange thing is that I'm beginning to feel a certain affection for Turkey.

In saying goodbye to Von Falkenhayn, I said to him: 'Good evening.' The general looked at me and said, 'Until we meet again... without war.' I hope so. Shining at the general's collar was the Order of Merit, as well as the splendid Iftihar medallion [Order of Glory], the Iron Cross and the Turkish Crescent.

This coming week promises to be very lively: Tomorrow I'm having lunch at my place with Kraus and Captain Moro; the day after tomorrow an excursion by car to Artas and lunch in the convent garden; Tuesday, a visit to the Mount of Olives and a meal with Ziemke and Wednesday, poker with the general and the Minister of the Navy attending; the following Sunday, a party for the king of Greece and poker at my Greek colleague's house.

1 June, 1917

As I already said, the General called us colleagues to say that the news agency, Havas, had published some information according to which the Turks had decided on the destruction of the religious establishments, had committed slaughters of Christians and Jews and, in short, poor Palestine was devastated by its current possessors. Much of the 'beast' you have to take out, but a 'little bit' of all of it... except the part about the killings. Djemal Pasha wanted each one of us to make a report to our respective leaders to refute these rumors. I plan to do mine, except for a few little provisos.

With the conference finished we went to have coffee with Captain Moro, and, in a little while, an officer came to tell me that His Excellency wanted to see me again and... to my surprise, Djemal began by telling me that he had received a telegram related to the robbery committed in 'the Spanish convent of Ramla.' He, who had never wanted to hear talk of this being 'Spanish'! But my surprise increased when he told me that he wanted me to personally go to the convent by automobile, with one of the officers of the Headquarters, to verify what happened and what stolen property could be vouched for. So this morning at 7:00 I went to Ramla with an officer and my *dragoman*, in an elegant Rolls Royce that runs wonderfully, taken from the British by the Turks. We concluded the official dossier, and, from there, we went to the convent of al-Atrun, which we visited, and I even reviewed the students. The unfortunate Trappist convent is an Ottoman farm school. The church has been transformed by the Turks into a student dormitory, and one of the professors who was accompanying me had the nerve to tell me that, 'after the war, God and the Virgin will occupy the church again.' This is a very interesting fact that is worth the effort to write down, and which I will point out in the report to my government that Djemal Pasha asked for, and to which I alluded before.

We drank some good wine from the farm, and, when we left, the teachers gave me an excellent cheese from the ones the friars made. A small detail: The students were dressed in a cloth so heavy for the heat that they inspired pity in me. The teacher told me, 'What do you want us to do? They are their winter outfits. We asked for summer ones long ago, but you know the difficulties there are for everything in this country, so who knows when they will get them…' The patriotism of this professor is a common matter there.

Another detail: One Murad Bey, chief of a battalion that occupied al-Atrun more than a year ago, sold a gold chalice from the convent to a Jew of Artuf for 600 Francs. And if, reader, you say I lie, I'm just telling what they told me.[19]

According to some, Nogales Bey has been taken prisoner by the British, and according to others he has gone over to the enemy.

During my stay in Ramla I visited the dining room (the former refectory of the friars), the bar – which is no more than the convent wine cellar - the photography workshop and the press that occupies the spot that was inhabited by the Sisters of St. Joseph. They showed me a cart transformed into a magnificent dark room, with electric light, as much water as wanted, filing cabinets, gadgets to dry the proofs: In short, the work that transforms everything here. In the press they were making a copy of a map done by the British, according to notes taken while attacking Gaza and which will be reprinted for the Germans. They also showed me a film map, taken from a plane by an observer provided with a movie camera. Clearly topographical mapping will be very simple in the future.

6 June, 1917

Enormous work with the Spanish, French, English, Russian, American and Romanian book-keeping. My health, thank God, is sufficiently robust to bear not only the arduous work of representing so many countries, but also to put up with meals with the Germans, and that's saying something! The last meal of this type was last night in the Benedictine convent of the Mount of Olives, in the current headquarters of a column of drivers. (…)

New Austrian 104 mm. howitzers have arrived that shoot 15, even 17 kilometers. Some German cannons have also arrived, or will arrive. We don't know anything more about the war in this area.

Sunday, the 3rd of this month, was the birthday of the king of Greece. I promised Raphaël I would be back from my excursion to the east of Jordan with Austrian and German military men by that day, and I kept my word. The road to Jericho was completely destroyed by the trucks. The heat on that plain, at 400 meters below sea level and in this season, was really getting oppressive, so much so that when we got to the shore of the river, the thermometer was registering 61°C in the sun. (…)

We crossed the plain and went up to al-Salt, along the Wadi Nimrin, narrow at its mouth, but it widens out among the mountains covered with thorny bushes and mallow in bloom. (…) The highway, built during the war, is good, although in some places it is dangerous because of very fast turns next to a real precipice. The air and the sun toasted us more than you would think, and we could hardly breathe.

We passed a provisional wooden bridge that has been constructed, in hopes that the completion of a better one will permit the crossing of the upper course of the Nimrin. The air was a little fresher now, the sun didn't bother us so much and, finally, we stopped in the shade of some magnificent fig trees very near al-Salt to have breakfast. (…)

We did not stop in al-Salt, but we did admire the mountainsides, well cultivated and covered with grapevines from which they get raisins, famous in all Palestine. At 10:00 A.M. we were going through a *tcherkes* town. To my great surprise I admired the surroundings of the town, which were much better cultivated than the lands nearby. One could see that the people worked hard: The houses were as white as snow, and big; the inhabitants wear with elegance their classic outfit, the *kalpak*, a type of tunic with two daggers crossed in front of the chest. Some of them wore magnificent arms that I would have gladly bought. What a difference between these people and the Arabs sunk in the most frightful misery and filth, blind or nearly so for the most part, apathetic and unkempt to an incredible degree!

A little later we arrived at Amman, where a crowd was waiting to 'admire' us. The chief who was accompanying me gave orders to the military commander, and right away we headed for the Roman circus, rather well preserved and preceded by some columns that form part of the ruins of ancient Philadelphia. (…)

Since the altitude is about 800 meters, the temperature is very bearable. The Roman circus was occupied by Turkish forces, or rather Arabs whom we 'reviewed,' and I say this because the Ottomans took me for a German 'pasha.' Without time for anything more, we came back and stopped in al-

Salt, which is the ancient Gadara that now counts about 25,000 inhabitants. It has a cobblestone street, an extraordinary luxury in this country, and we went up it by car; I said we went up because the village is in an amphitheater, occupying the side of a mountain.

Dr. Rhodes visited a typhus victim with me, and I served as his *dragoman*, translating from English to French and vice versa. As there was an English doctor here before the war, almost all of those Arabs, sedentary Bedouins, spoke English. Among these Arabs there are some extremely wealthy people. One of the most affluent is the sick man that we visited. This wealth did not surprise me, for everywhere you see great fields of wheat, and certainly, the harvest is not so bad, despite the news I had been given in Jerusalem. In other hands, that country would be a paradise.

When we reached the Jordan plain I thought I would be asphyxiated by the searing wind that was blowing from the west. We felt the sun on our necks, in spite of keeping the hood of the car up. I understand very well why the inhabitants of Jericho are so indolent, since with this climate no one can work.

As I said before, we arrived in time to congratulate our Greek colleague and for the customary poker game with him, the German colleague and Djemal Pasha. The country is saved!

10 June, 1917

Yesterday afternoon, Djemal Pasha invited me for a tea with some colleagues and Djamil Bey, Mr. and Mrs. Verber and Mr. Spafford as well, in Gethsemane in honor of Prince Osman Fuad Effendi, son of the crown prince who committed suicide. His Royal Highness is a young cavalry captain who will depart tomorrow to take charge of a squadron on the Gaza front. Unfortunately, he doesn't speak anything other than German, and Djemal Pasha had to act as a Franco-Turkish interpreter.

Djemal Pasha told me that there were rumors about the resignation of Poincaré, but it seems to me that the news cannot be very exact. What is certain, to the contrary, is the probability of a great naval battle that could possibly decide the war. The British and the rest of the allies, according to this version, would be likely to attack the German submarine bases.

11 June, 1917

Oh, surprise! Nogales has not been taken prisoner, nor has he gone over to the British, since yesterday he sent one of his officers, Zacarias Effendi, to pay me a visit on his behalf and tell me that they had made a raid into enemy territory and had gotten to al-'Arish, Magdaba, and close to al-Hafir. They cut the railroad in four or five places, burning the Magdaba installations, cutting a water conduit from the Nile, and various other feats, without having lost more than one man, the cook. Today Nogales has returned and confirmed his lieutenant's story. He commands 500 horsemen, 250 of them regulars and 250 Bedouins, the majority of them *meharistas*.[20] He had tremendous praise for the military capability of Von Kressenstein, to whom Turkey owes a great deal for the rest; I think the general, such a nice man, has been 'Turkified.' His Chief of Staff, [Karl] Mühlmann Bey, is returning to his country and has been replaced by a Turk, 'Ali Fuad Bey. (...)

The French press talked about the speech of the German chancellor who promised Spain help to retake Gibraltar from the British. Such a beautiful thing couldn't be true!

I have made my official visit to the new *mutasarrif*, 'Izzet Bey, a relative of Djemal Pasha. The new authority struck me as a tough bird, with nothing spit and polish about him, but it may be that he will turn out better than his predecessors because, when I sang the praises of Djemal Pasha, he assured us that the latter had recommended to him above all to worry about the population and 'take care of the convents' in which he should commit no abuses. I could not get over my surprise at hearing these assurances which, naturally, were directed especially at me. But will this actually come to pass?

News from the office: I got some today, and it was a groovy, for sure. Arroyo telegraphed me in code, by means of the embassy of Germany, the following: 'Please accept the invitation that the German military authority will make you, to serve as an official observer of the territory in Syria and Palestine...' So I will probably have to make an inspection tour and draw up a rather tricky report because, with it, I will displease the Turks, the Germans or the Jews. And the three of them are terrible enemies. To make all three happy is impossible, but I will tell the truth and fulfill my duty, come what may. I have talked to Brode about the matter, and my colleague assured me that there was, some time ago, a project to send a commission from Europe to clarify this question and that it was Djemal Pasha who proposed it. He did not bring it up again, but it is known that now it has been decided to entrust the mission to a representative of a neutral country and selection has fallen to me, accompanied, perhaps, by other consuls or functionaries. Let's wait for the invitation from the German military authorities, and we'll see what happens then.[21]

12 June, 1917

Brode has telegraphed his government that the idea of which I just spoke seems excellent to him and that they should do it right away.

The Dominican Republic is following the example of Haiti, declaring war on the Germans.

17 June, 1917

Yesterday we had tea at Kuebler's home to celebrate the birthday of the king of Sweden, Gustaf V. Some people told me they believe in the possible entry of Spain into the war, since García Prieto's cabinet has been replaced by Eduardo Dato, and the latter (according to *Le Petit Parisien*) had declared not long ago that he did not agree with the Allies. Moreover, my Greek colleague is preparing his bags now because King Constantine has had to abdicate and has been substituted by his second son, Prince Alexander.

A few days ago I attended a circumcision, a curious ceremony and, above all, painful for the patient. Fortunately, the Jews practice it eight days after the birth, not like the Muslims who operate at the age of 14 or 15 years. The lucky soul this time was son of Mr. Angel, nephew of Farhi, director of the Alliance Israélite. Dr. Wallach cut and right away treated and bandaged the lesion, not without having first absorbed the blood that escaped from the little wound by a procedure that must be very pious and in accordance with all the ancient ceremonies, but which is, simply, disgusting. There were two big chairs covered with Jewish emblems, in which were seated the father of the little tyke and a godfather who was the one who held him in his arms during the entire event. This was preceded and followed by a series of prayers led by the singing voice of the doctor who performs the operation, and the rabbis. Once this was finished they wished 'good luck' to the circumcised child and to his father and 'executor.' During the ceremony it was *de rigueur* to hold in one's hand and smell a little branch of rosemary or some such plant. (…)

26 June, 1917

It is 6:30 A.M. and I have been awakened by two British airplanes that have made a reconnaissance flight over Jerusalem. I woke up to the noise of the defense cannons that were firing against them and the murmuring of the people who were commenting about it all in the middle of the street. Is this just a token appearance, or are the British planning something serious against the city? I hope to God they leave us alone and that they don't advance much more than their current positions for, if not, the Turks are going to give us some trouble.

I have received orders to come to an arrangement directly with the Minister of Sweden, Auschwaerd, about the American affairs. I also correspond with Mr. Van der Does de Willebois, the Minister of Holland for the other protectorates: France, Russia, England, Serbia and Montenegro.

The situation has cleared up, since according to the news from Spain, Mr. Dato has demonstrated that he will follow the policy of the Conservative party.

6 July, 1917 (Friday, the month of Ramadan)

This week I have had events of all sorts, including astronomical. On the 4th, the U.S. national holiday just to clinch it, a numerous group of us, among them the mayor of Tel Aviv, Dizengoff, was having tea in the garden of Mrs. Shaykh Asiri. The invitation was to admire the full moon that converted the rather vulgar garden into a marvelous one, but we were not counting on the hostess, who produced in due form a total eclipse of the moon. I don't believe there is another place in the world where a better one was seen. It began at 10:00 and at 11:00 the clearing was beginning, which lasted a full two hours. (...)

As expected, the Arabs considered the eclipse a sign of evil. The one who shouldn't consider it so is Djemal Pasha. If the following scheme they are telling me is confirmed, he will be named the supreme commander and Minister of War; Enver Pasha will be the Kaiser's adjutant, or ambassador in Berlin. If this materializes, 'Izzet Pasha, the former Minister of War and current chief of the II and III armies, would come here in his place.

On Tuesday, I visited Djemal again, who had called me to remind me about the famous report on the pretended atrocities against the Jews, to which I alluded before. I talked to His Excellency about the church of al-Atrun, and the chapel of the Brothers of the Christian Doctrine which had been transformed into dormitories and conference rooms, to which he answered: 'The Ottoman government, being the current proprietor of these places of worship, can do with them as it pleases. Besides, I myself ordered the al-Atrun part.' I also spoke to him about the bell that they have taken from the Russian cathedral... and the same failure. There's more: The Pasha told me he would convert the cathedral into a library.

Last Sunday I gave a dinner in honor of Prince Osman Fuad. Several friends attended and His Highness ate, sang and danced like a good comrade. Really, a very nice prince.

8 July, 1917

I had forgotten to give more details about the 'visit' of the British. There were eight planes, and the noise that I heard was the bombs exploding above the Mount of Olives. They dropped 50, and only one fell on the sanatorium, causing some damage. There were two horses dead and that was all. The German and Turkish presses have taken it as a pretext to say that the British have bombed Jerusalem, a holy city for Jews, Christians and Muslims. However, this affirmation is absolutely false, because they have bombed the headquarters, which they had a perfect right to do, according to the Turkish and German officials themselves. What's going on is that a military action has been converted into a political one. But the thing is, besides this being such a holy city, the mere act of the Turks having fortified and occupied it as a center of operations would justify their attack, so the ones who have profaned the city are the Turks. And I say this, although I am perfectly neutral.

Raphaël is disposed to leave in view of the breaking of relations with Greece. He has told me that, when he was in the headquarters to say goodbye they received him with an ovation. The Pasha was very friendly and told him that he would travel like a prince, but he did not consent to his going through Tel-Sharin, doubtless for military reasons.

An important detail: Djemal Pasha's adjutant asked Raphaël, 'When is it Spain's turn?'

On the other hand, I know that Djemal Pasha said a while ago, 'If it is written that Turkey must be conquered and divided and crushed; the entire Christian element that is found in my country will fall with us.' As you see, this is a phrase to calm anyone, above all me, the only consul who will probably stay until the end of the war. Foreseeing the possible entry of Spain in the war, I already have a coded message arranged with our Legation in Constantinople, that they will telegraph me saying, 'Excellent news about the health of Zaragoza.'

17 July, 1917

(...) Raphaël has received authorization to depart in no less than a special train that Djemal Pasha is putting at his disposal. A Turkish official will accompany him to the Bulgarian border. With all this, he does not know to whom to turn over the consulate, since his minister left Constantinople without giving him instructions.

Among the services that I have been able to do for the prisoners is that of notifying their families, doing it almost always through the mediation of the Minister of Holland.

Kuebler is in Petah-Tiqwa to clear up the matter of the falsification of documents. Clearly, these bandits abound everywhere.

12 August, 1917

I've made quite a leap from the last notes; it's really true that I had neither time nor inclination to write, nor news to record. But since quite a few days ago I have had a lot to record: An incident with 'Izzet Bey, the new governor, that will demonstrate to anyone who does not know this country how far the diplomacy and hypocrisy of the Turks will go. Look at the proof.

Some time ago, the governor requested that the consulate open a room that was sealed by the American consul in a Turkish military hospital – the ex-convent of the Italian Salesian Fathers – to install patients with dysentery. I sent my *dragoman* Rauf to see what it was about. He took off the seals (which were not American, but rather from the Spanish consulate, the original ones having been replaced by mine before the departure of the Yankee consul), and, seeing that it was the chapel of the Salesians and not just any room as the governor pretended, he returned to forewarn me. I then sent the *konak* to warn the governor what was happening, I had the chapel sealed again by my *cavas* with the permission of the director of the hospital, and I wrote to the governor an official communication telling him that, since it was a chapel, I could not give my consent that it be occupied and that he must keep in mind that it was closed by me. Well, what do you expect? The following day, and without further warning, the military removed the seals, emptied the room and occupied it.

Naturally, I protested vigorously, and I telegraphed the matter to the Legation. Furthermore, I decided to go to Damascus with Axster by car to tell what happened to Djemal Pasha. The 'good' governor refused me the *werko*, or permission, necessary for the trip, telling me that, for military reasons, the permission of Djemal Pasha was necessary, and to assure my 'rest' [not clear] it was indispensable that I await the order. In the meanwhile, he hoped that *My Excellency* would not do anything contrary to propriety and good friendship. Why this last paragraph? Well, because the day before, the Chief of Police had come to see me on behalf of the governor, and I told him that the gentleman was acting in bad faith, and that I preferred that he arrested me in case of my disobedience to his arbitrary measures.

Djemal Pasha ordered him to let me go to Damascus immediately, with which the governor saw himself obliged to send me the *werko*. I answered that it was already too late and that I didn't need to go to Damascus since I had already written to Djemal Pasha complaining about him.

In the whole matter, there were details that justify the affirmation that I have maintained from the beginning. The governor has recognized in front of Kuebler, Sabra Bey (*Mudhir al-Tahrirat* = chief of records and correspondence) and my *dragoman* that he was misinformed. Why, then, doesn't he want to reveal this in writing and end the matter? His Excellency pretends:

    I) That he was not previously given my communication that dealt with my seals until two days after receiving it in the *konak* because Muhammad Effendi had not translated it.

    II) That I, after my *dragoman* removed the seals, returned to put them on again without the knowledge of the authorities… As if, in my house, one could enter without permission and particularly in a hospital!

III) That I wanted to lock the room. This is ridiculous since I have not said a word about this invention.

And very many more details that would make these notes too tedious.

Having decided to finish for once and for all with similar questions, in which it is impossible for me to fight against due to passive resistance and the Oriental character, I decided to go to Constantinople to inform Arroyo of these and other matters. The governor has closed this incident, saying that it dealt with an unimportant matter and that he wanted to be in good official relations especially with me, for which reason he was returning my protests so there would not be any proof in his records of these poor relations that cropped up between the Spanish diplomatic representative and the Ottoman government. So his returning the communications, which in all the countries of the world is considered a breaking of relations, is interpreted by the governor as a demonstration of his desire for a good friendship... that's the way it is in Turkey!

After putting the ball back in our court, a news item in the Ottoman press says, 'In accordance with the declarations of Mr. Dato, Spain will persevere in its neutrality. On the other hand, this is the opinion of people who know the *matters of Spain* very well: Among them let us cite in first place His Excellency, Sezzy Bey, Minister of Turkey in Madrid.' The manner in which the Ottoman government treats us certainly does not correspond to this declaration.[22]

8 November, 1917

A truly sensational day. My German colleague, Erlberg, wrote me that Major General Von Falkenhayn would receive me at midday, and in the same letter my colleague told me to come see him before at the consulate. There, he explained to me that the military situation is rather grave, and the order has been given to evacuate the hospitals. The British, with troops of about 100,000 men, and provided with large caliber artillery and all kinds of materials, are advancing with the intention of occupying Hebron, Jaffa and Jerusalem.[23] The German troops they were hoping for have not arrived yet, and everything makes one presume the occupation of this city. Will Falkenhayn's strategy be able to prevent it?

The German vice consul, Ziemke, talked to me about the measures that I would be able to take. In taking charge of the German interests these will be very few, since the case is very different than the ones up until now, since there will be a military occupation in enemy territory.

At 12:00, Falkenhayn received me. Very friendly and nice, he told me that he remembered me perfectly. After a series of courteous phrases I told him that, since his time was precious and delicate, I was only going to inform him about a few matters. Next step, I explained to him the question of help for the Jews, proposing that a German official be charged with watching over this matter and that he exercises more or less direct control over the unofficial committee that I preside over. The project seemed fine to the general, and then he began to make allusions to the current military situation, saying that it is unpleasant, since the British are attacking seriously. I took advantage of the occasion to talk to him about my future post as the one in charge of the German interests.

These last few days, the news has increased in gravity. The first information I received was by M.B., who managed to escape on foot from al-Dahriyya, losing the majority of his baggage. The enemy (of the Germans, of course) has occupied Beersheba and, they say, Tel al-Shari'a. The last part I do not believe, since in that case the Turks would have had to withdraw more than escape. In any case, this attack seemed to have rather surprised the Turks. Hebron is very much threatened; and there the headquarters of the 7th Army is found, whose Chief of Staff is Von Falkenhausen, together with Von Arnim, my old friend. The other day both of them ate in my house with Hohenhole, who is now with Kress Pasha.

I have visited six British officer prisoners. Their leader is Lieutenant Colonel Newcombe. I gave them cigarettes, money and novels in English, for which they were very grateful. The Turks were very friendly and let me speak freely with the prisoners, permission for which I did not abuse in any way. (…) I also visited 30 Russian prisoners who are working in the station. The chief of the station made them fall in line, and I asked them by means of an interpreter what they wanted. They asked me for tobacco, shoes and blankets. As for the first item, I will pay for it out of my own pocket, because I do not have funds for Russian expenses, and as far as the rest I will telegraph the Office of Prisoners of War in Constantinople for them to send it if possible. These poor people. They eat rather well, since they give them almost a kilo of bread a day, but they need to increase their hot food. I will see if I can get it done.

10 November, 1917

We are in the most ridiculous situation one can imagine. The night before last, they woke me up at 11:30 to tell me that the danger of occupation was imminent, and that the colleagues were preparing to leave for Damascus. This was confirmed to me by Ziemke, whom I found in the morning in the hotel, making preparations, and by Brode, who turned over to me part of his official records. From 7:00 A.M. until 11:30 P.M. yesterday, I didn't stop making trips from the consulate to the offices of my Austrian and German colleagues, who sent me communications entrusting me with the interests of their respective countries.

I had an exchange of impressions with the director of the German Bank of Palestine, which will remain under my immediate direction. After receiving an endless number of business visits, I fell into bed exhausted, after having said goodbye to Brode and Ziemke, who were leaving on a truck around 10:00.

The *manzil*, the civil government and almost all the workshops and military offices and German and Turkish civil ones have been evacuated as quickly as possible. At 2:00 P.M. the governor, 'Izzet Bey, called me to tell me that the situation was very grave, that the British were very near Wadi Sarar, and that Major General Von Falkenhayn had ordered the evacuation of the city by the military and the government functionaries. He also told me that he planned to remain, to guarantee order, until the 7th Army arrived in Jerusalem and that although it was in a good military situation, it had to retreat now that the British occupied Tel al-Shari'a and the rest of the principal positions near the sea. When we left the governor's office we said goodbye to the *Mudhir al-Tahrirat*, Sabri Bey, as well as the director of public instruction, *Mudhir al-Ma'arif*.

The bad news from the governor was confirmed to me by the German consul, who assured me that the army had been completely routed, and had even lost their cannons.

So, it was obvious that it was right to suppose that the British would be there within four or five days. My Austrian colleague confirmed this to me, who told me that he could not save more than the strictly necessary equipment, which made one suppose that the situation was extremely urgent.

In the consulate, I received Mr. Rohrer, the president of the German colony of the Templars, Sister Teodora, the superior of the deaconesses of Oilberg (the Mount of Olives), the prelate Fellinger, the prior of Tantur, Rabbi Horovitz, Dr. Hirschin, Dr. Pascal, Dr. Feigenbaum, Dr. Thon and various others of my new Austro-Hungarian-German protégés.

Change of directions: And now comes the ridiculous situation to which I alluded before. This afternoon, much better news began to arrive from the battlefield. The Austrian batteries, which everyone considered lost, have arrived in perfect order at Wadi Sarar, without more casualties at their positions. Although the matter is always serious, they have hopes that the 20,000 Germans may arrive in time, which I suppose Falkenhayn hopes for like the Second Coming. It is true that this gentleman said, a few days ago to the German consul: 'Give me half the equipment the English have, and I'll win the battle.'

All in all, after having been in charge of both consulates, in which there has been a burning of suspicious papers and even destroying the seal of the consular general of Germany, it is very possible that, within a few days, I will once again return to them their respective interests and will have gone through a situation without precedent in the consulate annals: I will have been in charge of the interests of enemy countries, in an Allied country, while the respective consuls were still in the country.

15 November, 1917

New events. This morning my Austrian and German colleagues have left for Damascus, so I spent all day giving orders regarding the protection of their interests. Moments before Brode's departure, he received a telegram from the ambassador of Germany telling him that the Minister of Spain assured him he had received a telegram that said I would be obliged to leave the Spanish colony. However, this has been a poor interpretation of my (previous) telegram, since I simply said, 'the creditors are pushing me, and I see myself obliged to execute the instructions of letter No. 8 of 1916.' Because there was no possibility of sending coded telegrams, I came up with this trick, since in Spain they vulgarly call the English 'creditors.' The German ambassador was surprised when our minister told him that the English were going to enter Jerusalem, because the censors had very strict orders to prevent this news from becoming known in Constantinople, but the ambassador could not imagine that I had employed this stratagem to communicate the news to our minister.

Axster left me his car, with which I went to the Mount of Olives to talk to Falkenhayn about the question of the mills and engines of Jerusalem, which the Turks wanted to destroy. I explained to the general the situation in which the populace would be left: Tragically, without bread. Right away he picked up the telephone and said to the Turkish authorities, 'Doesn't the military have anything else to do but destroy mills? Do you think the British won't have the wheat they need without these few misbegotten mills?' The order was fulfilled right away, and they took away the dynamite that had been placed in all of them, as well as in the presses, above all in the magnificent one of the Franciscans, a gift of the emperor, Franz Joseph. The phrase that the major general used to direct the hubbub toward the Turks gave me a real shock, since he called their spokesman in German 'a big pig,' which is the greatest insult you can give a Muslim.

20 November, 1917

Much to my sorrow, I have not been able to write the story of these last few days for a real lack of time. The British have now taken control of Ramla, Wadi Sarar and Jaffa. Right now, it looks like they will continue through the Plain of Sharon, with the intention of surrounding Jerusalem while they also attack on the Abu Gosh side. The cannon fire can be heard quite well and is closer every day, assuring us that they are in Bayt Musa and near Saris. Every day various English aviators come to observe the movement of the Turks, but they have never attacked Jerusalem. Today, only one of them dropped a bomb towards Bethlehem, with what result I do not know.

The staff of the 7th Army has been here for several days. Before, it was in Bethlehem, where I went one night to dine with the officers. Prince George of Bavaria was there, the son of Prince Leopold and the cousin of our crown prince, Don Fernando. His Highness wore the uniform of a lieutenant colonel, and the Austrian Golden Fleece on his collar. Arnim, Count Galen, Axster and Falkenhausen also attended the meal. A very happy occasion.

Now that the staff is here, I have made use of it for the extremely delicate question of the order to intern the Patriarchs of all denominations, given by Enver Pasha. As it is a question that will be pretty juicy, I copied in its entirety the dispatch that I am directing to the Political Section [of the Ministry of Foreign Affairs]:[24]

No. 64. Political Section.

Dear Sir,
Because Your Excellency will confer great importance to this matter, it is my honor to inform you in all detail about a very serious question that has been presented to me in the last few days. The governor of this city, 'Izzet Bey, communicated to the Patriarchs of the different denominations that reside in Jerusalem (Catholic, Greek, Orthodox and Armenian), as well as the spiritual leaders of the other religious faiths (the Syrian and Coptic bishops, the great rabbis, etc.), the order that he had received to *invite them* to go to Nazareth and abandon Jerusalem before the British occupy this Holy City. I figured right away that it was dealing with a political measure and not the wish of the Ottoman government to distance them from this city, where they were running no risk due to their religious nature. I immediately began to put into action steps in union with my Austro-Hungarian colleague, steps that seemed to give results: General Von Falkenhayn telegraphed Djemal Pasha; the governor, after a discussion my Austrian colleague and me, communicated that he would not execute by force these instructions regarding the Catholic Patriarch (the only one in which I could interest myself), and finally, it seemed all finished.

But the governor, having called for all the Patriarchs in a meeting, announced to them that they should leave and that he would communicate the order to them in writing, which he did; that order (from Djemal Pasha according to some, and from Enver Pasha according to others) did not say that they should be conducted to Nazareth by force. Our Patriarch, Monsignor Camassei, answered that he was grateful to the government for their solicitude, but being in this city by order of His Holiness the Pope, he could not leave it without his order. It was all useless: The government insisted on its point of view in spite of Monsignor Camassei, having insisted that he would not abandon this city except by force, and in spite of me having directed a communiqué whose copy I attach. On the 19th of this month, the Chief of Police of this city presented himself in the Patriarchate, accompanied by various inspectors and in spite of finding the Patriarch in bed, in a delicate state of health because of the unpleasantness that this matter has occasioned, the police obliged him to get up and to leave via Nablus, in a poor carriage and accompanied by a priest of the Patriarchate and a policeman. In Ramla, the carriage was overtaken by an automobile which Lieutenant Colonel Von Falkenhausen had the kindness to send, and in which he continued on his way.

Up to here, that is what happened, and now I will permit myself to expose to Your Excellency my intervention in the matter and the very bad effect that that incomprehensible measure has produced.

Our Patriarch is the only one who resided in this city that is not an Ottoman functionary. All the rest are Ottomans, and their functions are absolutely and officially known by the Sublime Porte. The Catholic Patriarch does not have any *firman* and is, in addition, an Italian subject, being first and foremost a representative of His Holiness and, as such, of an international character. Even supposing that he were Ottoman, his condition would be the same, outside of matters of nationality. One of the infinite proofs of this is the fact that the consul of Austria accompanied me in the steps I took, despite the Patriarch being from Italy.

The manner in which the representative of His Holiness has been treated is truly iniquitous; he has been interned and lead away by force like a criminal or suspicious person. I understand that, for military reasons, a government can take measures by force, but to intern an elderly man of 70 years, ill and the spiritual leader of all the Catholics without distinction of nationality seems to me an arbitrary measure and without justification. Logically, we think he has been taken to the interior of the country as a hostage. It is up to the government of His Majesty and the rest of the interested governments to judge the question that I expose in the most faithful and exact detail that one may wish. Your Excellency may be certain that the many details I give are absolutely accurate.

The measure of which I speak has given me an extremely bad impression on the German military authorities; I have already made clear that General Von Falkenhayn did what was possible to avoid it, and I say the same of Lieutenant Colonel Von Falkenhausen, the Chief of Staff of the 7th Army, and of Commander Von Arnim, who hurried to let me telegraph His Majesty's Legation in Constantinople about the matter. They themselves telegraphed His Excellency Von Falkenhausen and, in short, expended all means available to prevent this measure from being executed. Seeing that they could not prevent it, they sent their car to Ramla so Monsignor Camassei could make his trip in greater comfort.

The governor, furious with my attitude (which I don't think could be more correct and justified) in the matter, threatened me with employing measures of violence against me, to which I answered what Your Excellency will be able to see in one of the two attached copies of the telegrams that, to express the question, I have remitted to the Minister of His Majesty in Constantinople and from which I have received no response.

Subsequently, the governor has come to make his excuses which, as Your Excellency will understand, I have accepted because I could do nothing else in these critical circumstances, and I am convinced that, at the first possible occasion, he will behave in the same manner with me again, or worse.

I believe that I have correctly interpreted the intentions of His Majesty's government with my conduct in this sad affair, and I must, however, make it clear to Your Excellency that I find myself incommunicado as far as being able to ask for instructions and receive them in time, so in all occasions I see myself obliged to work by myself and on my own authority. May God, etc.

The thefts are beginning to occur more frequently. Yesterday there were Turkish soldiers in the house of Marrum, the Secretary of the German legation, and, breaking down the doors, they carried off whatever they wanted. The same thing has happened at the convent of the Passionists of Bethany and the Benedictine one of the Mount of Olives. The governor has put me in charge of forming a police corps to watch over the homes of the allies and the belligerents, but I fear that such police are not to be trusted. In any case, I am preparing to defend myself in the consulate in case of danger. I am also copying the edict published by the military governor, which will not really calm anyone. Here it is:

Edict of 'Ali Fuad Bey

The city of Jerusalem, which, after thirteen centuries, is the second Muslim religious center and the first Christian religious center, has been preserved up to the present by the Ottoman troops under the protection of the Ottoman Empire. The Ottoman troops will defend themselves to their last breath against the enemy that opposes these Holy Places. We will not stop doing whatever is necessary to defend the empire; may each one of us be faithful to the directions of the Ottoman troops. The victory is God's.

I recommend to the populace of Jerusalem, without distinction of nationality or religion that they abide by the following articles:

1. Whoever believes they will be affected by the lack of supplies or by the combat should depart immediately for the places designated by the government.
2. If it is necessary, to preserve the city, I will ration the food supplies as well as other products.
3. I ask the population to maintain extraordinary calm and order.
4. Every person who does not carry a permit (*werko*) from the city commander is forbidden to leave home during the evening hours.
5. Those who do not abide by my orders will be promptly brought before the martial court, which will impose legal sanctions against them.

My dear compatriots: As long as you are faithful to our country and obey the orders given, you must recognize me as the first commander who will defend your rights. But those who behave in a contrary manner should know that they will be punished according to the formal and urgent orders given by the leadership, which has maintained its military dignity and its honor in many battles.

Jerusalem, November 18, 1917. Commander General of Jerusalem and its surroundings and of the 20th Army Corps. Colonel 'Ali Fuad.

The Patriarch, Camassei, granted me, before leaving, the Commendation of the Holy Sepulcher. In announcing it to me, he said, 'It is the custom ordained by the Holy Father to grant this honor to the consuls of the Catholic powers when they leave Jerusalem, but this time I want to interpret the will of His Holiness conferring it to you now.' Naturally, I have received many visits of congratulations.

The Custody, for his part, has sent me two communications that I copy also, one of which he said that thanks to me the Franciscans have been able to continue in the Holy Land. He referred especially to the fact that I managed to save the principal convent of the Custody, as I said before:

Communication of the Custody of the Holy Land[25]

Protocol, Jerusalem. November 15, 1917

Dear Consul,

I have the honor of acknowledging the receipt of your letter announcing the result of your steps before General Von Falkenhayn in favor of our mill and diesel motor. I hope that the General's order will be executed and respected by the Ottoman authorities and that we can thus continue lending aid to the poor Christian population of Jerusalem.

We offer our heartfelt thanks for this favor that you have allowed us to obtain, as well as so many other services that you do not stop offering in these sad circumstances and that the Custody of the Holy Land will never be able to forget.

Protocol, Jerusalem, November 20, 1917

We are pleased to announce to you that the civil governor has come in person to give us the good news that the Franciscan fathers, being for the most part pacific men, will not be bothered and will be able to stay peacefully. He has added that the Supreme Pontiff will probably have defended our cause before the Sublime Porte, given that the latter is doing us this favor. Be that as it may, we are more than ever convinced that it is thanks to your powerful mediation and your sincere devotion to the Catholic cause – what was in play here – which are the reasons for which we can remain in this place of honor that we have occupied for seven centuries.

Yes, dear Consul, we acknowledge that it is to you alone, after God, to whom we are grateful for this unexpected favor, and although we lack the words to express our gratitude, we nonetheless hope that time will permit us to prove it to you with deeds. Meanwhile we have the duty to offer you, in the name of all the Custody, sincere recognition, our greatest gratitude and the security of a religious devotion for which I have the honor of being, dear Consul, your obedient servant.

Signed, Father Castellani, Custodial President.

Didn't I say it was an historic letter?

21 November, 1917

The cannon fire has continued all day, ceasing as it got dark. Without a doubt, the British are getting closer and closer. The Turks have blown up the rolling stock from the railroad station. I hope to God they don't blow up the mills or the military establishments! I am very much afraid of this because I know the Turks.

Arnim came to say goodbye. He promised to send me a radiogram if what I was trying to the best of my ability to do was accomplished: Principally, that they not force the Patriarchs out of Jerusalem. I told him that I needed to know the truth of the military situation, to which he answered that the arrival of the British was a matter of three days.

I have gotten the Germans fit for military service, to be trained to become military police in case of necessity.

Airplanes dropped three bombs on the road from Bethlehem. I knew that from a nun who was going in a truck; when the driver saw the planes, he ordered the travelers to get out and hide themselves on the ground.

22 November, 1917 (2:30 P.M.)

I have installed myself in the American consulate to avoid its being sacked in my absence. Around noon, I witnessed a battle between a German airplane and two British ones, which took place just above the consulate. The German defended himself fiercely with his machinegun. Seeing that he could not sustain the battle, he descended at full speed towards the north in a majestic flight, which I contemplated with admiration since they were scarcely 200 meters over our heads. I had our flag hoisted above the terrace roof just in case, and, furthermore, I communicated to the governor that, in view of the notices and of the agreement that we had about the protection of the city, I was going to leave the flag raised.

They have given me some bad news: One of the Spanish Benedictines from Abu Gosh has been seriously wounded, or perhaps killed. A missile took both of his legs. I hope that this news is not confirmed. [*It later turned out to be a Trappist brother.*]

8:30 P.M. At 6:00 in the afternoon the governor came to see me, accompanied by my *dragoman*. At first I thought it would be to say goodbye to me, but I had several disappointments: In the first place, because he came to give me excuses for his rude behavior the other day, and in the second place because the British... have been pushed back. Rauf has gone with the governor to the front and has visited the Turkish positions; he said that the 53rd division, stationed to the north of the road from St. John ['Ayn Karim] with three batteries, many infantry forces and 2000 horsemen was in full engagement. The English do not have big cannons, only field or mountain guns with lots of machineguns; although they had managed to take control of Mons Gaudi [Mount of Joy] and to fortify the mosque of Nabi Samwil, they have been forced to withdraw by the concentrated fire of the Turkish batteries.

In any case, this cannot go on, and we can even be a little upset because one of the Turkish batteries is at the bifurcation of the Jaffa highway and the road from St. John. To destroy it, the English will have to destroy several houses in that neighborhood.

Let's go to bed, and we will wait to see what the next day will present us. But I don't know if I'll be able to sleep with the memory of the conversation that I had with the governor, who, no doubt, wanted to make me happy and is therefore going to severely punish the thieves of Siloe who robbed the convents to which I alluded. One of them will be hanged in Bethany, another in the Mount of Olives and the third... he wanted to hang him at the door of the consulate, but naturally I have not consented. I feel bad for what happened, but I understand that there has to be an exemplary punishment. [*Fortunately, I found out later that the president of the military tribunal refused to hang them because, since the Germans who were occupying the convent had left the doors open, 'there was no violence.' If I had known that, I would have slept more peacefully.*]

The governor has also had all the wheat that they had requisitioned returned to the German hospitals. He told me that, after the scene that had taken place with me, he had wept with sorrow. It could be that the proximity of the British may be the motive of this great kindness.

23 November, 1917

I have attended an interesting show: Two British airplanes have been violently attacked with gunfire from artillery, machineguns and rockets. A firing machinegun was situated next to the consulate, and since one of the planes was located almost on top I feared that a bomb would fall on us. Fortunately, the British seem determined not to touch Jerusalem, and scorn these attacks.

At 10:00 I went to the terrace of St. Peter of Ratisbonne to see the battle. I was there almost an hour contemplating the attacks and counterattacks, whose object was the mosque of Nabi Samwil. One could clearly see the encounters between the infantry of both sides. The English were not firing artillery, perhaps so as to not do so towards Jerusalem.

By cards received here from Sarona and Jaffa, I know that the British have behaved well towards the German colony, naming an administrator in Willhelma to take charge of that colony.

24 November, 1917

In the morning, several airplanes flew at a great altitude. Little or no shelling. At 1:00 P.M. cannon fire began again and rather heavy machinegun fire. From Ratisbonne one could see a Turkish battery that was firing from the St. John road; I suppose against the heights of the colony. Various battles took place in Nabi Samwil, which, if I am not mistaken, was bombarded by British artillery. At this time (5:00 P.M.) one hears nothing. One would say that the Holy City is as calm as always.

I have received a very odd telegram from Falkenhayn, directed to Brode, in which he communicates to him that he has been able to arrange that the expulsion of the Spanish consul is not to take place. I telegraphed him, asking if this is about me or is a mistake; actually, he was referring to the Patriarchate. With all this I sent my *dragoman* to see the governor, who swore and declared that he had not written anything against me, and the ones with whom he was furious were my German and Austrian colleagues. I know him too well to fall for that! He told Rauf that I have only done a few 'childish things,' like sending letters by means of the German officials, letters that are detained here and in Constantinople. What the good governor does not know is that my boss in Constantinople has found out about the British advance (which he was forbidden to know) by a camouflaged telegram of mine. Another 'childish' thing.

(...) It seems that they had promised the British soldiers to take Jerusalem by the 22nd, but now it is the 24th, and it still has not been accomplished. Nonetheless it seems the British are employing their artillery: If you think not, tell it to Dr. Wallach, whose hospital has been hit by a shell that has caused quite a bit of damage, although it appears there have been no victims.

I have written a long letter to the Major General Von Falkenhayn about the departure of the bishop, Monsignor Piccardo, and of members of the Patriarchate, indicating to him the conflicts that may develop in the Holy Sepulcher and in Bethlehem by Christmas if there is no prelate. I hope there are some results.

27 November, 1917

A second change of scenery. I find out that the Chief of Staff of a British division has been taken prisoner by the Turks, who have caused, up until now, about 4,000 casualties among the British. Upon confirming this news, the governor invited me to go for a ride by car along the 'front.' The excursion was reduced to a visit to the hospital and a ride up to the entrance of the road from St. John. In the hospital I managed to see that the mentioned shell had destroyed the top floor of the wing for contagious diseases. According to the governor [the damage] was produced by a 15 cm. British shell proceeding from al-Qastil, while according to a German officer friend of mine it was a Turkish cannon that fired on an airplane. Who to believe?

In the afternoon I visited Falkenhausen and Arnim. Neither they nor I hoped to meet each other again so soon. The minaret of the mosque of Nabi Samwil finally fell under the fire of the Turkish artillery. A British shell killed poor Ayyub, Hanna's brother.

Mustafa Bey decided to leave the consulate, as did the American, who was at home.

A splendid day: Least of all for killing oneself stupidly as almost all humanity is doing. With the binoculars, I have seen in detail a British balloon that day and night continues its observation duty.

30 November, 1917

Little or no cannon shelling. The earth must have swallowed the British! The observation balloon has been destroyed, according to the governor, by a German airplane. A couple of days ago it looked like the Turks took a real pounding in an attack across from Nabi Samwil. The British pretended to flee before the Turkish push, and three battalions that hurried to pursue them were annihilated by the English, who suddenly turned up attacking them with hand grenades: Those English were hidden in the many caves that are in the mountain. On the other hand, on the plain, the offensive of the 8th Army commanded by Djemal Pasha was a success. The Turks are southwest of Petah-Tiqwa.

We find ourselves in a complete mania of anti-Semite persecution, since the governor does nothing but arrest right and left all the Jewish notables: Dr. Thon, the leader of the Zionists, Astroc, director of the Rothschild hospital, Dr. Ticho, *Farhi* of the Israeli Alliance, Barouchan and Dr. Schatz of Bezalel, also the *dragoman* of the Franciscans and other notable Christians and even a Muslim from Jaffa. For this matter I went to the hospice of St. Paul to interview Major Schrecker, who transmitted my reports to General Falkenhayn. The general answered right away, giving me repeated thanks for my efforts on behalf of the Germans and Austrians, announcing that he telegraphed the Count of Bernstorff [German ambassador in Istanbul] directly so he would immediately send a consulate official from his country and another Austrian to Jerusalem, at my orders, at least until the British arrive.

I have freed Dr. Ticho from prison and arranged that the 35 Americans detained may go to Damascus by automobile instead of on foot. Bravo for Major Schrencker who granted it to me!

From this evening I have electric light in the consulate, coming from the engine of the drivers, my neighbors. The Baron Von Perfall has graciously granted it to me, and I hope to inaugurate it solemnly with a meal to celebrate my 32nd birthday, a meal to which only the baron and the major will attend, unless Axster decides to come from Nablus by car. I wish myself a good party.

1 December, 1917

The day of my birthday has begun very well. I have managed to see to it that the American Jews won't leave today (the Sabbath), and Mr. Astruc, Hoofien, Thon and Myouhas have been freed under my guarantee. But the most sensational news is that negotiations for peace with Russia have begun.[26] I have received visits from the Württemberg colony to thank me for some measures on their behalf.

2 December, 1917

I have received a telegram from Major General Von Falkenhayn. In it, he said that Jerusalem is a city attacked by the enemy, because of which the authorities have the right to take the measures they consider necessary, including the expulsion of the inhabitants without any distinction, which is the legal point of view, and if there is some hardship it is inevitable: Unfortunately, we find ourselves in times of war. He also said that they have no right to get involved with the measures of the interior political order that the Ottoman government may take, unless it deals with violations of rights. Nonetheless he tries to sweeten the measures referred to, and proof of this is that I can continue in Jerusalem. So, as far as I can tell, I do not have to intervene in any matter, which enormously simplifies my work. But the consequences of such an attitude from Turkey are not [clear?]. After the war we'll talk.

The governor is furious with me, as he has heard an earful from the Minister of the Interior, because of the crudeness with which he treated me when the Patriarch was expelled; the hubbub comes from a complaint from the Spanish Legation about this matter. My telegram has some teeth to it. See for yourself:

Urgent. Minister of Spain. Constantinople

Having sent a letter yesterday to the governor of Jerusalem asking very courteously that he does not make the Catholic Patriarch leave, this morning I went to solicit the governor that he postpone the departure until Your Excellency's reception. The governor, without allowing me time to direct a word to him, shouted at me that I should not meddle in the affairs of the government, threatening to take violent measures against me. I responded to him, 'I forbid you to speak to me in this manner, because if you represent your government, I represent mine.' After that violent scene which took place in front of German and Turkish officials in the German hotel, I went to say farewell to the Patriarch, and the governor forbade me to enter the Patriarchate. Stop. Under these conditions, and since my authority is not respected at all and my person threatened, I decline all responsibility concerning the Austro-German interests and others in my charge, and I await instructions from Your Excellency. Stop. Patriarch has left by force, taken by the Turkish police.[27]

4 December, 1917

To avenge himself for the hubbub caused by me, the governor decided just yesterday to send to Damascus the nine Jews whose provisional liberty I had asked him for, under my guarantee. The principal ones were Dr. Schatz, from Bezalel, Farhi of the Alliance and Grazosky of the German Bank of Palestine. This vengeance on innocents is worthy of the one who has executed it.

I received some good news from Arnim. The German vice consul, Ziemke, is returning to Jerusalem with two more civil servants, just as I had asked of General Falkenhayn. It seems that it has been decided to leave Mr. Astruc, the director of the Rothschild hospital here. Until Ziemke returns I do not believe Dr. Thon and Hoffien will leave.[28]

Other news of the war: Yesterday afternoon the cannons of the 'Moscowieh' fired ten more shots towards an airplane that calmly continued its observations without seeming to care a fig for the gun fire. Let's hope they don't get tired of putting up with these provocations! This morning, rather lively fire. In the afternoon too and it seems from large caliber guns. According to the Germans, the military situation is pretty good. They have occupied the Runtis plain and the Bayt Tabal mountains for a few days now.[29]

5 December, 1917

I am writing these lines at 9:00 P.M., in the middle of a fierce shelling that began half an hour ago. According to the Germans, the situation continues to be fairly good, and the Turks can count on new large caliber guns (15 cm.) But we civilians are ignorant of everything, even where the invaders are. The Turkish officials are rather more pessimistic and, according to them, they are on their last gasps, whatever they do being useless to resist.

The evacuation of the colony has been followed by that of St. John, which took place yesterday. The Franciscans came to me saying they had been given only an hour and a half of preparation time to leave the convent. I don't know if that measure obeys the military necessities or vengeance against the people of St. John, who have gone with the British in great numbers. To me it seems it must be the former, because the shelling of this evening is in that direction, and one can hear the whistling of the missiles amazingly well.

They assured me that, the day before yesterday, three British armored cars arrived which fired at a cavalry force they met along the road. It seems rather audacious to me.

Falkenhausen and Arnim came today. They are leaving tomorrow for Jericho and Amman, but they have promised to dine with me tomorrow. Arnim says that Ziemke will come tomorrow or the day after. Amen.

Today, Rauf convinced the governor to allow the four Jews in whom I took personal interest to stay here until Sunday. In the meanwhile I hope they will be safe. They have also detained Dr. Feigenbaum. I have given his wife a certificate making me her husband's guarantor, but I don't think it will really happen.

A German officer has told me that the 8th Army keeps on making progress. Petah-Tiqwa has been reoccupied. The Turks and the Germans are counting on occupying Jaffa, with the help of seven submarines that will not leave the Entente fleet in peace.

Almost unbelievable news: The great Rabbis of Jerusalem and Jaffa have returned. It seems that they saw Djemal Pasha, who told them, 'Do you want to go back to Jerusalem?' Naturally, their reply was affirmative, and here they are. But the Christian patriarchs have not yet come back. Decidedly, Turkish politics is beyond my poor intelligence, and I do not understand it at all.

8 December, 1917 (the Day of the Immaculate Conception)
If I'm still alive in a few days, a thing I do not know, I will be able to tell many a very curious tales.

It's six in the afternoon, and I doubt very much that I'll be able to eat peacefully and, above all, sleep tonight. Oh, really it's nothing at all that's going on now! I'll make a bit of history, which this time can be said to be the real thing. This morning at 2:30, cannon fire began, which very quickly became generalized, and which was joined by fire from machineguns and even rifles. Because of yesterday's rain there was a lot of fog during the night, and when I got up around 7:00, there was still fog, but the battle continued across the board. Captain Von Perfall told me that two attacks which took place during the night had been repulsed and that the military situation was fairly good. But every moment, more and more wounded were going by the consulate and the fire continued to be lively, so I was not very sure about what the military people were telling me.

The poor Turkish soldiers! The injured men that were passing by in front of my house were on foot, holding their wounds with their hands, full of blood, haggard. An officer came by on horseback with his arm bandaged and his body sustained by three soldiers on foot. The officer's face expressed the most horrible suffering. He, just as the soldiers and the wounded, went with his head down and looking sad, very sad. (…)

At 9:00 A.M. the fire had ceased in the part where I live and the enemy had been pushed back. Nonetheless, on the Lydda side, towards the [German] Colony, it continued in great intensity. I went to the German consulate, were Ziemke and Kuebler were planning their departure.

I then returned home, where my colleagues Kraus and Ermont came to eat lunch with me. A little later Perfall came and made my jaw drop with the following news: 'The 20th Army Corps will still defend the outskirts of this city this afternoon and will withdraw this evening, leaving only three regiments who will take the Jericho road.' I hurried to the Austrian hospice to advise Kraus to get away in all haste before he is taken prisoner. Not believing the matter to be very urgent, I was ready to take a walk around the municipal hospital, when I ran into the police inspector, 'Arif Bey, who advised me not to go 'because the missiles were falling in that direction.'

The advice seemed very sound to me, and I went back to the consulate, witnessing scenes of panic that cannot be described: Officers were running their horses at a gallop, soldiers as fast as their legs would carry them, women and children crying out loud. We asked (my servant Yusef was with me) what was happening, and they answered us that the British were already in the municipal hospital. Despite the not small dose of fear that ran through my body, I calmly continued my way towards the consulate, where I arrived without any novelty.

Kuebler has gone to the German colony to look for Ziemke and made him leave. When my vice consul returned with the former, he told me that in the colony, various missiles had exploded and that a German was seriously wounded. The fire has stopped, and one only hears (7:50 P.M.) an occasional gun shot.

Well, Lord, up until now I am still alive, but what is happening in the city? Have the British occupied it? Have they withdrawn? I tremble at the fate that may have befallen Ziemke and Kraus, who have no doubt left under enemy fire. I see it in the fact that the car in which Drs. Rhodes and

Bleiche came (which they stopped for five minutes, to have a cognac with me) has taken a machinegun fragment in the engine. So the road is not at all safe.

But, Lord, why is there no more than one cannon shot every five or ten minutes? It is a regularity that surprises me. Even if they were just maneuvers. And I very much doubt I can know before tomorrow… unless a missile gives me a solution that I don't at all want, frankly.

It's still the Day of the Immaculate Conception. At 8:30 P.M.

Everything is quiet, except the cannon shots fired at regular intervals to which I alluded before. I have gone up to the terrace of the consulate and, from there, I have seen and admired the sleeping city (it is not a bad dream I am having), some lights in houses, the splendor of a bonfire in Ratisbonne, the starry sky, not a breath of air, nor another sound but the barking of stray dogs.

I am beginning to believe that all this is an hallucination and that I have dreamed the bombardment, the panic in the streets, etc. But no, it isn't panic, I mean a dream that I had. I am almost convinced that the British have not entered the city, at least in all of it. If that were so, from where do they justify the famous cannon shots I spoke of before and that seem to be fired from the city towards the St. John road? After the detonation of the cannon fire, one always hears the explosion; so if my supposition is exact, the enemy is not far away, and I suppose that tomorrow we will have a terrible battle in the streets, unless the whole army leaves. The Turks have tried to blow up the mills: The order did not exist; doubtless they were trying to stir up a commotion, but they did not get what they wanted.

At this moment (8:50) I hear a car stopping in the parking area (Rosary convent). Another reason that confirms my belief that the Turks are still the owners of the city.

I wonder what has become of Hoofien and company. 'Arif Bey came this afternoon to ask me to turn in the Jews I have hidden in the consulate to the governor. I answered him that, since my promise is until tomorrow, I will not turn them in until that date. Hmmm, it seems to me that they should depart tomorrow.[30] [*When 'Arif knocked at the door, I signaled my protégés to hide behind a folding screen that was in my office, and since they heard my conversation with the policeman they began to tremble thinking, that on the following day, I would turn them in to the governor, but they were unaware that I knew the Turks would evacuate the city that night.*][31]

Oh, I forgot. This afternoon I saw the line cut that brings electric light to my house. Hadjdj 'Umar saw the driver of the automobile that just arrived, and it seems to him that it was for the Austrian consul. The latter will depart this evening. According to a *shawish al-qanun*, whom my *cavas* has questioned, the British are in Ratisbonne (the bonfire I saw?) and are surrounding the city on all side to attack it tomorrow morning. Let's hope there is no resistance and that it may be a pacific occupation. Amen.

I fear the police may detain the famous Zionists tonight. I am falling asleep because of the emotions of today. So I decided to take a horizontal position. At what time will the noise of the machineguns begin again? Yusuf came to tell me that Hadj has misunderstood and that Kraus left some time ago. May God keep him safe. I'm going peacefully to bed. Good night.

9 December, 1917, 8:00 P.M.

A date forever famous in history. We say in Spain that with a new year there is a new life, but this time I would have to say 'Dec. 9, 1917... New life.' But let's go a little at a time.

[*After I went to bed*], around 11:00 last night, the cannon shots began again in answer to the fire of British machineguns that were next to Ratisbonne, rather near my house. (...) I got up thinking that some rocket was going to fall on the consulate, but there was nothing of that sort, and I went back to bed peacefully, sleeping very well (it could be that I was the only one in Jerusalem who did so). I woke up around 7:00 A.M. to the weeping and shouting of the women and families of the Americans who, numbering about 35, were expelled on foot yesterday by 'Izzet Bey. The black man from the Fast Hotel brought me the news that the mayor, Husayn Salim al-Husayni, had left early in the morning towards the British lines on horseback and with a white flag, sign of the surrender of the city. This news was confirmed to me by Kuebler, with the natural rejoicing of my Jewish protégés (my four friends are saved).[32]

I went to the Fast Hotel where Mr. Rohrer was waiting for me with the entire German colony of the Templars. They were there by order of Ziemke, to avoid being the victims of the bombing of their colony (only two houses were destroyed). (N.B. That bombing, for the most part insignificant, was more than justified by the German soldiers, having filled the colony with machineguns without the consent of the inhabitants.) I calmed them down, promising to bring them news of the attitude of the British.

I went for a walk along Jaffa road, taking advantage of the splendid morning. The instincts of the inhabitants of Jerusalem were palpably shown. Everything that was capable of being stolen was disappearing into the hands of thieves of every caste, religion and nationality that was swarming around there. Telegraph wire, half-destroyed cars, wood, old cans, etc. The scene was not very uplifting. From one of the balconies of the Hotel Kaminitz I saw an armoire being lowered down by ropes. And the Turkish police were watching all this without turning a hair.

A little before the Wallach hospital I ran into the first British soldier, a cavalry man who asked us to inform him where he could water his horse. At the door of the hospital there was a British soldier with a fixed bayonet and two Turkish policemen, or rather Arabs, since the Turks had all left. They told me that the English were inside the hospital, and I entered. In the salon there was a colonel, whose name I do not remember, an officer lightly wounded in the hand, the mayor, Dr. Wallach, Mr. Mani and the engineer, Guini, from Jaffa. After the required introductions, the English colonel began to direct at me the questions of Cain, for example: When was Falkenhayn here, how many German soldiers were there, at what time did the Turks leave last night, etc. I answered him that I didn't know a single thing about any military news. That reply, I think, would teach him a lesson. I then asked him to take care of organizing British police for the city before all else, which he did immediately, because I know that, in the [British] colony, there were some and they provided excellent service.

A short while later General Watson came. Naturally, since he was very busy, I said goodbye before long, dedicating myself to strolling throughout the day to observe the effect of the arrival of the British on the population. And here one can apply all the wildly enthusiastic phrases that the newspapers utilize on grand occasions. Really, I have never seen a popular enthusiasm so spontaneous and great. Every British soldier that passed by was followed and escorted by a throng of admirers that touched his uniform, caressed his horse, talked to him in all the languages of the Orient and admired him like a hero. In this admiration were men and women, small and large, Christians and Jews. Through the streets there circled an enormous multitude, overwhelmed by a limitless satisfaction and understandable and excusable enthusiasm, because it is impossible to imagine a government more detested and detestable than the Turkish. In all the physiognomies one read the same emotions: 'The hour of freedom has arrived, a heavy weight has been lifted from our heart, at last one can breathe, life begins again for us, now one can go to bed without wondering if the next day he will be expelled, arrested or robbed.' I hope that these same sentiments have not been read in my face, since I have too much devotion to my role as a neutral, and I must hide all my happiness.

The balconies were full of people. Many people were hugging each other in the street, others were mutually congratulating each other and all were walking around in their best clothes, smiling at the English and greeting them as beloved liberators. I saw a portion of people who had hidden themselves recently to free themselves from the Turks, among them some who had been hidden for months and years. One of the disappeared was the British *dragoman*, who presented himself to me today and left right away to serve his friends. But I observe that I am getting too mundane in my revelations, and I'll go back to my serious and concise terms.

Two battalions of Scots infantry paraded by, very well equipped, some sections of cavalry and columns of supplies and munitions. All the soldiers I have seen are English, and not Indians or from other countries. With respect to my protégés, up to now the occupiers have behaved very well with the Germans, and proof of it is that, in the hospital of the Deaconesses, a military doctor presented himself and asked the Mother Superior very courteously: 'Is this hospital for civilians? Could you accept our wounded soldiers?' Naturally the Superior answered affirmatively.[33]

Up to now they are permitting the German school, which is from the German government and directed by the *Propst* [Prior/Provost], Jeremiah, to continue functioning. If they keep on like this, my work of protection will be greatly simplified.

This morning I witnessed an aerial combat: During the whole day various British planes have flown over the city. The shelling continued towards Shafat but now has stopped. Goodbye, hated Turks.

The British soldiers either really are very friendly or have received orders to be so. Upon withdrawing this evening to the consulate, I met a squadron of cavalry; I didn't see a thing because the night was so dark, but all the soldiers said good night to me as I passed by. The police inspector, 'Abd al-Qadir, as well as 'Ali Effendi have been imprisoned. They told me that when the French clerics departed two years ago, the former pulled one of them by the beard, and the cleric told him that he would remember him. If this is true one could apply to the police, 'He who lives by the sword, dies by the sword.' In any case, whether or not the incident is true, I remember very well that 'Abd al-Qadir was brutal with those who were leaving.

I thought a lot during this day about what the situation of my colleagues must be on the road to Damascus, but above all, I am extraordinarily grieved by the unfortunate death of Monsignor Piccardo, auxiliary bishop of Jerusalem. Without any doubt, it has occurred because of the trip the Turks forced him to make, without taking into account his delicate state of health.

I forgot to say that, in the taking of the *fortress* of Jerusalem, there have been no more than three wounded civilians, one of them a German for whom they will have to amputate an arm. The poor man is 65 years old and has remained very much on my mind because of the visit I made to him in the hospital.

10 December, 1917

The enthusiasm of the people seems to me to be still on the increase. Never, except for the arrival of Enver Pasha, have I seen so many people in the street. I followed the crowd, going where the people go, so I dedicated nearly the whole afternoon to strolling and seeing the English, Indian soldiers (now a few have arrived), policemen, Turkish prisoners, Ottoman ex-soldiers, etc. The German consulate has been occupied for the headquarters of the 53rd Division. The Russian establishment appears to be crowned with the British and Red Cross flags.

(…) Among the English officers came Simmons, the former director of the Ottoman Bank of this city, and who was the civilian prisoner of the Turks. They are bringing him in now as a financial advisor for the army. He told me that he had news for me by means of Yale, who is now in Egypt, and he confirmed the sad news that my poor colleague, Raphaël, had drowned, when the boat on which he was traveling was torpedoed.[34]

I visited General Burton, the military governor. He speaks French very well. I explained my situation to him and that by orders of our embassy in Constantinople, I should halt my functions as the one entrusted with the interests of the Allied countries of the Entente, which should pass to him. However, the general answered me that he did not plan to change anything for the moment and that I should continue until the Commander in Chief (Allenby) ordered something else. I spoke to him then about the misery of the civilian population and, above all, of the depreciation of the bank bills, for which he told me that I was in complete agreement with my friend Simmons. He kindly took charge of sending as many communications as I wanted to Egypt for our ambassador, Vallín.

During all this, the battle continued in east-northeast direction, the cannons and machineguns being frequently heard.

11 December, 1917

Another historic day: The solemn entrance of the Commander in Chief of the British army, Allenby. At 10:30 I headed home because I had heard that the French troops would arrive and with them some of my old acquaintances. When I arrived, I supposed that it was not a matter of just a few French, but rather the Commander in Chief himself, and so it turned out to be. With a splendid morning, the spectacle was magnificent. Before my balcony, in perfect formation, were British troops and a company of Indians. Generals Watson and Burton were going up and down the line inspecting the troops. The public was numerous and had the same faces of satisfaction as at the arrival of the first British soldiers. From my balconies a sea of people, above all Armenians, heaven forbid.

Shortly after noon I observed a British officer with two policemen, who was looking towards my balconies and asking out loud for me. I went down and the officer told me that General Burton was inviting me to go receive the Commander in Chief. I could do no less than accept, and the officer accompanied me to a sort of fountain situated next to the citadel of David, where the mayor and representatives of all the religious denominations were waiting, as well as Valero and a few other notables of the city.

General Allenby arrived a half hour later. An order was immediately proclaimed by the Military Governor that declared Jerusalem to be in a state of siege and promised absolute freedom of worship, as currently exercised. It was first read in English by Burton, then in French by a Franciscan father, then in Italian by Father Rosa and lastly in Arabic by the general's *dragoman*. The text of the declaration said this:

To the Inhabitants of Jerusalem the Blessed and the People Dwelling in Its Vicinity: The defeat inflicted upon the Turks by the troops under my command has resulted in the occupation of your city by my forces. I, therefore, here now proclaim it to be under martial law, under which form of administration it will remain so long as military considerations make necessary. However, lest any of you be alarmed by reason of your experience at the hands of the enemy who has retired, I hereby inform you that it is my desire that every person pursue his lawful business without fear of interruption.

Furthermore, since your city is regarded with affection by the adherents of three of the great religions of mankind, and its soil has been consecrated by the prayers and pilgrimages of multitudes of devout people of these three religions for many centuries, therefore, do I make it known to you that every sacred building, monument, holy spot, shrine, traditional site, endowment, pious bequest or customary place of prayer of whatsoever form of the three religions will be maintained and protected according to the existing customs and beliefs of those to whose faith they are sacred.

Guardians have been established at Bethlehem and on Rachel's Tomb. The tomb at Hebron has been placed under exclusive Moslem control. The hereditary custodians at the gates of the Holy Sepulcher have been requested to take up their accustomed duties in remembrance of the magnanimous act of the Caliph Omar, who protected that church.[35] [This last paragraph was not reported by Ballobar in his diary].

December 1917
Edmund Henry Hynman Allenby

Immediately afterwards, Allenby went to the great patio of the former military government (in the times of Zaki Bey), followed by his retinue and all of us. There, the official presentation took place, which began with the mayor, then the *mufti* with the religious leaders and continuing with my humble personage. Allenby was extremely friendly and thanked me for my interest in my protégés of so many nationalities, adding, 'hard work.' Then he introduced me to Colonel Piepape, French, and to the Italian who was at his left. Both were very expressive in telling me that they knew me perfectly and that we would talk more at leisure now. Since I am becoming a polyglot by necessity, I spoke to each one of them in their language.

During the event to which I just referred we were photographed and filmed endlessly, and I would be glad if that movie were seen by my father and… by Djemal Pasha, though for rather different reasons. To carry on, the general reviewed the forces of the three allied countries and continued his entry into the city. I forgot to say that the Italian to whom he introduced me was Lieutenant Colonel D'Agostino.

I dedicated the afternoon to visiting some French institutions like Notre Dame de France, which is in a lamentable state of filth, and the St. Louis Hospital, perfectly maintained by the Sisters of St. Joseph. The latter was occupied almost completely by British sick and injured, whom I visited, since I continue to be entrusted with the interests of their country. One of them speaks Spanish perfectly, having been born in Argentina, and assured me that there were many Argentine volunteers in the army.

My impression for the moment is that we can be calm; that the hated Turks will not return. I have found, among other friends, Father Burtin, a cleric of the Missionaries of Africa, who is coming as a nurse or something similar. They told me that Mr. Picot, the former French consul in Beirut, is coming as the resident general of France. What does this mean? I am very alarmed because, if our government doesn't hurry to reclaim our convents, the French will take control of them. Unless the Italians do it, and I'm very much afraid they have made great concessions in the matters of the Custody.

If I can avoid it, I will do so, because it seems to me that there is not much to hope for the *Casa* (Ministry of Foreign Affairs). Let's not anticipate events.

12 December, 1917

I spent the whole day in visits: The Sisters of Charity, the chief of the British police, Commander D'Agostino with various Italian officers and Fathers Rosa and Teofilo. All these visits I have to return right away. The Italians came to 'kill two birds with one stone,' which on this occasion was the Count: They asked me for my support in opening the consulate general of Italy, to which I immediately acceded while keeping my comments 'in petto' [to myself] about the reopening, which was done with all solemnity in the presence of four soldiers and a corporal, before whom he raised the flag.

In the afternoon, I took a walk near the asylum to admire the magnificent caterpillar tractors that the British have brought. I visited the Sisters of the Reparatrice and the Orphanage of the Sisters of St. Joseph of the Apparition, returning to the consulate to wait for the visit of Colonel Piepape and the Captain Count of San Quentin, a secretary who was from the embassy of France in Constantinople. The Colonel is a very fine man and of perfect friendliness and correctness. He told me that, since he arrived in Jaffa, he had not ceased to hear people speaking well of me, a phrase that clearly demonstrates that he is too kind. The visit lasted an hour and a quarter, the conversation dealing with the situation of France in the war, Djemal Pasha, Zaki Bey, Kuebler's position, that of the German and Austrian clerics, etc.

13 December, 1917

New visits: Lieutenant Albert Abramson of the 'Intelligence' with the universal system of initials G.S.J. Interesting conversation. He asked me the list of the Germans and Austro-Hungarians, and I have decided to face the question of the treatment the British think to give to these people. I told my guest about the behavior of these people during the war as favorable to the interests of the Allied. Based on him and on British political interests, I told him that, according to me, they should proceed as follows: First, not to annoy or only to a small extent the clergy of any denomination; secondly, to guard, with some limitations, the White fathers, and ask them to present themselves to the police or similar. Will they accept my idea? I don't think so, but if they accept my victory it will be great.[36]

Dr. Thon and Hoofien came too. They thanked me, and they offered me a table, made in Bezalel, with a nice card as a souvenir for having saved them from prison.

I myself made several visits: Amongst them to the Italian commander Caccia, aid of the Duque of Turin and military attaché of the Italian Diplomatic Agency in Cairo. I have also visited the American chief, Davies, who speaks Spanish as bad as I speak English.

My Jewish protégés told me that they have included my name in a 'Gold Book' that they keep for those who have given a great service.

14 December, 1917

Lieutenant Abramson assured me that he has spoken about the question of the Germans to General Burton, who agreed completely with my point of view, so the religious people will remain calm, including the Protestants. Only a small number of people of the civilian population will be expelled, unless even that small number may be retained at my request. It's the first victory I have obtained for German interests. I also spoke to him about a person who will be able to render him great services... at the same time that he does so for me too. Tomorrow I will have lunch with him at the Hotel Fast, and if they agree, I will have done some good business, and I will have the Anglo-Arab police in my hand. *Inshallah.*

Besides continuing to receive visits from all the French that have come with the army, today I went to see Mr. Picot, that is, the Resident General of France. The first thing he did was to warmly thank me on behalf of his country, which he had been especially entrusted to do. He then extolled endless tributes to me and announced, that tomorrow at 10:00, he will come to visit me, in consequence of which I'm making my preparations.

16 December, 1917

Much political work yesterday and today. I have had various conferences with Picot, Colonel Deedes, Lieutenant Abramson and Rauf. For the most part I will not speak here of what was dealt with in them, because it is not convenient to do so. In a nutshell, there is the following news: Zaki Bey has obtained permission, by my petition, to be sent to Heluan with honors due to his rank as a colonel. Picot has proposed that I go with him by automobile to Egypt on the 25th or 26th to deal with the numerous matters that I have to decide with the embassy. Italy seems to have nothing to do with the Franco-British agreement about Palestine. In this agreement, an interesting thing, figures the clause that no European flag may wave in Jerusalem.[37] For this reason, the British have not made any demonstration of this type, nor have they hoisted the other diminutive flags that fly with those of the Red Cross on hospitals. France promised her help on the Spanish aspirations in the Holy Land. If I manage to get this done I will have fully accomplished the personal mission I proposed to carry out here for my personal friendships for one and all. Rauf will be named. (…) Something of all this I stated in the luncheon that Picot and Lieutenant Marignon had in my house today.

The offices of foreign mail will return here again, so too my friends who administered them.

1918

8 January, 1918

I have had a light attack of nervous exhaustion caused by the arduous work of years without a single leave of absence. Because of it I've been presenting myself every day, lately at 11:00 A.M., to the resulting surprise of my numerous employees of every nationality, so accustomed to seeing me get up at dawn. After the arrival of the British there have appeared some new employees: 'Ali (Armenian *cavas*), Nadji (French, ditto) and a Greek. All of them are deserting soldiers.

In spite of the agreement of which I spoke before, the Italian flag kept on flying over their consulate until the British horse police made them take it down.

Burton has departed, a failure, according to what the English themselves assured me. In his place R. Storrs has been named, who was the secretary to Lord Kitchener and is now the Oriental Secretary in Cairo, as well as a consummate polyglot. I introduced myself to him at New Year's, and he made the best impression on me. An excellent pianist, he knows Albéñiz and the modern Spanish musicians. He asked me for a French translation of *Blood and Sand*, the famous novel by Blasco Ibáñez.

Storrs has entrusted me with various things about Egypt; all was ready and my luggage packed with a shipment of letters when here, on New Year's Day itself, they brought me a letter at 11:00 in the evening in which one of the British officers told me, by order of the Governor, that there are impediments to my trip to Cairo and that they would explain it to me the following day. It's a reproduction of the fable of the milkmaid. All my projects for some fun in Cairo, excursions, shopping, important matters for our interests... it's all turned to mud. My hopes are dashed.

The following day, Governor Storrs, showed me a telegram from General Clayton, Director of Political Affairs, in which he said that, in the first place, he did not recognize me as entrusted with the Austro-German interests; and in the second place, he would permit me to go to Cairo, but I would not be able to return here because the Allied consuls were not permitted to come to Jerusalem.

The governor seemed very regretful about what happened and told me that he thought it must be a sort of reprisal for the conduct of the Germans with the foreign ambassadors in Romania. I responded with a number of forceful arguments: My case is different from that of the Allied consuls who were stopped in their functions by the interruption of diplomatic relations; but even if it were so, it is unfair that the British government take these measures against the one who was and is entrusted with British interests. Even if they did not bear in mind either international law or gratitude, the mere fact that the British high commissioner in Egypt [Wingate] has manifested the desire to speak to me (as General Clayton himself has told Kuebler) would have been enough to justify my making the trip. From among these allies there is no more than one who opposes the trip, and that is Italy. That is what I let Storrs understand this morning when he told me that it was not the Ministry of Foreign Affairs that had ordered it, and I answered him, '*Sicuro*.' He smiled and ended the conversation.[1]

This disagreeable matter seems to be on the road to repair because Storrs himself has made a report in my favor, and besides, Picot will return within a few days from Egypt: I hope that the conferences that he promised to have with Lord Wingate and our minister about the matter will have turned out well.

It is all cleared up, since the governor has just told me that the famous telegram was in error, and that I can take charge of the Austro-German interests. The telegram said, 'There is an objection' when its text actually was 'there was no objection.' To celebrate the arrangement, Storrs invited me to eat at the Hotel Fast.

The Turks are scarcely giving any signs of life, except for a little, very distant, cannon fire that was heard this morning. But up until the end of last year the matter was rather serious: On the 26th and 27th, if I recall correctly, the Turks tried to take back the Holy City and carried out seven successive attacks that were beaten back. I witnessed part of the battles from the home of Mr. Meyukras, and I managed to contemplate them to my enjoyment with binoculars. I counted 24 cannons on the side of the Mount of Olives. In addition, there were infantry and cavalry forces perfectly sheltered from the fire of the Turks. When it got dark, two batteries situated to the northeast (towards Ramla) opened fire against the Turks. To be sure, both batteries were so admirably hidden that, although I distinguished the flashes of the shots with the field glasses, I could not discover even a single gun.

These battles have been deadly for the Turks, who have lost a lot of people. Just in the areas near the Convent of Mar Saba they have counted 600 dead. The convent of St. Theodosius has been very damaged by the Turkish artillery. A few days ago Ramla fell to the British, and now we hope that it is Nablus' turn.

My old friend and colleague, Hough, the British vice consul in Jaffa, came to see me, and we had a lively luncheon. He was in the United States, entrusted with a 'special mission,' and here he seems to have another along that line, which makes me very happy because I am going to be more or less a main actor in it. (…)

8 April, 1918

An entire trimester without writing a single impression. It really is true, for what it's worth. I have had many reasons for doing it. First, I spent a month in January I wouldn't wish to anyone: An attack of nervous exhaustion that would have flattened Hercules. I, since I am not exactly an Attila, had some very bad moments, and only the air of Rehovot could end my illness. This gave me new proof of what one can expect from the persons for whom one does favors. I did not need those favors, because I was well-convinced that the inhabitants of Jerusalem, without distinction of religion or race, can figure among the most ungrateful of the world. But the proof was definitive. I will not speak of it in any more detail.

General Allenby sent me his doctor, who told me there was nothing to be done except take a period of rest without reading even a letter. In view of that I went to spend a little while at the Jewish colony of Rehovot, or Deir Tanneis [?], as the Arabs call it. (…)

My stay in the Jewish colony was much livelier and more entertaining than I thought it would be, thanks, above all, to the nice General Sir H. Chauvel, leader of the Australians, who are among this army. He invited me to eat several times, together with his officers and the New Zealand Lieutenant, Lion. They put at my disposal an automobile in which I made various excursions. (…)

I made a visit, at headquarters, to General Edmund Allenby, who received me very well. We had lunch with General Sir Philippe Chetwode, General Clayton and some other officials from the political camp. We served ourselves the lunch, since there was a big table on which was prepared a vast amount of cold cuts, salads, pastries, puddings and other such things. Every time one of us wanted to serve himself something he got up and went to the table, where he took what he wanted. The system is very practical and, at the same time, is a means of facilitating digestion with the little steps we saw ourselves obliged to take every little while. I, as the guest of honor, avoided many of those strolls, because the general's assistants hurried to serve me whatever I needed (and one of these improvised waiters was no less than Lord Percy, that is to say, the Duke of Northumberland).

The Commander in Chief speaks some Spanish, very little. He told me himself, 'I speak a little.' He has traveled a bit through Spain, and something of our country has stayed with him, at least in affection. He said to me, 'Why are there so many Germanophiles in Spain?' I answered him calmly, 'Very simple, because of Gibraltar.' I didn't know if he would like my frankness, but he began to laugh. He was amazed to see that I knew all his campaigns, from the one he did as an officer of the Dragons against Cetewayo and the Zulus, to the English-Boer war and his commands in the French front in the current war, on which front he directed the Third English Army.

Allenby promised to do everything possible so I could achieve my trip to Egypt, and thus it was accomplished. But I'm not going yet because the Marquis of Alhucemas begged me to delay my trip until Father Pardoa is substituted as Procurator for the Holy Land by another cleric more worthy of that duty.[2]

When the referred-to luncheon was finished, I went back to Jerusalem in General Chetwode's car. The general is a descendant from a direct line of the companions of Richard the Lion Heart and is a knight of the Order of Bath. He invited me to dine two more times in the sanatorium where the headquarters of the XX Army that he commands is installed. The first time was a 'political meal,' which was attended by the French high commissioner, an Italian, Lieutenant General Bulfin and Brigadier General Pearless. During the meal we had music, and after dinner, the theater company of the 60th division presented a whole comic-lyrical-dance program, of which I understood only the dances; the songs and observations about the British officers were made by a certain general. (…)

In all of this, in the meals to which I referred, the British stopped at nothing to praise the bravery and spirit of sacrifice of the Turkish army, or rather that of its soldiers, since they detest the officers. They told me of an incident that depicts the modesty of General Allenby: When Gaza was taken, the Commander in Chief published an order of the day, saying that the victory was not due to him but rather to General Chetwode, whose plan he had followed exactly, with Allenby limiting himself to approving it. (…)

8 July, 1918

Another good jump in these notes. I was, finally, in Egypt, and my trip was almost triumphal.[3] The governor did nothing but put it off, with the pretext that he had no news of what Allenby had telegraphed to London: He did it so much that he raised a hullabaloo, and a good one, from headquarters. In short, one fine day I left Jerusalem by car, I went to Jaffa to see how Kuebler was, who had just suffered a terrible attack of malaria (an illness I know by experience) and, from there, I made a visit to the British 'political camp' to eat with General Clayton, the Chief of Intelligence. Do you want to know what a British 'political camp' is? Well, very simply: Various magnificent tents, a big hut for the officers of the military staff, a dining tent, which is at the same time a waiting room, electric light everywhere and a telephone to the entire occupied territory. Well, from these tents all of occupied Palestine is governed, and the whole of Turkey would be.

I ate with Clayton, and I asked him, for diverse, complicated reasons, not to let the general of the Franciscan Order come here, my dear friend Father Cimino.[4] The general promised me and, right away, I went in a grand Rolls Royce to the Lydda station.

I had admired, as one must, the activity put forth by the British to fix the highways, but I was even more astonished to see transformed into practically a first-class station the wayside stopping point that there was in Lydda during the time of the Turks. I looked for the transportation officer, and that good man put me in a sleeper-coach from the ones that constitute the current service from Lydda to al-Qantar. Until 10:30 I was watching the coming and going of military trains. Among them, one loaded with Indians really caught my attention. These were traveling in about the same conditions, almost worse than if they were pigs. The train cars are hardly wonderful, not even close, nor is the train itself. But in any case, one can spend the night in a compartment equipped with a dining room.

I went to bed, sleeping peacefully through the night. When I woke up at 6:00 A.M. I saw, through the windows, the landscape which was a full desert of sand dunes, plains of an unpleasant and sad, yellow color, crows and birds of prey; that is to say, a marvel. From time to time the double track converted into a triple to pass by a siding where one saw some tents, a Scotsman washing himself in the open air and some Egyptian soldiers with curious hats. Dust, lots of dust that entered through the interstices of the windows, and from which one can in no way defend oneself. Suddenly, and without noticing any undulation in the plain, one discovers a species of anthill of gigantic termites; little by little, the anthill transforms into an immense encampment of yellowish tents (so it is more difficult to distinguish them from airplanes), and the soldier that runs up and down the train to make us sign the travelers' book tells me this anthill is al-Qantara.

At 7:00 we arrived at that species of city created by the art of enchantment, and the train pulls up alongside a magnificent dock, to which various trucks immediately close to load our honorable persons and luggage. I took one of the trucks by storm and crossed the Canal. (...)[5]

29 July, 1918

Today was the day set for the departure of the Germans and Austrians who are finally going to be interned in Egypt, but it has been postponed until later. For that reason, my work increases at an alarming rate, for the necessity of taking care of the interests of everyone who remains here, especially the two big groups formed by the Evangelical Church and the Württemberg colony. I have done the impossible so that Dr. Jeremias, head of the former group, can stay here, but it has all been in vain. Off they go!

Mr. Rohrer, the president of the Templegesellschaft, is one of the more 'restrained' types I have seen in my life, since he didn't want me to take any steps in order that he might stay here, despite the fact that the British were inclined in his favor, saying, 'From the moment that my colony departs, it would be cowardice to leave it.' So the good man is leaving to be interned, exposed perhaps to being torpedoed if they repatriate him to his country, but with a clean conscience. Few Jews would do that! At least the ones that I know in Jerusalem.

These last few days we have had parties of every type and stripe. One of the most significant ones was the placing of the first stone of the future Hebrew University of Mount Scopus.[6] The Jews have purchased the possession of Lady Gray Hill, near the German Sanatorium, and there they are inclined to spend a few millions. They began placing not one stone, but a collection of them. Beforehand, there was a small reception of the personalities who attended, among them I will cite Generals Allenby, Chauvel, Clayton and various others, the American ambassador in Cairo, Mr. Gary, the French and Italian detachments and Jewish personalities from Egypt.

After that, the ceremony proceeded with the reading of a statement in Hebrew, and right away the 'stoning,' in which Dr. Weizmann, other members of the Zionist commission, various notable of Jerusalem, like Hoofien, Meyohas, Eliazhar, the representative of the Jewish colonies, and a general chorus took part. To continue, Dr. Weizmann read us a pedantic speech of as many pretentions – despite his simple and modest style – as its author for whom I have no sympathy whatsoever. The same gentleman read a telegram of support and sympathy, signed by Lord Balfour. After, Captain Coulondre read another from the French government. This last one, it seems, had been discussed by the French Council of Ministers. But with the respect due to those gentlemen, it seemed to me a huge political error. Why? Well, for one of two reasons: Either it is dealing with the simple placement of the first stone of a university, or it is dealing with a transcending political act, and both, when put like that, benefit Zionism. This last alternative would be putting oneself out in front of the Muslim and Christian element, especially the former. I understand that they may want to butter up the Jews, who enjoy so much influence that they even have a voice and vote in the councils of war, but to the point of making a Catholic-Judeo policy in this country seems dangerous to me. For soon, the *mufti*, no less than a descendent of Muhammad, was obliged to place one of the famous stones. And you should have seen his face when he did so! Yellow as an over-ripe melon!

Another of those who placed their little stone was the Protestant bishop, MacInnes, who, in my judgment, is the one who runs everything in Jerusalem. This gentleman, an Anglican bishop, presented himself on the day of the Armenian Easter in the *Tiara* Convent, made the representative of the Armenian Patriarchate put him in charge of the *Tiara* and promptly read the gospel in English. That Anglo-Armenian entente: Is its object to prove we are all brothers? (No one would say) or is it trying to show that the differences of religion no longer exist in these democratic-warrior times? Whatever it may be, the fraternal feelings are extended to the Jews, since the bishop placed a stone, as has been said, on Scopus. Of course, as soon as he returns to his cathedral and magnificent residence he will tell his wife what happened and will probably talk about such Jews. Long live freedom of religion and freedom of conscience!

The conduct of all these people towards the Jews made me indignant, not because I have so much sympathy for the Jews, but because I can't bear the hypocrisy of which all the Protestants are masters. The aforementioned Bishop MacInnes is also the one who directs, behind the scenes, the Aid for Syria and Palestine, which is the most efficient instrument of the policy of English influence. With the propaganda in the press he takes in a lot, a great deal of money from Protestants and Catholics, and uses it to help both groups (but little, very little for the Catholics).[7]

To cover appearances, an Anglo-American committee has been formed, which is called the 'Educational German Institutions' and has assumed the direction of the Protestant institutions and schools. Of course, they wanted the Catholic and Protestant auxiliaries to unify, but I indicated that the Catholic schools should be administered by our clerics, and it seems it will be done that way. Meanwhile, they have made a very bad impression on the city, by having transformed the Austrian hospice, a purely Catholic institution, into a Protestant orphanage. The orphanage is under the direction of the mentioned bishop and a certain Miss Warburton, excessively disagreeable.

Let's leave these criticisms to the British administration, and move on to praise the advantages that have been brought to the city. Just the fact of being able to go out into the streets without fear that the famous Turkish police may do some barbarity would be enough that I would consider myself very fortunate with the British. I will never forget the reign of terror that there was during the last days of the Turks, although, in honor of the truth, I have to say that the years 1915 and part of 1916 were very peaceful, and I even doubt that one would have been better off in the countries currently at war. But 'Izzet Bey, the last governor... it's better not to remember him.

As I said before, one has to be grateful to the English for the public security, which is rather good, the relative good condition of the highways and the construction of other new ones, as well as the bringing of potable water from al Anum al-Kharrub (excellent, according to the analysis), and although now it only serves the military, it is an improvement that will remain.

The streets are, frankly, clean; the commerce, almost nil during the Turkish occupation, is now giving a lot of life to the city, which helps the farmers to whom they sell and transfer horses for the chores of the country, and lastly the railroad from Egypt, which seems like a dream. In short the advantages that the British administration always brings. All this gives work to thousands and thousands of workers, who, before were obliged to desert from the Turkish army, die of hunger or work for free: Three solutions that I think nobody would like.

Among the new highways it is worth mentioning the one from Ramla to al-Atrun, which seems to be very picturesque. A railroad from Jerusalem to Ramla will also be built, of narrow gauge for the moment. This railroad will keep on moving forward when the British advance, and there is no need to mention the advantages that it will bring.

What is needed now is a sanitary campaign against the trachoma and malaria that are the two calamities of this country (apart from its inhabitants, who constitute the worst calamity). Although the climate is very pleasant (in few countries will one spend the months from May to December without a cloud in the sky, nor a drop of water, and without having excessive heat more than some isolated days), the malaria offsets all these advantages, makes a mess of the appetite, stomach, head and nerves of one who suffers its attacks, which I say from experience.

To combat the focal points of malaria, we have to follow a complete plan, which is not a question of a month or even several but, rather, one of perhaps years and spending a lot of money, since we have to end this disease not only in Jerusalem but also in the countryside and in Jaffa. A system of vigilance and conservation of the cisterns, petroleum in the marshy areas and ponds, with the draining of those swampy territories, would finish off the mosquitoes and therefore the disease.

Another success that the British have achieved, perhaps the most important, is that the people accept the Egyptian money at its full worth. When the British occupied this region it produced a curious phenomenon: The Turkish Pound (paper, nominally 100 piasters) which was worth 15 piasters, dropped to 10 and then rose suddenly to 27 when the British arrived. For what reason? Well, because in Egypt the Muslims now pay 30 piasters for it, no doubt because they have confidence in the Ottoman state. Now then, the English government established the Egyptian Pound here as the common currency. The populace was accustomed to the little confidence that the Turkish Pound inspired in them, and began to refuse it at its nominal value of 100 piasters, and the moment came when gold reached an enormous premium over the Egyptian money. Well, such is the confidence that the British have known how to inspire; now it has gone up to be almost even. The benefits of bringing this up are incalculable, and it's beyond me to explain them all.

30 July, 1918

Last night the military governor, Storrs, came to dine with me. He declared during the meal that the best solution of the Jerusalem question would be to turn it over to the Americans. That idea, which has been backed by some, I think would be well-received by the Jews, who have so much strength in America, but it would not make a good impression among the Christians and Muslims. The governor told me that its possession was not agreeable to the United Kingdom, but I keep thinking that the British are not leaving here even at gunpoint. And I prefer them with all their defects, to any other solution.

We keep hearing cannon fire, and this time really close, since the Turks are bombarding Ramla with 24 cm guns, and 15 rockets have fallen near there since yesterday morning.

I have sealed the rooms of the Mount of Olives Sanatorium. Sister Theodora Barkhausen remains in Jerusalem but cannot live there. Seeing her this morning, I admired the strength of character that distinguishes the Germans, since she attended the act of her expulsion from the building laughing and joking, and who knows if she will ever see it in her hands again.

The Germans must leave Saturday at 5:00 A.M. Thank God. Thus they will be peaceful, so will the British and I.

2 August, 1918

Last night there was a concert in the Y.M.C.A. They invited governor Storrs, and General Money attended with many British, American and Italian leaders and officials. Of 'the ladies,' there were various English and American nurses (only one pretty) and some good-looking Jewish women. The company was formed by two British ladies of pure blood, tall and as slender as two canes and with a gracefulness that, if they are seen in Triana they'll be attacked with stones.[8] But since we are not in Sevilla here, they applauded them and even found them very funny (not I, mind you) singing couplets in the British choral style. One of the company was a captain of mediocre baritone voice, but with pretentions of rivaling Titta Ruffo: This good man sang 'Carmen' with a toreador air that left nothing to be desired. Goodbye, Belmonte! There was, of course, a grandiose number, the one of a perfect imitator of animals, who imitated the death of a fly by smashing it in such a way that there were women who screamed in horror. A curious detail: Monsignor Fellinger and representatives of the different Christian sects, including my great friend, the Dutch Father Van der Vliet, attended the party. What a revolution in the clerical customs of Jerusalem!

6 August, 1918

On the 3rd, a Saturday, the Germans left, or rather, they made the Germans leave. The little trip cost me a first-class morning, since I left by automobile (which the British army had placed at my disposition) at 4:30 A.M. The *dragoman* of the consulate general of Germany, Mr. Haddad, accompanied me, and we went to the station where the men and women were in correct formation, the majority of them women. In a little while, the military governor arrived in person to see if all was in order.

The special train left at 6:30 and was composed of a first-class coach in which we went; the *propst*, Jeremias with his family, Baroness Von Freytag, Father Müller, Mr. Rohere with his family and various deaconesses. Very proper attitude with each other. The interned people were installed in third-class coaches, but you have to keep in mind that only the generals and the high-ranking types travel in the first-class ones.

Matters of the Germanic character: If it had been in Spain, surely there would have been sobs and tears by the bushel on the part of those who were going into exile, abandoning their homes and interests, as well as on the part of those who remained here, who did not know what would become of them either. But nothing, not a tear, nor a sad face.

A splendid day. Parading before our eyes are the landscapes, at times savage, at times smiling, of the Sorek Valley. The train went by the ancient station of Dayr Aban, which by appearances has been destroyed by the Turks before they retreated, and arrived at Wadi Sarar. That is an immense encampment, workshops, offices, etc. The station building is still the Turkish one. This spot has the reputation that there is no way to take it, no doubt because of the famous malaria that almost all of us have suffered here. In the station, several Italian soldiers from those of their country's camp on the high ground that dominates the station.

Shortly before 9:00 we were arriving at the pass at the level of Ramla and, in the same moment, my automobile also arrived with my *cavas* 'Abed, who was greeted with an ovation by the Germans, to whom he had also given good service. (…) A little later we arrived at Lydda in the middle of a forest of olive and apricot trees. Kuebler was in the station with the Germans who still remained in Jaffa.

I say goodbye to my traveling companions with real feeling and install myself with Lieutenant Sachs, who had come to look for me on behalf of General Lloyd in the magnificent and extremely comfortable Sunbeam amidst the sea of horses. He drove me to Ramla, and the general's staff did the honors for me with great friendliness. (...) Because I should point out that our convent is the headquarters of that gentleman, who is no less than the head of the P.L.C. ('Palestine Lines of Communication'). This general has a very important position now that he has at his orders the thousands of automobiles and trucks that the army disposes. An excellent breakfast, quick visit to the fathers, who were on holiday because of St. Nicodemus Day, and at 11:00 I returned to Jerusalem in the General's own car. (...)

The only discordant note, which contrasted with the attitude of the British, has been that of Lieutenant Monckton, who has set out to lose the good accord that exists between the Germans and the English with his gross behavior. That gentleman, or whatever he is, dedicated this morning to stealing flowerpots, benches, etc. from the German colony, since he couldn't enter in the houses because the keys were in my possession. I'll write a letter to the governor about that, which reminded me of the good old days of the Ottoman Pashas.

17 August, 1918, Jaffa

Here I am, and I'm writing this seated on the balcony of Kuebler's new and lovely house; he has occupied the one of Pastor Von Ratnau, currently deported in Sidi Bishr. Not very fresh air, but views of the sea, a sky oh so beautiful and such a quantity of palms and orange trees that one even forgets the war.

It seems the British have retreated a little in this part. Just a month or so ago Turkish rockets fell in the city itself. Wonderful!

Yesterday afternoon I went to communicate to Father Mateo Hebreo that, thanks to the weakness of our government, which accept any measures that the 'Vatican Consult' society takes, he is removed from his position as Superior and replaced by Father Andrés Rodríguez, the deed of Father Pardoa and therefore of the afore-mentioned society. I could make a lot of comments here, but I do not want to be labeled anticlerical when in reality I am not, but faith is one thing and ecclesiastical discipline is another. (...)

The English government has sold 10,000 barrels of petroleum a month so that the farmers can maintain their irrigation motors. They have not been content with selling them; they have given credit to those who did not have the money. In Egypt, they are giving petroleum with promissory notes. It seems that the Worms House and Port-Said Company will take this matter into account.

Crédit Lyonnais sent me a large rug from Bukhara as a souvenir of my conduct as 'director' of the Jerusalem agency during the war and the Turkish occupation. That is what the real director, Miguel Antonio Guerássimo, told me.

The invitations continued; the night before last I attended a meal in the Sanatorium, that General Sir Philip Chetwode gave. The dinner guests were Captain Coulondre, the military governor; Colonel Finley of the American Red Cross, various other military people, and me.

The Jews were threatened by a serious blow: The expulsion or internment of the Austro-Germans. Nonetheless, the influence they have is so great that I doubt very much that the English dare to take this measure.

21 August, 1918

I have made a visit to General Clayton and Colonel Deedes, both from the general headquarters. Everyone was very friendly, but they continue the deportations to Hebron, among them that of my colleague, the honorary consul Dr. Einsler, the Schöneke family and three deaconesses from the Mount of Olives. Mrs. Schöneke came very hurriedly to tell me that the Zionists wanted to leave with the model of the Temple of Solomon that her husband made to take copies of it, taking away from the poor lady her only means of living. In view of it, I begged General Money not to do it, and I managed it, to the consequent satisfaction of all.

23 August, 1918

Yesterday I accompanied the new Superior, Father José Montero, to St. John. Since my car was not running very well, the French high commissioner granted me his. Tomorrow, the new Superiors of Ramla and Jaffa, Fathers Angel Ulibarri and Andrés Rodríguez, are leaving too.

Today, the cold we have been suffering for days fortunately has ceased. That takes away a little of the concentrated anger I have against the inhabitants of Jerusalem.

24 August, 1918

The correspondent of *L'Illustration*, Mr. Chausel, wrote to Captain Coulondre, asking him that I send him my information, which, according to him, is very interesting. The good man believes me to be a Francophile incarnate and very diplomatic besides, so he wants anecdotes all about my role during the war.

7 September, 1918

I am writing from my Emmaus office. This bit about 'my office' is a manner of speaking, because the delightful house of the German Order of St. Lazarus Fathers does not belong to me, of course, but it really is at my disposal. Since the British have not occupied it, I shut and sealed it in view of the fact that Father Dunkel was supposed to leave for Jerusalem with the Sisters of San Charles Borromeo, who were taking care of the building. I asked Storrs to let the sisters come here to cook during my stay and care for the house, which has been granted to me. I am now occupying two, royally-furnished and magnificent rooms, the office of which I spoke before and a bedroom. Anyone, to whom I say that I have, to put it like this, German nuns at my service and authorized by the British, will not believe it. They are very good and feed me wonderfully.

Here one hears the cannon fire all day from next to Nablus, and in the evening the explosions are perfectly distinguishable. Memories of the past! (...)

On the road from Jerusalem I have found endless cartridge caps, discharged airplane bombs and even a loaded hand grenade: I forbade the Arab who brought it to me to touch it, because there could have been an unfortunate incident due to carelessness, like the one that cost the lives of several people in St. John and in other towns.

The forest of pines and cypresses that surround this house is wonderful, and even more so keeping mind that it is the only one that there is in this country. There I dedicated myself to resting from the extremely busy days I have had because of the trip of the corvette captains, Lorenzo Moya and Arsenio Roji. For three-and-a-half days I had not one day of rest: They arrived on Monday, the 2nd, at Lydda, where I was waiting for them, warned by the authorities from Alexandria. The nice sailors did not believe their trip was possible and were very surprised when, in Alexandria, they let them know that the consul of Spain was claiming them. They are on Allied hospital ships to guarantee they are nothing more than hospitals, and that they should not be torpedoed.

The itinerary began with our visit to the convent of Jaffa, the sailors being delighted with the beautiful views that the convent has and with the fraternal welcome of our clerics. Then we visited General Clayton, who was very courteous with the Spanish leaders and indicated that the other Spanish sailors had been very jealous of their trip and wanted to come too, from which I suppose I will have a whole series of visits from the navy officers, an idea that, while *dear* to me, will be rather dear in cost.

We also visited Bethlehem, St. John and Artas. In Bethlehem we saw the wall that has been destroyed by order of the governor of that city. It was, in truth, anti-aesthetic and took away the view of the high altar of the

Greeks, which is located across from the door of the basilica and makes a good impression, but this is damaging to the Franciscans, who have protested, although to no avail. So you can see the difference in government: If it had been the Sublime Porte who had ordered it, there would have been uproar, deaths, injuries, and even the destitution of the *mutasarrif* and the mayor of Bethlehem, perhaps a ministerial crisis and even a threat of intervention by the Great Powers. But the British have done it, and everything has been reduced to simple protest, which I'm not even sure has taken place. It seems to me that the British are going to resolve the famous 'question of the Holy Places' little by little and in all its manifestations. (…)

In St. John, a repetition of the scenes of the Jaffa convent. I like this convent more than any other of the Franciscan Order in the Holy Land, and this is because (apart from the beauty) there are not different Christian denominations that live together and dispute, at gunshot, the right to sweep the floor or some such thing, in virtue of the principle 'let us love one another.'

The excursion on Wednesday was first-class. I went by car to look for my guests in Gethsemane, where there was no less than His Most Reverend Fatherhood, Father Ferdinando Diotallevi, *Custos* of the Holy Land.[9] While the sailors were visiting the Sepulcher of the Most Holy Virgin, I took advantage to have a few words with the *Custos*. I told him that the government of His Catholic Majesty would advise our sovereign the concession of an extraordinary, great boon as soon as the Vatican agreed to reappoint Procurator Pardoa. To my great surprise, the *Custos* told me that what we needed for that change (which he wanted more than anyone) was for the ambassador of Spain to the Holy See to *truly ask* the Holy Father for that substitution. The hint for the Marquis of Villasinda cannot be more direct and, just as Father Diotallevi told it to me, I will tell it to the Minister of State. An interesting note: When talking about Father Pardoa, the *Custos* told me that he had gone away from the convent to the famous Armenian lady. This hint is really direct, and I can imagine how the Procurator will be upon losing his girlfriend after having lost his friends, Father Teofilo Capri and Father Rosa.

Later, we continued towards Jericho. A little beyond that we saw the insignia of the Desert Mounted Corps, and we headed there. Several tents with ten or more initials (these British have a mania for initials), a very elegant Indian lancer saluted us in military fashion and there were no other sentinels; nor checkpoint, nor guard corps, nor all those very complicated precautions, for in peace-time we use the others. We arrived, without anyone asking us anything, at the tent of the nice General Couvel, my friend from Deiran.

If we were surprised at such a thing right on the front and in war time, we were still more surprised when my New Zealand friend, Lion, showed us the panorama that dominates from the headquarters. I am not a writer, nor even if I were would I be able to describe it for its grandeur, but I will at least give a very vague idea of it. The tents are on a little plateau. Suddenly, we found ourselves on the edge of it, seeing all the Jordan valley, the mountains of Moab and the entire desert of Judah. But all the grandeur of that view is eclipsed by the 'foreground,' because at our feet an abyss some 150 meters deep opened up, sharply cut off, with nearly vertical walls. (…)

The solemn silence of the place, and the grandiose vista, left us with such admiration I would have gladly stayed to live in that site as a highland dweller… if I had as lodging a tent like that of the general. You would have to see it! Built right on the very edge of the abyss, and made of sacks filled with earth as a shelter from the wind, the dust, the heat and the cold. I saw in it the 'salon,' which is magnificent, with extremely comfortable easy chairs, geographical maps and a table with the latest newspapers and magazines from Europe and Egypt, and a terrific bar. The dining room was almost sumptuous, and the lunch that they served us was excellent. We even had ice and every kind of beverage! What would the Bedouins say, up until now the only inhabitants of the desert?

After eating, Lion accompanied us to Jericho and the Dead Sea. We went in two cars, one of them from the Intelligence. If it had not been like that, I think we would have had to return on foot. We made the trip out to Jericho on the old road, which now is perfectly cared for, while before the war it was completely abandoned. Of course, we took advantage to admire the picturesque and moving site of the convent of St. George and to admire once again the work of the Romans, who built an aqueduct that is still maintained and functioning, carrying water to the depths of Wadi al-Qilt. Admirable hydraulic policy those people had!

To get to Jericho we thought we would choke on the clouds of dust raised in the desert sand by thousands of horses and mules that were going to get a drink. Contrasting with these scenes, a recently constructed narrow gauge railroad told us what we could expect from this country if the British continue. For me, the Jordan valley will become as rich as Egypt, at least in time.

A rapid visit to the ruins of the city and also to the fountain of Eliseus, whose exquisite water we tasted. To continue, we began a cross-country march, crossing ravines, traversing sand dunes and jumping in our seats like rubber balls. In this manner, we miraculously arrived without any breakdowns at the Dead Sea, where I could compare the work of the one with the other: The miserable tents and only faintly less disgusting huts of the Turks had been transformed into a series of provisional but magnificent installations, with workshops for naval construction, a canteen, electrical installations, baths, showers, etc. On the Biblical lake, I counted ten motor boats and also an old Turkish steamer that is under repair and will be launched again, armed with four cannons. Each boat has its corresponding anti-aircraft gun.

We had tea and, with the binoculars, contemplated the Turkish trenches, which are about ten kilometers away. I should mention that our visit was to see the front and that, although we were on it, we did not hear even a single cannonade or shot, and only one of the soldiers that we saw in the entire excursion (and there were very few of them) had a rifle. (…)

The day before yesterday we were supposed to go to the front of division 53, in Nablus, but we didn't because of a breakdown of my car. We went instead to Lydda, where I 'set aboard' for Alexandria our nice sailors, who I think considered me a 'supernatural being,' according to Moyá's declaration.

12 September, 1918

I have returned from Emmaus, and along the road, the servant from the Order of St. Lazarus was showing me the tombs of English but Muslim soldiers, so they were probably the Indians who fell in the battles that preceded the taking of Jerusalem. With the loquacity of the Arabs he was explaining to me point by point the details of the battle, which was an artillery duel, but since the explanation was in Arabic I only understood part of it.

This morning I went in uniform to a Te Deum, celebrated in the Holy Sepulcher by the Greek Orthodox to celebrate the name day of King Alexander I. I officially had to go because of being in charge of the Greek interests, and I did it as a 'schismatic.' The ceremony was, fortunately, rather brief, and Storrs presided at it, resorting to the well-known songs and *kyries*.

Afterward, and in solemn procession, preceded by the new Arab police (who, most assuredly, are dressed in rather good taste), all the religious dignitaries went to the Patriarchate. There, the Chief of the Executive Commission delivered to us a rather tendentious little speech in which he said that he was drinking to the health of 'our sovereign, Alexander,' and I applied this qualifier since the orator and all the Orthodox clergy are Ottoman subjects. Then he enlarged upon the considerations of Greece and the wishes to be bigger, a rather clear allusion to the territorial pretentions of that country against Turkey. He finished drinking to the health of the king of England, of the military governor and my own, a thing for which I am sincerely grateful: As they say in Spain, 'Here's to your health and may you enjoy it.' Since the translation of the toast was done for me by Governor Storrs himself, he was also a bit tendentious.

This evening there was a wonderful concert in the home of the military governor, Storrs, who was in the former German consulate. A new Italian colonel, Passenti, Lord Percy, General Money, a commander whose name I don't remember and I ate with Storrs. After the meal the concert began, which is the first real one I have heard in Jerusalem.

Tomorrow, a meal in the home of Colonel Findley, head of the American Red Cross. A change of decoration: Dollars instead of art.

15 September, 1918

We have had a meeting with the military government to establish a music school. They discussed the general lines of the project, and I tried to keep politics from mixing into it. Governor Storrs helped me and proposed that they call it the 'Jerusalem Music School' in place of the 'Anglo-Judeo Music School' as the Jews had proposed. Nonetheless, my proposal that a Muslim member be added to the committee, a natural thing since there were Christians and Jews, did not prosper. [*Finally, they all understood that I was right, and my plan was approved.*]

I have had news of the Germans interned in Egypt. They are satisfied with the treatment they are receiving and even with the temperature. On the other hand, here we have returned to the heat, and what is worse to the illnesses, since beside the flu, badly named 'Spanish,' we now have no less than the pernicious malaria. Because of this disease, a poor Christian girl, whom I met in the bank, has died, and she lasted no more than six hours.

23 September, 1918

We are in sensational and very historic times. The British have surprised the Turks and have made a substantial advance in very few days, occupying Samaria and part of Galilee. At the 'Intelligence' they assured me yesterday that the British line is currently Haifa-Tiberia. The number of prisoners is no less than 25,000; that is to say, almost the whole Turkish army to the north and northeast of Jerusalem.

On Thursday I was in Jaffa, and on arriving near Mikveh Israel, I encountered various regiments of Australian cavalry. Seeing them go in full gear, and the fact that the chiefs of staff were studying maps and giving orders at full speed, made me believe that they were dealing with something more serious on that side, but I never thought it would be that much. In Jaffa they confirmed to me that, before dawn, a furious bombardment began which lasted a short while. Other persons told me that the Jaffa-Jerusalem highway had been completely obstructed during the night because of the movement of artillery, cavalry, munitions, etc.

In the afternoon I began to see the consequences of it: Wounded and more wounded were arriving at the Tel-Aviv hospital and, among them, were Germans and Austrians. Upon returning to Jerusalem I stopped to have tea with Captain Hough, who is serving as interpreter in the Turkish prisoner camp of Lydda (Arimatea). While I was there, some 400 prisoners arrived. They were all well dressed and seemed to be good troops. According to what they assured me later, they were from the 22nd Army Corps, which even lost its Chief of Staff, who fell into British hands.

In Jerusalem I keep on seeing more prisoners and, every day that passes, I learn more details of the operation, which will give a huge reputation to General Allenby. The operation was the following: The British advanced along the coast up to Yaqum, heading from there towards the interior to cut off the retreat of the Turkish army. Pushed by the troops who were towards Nablus, the Turks found themselves in a crossfire and without any retreat, except a difficult or impossible one towards the Jordan. The result was that the entire army has been surrounded. A curious detail: The British cut the railroad in various places and four German airplanes, completely unaware of what happened, calmly landed in al-Tula, occupied by the Australians, who took away the mail they were carrying.

Artillery forces have now passed through Nazareth, and I hope for other interesting details any moment. With all this, the Turks who are on the east of the Jordan seem to be ignorant of what happened, and calmly continue bombing Jericho. In the surrounding of Lorenzo's house various projectiles have fallen. Those troops are probably going to find themselves surprised to see themselves trapped by the north. I hope that puts an end to them, because they have been committing brutalities with the Armenians, whom they are stoning in Kerak, according to my information.

To follow the campaign well, I am going to copy and translate the official dispatches that they are publishing. I have here the first:[10]

Palestine Front – Official – Cairo

Last night troops from India and the country of Wales attacked the enemy positions to the east of the al-Bira-Nablus highway, on a four-mile front, and advanced to a maximum depth of 5,000 yards. Some 400 prisoners were taken.

At 4:30 this morning English, Scottish, Irish, Jewish and French troops, after a short bombing, attacked between Rafat and the sea in a 15 mile front, the whole of the enemy defense front at the foot of the colonies to the southeast of Djildjiliya and from Bir 'Adus to the sea was taken very early. The second enemy defense system from al-Bira to the mouth of the Falik River and the towns, strongly fortified, from Djildjiliya and Qalqiliya, were in our hands by mid-day. The enemy is withdrawing in disorder, pursued by our cavalry. We have occupied the important rendezvous station of Tul Karam. The R.A.F. bombed the enemy headquarters and the railroad stations last night and, during the day, getting many targets among the troops and transports. They calculate some 3,000 prisoners, but they are taking many more. We have also captured many guns and materials.

Friday.

The divisions who broke the enemy defenses on the coastal plain yesterday are advancing today towards the east, through the hills, and are converging towards Samaria and Mas'udiyya. To the west of the al-Bira-Nablus road, the Irish and Indians have reached Kafar Haris and Salfit. To the east of the road, Indians and troops from the country of Wales have continued their advance towards the north. They have found considerable resistance at first, but the enemy is now in full retreat along the length of the road that leads to al'Alfula and Raysan. The cavalry that reached Qaqun and Siktera yesterday is now in al'Afula, the enemy line of retreat. The road from Mas'udiyya to al'Afula is full of Turkish troops, and transports going north fell into the hands of our cavalry. The Turkish communications by railroad have been cut to the north, south and west of Der'a by Arab Regulars and Bedouins.

The total number of prisoners is unknown, but they have counted more than 8,000. The loot is comprised of a great quantity of transport material, munitions and military depots. The airplanes have attacked the enemy columns with bombs and machine guns.

28 September, 1918

I will not keep on copying the official dispatches because I will have them all in our great newspaper, *Palestine News*. Besides, I am prepared to verify with my own eyes the British advance, since I will leave tomorrow for Nazareth, Haifa and Tiberias, provided with the necessary documentation. The military has made no objections, and it is clear that I am the first civilian to make that trip. The Zionist Commission, with all their power and influence, has not been able to do it up to now. I'm taking Haddad and 'Abed. The Zionist Commission has not given me any assignment for the Galilee colonies, no doubt out of spite.[11] Oh, I will also be accompanied by some boils, which have been giving me trouble for a couple of weeks. I'm carrying commissions of all types, including one of turning over 500 British Pounds to the governor of Nablus, my friend consul Kerny.

The day before yesterday I was in Jaffa once again for two actions: To visit General Lloyd and Father Ulibarri, to make a claim for the effects requisitioned in their convent, and to see the German officer prisoners who are in Lydda. Since my friend and colleague Hough is precisely the one in charge of them, it was not inconvenient to see them.

The camp is very well organized, surrounded by an extremely tall stockade of wire and distributed in different sections, also separated by barbed-wire entanglements; there is a canteen and all the necessary outbuildings. I first visited five officers, all of them very young. Through them I found out that my friends Hohenlohe, Falkenhausen, Arnim and Axster are in Germany. They asked me for news of the French front which, naturally, I did not give them. The poor men told me, 'We don't believe what the British are telling us.' The truth is that, if what the British are saying in their telegrams is true, Germany is on its last legs. Beaten in France, the Bulgarians asking for an armistice and Turkey destroyed. What else is left for them?

It is 10:15 P.M. and, in the orphanage across from my house, the Germans are being a nuisance, as every night there is a party.[12] I've had it up to here with Jewish song, some of which are very pleasant, but some of them go down like the pigeons they eat every day. At least at this moment they are preparing, the children, not the pigeons, to sing 'Tiqwa,' that is 'Hope', the Jewish national anthem. Since they always sing it at the end of every party it is a sort of 'invitation' to say goodbye; in view of that, I also bid farewell to my very patient readers or 'listeners'.

5 October, 1918

I'm on the way back from my trip, and it seems as if I attended a cinema production instead of taking a trip. I have had many surprises, some pleasant; I have admired the incredible effort carried out by the British to assure victory, and, on the other hand, I have witnessed macabre scenes I will never forget.

Last Sunday I set out on my journey at 7:00 on a morning worthy of Palestine. Air and sky extremely pure, without a gust of wind and me in a state of enthusiasm thinking that I was going to visit the areas liberated from the Turkish yoke, and I was going to see the country where our Lord lived for 32 years. No doubt, that idea of freedom from the Saracen yoke, as a common poet would say, to a country so sacred to us, would make me sympathize with the British... but I was afraid to find (as I did find) too many signs of the evils for which that liberation had been necessary. (...)

But let's get to the point. A short while after leaving we began to meet people whom my *cavas* recognized by their outfits and turbans, which, as everyone knows, vary according to the region to which their owners belong. Little military movement until al-Bira, where we met some troops and a great camp, continuing along a highway that is no marvel, but will be in short order if the thousands of Egyptian laborers who are working on it do their duty.

We passed the precious Wadi Djifna and arrived at the famous Sirnia, descending to the no-less famous 'Ayn al-Harammi ('Fountain of Thieves'). In all this, interminable lines of ants, or at least Egyptians who carry thousands of pails of water, straw for the horses, and all that is necessary for the provisioning of the army.

Soon we began to distinguish the remains of what was the Turkish army: Wagons, wires and some abandoned shells. On the tremendous slope down to Khan Lubban there were several British police directing the traffic to avoid accidents on the turns of the road. We stopped a little while in Khan to water my 20 horses. We drank water from the ancient spring which the British have transformed in a few days, converting it with a framework of wood and waterproof sacks into a big reservoir. We began to see the holes made in the earth by the explosion of large caliber missiles and we also began… to have breakdowns. While my mechanic, Davids, was changing a tire, an Indian mountain battery went by towards Jerusalem. (…)

At 10:30 we arrived in Nablus, but before then I managed to notice more than a hundred guns taken from the Turks. Almost all of them were in good shape and among them there were some large caliber. To be sure, on my return I found some of these pieces that, dragged by tractors, were going to lob shrapnel at their former owners.

Nablus is boxed in between Mount Ebal and the Gerizim. It was atrociously hot there. Those two so-celebrated mountains have no vegetation, nor the height that I supposed either. The town, as is well known, is very fanatic and, for this reason Colonel Kerny has declared it 'out of bounds,' to avoid a big mess, above all keeping in mind that men and women of the imprisoned Turkish officers have stayed there, and one must be careful with the Indians. In the city was D. Giorgio, the Austrian priest of the Patriarchy. I also found General Chetwode, the leader of the 20th Army Corps. Poor Kerny is supremely bored in that one-horse town. With surprise, I saw the railroad that goes from that city to Mas'udiyya, of whose existence I was completely ignorant.

The priest's house was decorated with al fresco paintings (and fresh they were) representing nude women serving champagne. And in such a place the Sisters of the Rosary worked, the poor ladies hoping that a dose of lime would free them from that view. The paintings are the work of the Germans who had occupied the house.

We left Nablus and crossed a little oasis that has nothing special about it except its smallness. I don't want to remember the time we spent in my Ford crossing the first kilometers beyond the city. Not even the Turks had prepared the road before getting cut off! I have never in my life seen a worse road. At every step we hit our heads against the sunshade of the car, but the worst was that the road was brightened by the smell of dead horses and camels that were along the sides.

It must be pointed out that the defense of Nablus was not very energetic. Just a few French soldiers made prisoners of hundreds of Turks. The beautiful olive trees that were there have been devastated in an incredible manner by the Turks. We kept on finding rockets, the remains of boxes, tents, empty cans, etc. When I was amazed to see six planes that were flying slowly because they were loaded with bombs, Davids told me that he had seen 49 of them together the other day.

At 12:30 we arrived at the station of Mas'udiyya. The impression I got was that of finding myself in an immense cemetery. The station, and the numerous shanties that constituted its outbuildings, were completely destroyed. We got out of the car and dedicated ourselves to picking up souvenirs of the war. We could have filled several trucks, since there were damaged automobiles, missiles, cartridges, bayonets... a veritable arsenal. Backed up to a hill was a depot of rifle cartridges with the door open. The heat was suffocating, and, with that silence of death, one could almost form an idea of hell. We hurried to leave that place, and we continued down the road without finding a soul, with a sun that began to oppress our hearts more than justice in spite of the beauty of the heights that surround Siloe, and from which one sees the sea, Carmel, the great Hermon, etc.

The horrors of the solitude and the heat united when we found a Turk half-eaten by animals. Ghastly! Since the road was dreadful, I feared that night would overtake us before reaching Nazareth. My car does not have headlights, and without knowing the road, the prospect was not very calming. The abandoned automobiles and wagons were multiplying to an incredible extreme.

Finally we saw people upon arriving at Djenin, which is occupied by soldiers from Nepal (*gurkas*). We drank a glass of water to refresh our throats, dry from the dust of the desert we have just traversed and, while we spoke with an interpreter, we saw many Turkish prisoners go by. (...) At the exit of the town we crossed two camps of prisoners, and we saw two captured German airplanes, one of them completely carbonized. Then the most horrible spectacle of the road: A column of fifteen trucks had been bombarded and strafed by British planes and of them there remained scraps, empty bottles, an enormous quantity of papers on the ground...

and many Turkish soldiers, dead, blackened, and in a state of which I prefer not to speak.

More dead on the highway: A group of horses, probably sacrificed by the British for having arrived at that site all worn out. Finally, we arrived at al-'Afula. There was an endless number of German cars seized by the British there. We only had an hour left to cover the enormous slope one has to go up to get to Nazareth, but we were still supposed to meet a German officer who was arranging with some soldiers for their own cars fallen into the hands of the enemy.

When it was almost nightfall we got up the steep slope and still saw many German cars that doubtless before the fire from the Turkish airplanes were in such a panic that some of them hurled themselves over the earthen bank fleeing from that inferno. This is the novelesque interpretation of the matter, since some of the common folks would probably suppose that the drivers tossed the cars to prevent them from falling into enemy hands.

Nazareth has an admirable look. It is a happy city with a pleasant climate. Its inhabitants are also happy, or they were when I went because of the arrival of the British. The Nazarenes remind of the people of Bethlehem, although at heart I suppose they will be like all the Arabs: At first glance they seem better.

I gave a big surprise to the Franciscans and to the Guardian, Father Serafin Lavarez. Father Marcelo Martin Plata and some laymen were very eager to honor us. Surprise: Mustafa Bey has stayed in Nazareth. I received visits from various of my *mixed* protégés, and the following day we left for Haifa.

The road, rather good, crosses the mountain, but it is very average in the plain and got worse to the point that we had a breakdown. (...) After finally getting down off the slope, there before our eyes was the majestic Bay of Acre, making a worthy background to the landscape in front: Mount Carmel and the admirable Plain of Esdraelon. Finally, we saw British forces again: Cavalry and small and medium-caliber artillery. They occupied the foot of the mountain and spread out to the city itself.

My first visit to Haifa was for the Patriarch, who was lodged in the convent of the monks of Mt. Carmel. Monsignor Camassei showed himself to be very content and grateful. I was truly happy to see again the man who so well deserves the name and description of Patriarch. Later, I visited the Chief of Police, who is none other than my *dragoman*, Rauf. After two days he left, with the same post, for St. John of Acre, with Major Abramson as chief.

Haifa must be an ideal winter residence. If it is hot, one has only to take a walk up Mt. Carmel between the breeze from the sea and the perfume of the pine forests. The city has a very happy aspect, with charming houses in the German colony and a very lively bazaar. There I ran into good friends, like Dizengoff, the famous mayor of Tel-Aviv, Storrs, Captain Harrington (governor of Samaria), Simmons, Kaiserman (director of the Anglo-Palestine Company Ltd.) and Fakhri Bey. They all made me spend pleasant hours with the ones who contributed the courtesies of the German colony. We ate in the Hotel Karmel, and there I learned about the taking of Damascus, but since I also found out that there are cases of cholera in Tiberias, I decided as a matter of prudence not to go to said city and to return from Nazareth directly to Jerusalem.

The only one who was not happy with my trip to Haifa was our vice consul, Scopinish, nor his comical wife. But what are we going to do for him?

To return to Nazareth I took another road, more to the north which, besides being better, is much more interesting. My car was advancing in the middle of a strong rain shower (the first of the season) crossing thickets of oak shrubs and other mountain plants. The rain stopped when we got to a German colony, Waldheim, delightful and well-cultivated. We stopped a moment and did the same in the home of the mayor of another new and flourishing German colony that is called 'Bethlehem.' It has been established for a dozen years and has 700 hectares of crop land, vineyards and wooded areas. A rustic mayor honored us with fresh lard, cheese, olives and excellent bread; a rather simple lunch, but in these times of war it is an unheard of luxury. One of the colonists told me that the wheat produces for them at a rate of 18 and even 20 to one, which is to say, a marvelous land.

Some kilometers farther along we crossed a delicious oasis, an orchard of great extension perfectly cultivated and irrigated, and planted with pomegranates and other fruit trees. We stopped, and while 'Abed was buying some pomegranates, I took a stroll through that little forest, listening to a sort of flute, played by the peasants of that country that took me back to other times and ages, not these of Enver Pasha and Hindenburg. But, *alas*, as the English say, I had to go back to my car, finding newly dead horses, abandoned missiles (times of Enver Pasha) and other reminders of war.

At last, after a British wireless telegraph station, we wound up in Nazareth. New acts of kindness from the friars with whom I visited the sanctuary, the description of which I need not bother, it being sufficiently well-known, just as the new church designed and directed by the nice Father Prospero Viaud, vicar of the Holy Land, in the site of St. Joseph's workshop. I was also in the hospital of the Brother of St. John of God, where I met an old friend, the German officer Lübke, who was directing the loading of the sick and injured Austro-Germans in trucks from the English Red Cross. I took note of all of them, to send it to the German government and an acknowledgment to their respective families.

They told me that the arrival of the British forces was so unexpected that Liman von Sanders, the Turkish-German General in Chief, escaped from the city when the British had already entered it. His daughters accompanied him and left some 70,000 prisoners in the hands of the enemy. It may be that, in his place, I would have done the same, but it is possible that it would have been better to be taken prisoner also.

The return to Jerusalem was 4 ½ hours and without any breakdowns but the same spectacle as leaving: More dead than before, and a delicious coolness.

I have found in Jerusalem as many Zionists as when I left, and the people with great hope that Turkey will sign the peace this month. If it is so, I will have guessed it, and I will be *Nabi* (Arabic for prophet).

31 October, 1918

Hanna Rahil has told me this morning that Turkey has accepted the peace without conditions and that at noon, the armistice should begin. The rest of the news of the war this month is incredible but must be true. Germany is completely defeated and will have to turn itself over to its enemies tied hand and foot, as its other allies have already done.

I have taken another trip towards the north, although more interesting than the previous one. On the 19th in the company of Father Dunkel, of the Order of St. Lazarus, I went again to Nazareth. I stopped in Nablus to have coffee with 'don' Giorgio Golubovich, seeing along the road the usual: Abandoned cars and remains of all kinds from the Turkish army, now belonging to history.[13] In Djenin I took a shortcut that led me to the former aviation field of the Germans. There, I took the opportunity to photograph a monument dedicated by the aviators to their dead or missing companions.

In Nazareth I only stopped just long enough for a light lunch. I continued my road along a delightful highway up to Cana of Galilee, situated in a valley that made me hope for an ideal landscape all the way to Tiberias. But, wouldn't you know it, as soon as we left Cana, the delightful highway transformed into an impossible road on which my companion and I did not break our heads a hundred times against the roof of the car... only because the car was without roof. To make the journey even more attractive, all the verdure disappeared and we saw nothing but masses of basalt and dark earth that, I think, will be more fertile when this country is in other hands but that carried a bit of sadness with it.

As it got dark we made out Lake Tiberias, which at that hour was fantastically beautiful. The full moon was reflected in its waters and the white of its reflection alternated with the dark gray of the rest of the waters and brilliant red of the innumerable bonfires that the Bedouins had lighted on the east shore and in the mountains of the same side. With all this, we had Tiberias at our feet, and I say at our feet because the road dropped off sharply towards the lake with a slope that was almost vertical. The car went down without the engine running but with the necessary precautions so as not to run off on one of the fast curves of the highway, with a heavy, suffocating heat, appropriate for the month of October in this country. The city is evidently a Jewish colony: Since my arrival I have seen nothing but Jews. I stopped only to put some gas in the car, and I was not sorry for it, because there have been some cases of cholera in the town. Probably the water of the lake is contaminated, which makes the decision for me not to take a bath in the sacred water.

We continue our road to Damascus, going along the coast of the lake and passing through Magdala, the home of Mary Magdalene. The heat was unbearable, but to the northwest of the lake there is a wonderful spot, the home of Tabgha, of the German order of St. Lazarus, and there I spent the night.[14] I couldn't sleep because of the heat, even though my bed faced an open gallery, protected only by a metallic cloth. The gallery faces the lake and, from it, I watched the dawn the following day. One of the most pleasant impressions of my life will surely be that dawn, the proximity of the lake, so blue, of memories so sacred to every Christian, seeing golden clouds, blue mountains, ducks swimming in the lake, fish jumping out to the water (descendents of those the St. Peter fished for), and all this from a forest of tropical trees and hearing the singing of thousands of birds greeting the dawning of the sun. I'm getting too maudlin, but there is no one who would not be ecstatic before such a marvel.

(...) At 6:30, on the morning of the 20th I left for Damascus. First the road went up a mountain on whose top there was a house that the Italian National Association bought some time ago.[15] It went on then, crossing a country infested with Bedouins, dark and burnished by the sun. It all changed appearance as soon as one arrives at a Jewish colony whose name I do not recall, and in which one sees the hand of man: Poplars and little forests of eucalyptus separate very well cultivated fields and comfortable houses, although not as clean as one would wish.

Soon the view of Lake Hula or Merom appeared, small compared to Tiberias but deliciously blue. To the north there extended an immense marshy territory that must be paradise for the duck hunters in winter, if the malaria permits them to approach it. The highway descended abruptly to the Jordan valley, and I could contemplate to my own taste the holy river, narrow and tumultuous, in which Christians and Muslims, Indians and English all bathe. I crossed the river by the bridge of the Daughters of Jacob, which has just been repaired by the British. Then we set off on a road that is so in name only, since the ground has disappeared completely, and the car marched along on pieces of basalt that miraculously did not ruin any of our tires. Numerous Egyptians and people from the country were working on the repair of the road.

From quite a few meters below the level of the Mediterranean we rose to a very respectable height. The fresh air brought me back to life, because I could not bear the temperature of the valley. The road up to al-Qunaytira is not bad but not at all interesting, if one exempts the beautiful massif of Hermon on whose peak there is still a bit of snow. Al-Qunaytira is a little city with houses of basalt and streets laid out in straight lines. In the streets one saw nothing but Australian soldiers and the occasional *Tcherkes*, with their typical outfits and weapons. From there to Damascus we met at least 3,000 Turks, many of them very tired; they were not able to follow their companions and were left far behind, a thing that, in these solitary places, can be dangerous with the abundance of jackals and hyenas.

Some isolated little forests and a little more greenness announced to us the proximity of the magnificent oasis of Damascus, where we arrived a little after midday. Before arriving, we met the first troops of the Sharif that I have seen: Several horsemen with an outfit very similar to the Turks with rather bandit-like characters, flourishing a flag with three horizontal stripes, black, green and white, with a reddish triangle near the shaft: As they call it, a rainbow... Well that is no less than the flag of His Majesty the king of Hedjaz.

I spent two and a half days in Damascus, lodged and treated like a king in the home of the consul Amigó, my dear comrade. The Jews expelled from Jerusalem in the times of the Turks visited me en masse: David Yellin, Mr. Massié with Margot, Moisé Valero and Berta, his wife, Dr. Krüger, Rabinowitz from Jaffa. (...)

The Greeks did no less, and Monsignor Damianos (the ex-Patriarch), Glykeris and Meletios hurried to come 'killing two birds with one stone.' They were trying to find out the impression the measure taken by the Greek convent had produced in Jerusalem: The convent was reduced to friars and some Archimandrites who decided not long ago to dismiss Monsignor Damianos and substitute for him the Archbishop of Sinai, Porfirios II. This all seems to be a matter of (the Greek prime minister) Venizelos, who is trying to Hellenize the Jerusalem church. Supported by Metxakis, a metropolitan from Athens, Venizelos has gotten the British government to take his side, so that, despite the opposition of the Orthodox nation of Jerusalem, what I relate is a consummated deed. In support of this belief, there exists the circumstance of the Inspector General of the National Bank of Greece being in Jerusalem, apparently with the object of paying off the great debts of the Greek convent, which amount to 12 or 14 millions of Francs. A trifle! (...)[16]

The British also came to see me in Damascus. I had tea one of the days with Commander Cornwallis and Colonel Stirling. The latter came with the Sharif's army and was wearing a khaki suit with the *kefie*, a very odd combination. Another day I had tea with none other than His Highness the Emir Faysal, the older son of the Sharif. His Highness received me with Amigó in a salon furnished in the damascene style and dress in the *kefiah* and an *abaia* embroidered in gold. Since His Highness speaks only Arabic, an officer of his army who is his assistant and, until quite recently was an officer in the Turkish army, served as interpreter. That's life! His Highness really has a very distinguished physique, and represents his role very well. Damascus currently has an army of the Sharif and the governor of the city is an Arab, 'Ali Riza Pasha. One sees the flag of the Sharif flown everywhere. There are two officials, one Engish and the other French, in charge of maintaining the relationship with the Arabs: The Englishman of whom I have spoken, and Captain Mercier. What does the population of Damascus think of this trinity? From what I could determine, they are fed up with the Arab government, except perhaps the Muslim element, and want a European government, preferably English. So I also believe that, sooner or later, Albion will take possession of that country. In the meanwhile, the Turkish system of *baksheesh* keeps on functioning, and I even think it has been perfected. A short while ago the emir told our consul that they still don't know how they govern themselves and that they need the help of England, France... and Spain, meaning that above all what they need is engineers and financiers. How little His Highness knows us!

The streets of Damascus are cleaned every day by the Turkish prisoners, who surely never suspected the role of street sweepers they were going to have. The misery of the population is great, and it seems to me that, for a while, they will just have to hope that the Arab government remedies the situation. As for the rest, I found the city to have the same Oriental character as always. The interesting and malodorous bazaars contrasting with that the illumination and the electric trolley cars. The Turks made a kind of avenue called Djemal Pasha and finished it, practically coinciding with the arrival of their enemies.

I visited the Red Crescent hospital, which is very near the home of that nice Nur al-Din Bey, at the foot of the mountain that dominates Damascus, with a marvelous view. There they described to me the entry of the

Anglo-Arab troops into the city: Bloody battles shortly before arriving, but the occupation was done with tranquility and only the thefts of the Bedouins who, following their customs, took advantage of the confusion of the first moments.

Naturally, I dedicated much time to the friars, my compatriots who were Fathers Luis Tuesta, Pedro Larrucia, José Vázquez, Fuster and Brother Domingo Alcorta, who are very good and conduct themselves admirably. It's only that they are not at all diplomatic with the people of the country, and, unfortunately, that is a defect common to all our clergy, with rare exceptions such as Father Juan Setón, who bowls over everyone.

The architect Aranda has a delightful new house that he himself has built, in the style peculiar to Damascus. Certainly, the first time that I arrived in this city, seeing the Arab style of the station, I did not know that its author was the same Aranda.

The Massié family told me about René's evasion. Condemned to three years in prison on suspicion of espionage he was sent, together with some 40 prisoners of all races and religions on a train that was headed for Aleppo. When the train arrived at the Rayak station, the British aviators began to bomb it, and then the officer who was leading them decided to take flight, yelling at the soldiers, 'If you love the Turkish homeland, follow me!' Naturally, only a few Turkish soldiers followed him, and the rest escaped, fleeing during the night and hiding during the day, sleeping among the trees. Poor René is now in Damascus, but full of bandages to cure his numerous rips and tears.

On Wednesday the 23rd I set off en route for Beirut. At first the road stayed along the edge of the Barada River with a little forest of black and white poplars, but after a short while it transforms into something more appropriate to the country, that is to say, it's pretty bad and crosses desert area, burned by the sun and of a crushing monotony. But the view of the *Gebel esh Sharqi* that appeared before long on our right (I say 'our' because Mr. Yellin is coming along with me) gladdened our eyes a bit. After finishing the rise to a hilltop there appeared before our eyes the beautiful plain of Celesyria, which we crossed at good speed, admiring its extraordinary fertility.

We went close by the famous agricultural farm of Shtoar, the property of the Jesuits, very well cultivated, and a little while later we began the ascent of the mountain range of Lebanon, by an admirable highway, crossing the railroad tracks many times and passing through little towns with European houses and almost-civilized people. Little by little we were seeing the Hermon in all its majesty, and the *Gebel esh Sharqi*, both behind the plain that we have just crossed. The air was becoming refreshing with the altitude, and as we got to the top of the mountain, we admired the Mediterranean slope, incomparably more beautiful than the other. (...)

We went down toward the sea and crossed through delightful towns in which there were magnificent hotels, terrific country houses and lots of money; that is to say, what was there before the war was lost happily in baccarat or poker games. During the war many of the inhabitants died of hunger. The French say that 150,000 people perished from hunger, thanks to the fraternal Turk. I don't know if the matter is exaggerated but, by the guys I have seen along the highway, there must be something of the truth in it. Besides, almost all the houses I have seen in the towns were closed. They tell of macabre details, like the one of the mother who, when a starving wild dog came by and threw itself on her child, did not have sufficient strength to stop the dog from devouring it... and I will not continue.

We arrived at Beirut at 1:30 in the afternoon, and I ate lunch in the Gasmann Hotel, which is now called the Royal Hotel. The following day I attended a luncheon in the home of Colonel Piepape, who had also invited Generals Wukfin and Money, with Piepape's Chief of Staff and Commander Dapdezele. The colonel is very nice and has made the best impression on the local population, but it seems that has not been the case with the rest of the French. I spoke with various people from different social categories, and in complete unanimity they told me they prefer the British to the French. I confess that I was surprised since, before the war, all the sympathies were for France and, in fact, everybody speaks French. But some time ago I was told that the absence of the consul general of France, Picot, who left in the archives compromising papers that in the hands of Djemal Pasha caused the death of many notable people of the city, hanged by my dear friend, had greatly cooled that enthusiasm.

What consequences will this antipathy bring? Is it owed to what I mentioned before, or that the English have more money and more means and that guides the Phoenician inhabitants of this country? I think it is a little of all of that and that it is not only patriotism that guides their sentiments. The British show themselves to be extremely correct with the French and, given the importance of the relations between the two, have named as 'Liaison Officer' none other than Colonel Deedes. Piepape is the governor of the city and, at the same time, 'Chief Administrator of the Occupied Territories of the Northern Zone'. I don't know why, but I figure that northern zone will be transported someday very far to the north... of Beirut.

Father Brégill, Jesuit with, I don't know, a more or less secret job in the French army, spoke to me of the projects that France is carrying out: The creation of a refuge for 3,000 children, large scale aid sent to Lebanon...

by the American Red Cross, which is doubtlessly considered an institution under French protection, if it is not actually the opposite.

A French officer told me (a rare thing) about a feat of the Germans. On the advance to the north of Jaffa, his regiment was detained for many hours by the fire of German machine guns; as soon as anyone poked his head out of the trenches, he fell down dead. At last they advanced, but who had stopped them? Well, simply three German officers, each with his own machinegun, put up that desperate resistance, thus protecting the retreat of the rest. The three officers knew they were sacrificing themselves, and, in fact, they were dead at the feet of their guns.

Speaking of the misery in Lebanon, they told me that in one town that had 12,000 inhabitants there were only 60 left.

In Beirut they were waiting for Mr. Picot on a cruiser, and on that boat, they believed that 60 civilian people were coming, charged with the administration of the country, which is greatly needed. Colonel Piepape occupies as an office the former palace of the *Nabi* of Beirut. They gave him guards from the Armenian legion, which does not seem very normal. In short, the current organization of the occupied territories is in three zones: Palestine (British), Syria (French) and the East (Sharif's). And I ask myself, for how long?

In Beirut I visited Musa and Alfredo Sursoc, of the famous family of millionaires, and I took a car ride through the pretty suburbs. I finished my limit of visits with one from Adel Bariash and Negir Abusswan who, with his wife and Salim, have been living in Hauran for four years. I was the first person from Jerusalem who visited them since they were expelled by Djemal Pasha, so they wouldn't let me go for love nor money.

On Friday the 25th I undertook the trip to Haifa. A very good highway up to Tyre. First you cross, at the exit from Beirut, some magnificent olives groves, and then the highway draws close to the sea, whose shore is followed constantly. (…) I continued up to the ancient Sidon (Saida), a city that is surrounded by wonderful gardens in which the flora of Europe is joined with that of Africa; the trees are magnificent and very tall. In a fountain of very abundant and fresh water we stopped and admired some of the real forests that abound there, formed by apricot, pomegranate and palm trees. I suppose that, if the French take care of this privileged region as it deserves, it will be a paradise within a few years.

We did not stop in Sidon, but did in Tyre, where we arrived later after an hour of crossing the coasts of Phoenicia. (…) Tyre is situated in a sort of peninsula, with a little port in which only fishing boats enter. That being so, anyone who lives there will never lack iodine, nor the sound of the waves in winter, nor the bad smell of the houses and their inhabitants in summer. But for what reason do the Arabs call the Jews dirty? He who wants to convince himself of this should go to the famous kingdom of Hiram and contemplate the bazaar and the houses of the city. I consider myself the most fortunate of mortals to live in Jerusalem, if I compare myself with the poor Lieutenant Angot, who has the high honor of being governor of the city. I only envy one thing of his: The balcony of his house which faces directly towards the sea. Sitting on it one can have the perfect illusion of being on a ship without the inconveniences of seasickness. Besides, it can be useful for suicide if they do you the honor of leaving you there as governor for several years. I had lunch with Sancho Panza, I mean with Lieutenant Angot, together with various convalescent French officers (besides being boring it is apparently not very healthy) in the convent of the Holy Land where Sir Governor resides.

Dear Angot told me a thing that demonstrates how far the public spirit of the bureaucrats of the country extends. While speaking with the mayor who has remained in the city of the Turks, he said that they were all thieves, to which Angot answered, saying, 'Naturally, with the exception of yourself.' And the good Arab with all frankness responded, 'Perhaps I am as much a thief as the others.' When we left Tyre we took not the road that kept on following the seashore, but rather an old one fixed up in a few days by the British. That road joins the other at precisely the most dangerous place of the route, where I glanced to see that the Phoenician coast also has cliffs. Ras al-Naqura is a bad pass in every sense of the word, but it's ideal for a bandit attack. (…)

A little further along the road twists towards the interior, with said spot lending itself very well to giving you a fright, if you're going by coach and with tired horses, shooting at you from perfect safety or shoving you nicely into the sea, which is what happened in the good old days of the Turkish domination to he who ventured to pass by there. Fortunately, that now belongs to history. When I arrived this time, a convoy of artillery and service corps had just gone through with at least 3,000 men, and I don't know how many thousands of horses. Farther along there is another site almost as 'pleasant' as the previous, except that it is not near the sea. There, my car passed the ones from Cain to get up the little slope. Since the British are so prudent we had found beforehand a warning that said 'three dangerous turns;' so dangerous that we almost stayed to keep company with a German automobile (from the factory of my friend, Opel) for which there was no way it could get by the slope.

With all this, nightfall was drawing nigh. Shortly before arriving at St. John of Acre, night fell definitively because we lost at least an hour with two consecutive breakdowns. The last one was very interesting now that, by the light of the headlamp of the automobile, the night presented a fantastic aspect: Behind the others there fell lightening strikes and flashes, and when my mechanic announced that he was putting on the last tire we had, I prepared to spend the night in the open air, listening to the symphony of the jackals and wild dogs whose eyes shone in the darkness, and exposed to an attack from the people of the country, which is the worst little problem with breaking down out here.

As all thing come, so too came the moment of fixing the tire as best we could, and, with a night darker than the inside of a wolf's mouth, we continued on our road. This bit about continuing our road is just a saying, because since there was no indication of any kind, we got lost and wound up running headlong into a marsh. Fortunately, we found a rich Muslim's house in the middle of the countryside, and, as the ultimate good luck, a boy who lived near there told us that he had to go to Haifa by donkey and, of course, was delighted to accept the proposition we made him, that he come in the car with us to show us the way.

We managed to leave for the beach in such agreeable company. We crossed two bridges on the famous Kishon River, but when we got to within a scant 400 meters of the town of Haifa, drat, our last tire blew. But beggars can't be choosers, and any port in a storm. At least that's what the mechanic must have thought, who put an old blanket in the interior of the hood, and thus very slowly, and having to stop all the time, we managed to get to Hotel Karmel at 10:00 P.M. The delights of touring by automobile!

I was in Haifa only a short time, sufficient for the visits and work appropriate to my job. From Haifa I came to Jaffa along the coast, in which there was nothing notable. I passed by sites famous in history, but of them nothing but the name remains. The opposite is happening in the magnificent, prosperous colony of Zichron Yaqob, a colony situated near the sea, well-cultivated and with great storerooms. The governor there was a relative of Rothschild, Captain Walley.

From there, and by a road which I suppose will be a swamp in winter, I went on to Tulkarem, an extremely important hub of railroad connections in the times of the Turks and even more under the British. The latter are making a railroad that goes from there to Haifa, which will make that city (which also has the railroad from Damascus) convert, according to all the prophets of the country, into a port much more important than Jaffa, and perhaps of greater movement than Beirut itself. To the reasonings of these prophets I will add another: If Beirut finds itself in the hands of the French, Haifa is in the hands of the British... enough said.

We left Tulkarem and got lost again. Fortunately it was morning now, and since there were people in the countryside now, asking one after another we went successively through Kafar Saba, a Jewish colony that used to be, because all its houses were destroyed by the bombing of British gunfire. There the Turks were defending themselves from the taking of

Jerusalem to the last great British offensive. And one saw evidence of them everywhere. The road was full of discharged missiles; to the right and left one saw Turkish trenches, ruined wire defenses, shoes (many shoes), that you know had been left there by their owners so they could run better, empty tins of preserves, 'quixotic' helmets of British soldiers and camels and horses almost consumed now by the dogs and the sun. Quite lovely!

After many turns and doubling back and having to push our famous Ford several times so it could get out of the sand we had gotten ourselves into, we arrived at a rustic bridge over the Audja River, and, from there, in a few moments we were at Sarona and Jaffa. The poor German colony of Sarona had been robbed and plundered by its current military occupants (there are even Italians among them!). It seems to me that its former inhabitants will not recognize it when they return from their deportation from Egypt.

From Jaffa to Jerusalem there was nothing in particular, except the pleasant surprise that the highway had been nicely resurfaced by the British, so our car sailed along at all the speed its tired 'horses' allowed it.

6 November, 1918

The first day of winter, or better said, the first night of winter, since the day was delightful and only after it got dark there arose a real cold and disagreeable hurricane, and I don't know if it will leave me in good health to get to the Mount of Olives, where General Money has invited me to dine. There are so many cases of pneumonia lately! The sadly famous flu transforms into pneumonia, and in three days one is making the trip to the next world. Mrs. Bandakech died of it and, yesterday, a girl only 20 years old. They say the latter got to a temperature of 43°C. She died, so to say, all burned up.

Last Saturday, I attended the arrival reception for David Yellin, who was in the Samuel School, a place of so many intrigues... Many speeches in Hebrew. I only understood that the Jews are not showing themselves to be as ungrateful as I thought, and maybe, I even believe it. Perhaps it was because of my presence at the meeting.

Sunday morning, the American Zionist Medical Unit was inaugurated with all solemnity and with a series of speeches in Hebrew, closed with one simple, but eloquent, by General Money. Dr. Segal introduced me to James Rothschild. Certainly, the famous multimillionaire was very friendly.

In the afternoon there were two events: The arrival of the Latin Patriarch and the celebration by the Jews of the first anniversary of the Balfour Declaration. I attended the first with great pleasure, and even endured the innumerable speeches in Arabic to which they submitted poor Monsignor

Camassei, who didn't have the heart for much more after his trip from Haifa. The society of Catholic Literary Youth, the representatives of the local press (!) and all the Christian denominations gave the most affectionate and well-deserved reception for the Monsignor. The day before I had made my first visit to the new auxiliary bishop, Monsignor Luigi Barlassina who, up until now, was the priest of St. John Lateran. They are all delighted with him, but for me, I'd rather not be under his authority. He is intelligent, young and they say very energetic, but for some reason I find him to be excessively, utterly Italian.

I saw the solemn entrance of the Patriarch into the city from the balconies of the Hotel Marcos, and I could observe what the protection of the Catholic Church means for France and Italy, which seem to be the two most Catholic countries in the world. In the Holy Sepulcher they would have repeated, if I had attended, the scene that took place for the Te Deum, for the liberation of the Holy Places: That is, they would have placed before me an Italian captain... So I didn't go.[17]

Having to receive the Patriarch freed us from a big promise, which was attending the Jewish celebration. For that one it was announced that 'there would be trouble,' and there was. Some young Muslims and Christians gave a beating to various Jews, which was followed on Monday by a demonstration by those religious groups before the military governor, whom they asked to telegraph their protest against the Jews to the British government. The aggressors were condemned to several months in prison (keep in mind that the interim president of the Tribunal of Justice is a Jew, the elder Bentwich, a good friend of mine).[18] Yesterday, it was announced that they were inclined to let them go free if they asked the Jews for forgiveness, to which the detainees or their families answered that they preferred to rot in jail before doing that. From which one can see that my forecasts are coming true about Lord Balfour's promises being well beyond his grasp.

16 November, 1918

I went to Jaffa with the intention of seeing Picot, but he wasn't there. Instead I greeted the new high commissioner that they sent to this country. This time we're dealing with an Englishman and no less than an adjunct of Lord Balfour, which made me suppose that he will bring with him a civilian staff from the Foreign Office. What I don't know is, if they will make things better or worse in this country. Things are getting murky and are beginning to smell rotten. Meanwhile, Christians and Muslims of Jerusalem are organizing meetings and commissions to fight against the Jewish influence. While they are doing that, the Jews have complained to the authorities in Jaffa that the latter are protecting the Christians too much! The

Christian-Muslims have organized a protest this morning in Jaffa to celebrate the occupation of the city and have begged the governor to telegraph to His British Majesty.[19] Before, they gave speeches, in which they got to the point of saying the following: 'The Jews claiming this country is the same as if we Arabs claimed Spain... The Jews are worse than the Turks.' Oh, what a great country! Oh, what a great country!

Monday was the celebration for the king of Italy, at which I presided (!!!), the Italian officials coming in the afternoon to congratulate me.

4 December, 1918

On the 1st I turned 33. I received demonstrations of affection and presents in abundance, including from people from whom I had not expected it. (...)

I don't worry about the 'ex-war,' in hopes that what the winners decide to do with this tired old world will be to renew and transform it... naturally, in their favor.

To distract myself, tomorrow I will go hunting with Durieux and Jean Rahil. The very famous Fathers Lagrange and Abel came to see me again, as well as Brother Luis of the Missionaries of Africa. Once again, I saw myself thrust into the middle of a thousand questions: Pro and anti-Semite politics (or rather, pro or anti-Zionist), the substitution of Monsignor Damianos for Porfirio II, Muslim petitions in favor of the Sharif, Christian aspiration for the internationalization of the country, ad nauseam.[20]

9 December, 1918

First anniversary of the entrance of the British. After three days of cold, rain and terrible wind, today we are enjoying splendid weather, fitting to celebrate that anniversary. The populace celebrated it each in his own way. In the morning, I went to the municipality to congratulate the military governor and then to the French high commissioner and Italian officials. A musical band was going around the town, followed by a numerous group of Armenians, with an Armenian flag and an English one. The Zionists refused to accompany the people from the town hall because the latter refused to translate into Hebrew a speech that the mayor had given in Arabic, although they put the invitations for the tea this afternoon in Arabic and Hebrew. This has been the first serious skirmish between the Jews and the Christian-Muslims. I will go to the tea and see what happens, but I imagine it will be nothing. We are in the East, and to everything one must respond *ma'alish*.[21]

The night before last, the society of the 'Jeunesse Catholique' (Catholic Youth) was inaugurated. I attended along with Durieux, the representative of the high commissioner of France. Captain Soragna limited himself to sending his representative. The society is beginning modestly, but I think it has a future. For it I have given 25 [British] Pounds that I hope His Majesty's government will pay. They will teach English, French, Spanish and Italian. I will endeavor to send books and help of all kinds, in accordance with the very Father Pardoa himself.

In the inauguration there were no more than two speeches: One by the president, Mr. Gebríe (from Madrid and speaking in Spanish), and another from one Danil, who had a rather picturesque idea, since upon finishing his speech in Arabic, he spoke about how the new society was counting on the support of Catholic Spain, France, the daughter of the Church and Italy, in which the Pope has his seat! The hint probably did not much please the representative of the one in charge of the civil affairs of Italy.

15 December, 1918

Really, there was nothing at the tea that took place at City Hall to commemorate the entrance of the British, if you exempt the good tea and jokes from Colonel Storrs, who presided over the event. Several speeches were made in Arabic and one in Hebrew, but on behalf of one and all there was much propriety; that is to say, there was what had to be.

Today, I have been in Ramla and Jaffa. For once I am convinced that I no longer believe in God and the holy Church. But in this lowly world there is no one who deserves the trouble of helping him… All these reflections are inspired by the attitude of some of those 'of the cloth.'

1919

26 February, 1919

I've made quite a jump in these notes, since two months have gone by since the last ones, but it hasn't been worth the trouble to bother about them for anyone, not even me. (...)

Storrs, a general now, invited me to a meal in the Augusta Victoria, which was attended by James Rothschild, the famous archeologist, Paribeni, and Father Abel. I don't think these things are seen anywhere but here. During the meal someone said that the Talmud is the best book to form a man's culture. Father Abel attacked such an idea with such enthusiasm that Rothschild dedicated himself to eating oranges with real enthusiasm, to disguise his emotions.

The music school is now up and running and has named Storrs as president and me as 'honorary treasurer,' Mrs. Hoofien being the honorary secretary. What an honor for the family! Of course, in tomorrow's session I plan to ask what my duties are.

There is another ceremony: The inauguration of the ophthalmology hospital of the Order of St. John. Commander in Chief Allenby presided, who bestowed the medals of the order upon General Storrs and Colonel Gardner. Storrs then gave a speech about the contrast between the conduct of the Turks and the Germans, who occupied the building as a munitions depot, and that of the British who are caring for those with vision problems. It is clear that the orator was forgetting at that moment that the French communities said publicly that the British have caused more damage than the Turco-Germans. But that's life and that's politics: A series of lies and calumnies that do not surpass, nonetheless, those of private life. I believe in the Society of Nations and the time of rights and of the oppressed as much as in the sincerity of Storrs.

I exchanged a few words with the good General Allenby, as well as with some of my old friends, British or anglophiles. And, head home when it rains, never more opportune this expression because it was pouring.

I was in Egypt again, from which trip I have come back delighted, above all with the most wonderful Vallín family and some friends that I have there.[1]

1 April, 1919

I have taken an excursion to visit the Salesians of Bayt Djemal, who have a very extensive farm with crop land, vineyards, almonds, some orchards and a tree nursery. Captain Meli Lupi di Soragna, head of the Italian military mission, took me in his Ford. Father Sacchetti, who is the Superior there, came with us. (. . .)

The Bayt Djemal house is situated on the high part of a hill, directly across from where Sampson lived. I even asked myself if one of the burros I saw in that country (I refer to the four-footed kind) might be a descendent of the one whose jaw afforded the celebrated judge the chance to kill so many Philistines. Above the door of the house is the following inscription: 'Agricultural School of St. Joseph.' We entered the villa and visited a large, stoutly made and unsightly convent, but with views from the terrace that can compare with those of Lebanon. The mountains are not grandiose, nor the valleys as sunny as in that mountain range, but there is not a hill nor a valley that does not have a name celebrated in the history of Jerusalem. One sees from there the mountain that hides Jerusalem, the Plain of Sharon, the valley of the Sorec, the Trevinto, where David killed Goliath. (…)

The Salesians explained everything to me, and I stirred up trouble with so many Biblical names, and the moment came in which I decided to take flight and leave to see the gas-engine wheat mill at the entrance of the house. Don Ricaldone told me that he wants to have an olive mill from Spain and that he wished it to be from the Acapulco system, in his judgment, the best. (…)

9 April, 1919

(…) Dr. Otis Glazebrook arrived, and I have handed over to him the interests of his country. I hope to do the same with the British, Italians and Russians. I have presented my resignation to the diplomatic agent in Egypt, or better put, my unemployment, effective three months from now.

The School of Music was inaugurated, and there was one detail that had more to it than meets the eye. As the concert ended, they played the Zionist hymn. All the Jews stood up, except Miss Landow. Storrs remained seated and after a while got up… and immediately sat down again. Oh, the commentaries there were! Of course the British and Italian officials and I all did the same. The commotion that was stirred up can scarcely be explained. In a few days there was a fancy dress dance in the home of Miss Landow. The party was boycotted by the Jews, who gave in at last to the requests of Storrs and went to the dance after the previous excuses. Mrs. Feigenbaum took the first prize for her disguise as a Yemeni woman.

The nice Father Damian Amschl died. The poor man was a victim of his own charity, because while doing an ear operation on a boy, the sort of thing he always did for free, he caught an infection that carried him off in less than a week. I attended his burial with the prior of Tantur, Father Lorenzo Hirzi and the military governor of Bethlehem. We all went on foot as far as Bayt Djala, and before burying him, there were moving panegyrics from the mayor of the town, the Superior of the schismatic Greek convent (which was admirable) and from one of the notables of Bethlehem, Salomon Yacir. It was the most sincere expression of feeling I have seen in this country.

I also got word of another sensitive death, that of Father Atanasio Vanhove, who was the superior of Notre Dame de France, and he died on January 15th in the shipwreck of the steamer 'Chaouia.' Extremely intelligent and with a very pleasant manner, he had always showed me a great sympathy, which I returned.

3 May, 1919

This morning I attended an interesting ceremony, the Saturday prayer done by the Jews. Mr. Sola Pool, a member of the Zionist Commission, had invited me, and in truth I am not sorry for it. The synagogue is the one of the Sephardic, and it was full of Jews: Among other notables, Mr. Hany Friedenwald, the president of the Zionist Commission, the great Rabbi Eliazhar, the one from Jaffa, Oriziel and the ones from Tiberias and Safed.

The ceremony began with prayers, which were followed by the triumphal procession of the Torah, the five books, or rather the five scrolls that were carried around by Sola Pool, who wore around his neck (as did all the other Jews) a sort of shawl, which is ritual. The people milled around at his step, and touched the wood and silver case in which the scrolls were enclosed and, afterwards, kissed their fingers. During the whole ceremony it remained deposited on a sort of altar, situated in the center of the synagogue. Chapters IX and XX of Leviticus were read by the celebrant, which was translated for me directly from the Hebrew text by the Great Rabbi of Jaffa, who was at my side.

Every week one or a few chapters are read so that, within the year, the entirety of the five holy books has been gone over. To continue, a rabbi went up into one of the pulpits, where he gave a long speech about my humble person in Hebrew, but afterwards, directing himself to me, repeated it in the Sephardic dialect of Spanish. I understood everything perfectly, thanks to the habit I have of listening to that type of Spanish of the Middle Ages, but degenerated by the mix with other languages. The ceremony ended with a prayer for the English royal family and another for me to which they all responded, 'amen.' Truly, if I were capable of believing in something in this world, I would believe in the gratitude the Jews showed me.

Holy Week went by without anything in particular to record. Because of the exasperating *Status Quo* I did not attend anything but the 'Greek Fire'. Certainly, a hornet's nest erupted between the Orthodox of Jerusalem and those of Jaffa over who had the right to be closest to the site from which the fire leaves. The temple, which should be the most august and respected site in the world, was converted into a sort of a *café concert* since the Greeks of the country were singing in chorus, dancing and even playing a type of drum. What a profanity! Of course, the priests who spiritually directed these people were worthy of them. A Greek lady told me in that same temple that every Orthodox priest had his sweetheart, and even the Patriarch himself has his weaknesses. Oh, Holy City!

There also took place a Muslim holiday: The pilgrimage of the Nebi Musa. This is another farce: The Muslims know very well that Moses is buried on the other side of the Dead Sea and that nobody knows where his tomb is, but to counteract the influx of Christians during Holy Week, they 'invented' a tomb that gives rise every year at this time to a very well attended pilgrimage. This year there was considerable panic among the Jews, since horrific announcements of killings, pogroms, etc. were made… and nothing happened, as is almost always the case when something is announced and above all in this country.

Storrs attended with his mother and sister, as well as many officers and notable Christians and Jews. At the head of the cortege marched a squad of Arab 'explorers,' who executed some exercises in front of the governor, and then one of the above-mentioned made a markedly nationalist speech ending with a hymn in similar vein. Storrs answered four banalities in Arabic, and the party ended, with me returning to my quarters in a Fiat of the Italians. One detail: During the ceremony, an Indian band was playing. And what instruments do you think they were playing? Well, naturally, Scottish bagpipes. Of course, the lack of musical taste the British have is notable. You should hear them when some regiments parade by.

On the 6th there was a tea in the former Hughes Hotel, by the 'American Zionist Medical Unit' in honor of Mr. and Mrs. Glazebrook. There was quite a bit of merriment and lots of American flirting, at which the American women are quite accomplished.

The Italian hospital was inaugurated with a speech by Soragna, another by Dr. Mancini and another from Storrs, after which we visited the building. (…)

La Cronie has published a terrible article against the British. Since it is very interesting, I'm keeping a copy of the entire thing. It also speaks about me and says that my situation is false, with which I am in perfect agreement with the author of the short article, which is a bit awkward. Consequently, General Allenby has telegraphed to the Governor of Haifa that they should evacuate all the French establishments in 24 hours. The brave British will certainly be busy! The article is the best I have seen about the current situation in Palestine, and fearing that it may be lost I am copying it whole:[2]

La Cronie. Thursday, April 3, 1919

The English occupation has removed Palestine from the Turkish occupation. To conclude from this that the country has been opened and that access to it is easy would go against everything true. In fact, it has been closed in a form so systematic that the exclusively military reasons are not enough to explain this rigorous measure.

Everyone knows that our clerics have needed entire months to obtain permission from the English to land in Port Said and entire weeks to be able to cross the Egyptian border. As a consequence, the establishments or jobs that they would have been able to reclaim have remained unoccupied. This vacuum has attracted the attention of the military authorities, and, while certain German houses were respected, the French establishments have been occupied, without the corresponding requisitions, and considered enemy property. This word has been said by the governor of Jerusalem to a certain person, who had allowed a very legitimate reclamation.

Such principles explain, without justifying them, the depredations and usurpations of all kinds that need to be registered to the account of our allies. The detail of all this would be interminable.

In Jerusalem, if I exempt two or three establishments that have owed their not having been occupied to their location in the interior of the city walls, all the establishments could present complaints, some of them very serious. One can say the same for the situation in Bethlehem, al-Atrun, Jaffa, Haifa and Nazareth. What a suggestive chapter one could write entitled, 'what the Turks haven't done'!

Perhaps we have a certain right to more amicable treatment; they have even been careless of the formalities as if they wanted to establish that, in the army, everything must necessarily be brutal. I do not find any other terms to describe, for example, their attitude in Haifa concerning the Sisters of St. Vincent de Paul. There, the poor sisters are obliged to rent a house and crowd together with their orphans because the English seem to find their establishment extremely convenient for their services and, above all, perfectly situated. Nonetheless the governor has judged it convenient to grant them a corner of his own grain barn in which to deposit the reclaimed goods.

Or the Brothers of the Christian Schools, who can't even enter their establishments, under the pretext that new prisoners should be arriving. Two months after the armistice! Or the Carmelites, recently arrived from France and obliged to look for shelter across from their convent, newly reoccupied by the English, who doubtlessly regret having abandoned it too soon.

These are the deeds of yesterday. At the time I write, we are observing the forced requisition of objects of great value for motives quite distinct from military necessities. The reiterated claims of the interested parties serve to make the ill will of the authorities notorious. For example, the bedding material, dispersed by the Turks and found again, after their departure, in hospitals or crowded into unoccupied locales: Why haven't the owners been able to reclaim this material? Official reply: This material would need to be used in case of an epidemic of typhus. However this material has been granted by the English, without prior agreement with the owners, to the personnel of the American Red Cross for their private use, and even transported in private tents to the Plain of Sharon or to other places.

Should I add, to finish this demonstration, that lately the governor has refused to accept the claims drawn up in French under the pretext that the appropriate office does not have an interpreter for this language? This latest act is symptomatic and can serve to make manifest the English tendencies against us in this country.

We have no one to give us justice. France has sent a high commissioner here. He entered Jerusalem at the same time as General Allenby and remains there. From the beginning the official relations have lacked cordiality; neither the time nor the prolonged relationship has improved them. Quite the opposite: In the eyes of the English, France has nothing to protect here, not even its national citizens. Here we have why the past claims by the consul or the high commissioner have been without effectiveness and even without reply. We are always at the same point: That is, treated worse and less safeguarded than the German or Austrian subjects the consul of Spain takes care of. This latter gentleman is the only foreign consul accredited before the government. He represents friends and enemies at the same time, to such an extent that one could jokingly grant him the title of 'ecumenical consul.' Others have already given testimony about his activity and energy, and our government has recognized them granting him a high honorary distinction. But which will be his role in questions among allies, the ones who have militarily occupied the country and the others who are represented by an extraordinary diplomatic mission? His situation is false and, supposing that he echoed our complaints, he would not be able to speak with the same firmness as if he were dealing with the complaints of other foreigners, including enemies.

So many shackles, delays, tricks and rejections must have a cause. To explain the slowness of the trips and the long waits in Egypt, they speak to us of the difficulties of provisioning and of the number of needy to maintain. What shamelessness to increase them even more! Our country, nevertheless, has responded to this difficulty for some time by means of aid about which I should say a word or two. To justify the occupation of the premises or the conservation of materials, they imagine absolutely problematic events. The fact is that there has been the necessary time, too much time, to obtain the free possession of our properties and to reinitiate our public works. But then the English charity works are fully active, which may perhaps give us the real reason for all this. At their arrival in the region of the important cities of Jaffa, Jerusalem and Bethlehem, our allies have had the revelation of a state of things absolutely unheard of for them. The vision of the numerous French establishments has deeply surprised them. Evidently, to permit all the French scholarly and hospital works to revive would put the conquerors in a state of inferiority in the eyes of the liberated populations. The English would not take it well, to have worked to open the doors for others, without taking some benefit for themselves. Very natural reasoning, which explains the national and denominational organization of the orphanages, schools and civil hospitals with emergency personnel and at whose backs the Egyptian border has been closed. And while our missionaries are held up in Marseille for months, Jerusalem sees new faces appear every day. We appreciate even more that they are opening schools, including in Christian towns where the missionaries of the Latin Patriarchy have been working for quite some time protected and aided by France. I would not want to insist of the denominational nature of this help. However they have immediately had a character so clearly anti-Catholic that it is impossible not to point it out. Let them explain, if they can, words such as the following, spoken too frequently before the poor people who cry: 'You are Catholic, we have nothing for you, go to the French.'

Consequently, between the important aid received from America and from other places, there is Catholic money, lots of money, readily absorbed by the Anglican bishop. The donors count on the good faith of the intermediary, and the intermediary has deceived them.

There have been complaints; coming to the attention of the English, these complaints have not fallen on deaf ears during the trip Cardinal Bourne has made through the eastern Mediterranean. His Excellency has strongly encouraged the Catholic public works to consolidate and to appeal to the services of England. Afterwards the governor of Jerusalem has felt obliged to offer inducements.

For having arrived later, I dare to believe that France has not gone unnoticed. It has fulfilled and still fulfills its role of generous and liberal charity. The hospitals function in Jaffa, Bethlehem, Jerusalem and Nazareth (I speak only of Palestine). The orphanages receive attention in the same places thanks to the care of the Sisters of St. Vincent de Paul, St. Joseph of the Apparition, the Ladies of Zion, the Sisters of Nazareth and the Franciscans of Mary. The same religious women, to whom one must add the Brothers of the Christian Schools, direct the schools which are frequented as in yesteryear and even more.

All this represents an expenditure of one million for the clerics. This enormous sum is doubled if one keeps in mind the aid in cash and goods distributed to the poor of the city and to the numerous refugees of the localities sacked by the Turks. More than a hundred tons of wheat have thus been passed to the hands of the needy without distinction of nationality or religion. Likewise the organization of two works has permitted the distribution of more than 10,000 pieces of clothing. I cannot cite all the works of charity, since some have already asked to be silent.

To sum up, such an act of great piety has been carried out by our country in a land that is theirs. It will remain. But it is regrettable that France has not been seen in it and that it has not been seen before.

It is not sufficient: They need more troops that have an aspect different from that of a badly equipped regiment. To leave to England alone the conquest of this country exposes us to competitions, I should say victorious ones, of which we are both witnesses and victims. (…)

We have been damaged, it must be said, and we still are by the active propaganda that is made against us in favor of England. Numerous agencies roam around the country, distributing money and promises. For the peasants they procure seeds, work tools and field animals to revive the devastated farms, trees to reforest the mountains, etc.

The press itself is beginning to interpret its role. Up until a very short while ago, the sale of newspapers from Egypt was forbidden.

Nowadays, the vendors offer us the *Bourse Egyptienne*, but only the *Bourse Egyptienne*. The rest of the newspapers do not sufficiently reflect the English mentality. The newspaper has been won over to the British cause, and its principal editor signs off with a very French name on articles that praise England to the high heavens. Upon reading them, one does not recognize the Palestine of yesteryear. The English administration produces surprising transformations every day. The marvels of the present, apparently, are nothing compared to the surprise of the future. A useless memory of a too recent past! A premature glimpse of a problematic future! But even this prose that comes from Egypt, and is French, produces its effects. One has always seen the merchants exalt their merchandise; it is rarer to hear them denigrate the competition. Here we witness this rare practice. How much slanderous noise is scattered in the towns by these same vendors of the influence, of those of whom I have spoken above!

Our Palestinian peasants do not know a great deal about the Great War in the West. They haven't followed the terrible vicissitudes, and suddenly in front of them they find victorious armies that have done nothing more than cross a badly defended territory. It has been told to them that the brothers of these soldiers had also achieved victory on the western front. They forget about the others.

And nonetheless, in Palestine itself our little soldiers have overtaken hilltops bristling with machine guns manned by the Germans, and our cavalry, in a magnificent balance, has occupied Nablus before the eyes of an English cavalry hesitant and fearful before the machines guns that were spitting death, hidden behind the Hebal. This is not told.

We are allies in France; here we are competitors. Such is the word from Egypt to Constantinople, passing through this street from Syria. All the indications lead one to understand that our part in this country will be minimal. The longest and most satisfactory formulas are mistaken ones. The two rivals do not speak of a Palestine bound to Syria. In fact, the English distinguish between a French Syria and an Arab Syria. It is not my place to outline the limits of each one, but I do know that French Syria is comprised of scarcely more than the cities of the Syrian coast, from Tyre to Alexandretta: That is, a long strip of territory without much depth. The other Syria, the Arab Syria, is all the rest: It is Aleppo, it is Lebanon, the Antilebanon with the immense and fertile plain of Celesyria, it is Damascus; they are the infinite high plains that extend parallel to the Jordan and the Dead Sea and that are going to be found with the ill-defined dominions of the king of the Hidjaz, Husayn. It is to this Syria that England wants to attach Palestine.

Since we accept the principle that the populations of the occupied territories themselves choose the statute that should rule them, or the European power that will protect them, it is necessary to know the voice of the Palestinian people.

Under which regime do the Islamic-Christians wish to live? The question has been long debated in the meetings to which the chiefs of the most important locales have been summoned. With unanimity and unyielding firmness, the delegates reject a Jewish regime, whose specter the English have imprudently agitated before their eyes. One can sustain that Zionism has been the great scandal of the Muslims and Christians; this is the great majority of the population. That the Jews have been the object of favors on the part of the English government does nothing more than increase the already profound antipathy of the Islamic-Christians against them. There have been violent demonstrations in the open streets. Before the hostile attitude of the Muslims and Christians, the Jews have had to guard their banners and stars, while the English government is no longer continuing the stimuli to a premature nationalism by means of official channels.

One must remember that, at the moment that produced the expulsion of the German subjects, quite a few Jews affected by the measure have remained in Jerusalem. It has been sufficient for them to give their names to Zionism; this was a guarantee of loyalty. It will also be remembered that, in the official proclamations, the government has admitted to equal status the Hebrew language and the Arabic language and, at times, even the first in defiance of the second. It also must be remembered that the leaders of the Jewish community have obtained the privilege of facilitating means of transport for their co-religionists by the military railroads, and while the remaining indigenous peoples are obliged to solicit the same measures for weeks, the Jews come and go, traveling to Egypt and returning to their colonies without difficulty.

The signs of an interested favoritism, exalting the Jewish nationalism, have produced alarm and exasperation among the indigenous peoples. I have heard an old imam in a meeting of more than 300 notables make this suggestive declaration, 'If the Jews come to govern the country, we will have no recourse but to flee to other lands.' That is, not to the Jewish government. On the point the resolution of the indigenous people is clear.

(N.B.) The article concludes examining the different solutions of the Palestinian problem and saying, naturally, that the Islamic-Christians are all in favor of France. This is not completely exact, on the contrary to what it seems, and therefore I do not copy it.

A very funny thing happened to me in Jaffa. En route towards Haifa I stopped there to eat with the Zionist commission. Over the desserts it occurred to me to say that I would like to speak with Professor Bagrachoff, the ex-director of the school in Jaffa, who had just arrived from Spain and undoubtedly brought interesting impressions of my country. In short, the professor was introduced in a little while, and upon me asking him, he answered point-blank, 'The best part of Spain is that there are no Jews.' I couldn't get over my surprise at such a departure from good taste, and consequently I was so out of it that until the end of our conversation I didn't understand that he didn't know who I was. After having laid down that axiom, he began to get into it with the Count of Romanones. He said that the count had earned 300 million Pesetas negotiating export permits that are reserved for minerals. Then he touched upon the Jewish question in the following manner: 'The Spaniards are like the Arabs. The Count of Romanones received fifty people at the same time. He called me and told me, come here. 'The Jew who is a Zionist can stay in Spain, and the one who is not, we're going to expel him if he is Russian, as France has done and almost every country does for fear that they are Bolsheviks.'

With all this, I didn't know what to say. Friedman pretended to sleep, another had left and the rest looked as if they were on tenterhooks. Thus I understood him, and in a little while I left but not before having heard the famous professor affirm that Max Nordau is writing a magnificent book about the art of Spain and that he is well paid and thought of: That Father Fita was admirably knowledgeable about the history of the Jews in Spain, and he had been a very good friend of his, and he had told him that he was of Jewish origins.

As I was leaving, he found out that I was the Spanish consul and he came to give all sorts of excuses and to tell me that Max Nordau and Dr. Yehuda had charged him to thank me in their name for my services to the Jews. I was laughing for an hour, and I couldn't sleep, remembering the 'impressions' of Spain that I had heard.

I made the trip from Jaffa to Lydda in the car of the Zionists and from Lydda to Haifa in a train that truly does not honor the occupants of the country, because I have never swallowed so much dust as in the uncomfortable and dirty coaches that they gave us. With all this, the trip (of 100 km) cost me 104 piasters, so it is one of the most expensive railroads of the globe. The landscape is monotonous until arriving at the castle of Atlit, from where it follows the seashore and is very picturesque. The Carmel seems much less tall when seen from the south side.

In the station of Haifa, Gabriel Hadad was waiting for me. Together, we went to 'my house,' that is, to banker Dyck's house, which I have occupied to save it from the British. I visited the military governor, Major Kerr, and I received innumerable visits, among them ones from Rothschild with his wife, a nephew of the famous 'Abbas Effendi, the Franciscan Father Gabino Martín Montora and from Father Florencio del Carmelo. In the morning, I was on the mountain, and I was sorry not to stay for the solemn procession to enthrone in the convent the Most Holy Virgin of Carmel, which had been in the city during all the war.

Saturday, I spent a very pleasant day in the German colony of Bethlehem, and I thought I had returned to Spain already since the fruit trees, vineyards, almonds, oaks and grain fields surround the town everywhere, and one breathed in such an atmosphere of peace, tranquility, well-being and integrity that I would willingly have stayed several days with those nice Germans. They told me that some British officials said, upon visiting the colony and its inhabitants, 'And these are the barbarians (Germans) of whom they speak to us in the newspapers?' (…)

I was examining the work of the few but very useful agricultural machines that the colony possesses, and to rest we sat down in the shade of an oak that surely must be many centuries old and that the Germans care for with their love of the woodlands. They certainly told me a curious anecdote: The proprietor of that field sold it to the Germans, but reserved the oak and its shade. The terrain of the colony is divided among the agriculturists who each have their own property and also possess a common fund. A very well-arranged system.

On Sunday, I went to mass in the Carmelite Parish, and I received gifts from the nice Father Florencio, with whose ideas, religiosity and patriotism I remain delighted. We spoke of my project to have more Carmelites come to the Holy Land and to found a school of Spanish mysticism in honor of St. Theresa. May God grant it!

5 May, 1919

I received a long letter from Father Gonzalo de la Puerta, announcing that my project of a navigation line with the Orient will soon be a fact. *Inshallah*. I also attended a session of the Congress of Rabbis of Palestine. Upon entering, the Great Rabbi of Jaffa, Ouziel, made a speech introducing me, and I saw myself obliged to answer him, for which he made me go up into the pulpit of the synagogue, and from there I thanked him and I dedicated a few nice words to them, which Ouziel translated to Hebrew. He finished with the traditional *toda raba*, which means 'thank you very much.'

7 May, 1919

Last Saturday there occurred, in my judgment, a very serious incident. The British authorities from Nablus detained the delegate of the high commissioner of France, Pierre Durieux. I'm going to relate the version that the interested party himself gave me. Upon returning from Haifa, he stopped in Nablus to turn over the insignias of the Legion of Honor to a notable Arab whose father had been hanged by the Turks because of his love for France. As he was leaving the home of a relative of the recipient, to whom he had given the medal in the absence of the notable to whom I alluded, Mr. Durieux was arrested by an Arab policeman and a gendarme, who gave him the order to follow him to the military government. There, the governor (I don't know if his name is Howard Herbert) received him rather badly, but changed his attitude when he [Durieux] told him who he was. He then became very apologetic, meeting during the night with some 30 notables of the city, before whom he gave excuses to my speaker for what the latter considers a British blunder. But, in excusing himself, the governor made another gaffe (always in the judgment of Durieux): He confirmed that he had stopped him believing that he was dealing with a simple French agent who was running around the country doing politics on behalf of the pretentions of his country. Then Durieux assured the notables that the British had nothing more than force, and that's why they were occupying Palestine but that the indigenous people were free to opt for France if they believed that to be convenient.

Up to here is Durieux's version, which he considers to be a great triumph for the French cause. But someone who seems to be well-informed about what the British think told me that the object of this was to make the population see that France has neither power nor influence, proving it by the fact that they have been able to detain the French representative with impunity. According to this version, the British knew who the detainee was, and his detention was done on purpose.

I don't know which of the two versions is the truthful one, but if I were in Durieux's place, I would not have let myself be led away, arrested by the police, being a French official and in uniform. Probably, there would have been a serious incident, but I don't know if it would have been better. I suppose that the governor of Nablus will receive this incident with an official chill, a relief of office... or a raise. I could be mistaken.

On a visit to Storrs this morning, he gave me to read the excerpts of the Spanish press that the English Secret Service publishes. It seems that they are supporting us on the question of Tangier because the newspaper *The Mauritanian Echo*, sustained by British capital, advocates that we be granted this city. I also read that France offered to contribute to the Count of Romanones' half of the expenses for the construction of the railroad from the border over to Algiers. The count refused, saying that the capital that made it should be exclusively Spanish, and besides, the government would confiscate some railroads from the south of Spain.

Still, according to these news items, González Hontoria asked the Conference of Nations, which is going to constitute the famous 'League,' that Spain have the rank of 'great power' in it. It seems that France is supporting us in that sense. Another thing that I did not expect is that Lerroux and the Republicans have made an about-face on the question of Morocco, declaring that we Spaniards are very interested in the matter, which is vital for our interests, and even defending the Spanish colonial administration.

27 May, 1919

The king's birthday. A very well attended reception and not very solemn mass.

I had tea with General and Lady Money, as well as with Carton of Wiart. Very ceremonial. Before, I ate with Allenby, and I was bored there too. During these days I received a telegram from Hontoria, telling me that he cannot accept my resignation, but that he is soon granting me two months leave so I can come to Spain and *reflect*.

NOTES

Preface

1   Conde de Ballobar is not clearly a name but a nobiliar title: I chose to use this rather than the name, as in the sources available contermporary of the diary; Antonio de la Cierva was often identified as the Conde de Ballobar.
2   According to the diary, the last time Ballobar met Cemal Paşa was on 6 July 1917. It is possible they met again after this date, but nothing has been reported in the diary.

Introduction

1   R. Storrs, *The Memoirs of Sir Ronald Storrs* (New York: G.P. Putnam's Sons, 1937), 303.
2   Diary, *7 April 1915*.
3   M.S. Anderson, *The Eastern Question* (London: Macmillan, 1970), 1-6; W.L. Cleveland, *A History of the Modern Middle East* 3rd ed. (Cambridge: Westview Press, 2004), 49-51.
4   E.J. Zürcher, *Turkey. A Modern History* (London: I.B. Tauris, 1993), 21.
5   M.E. Yapp, *The Making of the Modern Near East 1792-1923* (London: Longman, 1987), 92-96.
6   Cleveland, *A History of the Modern Middle East*, 87-89.
7   For a detailed discussion of the Eastern Question, besides M.S. Anderson, *The Eastern Question*, see A.L. MacFie, *The Eastern Question 1774-1923* (London: Longman, 1996).
8   Following the failed attempt by Napoleon to invade the Middle East in 1798, Muhammad 'Ali, originally sent to fight against the French, came to control Egypt by 1805, and later also Syria. Although we can look at the establishment of Muhammad 'Ali's rule in Egypt as an internal matter of the Ottoman Empire, this was achieved in the main framework of the Eastern Question. Muhammad 'Ali and his son, Ibrahim Paşa, were eventually stopped by European powers, when

they became a clear threat to the Ottoman state and its own existence.
9 Yapp, *The Making of the Modern Near East*, 59-60.
10 M.S. Hanioğlu, *A Brief History of the Late Ottoman Empire* (Princeton: Princeton University Press, 2008), 69-71.
11 A. Pacini, ed., *Christian Communities in the Arab Middle East*, (Oxford: Clarendon Press, 1998), 342; S.P. Colbi, *Christianity* (Tel Aviv: Am Hassefer, 1969), 67; A.H. De Groot, 'The Historical Development of the Capitulary Regime in the Ottoman Middle East from the 15th to the 19th Centuries', *Oriente Moderno* 3 (2003): 596.
12 De Groot, 'The Historical Development', 577.
13 J.B. Angell, 'The Turkish Capitulations', *The American Historical Review* 6, no. 2 (January 1901): 256.
14 M.H. Van den Boogert, *The Capitulations and the Ottoman Legal System*, (Leiden: Brill, 2005), 7.
15 D. Goffman, *The Ottoman Empire and Early Modern Europe*, (Cambridge: Cambridge University Press, 2002), 187-188.
16 Goffman, *The Ottoman Empire*, 228-229.
17 Hanioğlu, *A Brief History of the Late Ottoman Empire*, 135-136; Cleveland, *A History of the Modern Middle East*, 86-87.
18 R. Mazza, *Jerusalem from the Ottomans to the British* (London: I.B.Tauris, 2009), 1-7.
19 A. Singer, *Palestinian Peasants and Ottoman Officials* (Cambridge: Cambridge University Press, 1994), 4.
20 Singer, *Palestinian Peasants*, 7.
21 Kudüs was the name of Jerusalem in Ottoman Turkish, meaning Sacred City. In Arabic, the name of the city is al-Quds. Singer, *Palestinian Peasants*, 7; A. Cohen, *Palestine in the 18th Century*, (Jerusalem: The Magnes Press, 1973), 169.
22 S. Noja, *Storia dei Popoli dell'Islam. L'Islam Moderno*. Vol. 5 (Milan: Oscar Mondadori, 1990), 11-13.
23 The Ottoman Decree of 3 November 1839, defined the *Tanzimat* era. The edict promoted a set of reforms which, in essence, were meant to change the idea of the state, and the official ideology of the state itself. Amongst the many publications available on the topic, for reference see J. McCarthy, *The Ottoman Turks*, (London: Longman, 1997), 296-301; Hanioğlu, *A Brief History of the Late Ottoman Empire*, 75-76; Zürcher, *Turkey. A Modern History*, 52-74. To contex-

tualise the *Tanzimat* reforms in Palestine see H. Gerber, 'A New Look at the *Tanzimat*: The Case of the Province of Jerusalem', in *Palestine in the Late Ottoman Period: Political, Social and Economic Transformation*, ed. David Kushner (Jerusalem: Yad Izhak Ben-Zvi Institute, 1986), 31-45.
24 R. Brunelli, *Storia di Gerusalemme* (Milan: Oscar Mondadori, 1990), 258.
25 D.R. Divine, *Politics and Society in Ottoman Palestine* (Boulder: Lynne Rienner, 1994), 115.
26 Divine, *Politics and Society*, 23.
27 H. Gerber, *Ottoman Rule in Jerusalem* (Berlin: K. Schwarz, 1985), 96.
28 Gerber, *Ottoman Rule*, 276.
29 R. Kark, 'The Jerusalem Municipality', *Asian and African Studies* 14 (1980), 119.
30 Kark, 'The Jerusalem Municipality', 125; Y. Ben-Arieh, *Jerusalem in the 19th Century. The Old City* (New York: St Martin's Press, 1984), 123.
31 H. Gerber, 'The Administration of the Sanjaq of Jerusalem 1890-1908', *Asia and African Studies* 12, no. 1 (1978), 55.
32 P.P. Khoury, *Urban Notables and Arab Nationalism* (Cambridge: Cambridge University Press, 1983), 10.
33 See Ben-Arieh, *The Old City*.
34 McCarthy, *The Ottoman Turks*, 202-203.
35 NARA, Consular Post, Vol. 69, Governor of Jerusalem to Glazebrook, 22 September 1914, Jerusalem: 'With the abolition of the capitulations in the Ottoman Empire, the foreign offices will have to close on the morning of 1 October 1914.'
36 ASMAE, Serie Politica P, Busta 498, Conte Senni to Italian embassy in Istanbul, Jerusalem, 20 September 1914.
37 Christian Churches relied on incomes coming from pilgrims and remittances from foreign countries; however, churches also established local enterprises.
38 A. Jacobson, 'From Empire to Empire: Jerusalem in the Transition Between Ottoman and British Rule 1912-1920' (PhD thesis, The University of Chicago, Chicago, 2006), 42-43.
39 Diary, *Efemerides September 1914*.
40 A. Bruce, *The Last Crusade* (London: John Murray, 2002), 6.
41 Hanioğlu, *A Brief History*, 150-177; Zürcher, *Turkey*, 115-116.
42 Hanioğlu, *A Brief History*, 177.

43 J. Nevakivi, *Britain, France and the Arab Middle East* (London: The Athlone Press, 1969), 2.
44 For a thorough overview of the diplomatic situation of the Ottoman Empire at the outbreak of the First World War, see M. Aksakal, *The Ottoman Road to War in 1914* (Cambridge: Cambridge University Press, 2008).
45 M.E. Yapp and V.J. Parry, eds. *War, Technology and Society in the Middle East* (London: Oxford University Press, 1975), 367.
46 Zürcher, *Turkey*, 116.
47 F. Ahmad, 'The Late Ottoman Empire', in *The Great Powers and the end of the Ottoman Empire*, ed. M. Kent, 18 (London: George Allen & Unwin, 1984).
48 U. Trumpener, 'Germany and the End of the Ottoman Empire', in *The Great Powers and the end of the Ottoman Empire*, ed. M. Kent, 18 (London: George Allen & Unwin, 1984).
49 D. Fromkin, *A Peace to End All Peace* (New York: Owl Books, 2001), 49; Ahmad, 'The Late Ottoman Empire', 13.
50 Fromkin, *A Peace to End All Peace*, 48; U. Trumpener, *Germany and the Ottoman Empire* (New York: Caravan Books, 1989), 15. The Ottoman government proposed a closer relationship with Germany on 22 July, but the German Ambassador turned down this proposal.
51 Zürcher, *Turkey*, 116; Ahmad, 'The Late Ottoman Empire', 11, a thorough discussion of these events can be found in Aksakal, *The Ottoman Road to War in 1914*, 119-152.
52 D. Nicolle, *The Ottoman Army 1914-18* (London: Osprey, 1994), 20; Zürcher, *Turkey*, 117.
53 M. Roubiçek, *Modern Ottoman Troops 1790-1915* (Jerusalem: Franciscan Printing Press, 1978), 20-21.
54 Bruce, *The Last Crusade*, 8.
55 In the diary there are several entries enlighiting us on the tensions between German and Ottoman officials.
56 Bruce, *The Last Crusade*, 43.
57 A debate on the Yıldırım army group can be found in E.J. Erickson, *Ordered to Die* (Westport: Greenwood Press, 2001).
58 Erickson, *Ordered to Die*, 171.
59 Quoted in D.L. Bullock, *Allenby's War* (London: Blandford Press, 1988), 66.

60 M. Hughes, *Allenby and British Strategy in the Middle East 1917-1919* (London: Frank Cass, 1999), 1.
61 The Local Government Board was a ministerial post with responsibility for local government. In 1919, it was abolished, and its functions fell to the ministry of health.
62 Nevakivi, *Britain, France and the Arab Middle East*, 13-16.
63 Nevakivi, *Britain, France and the Arab Middle East*, 19.
64 Yapp, *The Making of the Modern Near East*, 277-286. The position of Jerusalem in the Sykes-Picot agreement remained vague. Palestine (a part from Haifa and Acre, which were to be placed under British administration) was to be placed under international administration with no indication of how this administration should work. In the Husayn-McMahon correspondence, the questions of Palestine and of Jerusalem were not discussed.
65 Jacobson, 'From Empire to Empire', 35-41.
66 His father was Plácido de la Cierva y Nuevo and his mother was Marie Luise Frankenstein-Lewi. Conde de Ballobar, *Diario de Jerusalen* (Madrid: Nerea, 1996), 25-26.
67 AMAE, Madrid, P481/33813, Personnel files Antonio de la Cierva y Lewita.
68 The reasons for the argument between the Spanish consular mission and the Custody are discussed later, and more details are to be found in G. Barriuso, *España en la Historia de Tierra Santa*, Vol. 2 (Madrid: MAE, 1992-94), 625-630.
69 AMAE, P481/33813, Personnel files Antonio de la Cierva y Lewita.
70 AMAE, P481/33813, Minutes of Secretary of States, 22 October 1921, Madrid.
71 Interview with the family of Ballobar, 12/01/2010 Madrid.
72 AMAE, P481/33813, Spanish embassy to the Holy See, 21 May 1939, Vatican City.
73 A complete picture of the positions offered can be found in the personnel files. AMAE, P481, Personnel files Antonio de la Cierva y Lewita.
74 Officially, the Spanish government did not recognize the State of Israel; however, Franco wanted to open a consulate in Jerusalem in order to open a dialogue with the Israeli authorities. It was only in 1986 that full diplomatic relations were established between Spain and Israel.

75 Other details in relation to the life of Conde de Ballobar can be found in the obituary published by *Tierra Santa* (January 1972): 24-25.
76 I. Mancini, 'Cenni Storici sulla Custodia di Terra Santa', in *La Custodia di Terra Santa e l'Europa*, ed. M. Piccirillo (Rome: Il Veltro Editrice, 1983), 16.
77 A. Giovannelli, *La Santa Sede e la Palestina* (Rome: Edizioni Studium, 2000), 3.
78 ASMAE, Archivio di Gabinetto, Pacco 185, Diotallevi to Cimino, Jerusalem, 6 March 1918.
79 Ottoman law permitted only individuals, and not institutions, to be the owners of religious estates. A change took place in 1912, allowing for property to be in the name of an institution rather than an individual; however, ownership still belonged to the individual and not the institution.
80 For an overview of the relations between the Vatican and the Ottoman Empire see G. del Zanna, *L'Oriente e Roma* (Milan: Guerini Associati, 2003).
81 Fr. Eutimio Castellani was in charge of the daily businesses of the Custody, due to the absence of the *Custos* who, after travelling to Istanbul, was recalled to Italy. This diary is available in the archives of the Custody of the Holy Land: Diario della Guerra.
82 ACTS, Diario della Guerra, 1914.
83 ACTS, Diario della Guerra, November 1914: '3 November. […] 24 Franciscan nuns, 19 Carmelitan nuns, 20 Benedictine nuns, 17 Franciscan of the tertiary order nuns, 60 orphans and other 12 nuns came to Casa Nova.' '7 November 15 White Fathers came to St Saviour.'
84 ACTS, Diario di Guerra, 1915.
85 ASV, *Sacra Congregazione degli Affari Ecclesiastici Straordinari Africa-Asia-Oceania,* Pos. 13. Fasc. 5, Card Dolci to Card Gasparri, Istanbul, 5 April 1915.
86 ASV, *Segreteria di Stato-Guerra-111*, Card Gasparri to Card Dolci, Vatican City, 3 September 1915.
87 NARA, Consular Post, Vol. 69, Governor of Jerusalem to Glazebrook, Jerusalem, 22 December 1914.
88 ACTS, Diario della Guerra, 1915.
89 NARA, Consular Post, Vol. 73, Custody of the Holy Land, 8 November 1915.

90 NARA, Consular Post, Vol. 69, Government of Jerusalem, 20 December 1914.
91 ACTS, Diario della Guerra, April-June 1916.
92 E. Barcena, 'La Spagna in Terra Santa', in *La Custodia di Terra Santa e l'Europa*, ed. M. Piccirillo (Rome: Il Veltro Editrice, 1983), 99-100.
93 Barcena, 'La Spagna in Terra Santa,' 102-104.
94 ASMAE, Affari Politici 1919-1930, Palestina Pacco 1457, Report of the Italian consul in Jerusalem to the Minister of Foreign Affairs, Jerusalem, 28 June 1922.
95 D. Fabrizio, *Identitá Nazionali e Identitá Religiose* (Rome: Edizioni Studium, 2004), 186.
96 Barcena, 'La Spagna in Terra Santa,' 107.
97 Fabrizio, *Identitá Nazionali e Identitá Religiose*, 187-189; Giovannelli, *La Santa Sede e la Palestina*, 48-49.
98 Today the *Obra Pia* is under the control of the Spanish Ministry of Foreign Affairs.
99 The Latin Patriarchate of Jerusalem was re-opened in 1847, and by 1853, the Patriarch Valerga was trying to defend national privileges and, above all, to look for money necessary to maintain the newly-established institution. In 1847, the authority and tasks of the Patriarchate were not fixed, and this contributed to a larger conflict between the Patriarchate and the Custody. See Giovannelli, *La Santa Sede e la Palestina*, 82-86.
100 Fabrizio, *Identitá Nazionali e Identitá Religiose*, 192.
101 ACTS, Razzoli to Schuler, Jerusalem, 18 February 1906.
102 Fabrizio, *Identitá Nazionali e Identitá Religiose*, 202.
103 Fabrizio, *Identitá Nazionali e Identitá Religiose*, 219-220.
104 Fabrizio, *Identitá Nazionali e Identitá Religiose*, 240.
105 Fabrizio, *Identitá Nazionali e Identitá Religiose*, 256-259.
106 Diary, *16 December 1914*.
107 Diary, *15 January 1915*.
108 Fabrizio, *Identitá Nazionali e Identitá Religiose*, 262-263. For the occupation of the convents see Mazza, *Jerusalem from the Ottomans to the British*, 58-62.
109 Giovannelli, *La Santa Sede e la Palestina*, 50-51; Mazza, *Jerusalem from the Ottomans to the British*, 199.
110 On this, see Fabrizio, *Identitá Nazionali e Identitá Religiose*, 264-294; Giovannelli, *La Santa Sede e la Palestina*, 50-63.

111 AMAE, H3069/008, numerous receipts are collected in this file as evidence of the consul's work towards the distribution of financial aid to the Jews.
112 On this topic, see J. Renton, *The Zionist Masquerade* (New York: Palgrave Macmillan, 2007); L. Stein, *The Balfour Declaration* (New York: Simon and Schuster, 1961); M. Levene, 'The Balfour Declaration. A Case of Mistaken Identity', *The English Historical Review 107*, no. 422 (January 1922): 54-77; J. Reinharz, 'The Balfour Declaration and Its Makers: a Reassessment', *The Journal of Modern History 64*, no. 3 (September 1992): 455-499.
113 Diary, *29 March 1917*.
114 I. Friedman, *Germany Turkey and Zionism 1897-1918* (Oxford: Oxford University Press, 1977), 347-348.
115 Diary, *11 April 1917*. According to Friedman, no shelter or food was provided and the evacuees traveled on foot; Friedman, *Germany Turkey and Zionism*, 350. Nevertheless, according to a report of the German Aid Association for the Jews, *Hilfsverein der Deutchen Juden*, the evacuation did not show any anti-Semitic character, and some form of transportation was provided, and about seventy watchmen were left behind to take care of Jewish properties; AMEA, H3025/020, Spanish embassy in Berlin to Spanish Foreign Office, Berlin 9 June 1917.
116 TNA: PRO FO 371/3055, Wingate, Cairo 28 April 1917.
117 Diary, *11 June 1917*.
118 TNA: PRO FO 371/3055, British Ambassador to Balfour, Madrid 19 June 1917.
119 TNA: PRO FO 371/3055, Copy of a note of the Dutch Foreign Office to Balfour, The Hague 10 August 1917.
120 An interesting article, published in 2003, reconginzed the role played by Ballobar in the protection of the French interests in Palestine during the First World War. Though the piece is more concerned with issues of international relations and, in particular, the role of neutral countries, it nevertheless underlines the historical agency of Ballobar. J-M. Delaunay, 'L'Espagne, Protectrice des Interets Français en Palestine au Crepuscole de la Domination Ottomane 1914-1918', in *Mediterranee, Moyen-Orient: Duex Siecles de Relations Internationales*, ed. W. Arbid, S. Kançal, J-D. Mizrahi and S. Saul (Paris: l'Harmattan, 2003), 93-107.

121 NARA, Consular Post Vol. 69/A, Governor of Jerusalem, 3 August 1914.
122 See Mazza, *Jerusalem from the Ottomans to the British*, 116; Jacobson, 'From Empire to Empire', 36-37.
123 NARA, Consular Post Vol. 69, Macid Şevket to Glazebrook, Jerusalem, 22 September 1914; Diary, *19 November 1914*; see Jacobson, 'From Empire to Empire', 37.
124 Diary, *Efemerides September*; Mazza, *Jerusalem from the Ottomans to the British*, 56; A. Jacobson, 'A City Living Through Crisis: Jerusalem During World War I', *British Journal of Middle Eastern Studies* 36, no. 1, (2009): 78.
125 Jacobson, 'A City Living Through Crisis,' 78.
126 Diary, *Efemerides September 1914*.
127 Diary, *22 November 1914*.
128 See several entries in the Diary, *16 December 1914* to *23 December 1914*.
129 Diary, *6 April 1915* and *29 May 1915*.
130 Diary, *23 March 1915*.
131 Jacobson, 'From Empire to Empire', 69-70.
132 A table compiled by the American consul, Dr. Otis Glazebrook, in November 1914 provides a good idea of the increase in prices, such as 40% for rice, 70% for potatoes and 50% for coal. NARA, Consular Post Vol. 69/A, Glazebrook to Morgenthau, Jerusalem, 17 November 1914.
133 See S. Tamari, 'The Short Life of Private Ihsan: Jerusalem 1915', *Jerusalem Quarterly* 30 (2007): 26-58; A. Jacobson, 'Negotiating Ottomanism in Times of War: Jerusalem During World War I Through the Eyes of a Local Muslim Resident', *Int. J. Middle East Studies* 40 (2008): 69-88; S. Tamari, 'Jerusalem's Ottoman Modernity: The Times and Lives of Wasif Jawhariyyeh', *Jerusalem Quarterly File* 9 (2000): 5-27; S. Tamari, *Mountain Against the Sea* (Berkeley: University of California Press, 2009).
134 Wasif Jawhariyyeh was born in 1897; his father, Jirys was a member of the Municipal Council and *mukhtar* (head) of the Christian Orthodox community in the old city. Wasif came to be a very popular 'oud player and musician, often performing at public and private events. Wasif was a protégé of the Husayni family; educated in several schools in Jerusalem, he took several subjects including Quranic

studies for Christians, as offered by the famous Palestinian educator Khalil Sakakini. Wasif spent most of his life performing in environments which were very different from each other, clearly marking the fact that borders between communities were not fixed, and clearly imposed as a result of British rule and Zionism.

135 Tamari, *Mountain Against the Sea*, 72.
136 See B. Vester Spafford, *Our Jerusalem* (New York: Arno Press, 1977).
137 Tamari, *Mountain Against the Sea*, 84-85.
138 Jacobson, 'Negotiating Ottomanism in Times of War'. 76.

1914

1 The diary began to be written only on November 16: The first three entries were added later to report on major events – *efemerides* – that occurred earlier. Eduardo Manzano Moreno has correctly decided to keep a full chronological order and to add these entries at the beginning of the diary.
2 Details on Georges Gueyrand can be found in V. Lemire, 'L'Eau, le Consul et l'Ingénieur: Hydropolitique et Concurrences Diplomatique á Jérusalem, 1908-1914', in *France and the Middle East*, ed. M. Abitbol (Jerusalem: Hebrew University Magnes Press, 2004), 125-137.
3 Details on the Goeben and Breslau can be found in D. Fromkin, *A Peace to End All Peace* (New York: Henry Holt, 1989), 62-76.
4 Carlo Senni served as Italian consul in Jerusalem from 10/05/1907 to 01/08/1915; he left Palestine when Italy declared war against the Ottoman Empire in May 1915. His relation with Ballobar was complex, as they cooperated several times but also fought bitterly to defend their own national interests.
5 William Hough was the last British consul in Jerusalem, until the end of the British Mandate in 1948, see W. Hough, 'History of the British Consulate in Jerusalem', *Journal of the Middle East Society*, no. 1 (October-December 1946): 3-14. Antonio Barluzzi (1884-1960) worked as an architect in Jerusalem; he designed several churches and other building for the Franciscans of the Custody of the Holy Land.
6 Some details on Glazebrook can be found in R. Kark, *American Consuls in the Holy Land 1832-1914* (Jerusalem: The Magnes Press, 1994).

7   As Ballobar arrived a few weeks earlier, he had not yet found a house, and lived in the Hotel Marcos until he moved to the house of the Director of the Crédit Lyonnais Guerássimo.
8   Details on Notre Dame can be found in D. Trimbour, 'Une Présence Française en Palestine: Notre Dame de France', *Bulletin du CRFJ*, no. 3 (Autumn 1998): 32-58.
9   It is possible that Ballobar referred to the Dome of the Rock, but this place was often mistaken with the Mosque of Omar.
10 This is the first reference by Ballobar to the problematic relationship between the Custody, Spain and the Italian monks.
11 The Christian Brothers is a French Catholic Congregation: They opened a school in Jerusalem in 1892.
12 The convent of the Sisters of Marie Reparatrice was opened in 1888 and located outside the walls of Jerusalem, close to the New Gate.
13 This line was clearly added later.
14 According to the constitution of the Custody of the Holy Land, the superior of the convents of Jaffa and Ramla were to be Spanish.
15 On 7 December 1914, through the American Ambassador in Istanbul, the British acknowledged the Ottoman request to exchange hostages for the promise not to bombard the Ottoman ports in Syria and Palestine. The US Department of State tried to lobby the Ottoman government, in order to release the enemy non-combatants (including clergy and diplomatic personnel) and leave them free to depart the Ottoman Empire. Eventually, from a letter of the American Ambassador, Morgenthau, to the Secretary of State, dated 18 December 1914, we understand that a number of men of French and British citizenship were deported to Damascus but no women and children. See United States Department of State, *Papers Relating to the Foreign Relations of the United States, 1914. Supplement, The World War* (Washington DC: U.S. Government Printing Office, 1914), 784-789. Available at http://digital. library. wisc. edu/ 1711.dl/ FRUS. FRUS 1914 Supp (last accessed 14 September 2010).
16 St. Steven is the French convent of St. Etienne, next to the École Biblique.
17 Père Antonin Jaussen was a very famous Dominican priest and academic. He would later work as French agent in Egypt, gathering intelligence on the Middle East during the war. See Henry Laurens, 'Jaussen et les Services de Renseignement Français (1915-1919),' in

Antonin Jaussen: Sciences Sociales Occidentales et Patrimoine Arabe, ed. G. Chatelard and M. Tarawneh (Paris: Cermoc, 1999), 23-35.
18 The convent of San Savior in the old city is the seat of the Custody of the Holy Land. The office of the Procurator was also located in San Savior; according to tradition, the Procurator has always been a Spaniard.
19 This note was clearly added later.

1915

1 Ballobar added the adjective 'great' to differentiate Cemal Paşa, the Commander of the fourth army, Minister of the Navy and Governor of Syria, from Mersinli Cemal Paşa, commander of the 8th Army, also known as Küçük (little). On Cemal Paşa see T. Çiçek, *War and State Formation in Syria: Cemal Pasha's Governatorate During World War I, 1914-1917* (New York: Routledge, 2014).
2 Ballobar gave to Cemal Paşa many nicknames, most of them quite sarcastic.
3 Clearly, Ballobar spoke Spanish, French, Italian and a bit of English; as proved by some entries he knew some Arabic, probably just words. It is difficult to say about other languages, though he admitted he did not speak German.
4 It is not clear what happened to Nur al-Din Bey, as he was mentioned by the consul on 9 December 1915, still in charge of the police in Jerusalem.
5 Romania entered the war in 1916.
6 On the contrary, the description reported by Ballobar was not far from reality; see Fromkin, *A Peace to End All Peace*, 121.
7 *Mehar* is the leading rein of a camel; I suspect Ballobar meant some sort of camel-mounted troops.
8 On the Husayni see I. Pappé, 'The Husayni Family Faces New Challenges', *Jerusalem Quarterly File*, Issue 11-12 (2001), and I. Pappé, 'The Rise and Fall of the Husaynis, 1840-1922', *Jerusalem Quarterly File*, Issue 10 (2000).
9 On the invasion of locusts there are several works available, see for instance: P. Goldstone, *Aaronsohn's Maps* (Orlando: Harcourt, 2007); A. Jacobson, 'A City Living Through Crisis: Jerusalem During World War I,' *BJMES 36*, no. 1 (April 2009): 73-92.

10 See A. Halabi, 'The Transformation of the Prophet Moses Festival in Jerusalem, 1917-1937: From Local and Islamic to Modern and Nationalist Celebration' (PhD thesis, University of Toronto, Toronto, 2007); Mazza, *Jerusalem from the Ottomans to the British*, 165-178.
11 By this date, the hostilities in the Dardanelles were already underway; see Fromkin, *A Peace to End All Peace*, 130-136.
12 The ceremony of the *Holy Fire* is a ritual of the Greek Orthodox Church in Jerusalem that takes places every year in the Holy Sepulchre on Holy Saturday. Traditionally the Greek Orthodox Patriarch enters the sepulchre, and there the 'miracle' takes place: The spontaneous ignition of lamps, which symbolize the resurrection of Jesus. See V. Clark, *Holy Fire* (London: Macmillan, 2005).
13 Ballobar refers to the traditional place which, according to the Gospels, Jesus resisted many temptations for forty days and forty nights.
14 C. Paşa, *Memories of a Turkish Statesman 1913-1919* (New York: Doran, 1922).
15 Italy declared war against the Austro-Hungarian Empire on 24 May 1915.
16 The American Colony was established by American and Swedish millenialists at the end of the 19th century. Often in Jerusalem, rumors spread about the practices of the members of the Colony. See J. Fletcher Geniesse, *American Priestess* (New York: Doubleday, 2008).
17 On the Dardanelles Campaign see Fromkin, *A Peace to End All Peace*, 150-154.
18 This name does not really sound German; unfortunately I was not able to find neither the correct name nor the name of the officer in charge of the German forces in Ramla.
19 Clearly, Ballobar had a negative opinion of the emerging Arab nationalism.
20 This comment was clearly added later.
21 See H. Morgenthau, *Ambassador Morgenthau's Story* (New York: Doubleday, 1918).
22 Sarona, near Jaffa, was established by German Templers in 1871; today it is part of Tel Aviv. See H. Glenk, ed., *From Desert Sands to Golden Oranges* (Victoria: Trafford, 2005).
23 Curt Prüfer was, in fact, a German diplomat and agent. See D. McKale, *War by Revolution* (Kent: Kent State University Press, 1998);

D. McKale, *Curt Prüfer, German Diplomat from the Kaiser to Hitler* (Kent: Kent State University Press, 1987).

24 The letters were addressed to the Sanusiyya, a religious anti-imperialistic movement who fought against the Italian occupation of Libya. See D. Vandewalle, *A History of Modern Libya* (Cambridge: Cambridge University Press, 2006).

25 The *Custos*, Father Cimino, left Jerusalem in 1914 as he was elected General of the Franciscan Order and due to the war conditions; it was not possible to elect a new *Custos*. In these conditions, Father Eutimio Castellani was elected President of the Custody, an office which was given to an Italian by tradition. See Fabrizio, *Identitá Nazionali e Identitá Religiose*, 142-144.

26 The Calvary is a small chapel inside the Holy Sepulcher.

1916

1 The *Barracas de Valencia* are traditional rural houses, common in the region surrounding Valencia, made of mud and other raw materials, and were very poor constructions.

2 In the original manuscript appeared only the letter 'P'. Considering the place and the kind of news the Spanish editor of the diary, Professor Manzano Moreno and myself believe 'P' refers to Prüfer.

3 Erzerum was taken by Russian troops a month earlier.

4 See Fromkin, *A Peace to End All Peace*, 200-203.

5 Ballobar, as the majority of western travelers and residents in the Middle East at that time, affected by a strong Orientalism, believed in a sort of Oriental fatalism, according to which people in the region inactively awaited for the destiny to fulfil itself.

6 On the Abyssinians in Jerusalem see S.Colbi, *Christianity in the Holy Land* (Tel Aviv: Am Hassefer, 1969); H. Kildani, *Modern Christianity in the Middle East* (Bloomington: Author House, 2010).

7 Disease and epidemics throughout the Ottoman Empire caused more victims than battle wounds, for more on this see H. Özdemir, *The Ottoman Army 1914-194. Disease and Death on the Battlefield* (Salt Lake City: The University of Utah Press, 2008).

8 Ballobar refers to the Battle of Jutland which took place in the North Sea between 31 May and 1 June 1916.

9   The superior of the convent of St. John ('Ayn Karim) was traditionally a Spanish friar.
10 Arthur Ruppin (1870-1943) was a leading Zionist, resident in Jaffa during the war, and was expelled by Cemal Paşa on suspicion of activity against the Ottomans. See A. Ruppin, *Memoirs, Diaries, Letters* (London: Weidenfeld and Nicolson, 1971).
11 The Arab Revolt began in June 1916 with the hope that at least 100,000 troops would join the Sharif of Mecca, but this did not materialize. The revolt then became more a guerrilla movement against the Ottomans, led by T.E. Lawrence. See Fromkin, *A Peace to End All Peace*, 218-228; P. Mohs, *Military Intelligence and the Arab Revolt* (London: Routledge, 2008); P. Satia, *Spies in Arabia* (New York: Oxford University Press, 2008).
12 The original is in French.
13 Details of the British campaign in Palestine can be found in M. Hughes, *Allenby and British Strategy in the Middle East 1917-1919* (London: Frank Cass, 1999); Y. Sheffy, *British Military Intelligence in the Palestine Campaign 1914-1918* (London: Frank Cass, 1998).
14 Here it seems Ballobar did not know Arabic, but in other parts of the diary it seems he could understand a few words.
15 Clearly, Ballobar tried to help the Sephardim of Jerusalem, as proved by an article that eventually acknowledges the positive contribution of the consul toward the Sephardi community of Jerusalem; see I. Abbady, 'Una Crónica Personal', *Ariel*, no. 17 (1969), 60-72.
16 The Jewish community of Palestine was helped through the war in particular by money and funds coming from the United States, and it was managed and distributed by Glazebrook. When the United States joined the war the relief work was taken over by Ballobar. For instance, see AMAE, H3069/008, a copy of a report prepared by Ballobar on the payments made to Jewish residents of Palestine in 1917. On this topic see also Jacobson, 'From Empire to Empire,' 52-61.
17 As with Arabic, Ballobar was likely able to understand some German, but he was not fluent.

1917

1. The *Cierzo* is a Spanish wind, dry and chilly, common in Aragon and Navarra.
2. The Amanus Mountains are a key passage between Syria and Mesopotamia, and the construction of tunnels in this area was considered strategically vital. See Erickson, *Ordered to Die*, 232-233.
3. The Basilica was traditionally used for Greek Orthodox celebrations.
4. It is not clear if this is a mistake in writing the date or addenda to the previous entry.
5. Boutrus Ghali Paşa, Prime Minister of Egypt between 1908 and 1910 – a Christian Copt – was killed by Egyptian nationalists, accused of being a British puppet. See V. Ibrahim, *The Copts of Egypt: Challenges of Modernisation and Identity* (London: I.B.Tauris, 2010), 54-56.
6. A *rotal* is a weight measure that corresponds to Kg 0.450 – 1 lbs.
7. Ballobar was correct not to believe this news; in fact Fakhri Paşa, appointed by Cemal Paşa as governor of Medina, surrendered the city only in January 1919. See Fromkin, *A Peace to End All Peace*, 228; Pohs, *Military Intelligence and the Arab Revolt*, 120-123.
8. Like Sarona, Wilhelma was established by German settlers at the beginning of the twentieth century. See, Glenk, *From Desert Sands to Golden Oranges*.
9. Most likely, Ballobar visited the Herzliya Hebrew Gymnasium, see A.B. Saposnik, *Becoming Hebrew* (New York: Oxford University Press, 2008), 62-63.
10. Rehovot was established by Polish Jews at the end of the nineteenth century, south of Jaffa.
11. Petah Tikva was established at the end of the nineteenth century by Jewish religious pioneers from Europe, as an agricultural settlement.
12. Tsar Nicholas II abdicated on 15 March 1917. See R.D Warth, *Nicholas II: the Life and Reign of Russia's Last Monarch* (Westport: Praeger, 1997).
13. The failure of the British campaign eventually led to a change in strategy and leadership. General Archibald Murray was eventually replaced by General Edmund Allenby. See Mazza, *Jerusalem from the Ottomans to the British*, 124-125.
14. Ballobar refers to the incidents that occurred in November 1901 between Greek Orthodox clergy and some Franciscans. This inci-

dent sparked major diplomatic tension amongst the European powers including the Holy See. Fabrizio, *Fascino d'Oriente*, 158-198.

15 The Ottoman Empire severed relations with the United States on 20 April 1917; nevertheless, the relationship between the two did not deteriorate, and many American activities in the Empire did not suffer from the changed diplomatic situation. See the various documents in J.C. Hurewitz, *The Middle East and North Africa in World Politics: a Documentary Record* (New Haven: Yale, 1979), 96-101.

16 This was clearly a rumor, as Gaza was taken only in the autumn of 1917.

17 The original is in French.

18 Abraham Elkus was the American Ambassador in Istanbul from 1916 to 1917; he followed Henry Morgenthau. See *New York Times*, 6 August 1916.

19 This is the only passage that suggests the consul might have thought about the publication of his diary.

20 See R. de Nogales, *Four Years Beneath the Crescent* (London: Charles Scribner's Son, 1926).

21 Following the evacuation of Jaffa, rumors spread of massacres committed against the Jews. A commission was formed to investigate, and Ballobar was called to be part of it. See the introduction for more details.

22 The gap in the diary from August to November is due to a trip to Istanbul. In the original there are several white pages; according to Manzano Moreno, Ballobar meant to write his impression of this journey later on.

23 With the change in strategy and leadership of the British while Ballobar was in Istanbul, the Ottomans were now on the defensive, following a new offensive launched by the British under the command of General Allenby.

24 In the original manuscript the text of this telegram is found later.

25 The originals are in ACTS, Guerra, Jerusalem.

26 Eventually, an agreement was signed in March 1918. See Fromkin, *A Peace to End All Peace*, 241-249.

27 The original is in French.

28 Though the reasons are not clear, in the last few days of Ottoman rule of Jerusalem, several Zionists were arrested including Dr. Jacob

Thon (head of the Zionist Office in Jerusalem) and Eliezer Ziegfried Hoofien of the Anglo-Palestine Bank.
29 These names may be incorrect, as they are not legible in the diary.
30 To the good fortune of Dr. Thon and Hoofien, Ballobar was correct in thinking that the Ottomans were certainly leaving in a matter of hours. Interestingly, Thon acknowledged the attempts made by German authorities to protect Jews and Zionists in Jerusalem and Palestine. See Friedman, *Germany Turkey and Zionism*, 372-373.
31 It is difficult to explain this paragraph; either Ballobar added it later, or in some way he was aware of the withdrawal of the Ottomans and Germans from the city but did not mention this earlier in the diary.
32 On the surrender see Mazza, *Jerusalem from the Ottomans to the British*, 132-136.
33 Though it is not clear as to which hospital Ballobar is referring, as he mentioned the presence of deaconesses, it may be possible he was describing the Augusta Victoria hospital which was, in fact, run by German Protestant clergy.
34 William Yale was an American citizen, resident in Jerusalem until the breaking of the diplomatic relations between the Ottoman Empire and the United States. Yale was employed by the Standard Oil Company of New York; early in 1917, he also worked for the US State Department, reporting on Middle Eastern issues. See A. Vincent-Barwood, 'The Many Hats of William Yale', *Saudi Aramco World 35*, no. 4 (Sept.-October 1984): 38-40. See also an interesting report by Yale on Palestine in the summer of 1917; TNA: PRO FO 371/3050, Report by William Yale, Washington DC, 13 July 1917.
35 TNA: PRO FO 371/3061, General Allenby reports, Jerusalem 11 December 1917.
36 TNA: PRO FO 371/3061, Mark Sykes, London 13 November 1917. Sykes, planning the occupation of Jerusalem, also cared about relationships between Italians and French: 'Jerusalem should be kept under martial law as to avoid Franco-Italian complications […]', 'No Austrian or German priest, monk or friar should be allowed to remain in Jerusalem unless it can be shown that a necessary indispensable service is performed by him.'
37 The agreement Ballobar is mentioning is the Sykes-Picot agreement, which sanctioned the partition of the Ottoman Empire between France and Britain. The literature on this is vast, see Fromkin, *A*

Peace to End All Peace, 188-199; D.K. Fieldhouse, *Western Imperialism in the Middle East 1914-1958* (Oxford: Oxford University Press, 2006).

1918

1. Ballobar was anxious to leave Jerusalem for Egypt, but he was informed that, if he was to travel to Egypt, he may not be allowed to return to the city. The measure was adopted to avoid diplomatic interference while the war was still going on. TNA: PRO CAB 27/23, Summary of Information, London 25 January 1918; TNA: PRO FO 371/3396, Wingate, Cairo 28 January 1918.
2. Emanuel Garcia Pardoa was elected Procurator and Spanish member of the Discretory in March 1914. Ballobar disagreed with the election of Pardoa, causing the incident of the seals that Ballobar fixed on the door of the office of the Procurator. Pardoa was considered an Italianophile, which is why Ballobar considered him not worthy of his role. See TNA: PRO FO 371/3389, Francis Rodd to Colonel Deedes, Jerusalem 3 February 1918. Pardoa eventually resigned in the summer of 1919, and Gabino Martin Montoro was elected Procurator. ASV, *Sacra Congregazione degli Affari Ecclesiastici Straordinari Africa-Asia-Oceania*, Pos. 9 Fasc. 2, Diotallevi a Gasparri, Jerusalem 30 August 1919.
3. Ballobar was eventually given permission to travel to Cairo for a period of rest, though he was not replaced by any Spanish official in Jerusalem. TNA: PRO FO 371/3396, Foreign Office to Merry del Val (Spanish Ambassador in London), London 11 March 1918. Details of the journey to Egypt can be found in AMAE, Madrid, H3025-020, Viaje del Consul en Jerusalen 1914-1919.
4. Following the main policy adopted by the British, Cimino, as a religious authority, was not allowed to travel to Jerusalem, to avoid the emergence of Franco-Italian tensions; in fact, Cimino, as General of the Franciscan Order, believed that with the end of the Ottoman regime, French protection over the Catholics of the Holy Land ceased too. See TNA: PRO FO 371/3403, Gaisford to Balfour, Rome 5 April 1918.
5. In the original manuscripts there are several white pages, which Ballobar likely left blank to discuss his journey to Egypt.

6   The Hebrew University eventually opened in 1925. See N. Shepherd, *Ploughing Sand: British Rule in Palestine* (New Brunswick: Rutgers University Press, 2000), 55-56; D. Trimbur, 'L'Université Hébraïque et les Puissances Européennes dans l'Entre-deux Guerres', in *De Balfour à Ben Gurion*, ed. D. Trimbur and R. Aaronsohn (Paris: CNRS Editions, 2008).

7   The Anglican Bishop in Jerusalem, MacInnes, established the Syria and Palestine Relief Fund to provide relief, re-organize hospitals and improve sanitation. For the activities of the Fund, see LPL, MS. 2611-2613.

8   Triana is a neighborhood of the city of Sevilla; it used to house Roma gypsy.

9   Ferdinando Diotallevi was appointed *Custos* at the beginning of 1918, and he reached Jerusalem in February of the same year. His relationships with Ballobar and the French were not at all easy, though it would be a mistake to define him a strong supporter of Italian interests in the Holy Land. See F. Diotallevi, ed. By D. Fabrizio, *Diario di Terrasanta* (Milano: EDF, 2002).

10 Reported in Spanish in the original manuscript.

11 For details on the Zionist Commission, see Mazza, *Jerusalem from the Ottomans to the British*, 148-157.

12 A word in this sentence is not legible, compromising the meaning of it.

13 Girolamo Golubovich, a Franciscan father, published several seminal works on the history of the Custody of the Holy Land.

14 This is the traditional place associated with the miracle of the multiplication of the loaves and the fishes.

15 The *Associazione nazionale per soccorrere i missionary all'estero* was established by Ernesto Schiapparelli, a famous Egyptologist, in 1886. The Association was not linked with the Italian state nor with the Catholic Church but was supported by both. See Fabrizio, *Fascino d'Oriente*, 81-82.

16 On the Greek Orthodox Church see D. Tsimhoni, 'The Greek Orthodox Patriarchate of Jerusalem', *Asian and African Studies 12*, no. 4 (March 1978): 77-121; S. Roussos, 'The Greek Orthodox Patriarchate and Community of Jerusalem: Church, State and Identity', in *The Christian Communities of Jerusalem and the Holy Land*, ed. A. O'Mahony (Cardiff: University of Wales Press, 2003).

17 The issue of the liturgical honors reserved for French diplomats, but also for Italian and Spanish officials in Jerusalem, was a major issue amongst the diplomats of these countries. The question was also linked to the broader issue of the protection of the Catholics in the Holy Land, traditionally in the hands of the French. See Giovannelli, *La Santa Sede e la Palestina*, 31-37; Fabrizio, *Fascino d'Oriente*, 83-87.

18 Ballobar is referring to Norman Bentwich, a British Jew and Zionist who served in the British administration in Palestine as Attorney General. See N. Bentwich, *Palestine* (London: Ernest Benn Limited, 1934); N. Bentwich, *England in Palestine* (London: Kegan Paul, 1932); N. and H. Bentwich, *Mandate Memories 1918-1948* (London: The Hogarth Press, 1965).

19 Ballobar is referring to the Christian-Muslims associations, which were created in the aftermath of the publication of the Balfour Declaration in Palestine to petition the British against Zionist immigration. See Mazza, *Jerusalem from the Ottomans to the British*.

20 Father Marie-Joseph Lagrange, Director of the École Biblique, believed that France should have ruled Palestine and that the internationalization proposed in the Sykes-Picot agreement was not going to work. See B. Montagnes, *The Story of the Father Marie-Joseph Lagrange* (New York: Paulist Press, 2006); S. Minerbi, *L'Italie et la Palestine 1914-1920* (Paris: Presse Universitaires de France, 1970), 165.

21 In Arabic it means 'no worries', 'it doesn't matter'.

1919

1 In the manuscript, a page was left blank. It is possible that Ballobar wanted to write some impressions of his trip to Egypt.

2 This is one of many articles that show the tensions between the French and the British in the Middle East.

BIBLIOGRAPHY

Archival Material:
Archives des Affaires Étrangères, Nantes
Archivo General des Asuntos Exteriores, Madrid
Archivio Segreto Vaticano, Vatican City
Archivio Storico Ministero degli Affari Esteri, Rome
Custodia di Terra Santa, Jerusalem
Lambeth Palace Library, London
National Archives and Record Administration, College Park MD
Patriarcato Latino, Jerusalem
The National Archives: Public Record Office, Kew Gardens

Unpublished Material:
Jacobson, Abigail. 'From Empire to Empire: Jerusalem in the Transition Between Ottoman and British Rule 1912-1920.' PhD thesis, Chicago University, 2006.
Halabi, E.A. 'The Transformation of the Prophet Moses Festival in Jerusalem, 1917-1937: From Local and Islamic to Modern Nationalist Celebration.' PhD thesis, University of Toronto, 2007.

Books:
Abitbol, Michel. *France and the Middle East.* Jerusalem : Hebrew University Magnes Press, 2004.
Aksakal, Mustafa. *The Ottoman Road to War in 1914.* Cambridge: Cambridge University Press, 2008.
Anderson, M.S. *The Eastern Question.* London: Macmillan, 1970.
Arbid, W., Kançal, S., Mizrahi J-D., Saul, S., eds. *Méditerranée, Moyen-Orient: Duex Siècles de Relations Internationales.* Paris: l'Harmattan, 2003.
Barriuso, Garcia. *España en la Historia de Tierra Santa.* Vol. 2, Madrid: Ministerio de Asuntos Exteriores, 1992-94.
Bein, Alex, ed. *Arthur Ruppin: Memoirs, Diaries, Letters.* London: Weidenfeld and Nicolson, 1971.
Ben-Arieh, Yehoshua. *Jerusalem in the 19th Century. The Old City.* New York: St Martin's Press, 1984.
Bentwich, Norman. *England in Palestine.* London: Kegan Paul, 1932.

— *Palestine*. London: Ernest Benn Limited, 1934.
— and Helen. *Mandate Memories 1918-1948*. London: The Hogarth Press, 1965.
Bruce, Anthony. *The Last Crusade*. London: John Murray, 2002.
Brunelli, Roberto. *Storia di Gerusalemme*. Milan: Oscar Mondadori, 1990
Bullock, David L. *Allenby's War*. London: Blandford Press, 1988.
Chatelard, G., Tarawneh, M., eds. *Antonin Jaussen: Sciences Sociales Occidentales et Patrimoine Arabe*. Paris: Cermoc, 1999.
Clark, Victoria. *Holy Fire*. London: Macmillan, 2005.
Cleveland, William L. *A History of the Modern Middle East*. 3rd ed. Boulder: Westview Press, 2004.
Colbi, Saul P. *Christianity in the Holy Land*. Tel Aviv: Am Hassefer, 1969.
Cohen, Amnon. *Palestine in the 18th Century*. Jerusalem: The Magnes Press, 1973.
Conde de Ballobar. Edited by Eduardo Manzano Moreno. *Diario de Jerusalén 1914-1919*, Madrid: Nerea, 1996.
Çiçek, Talha. *War and State Formation in Syria: Cemal Pasha's Governatorate During World War I, 1914-1917*. New York: Routledge, 2014.
De Nogales, Rafael. *Four Years Beneath the Crescent*. London: Charles Scribner's Son, 1926.
Del Zanna, Giorgio. *Roma e l'Oriente*. Milan: Guerini e Associati, 2003.
Diotallevi, F. Edited by Fabrizio Daniela. *Diario di Terra Santa*. Milan: EDF, 2002.
Divine Robinson, Donna. *Politics and Society in Ottoman Palestine: The Arab Struggle for Survival and Power*. Boulder: Lynne Rienner, 1994.
Erickson, Edward J. *Ordered to Die*. Westport: Greenwood Press, 2001.
Fabrizio, Daniela. *Identitá Nazionali e Identitá Religiose*. Rome: Edizioni Studium, 2004.
— *Fascino d'Oriente*. Genoa: Marietti, 2006.
Fieldhouse, D.K. *Western Imperialism in the Middle East 1914-1958*. Oxford: Oxford University Press, 2006.
Flatcher Geniesse, Jane. *American Priestess*. New York: Doubleday, 2008.
Fromkin, David. *A Peace to End All Peace*. New York: Owl Books, 2001.
Gerber, Haim. *Ottoman Rule in Jerusalem 1890-1914*. Berlin: K. Schwarz, 1985.
Giovannelli, Andrea. *La Santa Sede e la Palestina*. Rome: Edizioni Studium, 2000.
Glenk, H., ed. *From Desert Sands to Golden Oranges*. Victoria: Trafford, 2005.
Goffman, D. *The Ottoman Empire and Early Modern Europe*. Cambridge: Cambridge University Press, 2002.
Goldstone, Patricia. *Aaronsohn's Maps*. Orlando: Harcourt, 2007.

Hanioğlu, Şükrü. *A Brief History of the Late Ottoman Empire*. Princeton: Princeton University Press, 2008.
Hughes, Matthew. *Allenby and British Strategy in the Middle East 1917-1919*. London: Frank Cass, 1999.
Hurewitz, J.C. *The Middle East and North Africa in World Politics: a Documentary Record*. New Haven: Yale, 1979.
Ibrahim, Vivian. *The Copts of Egypt: Challenges of Modernisation and Identity*. London: I.B.Tauris, 2010.
Kark, Ruth. *American Consuls in the Holy Land 1832-1914*. Jerusalem: The Magnes Press, 1994.
Kent, Marian, ed. *The Great Powers and the End of the Ottoman Empire*. London: George Allen & Unwin, 1984)
Khoury, P.P. *Urban Notables and Arab Nationalism*. Cambridge: Cambridge University Press, 1983.
Kildani, H. *Modern Christianity in the Middle East*. Bloomington: Author House, 2010.
Lemire, Vincent. *La Soif de Jérusalem: Essay d'Hydrohistoire, 1840-1948*. Paris: Publications de la Sorbonne, 2011.
—*Jérusalem 1900. La Ville Sainte à l'Âge des Possibles*. Paris: Armand Colin, 2013.
MacFie, Alexander L. *The Eastern Question 1774-1923*. London: Longman, 1996.
Mazza, Roberto. *Jerusalem from the Ottomans to the British*. London: I.B.Tauris, 2009.
McCarthy, Justin. *The Ottoman Turks*. London: Longman, 1997.
McKale, Donald. *War by Revolution*. Kent: Kent State University, 1998.
— *Curt Prüfer, German Diplomat from the Kaiser to Hitler*. Kent: Kent State University Press, 1987.
Minerbi, I. Sergio. *L'Italie et la Palestine 1914-1920*. Paris: Presses Universitaires de France, 1970.
Mohs, Polly. *Military Intelligence and the Arab Revolt*. London: Routledge, 2008.
Montagnes, B. *The Atory of the Father Marie-Joseph Lagrange*. New York: Paulist Press, 2006.
Morgenthau, Henry. *Ambassador Morgenthau's Story*. New York: Doubleday, 1918.
Nevakivi, Jukka. *Britain, France and the Arab Middle East*. London: The Athlone Press, 1969.
Nicolle, David. *The Ottoman Army 1914-18*. London: Osprey, 1994.
Noja, Sergio. *Storia dei Popoli dell'Islam*. Milan: A. Mondadori, 1997.
O'Mahony, Anthony, ed. *The Christian Communities of Jerusalem and the Holy Land*. Cardiff: University of Wales Press, 2003.

Özdemir, Hikmet. *The Ottoman Army 1914-1918. Disease and Death on the Battlefield*. Salt Lake City: The University of Utah Press, 2008.
Pacini, Andrea, ed. *Christian Communities in the Arab Middle East*. Oxford: Clarendon Press, 1998.
Pappé, Ilan. *The Rise and Fall of a Palestinian Dynasty: the Husaynis 1700-1948*. Los Angeles: University of California Press, 2010.
Patrick, Andrew. *America's Forgotten Middle East Initiative: the King Crane Commission of 1919*. London: I.B. Tauris, 2014.
Piccirillo, Michele, ed. *La Custodia di Terra Santa e L'Europa*. Rome: Il Veltro Editrice, 1983.
Priestland, J. ed. *Records of Jerusalem*. Oxford: Archive Editions, 1988, Vol. 1.
Roubiçek, Marcel. *Modern Ottoman Troops 1790-1915*. Jerusalem: Franciscan Printing Press, 1978.
Saposnik, Arieh Bruce. *Becoming Hebrew*. New York: Oxford University Press, 2008.
Satia, Priya. *Spies in Arabia*. New York: Oxford University Press, 2008.
Singer, Amy. *Palestinian Peasants and Ottoman Officials*. Cambridge: Cambridge University Press, 1994).
Sheffy, Yigal. *British Military Intelligence in the Palestine Campaign 1914-1918*. London: Frank Cass, 1998.
Shepherd, Naomi. *Ploughing Sand*. New Brunswick: Rutgers University Press, 2000.
Storrs, Ronald. *The Memoirs of Sir Ronald Storrs*. New York: G.P. Putnam's Sons, 1937.
— *Orientations*. London: Nicholson & Watson, 1943.
Tamari, Salim. *Mountain Against the Sea*. Berkeley: University of California Press, 2009.
— *Year of the Locust*. Berkeley: University of California Press, 2011.
— & I. Nassar, *The Storyteller of Jerusalem*.Northampton, MA: Olive Branch Press, 2014.
Trimbur, D., and Aaronsohn, R., eds. *De Balfour à Ben Gourion*. Paris: CRFJ, 2008.
Trumpener, Ulrich. *Germany and the Ottoman Empire*. New York: Caravan Books, 1989.
United States Department of State. *Papers Relating to the Foreign Relation of the United States, 1914. Supplement, The World War*. Washington DC: U.S. Government Printing Office, 1914.
Van den Boogert, Maurits H. *The Capitulations and the Ottoman Legal System*. Leiden: E.J. Brill, 2005.
Vandewalle, D. *A History of Modern Libya*. Cambridge: Cambridge University Press, 2006.

Vester Spafford, Bertha. *Our Jerusalem*. New York: Arno Press, 1977.
Warth, R.D. *Nicholas II: the Life and Reign of Russia's Last Monarch*. Westport: Praeger, 1997.
Yapp, M.E. *The Making of the Near East 1792-1923*. London: Longman, 1987.
Yapp, M.E., and Parry, V.J., eds. *War, technology and Society in the Middle East*. London: Oxford University Press, 1975.
Zürcher, Erik. J. *Turkey. A Modern History*. London: I.B.Tauris, 1993.

Articles and Chapters:

Abbady, I. 'Una Crónica Personal', *Ariel*, no. 17, (1969).
Ahamad, Feroz. 'The Late Ottoman Empire', in *The Great Powers and the End of the Ottoman Empire*.
Angell, James B. 'The Turkish Capitulations', *The American Historical Review* 6, no. 2 (January 1901).
Barcena, E. 'La Spagna in Terra Santa', in *La Custodia di Terra Santa e l'Europa*.
De Groot, Alexander H. 'The Historical Development of the Capitulary Regime in the Ottoman Middle East from the 15th to the 19th Centuries', *Oriente Moderno* 22 (2003).
Delaunay, J-M. 'L'Espagne, Protectrice des Intérèts Français en Palestine au Crepuscole de la Domination Ottomane 1914-1918', in *Méditerranée, Moyen-Orient: Duex Siècles de Relations Internationales*. eds. W. Arbid, S. Kançal, J-D. Mizrahi and S. Saul (Paris: l'Harmattan, 2003).
Gerber, Haim. 'The Ottoman Administration of the Sanjaq of Jerusalem 1890-1908', *Asian and African Studies* 12 (1978).
Hough, William. 'History of the British Consulate in Jerusalem', *Journal of the Middle East Society*, no. 1 (October-December 1946).
Jacobson, Abigail. 'A City Living Through Crisis: Jerusalem During World War I', *British Journal of Middle Eastern Studies* 36, no. 1 (2009).
— 'Negotiating Ottomanism in Times of War: Jerusalem During World War I Through the Eyes of a Local Muslim Resident', *Int. J. Middle East Studies* 40 (2008).
Kark, Ruth. 'The Jerusalem Municipality at the End of Ottoman Rule', *Asian and African Studies* 14 (1981).
Laurens, H. 'Jaussen et les Services de Renseignement Français (1915-1919).' In *Antonin Jaussen : Sciences Sociales Occidentales et Patrimoine Arabe*.
Lemire, V. 'L'Eau, le Consul et l'Ingénieur: Hydropolitique et Concurrences Diplomatique à Jérusalem, 1908-1914', in *France and the Middle East*.
Mancini, I. 'Cenni Storici sulla Custodia di Terra Santa', in *La Custodia di Terra Santa e l'Europa*.

Mazza, R. 'The Spanish Consul in Jerusalem 1914-1920', *Jerusalem Quarterly* 40 (2009).
— 'Dining Out in Times of War: Jerusalem 1914-1918', *Jerusalem Quarterly* 41 (2010).
Pappé, Ilan. 'The Husayni Family Faces New Challenges', *Jerusalem Quarterly File*, Issue 11-12, (2001).
— 'The Rise and Fall of the Husaynis, 1840-1922', *Jerusalem Quarterly File*, Issue 10, (2000).
Roussos, S. 'The Greek Orthodox Patriarchate and Community of Jerusalem: Church, State and Identity', in *The Christian Communities of Jerusalem and the Holy Land*.
Tamari, Salim. 'The Short Live of Private Ihsan: Jerusalem 1915', *Jerusalem Quarterly* 30 (2007).
— 'Jerusalem's Ottoman Modernity: the Times and Lives of Wasif Jawhariyyeh', *Jerusalem Quarterly File* 9 (2000).
Trimbur, Dominique. 'Une Présence Française en Palestine: Notre Dame de France', *Bulletin du CRFJ*, no. 3 (Autumn 1998).
— 'L'Université Hébraïque et le Puissances Européennes dans l'Entre-deux Guerres', in *De Balfour á Ben Gurion*.
Trumpener, Ulrich. 'Germany and the End of the Ottoman Empire', in *The Great Powers and the End of the Ottoman Empire*.
Tsimhoni, Daphne. 'The Greek Orthodox Patriarchate of Jerusalem', *Asian and African Studies 12*, no 4 (March 1978).
Vincent-Barwood, A. 'The Many Hats of William Hale', *Saudi Aramco World 35*, no. 4 (September-October 1984).

GLOSSARY

Albert Antebi: (1873 – 1919) Jewish Ottoman citizen, director of the Alliance Israélite Universelle in Jerusalem, also worked alongside Cemal Paşa on economic and political issues related to Palestine
'aliyah: Jewish immigration to Palestine, and then to Israel after 1948
Alliance Israélite Universelle: Jewish organization established in Paris in 1860, promoted education for Jews outside France
Augusta Victoria: Originally a guest house for pilgrims, was built after the visit of German Emperor Wilhelm II to Palestine in 1898, and named after his wife. It was inaugurated in 1910, and it was the first building in Palestine to have electricity, generated by a diesel engine
A'yan: Notable Muslim and Christian families of Jerusalem and Palestine
Baksheesh: Bribe or tip in exchange of some sort of service
Belediye: Municipality
Beylerbeylik: Territorial subdivision which corresponded to a greater province
Capitulations: Treaties or grants which established a system of privileges and reductions in custom duties, as well as extraterritorial jurisdiction, favorable to Europeans
Celesyria: Ancient name given to the region of Southern Syria and Lebanon
(Ahmet) Cemal Paşa: (1872 – 1922) Member of the Young Turks and part of the triumvirate that ruled the Ottoman Empire during the war. In this period Cemal was in charge of the Fourth Army Corps, Ministry of the Navy and Governor of Syria. He crushed several Arab rebellions, and he was then known as *al-Saffah* (the blood shedder). He was killed by an Armenian nationalist in Tbilisi
CUP: Committee of Union and Progress
Custody of the Holy Land: Religious institution founded by the Franciscan order in the thirteenth century with the purpose of caring for Catholics in the Holy Land
Custos: Fr. Superior of the Franciscans in the Holy Land; he is resident in Jerusalem and by internal constitution, must be an Italian citizen
Curt Prüfer: (1881 – 1959) German *dragoman* and specialist in Arab culture and language, he worked as a German agent in Palestine and Syria during the war

GLOSSARY

David Yellin: (1864 – 1941) Teacher and activist, he founded a teacher association. He was elected in the Ottoman Parliament in 1913 and was an open Zionist: Due to his political activity he was exiled to Damascus during the First World War

Dragoman: Official translator and guide

École Biblique: Founded in 1890 by Father Lagrange in Jerusalem, the School is a French institution specializing in biblical archaeology and exegesis

Enver Paşa: (1881 – 1922) Leader of the Young Turks and then of the CUP: with Cemal and Talat Paşas, effectively ruled the Ottoman Empire during the war. As Minister of War, he pushed the empire towards an alliance with Germany and is considered one of the main people responsible for the Armenian genocide perpetrated during the war

Erich von Falkenhayn: (1861 – 1922) Chief of the General Staff of the German Army during the war, after the failure at Verdun was sent to take charge of the Palestine front and face the British Expeditionary Force commanded by Allenby

Firman/Irade: Decree/order issued by the Sultan in Istanbul and valid throughout the Ottoman Empire

Francesco D'Agostino: Colonel of the Bersaglieri in charge of the Italian detachment with the British Egyptian Expeditionary Force under the command of General Allenby

Friedrich Kress von Kressenstein: (1870 – 1948) German colonel who fought on the Palestine front with the mission of taking the Suez Canal

Guido Meli Lupo di Soragna: (1857-1931) Italian diplomat sent to Cairo in 1919 and later to Jerusalem to assess the local political situation

Halukka: Collection and distribution of funds for the Jewish residents of Palestine and Jerusalem

Hasan Bey Basri: Ottoman governor of Jaffa from 1914 to 1916

Jacob Thon: Head of the Zionist Office in Jerusalem

Karakol: Police station

Kavas (cavas): Messenger of an embassy or consulate, but also guard attending a dignitary

Kaymakam: Head official of a district

Kaza: Administrative unit, a subdivision of the *sancak*

Khedive: Equivalent of viceroy, this title was given to the dynasty established by Muhammad Ali Paşa early in 1805, by the Ottomans as recognition of their rule over Egypt and Sudan in 1867

Konak: Government house

Luigi Barlassina: (1872 – 1947) Ordained as priest in 1894, was appointed Latin Patriarch of Jerusalem in 1920

Manzil: Ballobar referred to the *Manzil* as the office in charge of the food rationing, which may also be defined as a logistics department; it was located in Notre Dame de France. It was also the seat of the Commissariat of the 4th Army

Maronite Church: Eastern Catholic Church in communion with the Holy See. Syriac is the liturgical language of the Church, its followers are mainly located in Lebanon

Max Nordau: (1849 – 1923) Writer and co-founder of the World Zionist Organization

Meclis: Council

Meclis-i Idare: Administrative Council

Meclis-i Umumi: General Council, usually of a province

Millet: State recognised community, defined according to religion

Miri: State lands, owned by the Sultan and available on the market

Moses Haim Montefiore: (1784 – 1885) Jewish philanthropist, chair of the Board of Deputies of British Jews, helped Jews all around the world and especially in Palestine

Mufti: Islamic scholar with the power of interpreting and expounding Islamic law

Muhdir (Müdür): Director

Mülk: Private property; privately owned land

Mutasarrıf: Governor of the *sancak* or *mutasarrıflık*; in Jerusalem he was appointed directly by Istanbul

Mutasarrıflık: Administrative unit corresponding to a province; synonymous with *sancak*

Nüfus: Population register

Paşa: Highest official Ottoman military and civil title

Pierre Durieux: French representative in Jerusalem after the war

Propaganda Fide (Sacra Congregatio de): The Sacred Congregation for the Propagation of the Faith was established in 1622 with the purpose of spreading Catholicism and to regulate Catholic life in non-Catholic countries

Rafael de Nogales: (1879 – 1936) Venezuelan mercenary at the beginning of the First World War, joined the Ottoman Army; after witnessing the massacre of the Armenians he was transferred to the Palestinian front

Reginald Wingate: (1861 – 1953) Wingate was appointed High Commissioner in Egypt in 1917, position held until 1919

Sancak: Administrative unit, province

Status Quo: Set of rules and customs ruling the disputes over the control and management of the holy places in Jerusalem and the Holy Land

Tanzimat: Name given to a set of reforms carried out in the Ottoman Empire in the nineteenth century

Tapu: Land and property registry
Tcherkes: Term that defines the people of Circassian originally living in Palestine
Vali: Governor of the *vilayet*
Vilayet: Administrative unit, a larger province which included a number of *sancaks*
Waqf: Charitable endowment; lands not available on the market
Werko: Tax imposed on land based on the value of the holdings
Zaki Bey: Military commander of Jerusalem and at the beginning of the war also civil governor

INDEX

A

Alliance Israélite Universelle 90, 104, 163, 179, 181
Allenby, General Edmund 11, 188, 189, 190, 196, 197, 199, 211, 232, 236, 237, 245
American (consul, consulate) 8, 15, 19, 28, 40, 45, 46, 62, 65, 70, 133, 151, 152, 154, 155, 156, 165, 166, 176, 179
American Colony 23, 66, 67
Antebi, Albert 62, 65, 111, 132
Armenian (s) 14, 20, 36, 53, 55, 80, 81, 95, 102, 103, 110, 114, 128, 131, 171, 188, 194, 200, 207, 211, 224, 229
Arroyo, Julian del 33, 34, 37, 44, 46, 53, 76, 78, 97, 114, 134, 156, 162, 167
Austria (Austrian) 2, 4, 9, 12, 14, 15, 20, 29, 35, 42, 44, 45, 46, 49, 56, 64, 65, 66, 69, 71, 74, 77, 83, 84, 85, 86, 87, 90, 91, 94, 96, 98, 99, 100, 101, 103, 104, 108, 109, 110, 113, 114, 115, 118, 122, 125, 126, 130, 135, 137, 146, 147, 148, 160, 168, 169, 170, 171, 172, 178, 179, 183, 184, 191, 199, 200, 211, 215, 237

B

British (administration, army, consul, consulate, government) 1, 3, 5, 7, 8, 9, 10, 11, 12, 13, 15, 19, 20, 22, 23, 28, 31, 35, 36, 38, 39, 48, 49, 51, 52, 53, 59, 61, 63, 66, 70, 72, 74, 76, 77, 79, 82, 83, 87, 92, 95, 96, 98, 100, 104, 106, 107, 108, 111, 113, 117, 118, 119, 122, 123, 125, 126, 127, 129, 130, 131, 132, 134, 135, 140, 142, 143, 144, 146, 147, 148, 149, 151 152, 153, 154, 156, 158, 159, 161, 163, 164, 167, 168, 169, 170, 171, 176, 177, 178, 179, 182, 183, 184, 185, 186, 187, 188, 189, 190, 191, 194, 195, 196, 197, 198, 199, 200, 201, 202, 203, 204, 205, 206, 207, 208, 209, 210, 211, 212, 213, 214, 216, 218, 220, 221, 222, 223, 224, 225, 226, 227, 228, 229, 230, 232, 233, 235, 236, 237, 238, 239, 240, 241, 243, 244
Brode, Johann 78, 97, 127, 148, 150, 155, 156, 162, 168, 169, 170

C

Cairo 53, 60, 98, 100, 191, 194, 199, 212
Camassei, Filippo 18, 28, 31, 37, 43, 48, 95, 113, 172, 173, 174, 217, 228

Capitulations 3, 4, 7, 8, 9, 21, 22, 27, 30, 54, 73, 90, 133
Castellani, Eutimio 14, 79, 83, 113, 143, 176
Catholic Church (institutions) 22, 47, 80, 124, 171, 172, 174, 180, 200, 207, 228, 230
Catholic (s) 12, 91, 112, 116, 175, 238, 239
Cemal Paşa 6, 9, 10, 20, 38, 44, 45, 46, 50, 51, 52, 55, 56, 62, 63, 64, 65, 66, 67, 68, 69, 70, 72, 75, 76, 77, 78, 79, 80, 82, 83, 86, 90, 91, 93, 95, 96, 97, 101, 102, 103, 105, 106, 108, 109, 110, 112, 113, 115, 125, 132, 136, 139, 142, 143, 146, 147, 148, 149, 151, 152, 153, 154, 155, 156, 157, 158, 159, 161, 162, 164, 165, 166, 171, 172, 179, 182, 189, 191, 222, 223
Church of the Holy Sepulcher 16, 57, 80, 91, 95, 113, 114, 116, 149, 150, 154, 157, 174, 178, 189, 209, 228
Christian (s) 3, 5, 7, 8, 13, 21, 24, 27, 29, 31, 48, 50, 51, 56, 57, 64, 80, 91, 92, 103, 105, 133, 148, 151, 158, 164, 165, 174, 175, 179, 182, 186, 200, 202, 203, 207, 210, 219, 220, 228, 229, 230, 235, 238, 239, 241, 242
Cimino, Serafino 18, 31, 37, 40, 45, 48, 198
Constantinople 27, 28, 30, 31, 33, 34, 35, 36, 37, 39, 43, 46, 51, 57, 65, 69, 70, 71, 72, 76, 82, 87, 91, 98, 110, 112, 114, 115, 120, 129, 133, 135, 138, 156, 157, 165, 167, 168, 170, 173, 178, 180, 188, 191, 240
Coptic Church 36, 171
Custody of the Holy Land 1, 12, 13, 14, 15, 16, 17, 18, 19, 28, 40, 43, 46, 54, 64, 79, 83, 85, 90, 113, 157, 175, 190
Custos 13, 14, 16, 17, 18, 30, 31, 37, 40, 45, 48, 109, 207

D

Damascus 5, 10, 12, 32, 33, 37, 38, 44, 48, 51, 54, 60, 66, 68, 69, 82, 85, 93, 94, 96, 99, 105, 108, 112, 113, 127, 133, 143, 145, 152, 154, 156, 166, 168, 170, 180, 181, 187, 217, 219, 220, 221, 222, 226, 240
De Marquet 90, 98, 99, 104, 135
De Nogales, Rafael 79, 80, 81, 82, 91, 119, 134, 159, 161, 162
Djemal Pasha: see Cemal
Durieux, Pierre 229, 230, 244

E

École Biblique 38, 66
Egypt 2, 3, 5, 10, 11, 13, 16, 22, 29, 31, 35, 36, 37, 40, 43, 44, 47, 48, 49, 50, 53, 55, 58, 63, 64, 70, 76, 77, 82, 104, 108, 118, 130, 155, 188, 192, 194, 195, 197, 199, 201, 202, 205, 208, 209, 210, 227, 232, 233, 238, 239, 240, 241
English: see British
Enver Paşa 9, 31, 65, 77, 80, 90, 91, 111, 132, 142, 144, 148, 164, 171, 172, 188, 218
Europe (Europeans) 2, 3, 4, 5, 6, 7, 8, 9, 14, 18, 20, 27, 28, 30, 31, 33, 43, 53, 58, 59, 66, 75,

80, 83, 91, 96, 99, 103, 105, 121, 142, 162, 192, 208, 221, 223, 224, 241

F

Firman 108, 172

France 4, 9, 10, 19, 27, 28, 29, 32, 33, 56, 77, 80, 82, 83, 93, 94, 107, 163, 190, 1491, 194, 213, 221, 223, 224, 228, 230, 237, 238, 239, 240, 242, 244, 245

Franciscan (s) 13, 14, 15, 16, 17, 18, 19, 28, 30, 31, 32, 37, 38, 53, 54, 56, 59, 78, 80, 96, 102, 112, 114, 116, 128, 129, 134, 137, 149, 170, 175, 179, 182, 189, 198, 207, 216, 239, 243

French (army, consul, consulate, institutions) 2, 3, 4, 5, 6, 9, 11, 13, 15, 22, 27, 28, 31, 32, 34, 35, 36, 37, 38, 39, 42, 43, 49, 51, 53, 64, 67, 68, 69, 70, 73, 74, 75, 76, 77, 79, 82, 83, 85, 86, 87, 90, 93, 94, 99, 103, 107, 109, 113, 116, 125, 129, 136, 137, 138, 153, 161, 162, 187, 188, 190, 192, 197, 199, 205, 212, 213, 215, 221, 223, 224, 225, 227, 229, 232, 236, 237, 238, 240, 244

G

German (army, troops, consul) 9, 10, 11, 12, 13, 20, 33, 35, 36, 42, 48, 57, 58, 59, 62, 64, 65, 66, 68, 69, 70, 74, 75, 76, 78, 79, 80, 82, 83, 84, 85, 86, 87, 89, 90, 91, 92, 93, 94, 97, 98, 99, 100, 101, 105, 108, 109, 112, 113, 115, 117, 118, 119, 123, 126, 127, 130, 131, 135, 137, 138, 142, 144, 146, 147, 148, 150, 155, 156, 157, 160, 161, 162, 164, 167, 168, 169, 170, 173, 176, 177, 178, 179, 181, 182, 183, 185, 186, 187, 188, 191, 192, 194, 195, 199, 200, 206, 210, 211, 213, 216, 218, 224, 236, 237, 241

Germany 9, 12, 20, 29, 45, 69, 83, 103, 11, 132, 133, 136, 150, 162, 169, 170, 203, 213, 218

Glazebrook, Otis 8, 12, 19, 21, 28, 39, 41, 50, 63, 65, 70, 72, 97, 133, 153, 154, 155, 156, 233, 235

Greece 36, 56, 62, 76, 77, 87, 102, 103, 109, 110, 158, 160, 165, 210, 221

Greek (s) 3, 34, 35, 36, 39, 46, 47, 48, 52, 56, 57, 58, 61, 62, 63, 64, 65, 72, 76, 77, 80, 87, 88, 95, 96, 103, 109, 110, 119, 126, 128, 131, 136, 147, 149, 154, 157, 158, 161, 163, 171, 194, 202, 209, 221, 234, 235

Greek Orthodox Church 2, 13, 14, 23, 57, 94, 126, 171, 209, 210, 221, 235

H

Hasan Bey Basri 29, 41, 47, 48, 72, 75, 78, 83, 84, 85, 88, 93, 97, 140

Holy Land 1, 5, 7, 14, 16, 17, 19, 38, 40, 53, 58, 89, 175, 192, 207, 225, 243

Holy Places 2, 3, 5, 6, 11, 14, 16, 17, 94, 174, 207, 228

Holy See: see Vatican

Husayni (family) 8, 129, 185

I

Istanbul 6, 7, 11, 15, 20, 179
Italy 15, 18, 19, 28, 36, 51, 62, 64, 66, 70, 77, 86, 172, 191, 192, 195, 228, 229, 230
Italian (army, consul, consulate, government, institutions) 13, 15, 17, 18, 19, 27, 29, 30, 35, 45, 46, 50, 60, 62, 65, 70, 75, 76, 83, 97, 153, 165, 172, 189, 190, 191, 194, 197, 199, 202, 203, 210, 228, 229, 233, 235
Izzet Bey 122, 125, 134, 162, 165, 169, 171, 185, 201

J

Jaffa 7, 15, 19, 20, 21, 28, 29, 31, 32, 33, 34, 35, 36, 37, 38, 39, 40, 41, 42, 45, 47, 48, 49, 56, 57, 58, 60, 67, 68, 69, 70, 71, 72, 73, 74, 75, 76, 78, 81, 82, 83, 84, 85, 86, 88, 89, 90, 93, 95, 96, 97, 98, 107, 108, 109, 111, 112, 113, 115, 116, 120, 121, 124, 134, 135, 136, 137, 138, 140, 142, 145, 146, 147, 148, 150, 151, 153, 154, 167, 170, 178, 1789, 182, 186, 191, 196, 197, 201, 204, 205, 206, 207, 211, 213, 220, 224, 226, 227, 228, 229, 230, 234, 235, 236, 238, 239, 242, 243
Jews 8, 19, 20, 21, 32, 42, 43, 45, 51, 58, 62, 65, 71, 72, 75, 114, 117, 128, 137, 140, 141, 145, 148, 151, 158, 162, 163, 164, 168, 180, 181, 182, 184, 186, 199, 200, 202, 205, 210, 219, 220, 225, 227, 228, 229, 230, 233, 234, 235, 241, 242

K

Kraus 29, 65, 71, 87, 97, 98, 105, 109, 113, 114, 150, 158, 183, 185
Kressenstein, Kress von 10, 78, 79, 82, 86, 88, 89, 90, 92, 99, 100, 106, 107, 108, 115, 116, 118, 126, 128, 129, 135, 146, 147, 154, 162
Kuebler 32, 33, 34, 37, 41, 47, 48, 67, 68, 75, 82, 89, 107, 112, 136, 137, 138, 147, 150, 151, 163, 165, 166, 183, 185, 191, 195, 197, 204

L

Latin (s) 64, 116
Latin Patriarch 13, 17, 28, 31, 36, 40, 95, 228
Latin Patriarchate 17, 45, 138

M

Madrid 2, 13, 17, 19, 33, 60, 116, 124, 142, 167, 230
Manzil 24, 144, 169
Marquis of Lema 30, 43, 45, 46, 60, 79
Meli Lupo di Soragna, Guido 230, 233, 235
Mesopotamia 10, 72, 92, 110, 134
Mount of Olives 49, 52, 61, 62, 76, 90, 105, 157, 158, 159, 164, 169, 170, 173, 177, 195, 202, 205, 227
Mount Zion 48, 70, 91, 102
Muslims 16, 24, 29, 30, 46, 48, 64, 66, 78, 80, 83, 86, 95, 102, 106, 112, 129, 130, 150, 151, 163, 164, 202, 220, 228, 229, 230, 235, 241

N

Nebi Musa 56, 93, 235
Notre Dame de France 29, 31, 37, 38, 50, 56, 62, 86, 96, 190, 234

O

Obra Pia 13, 16, 17
Ottoman Administration (army, troops, government) 1, 2, 3, 4, 5, 6, 7, 8, 9, 10, 11, 14, 15, 17, 19, 20, 21, 22, 24, 27, 30, 33, 34, 35, 36, 37, 42, 56, 62, 71, 75, 78, 87, 93, 96, 103, 105, 110, 124, 128, 132, 136, 139, 142, 148, 164, 167, 171, 172, 174, 175, 180, 188, 202, 204, 210

P

Palestine 1, 2, 3, 4, 5, 6, 7, 10, 11, 12, 13, 14, 19, 20, 21, 22, 24, 28, 40, 67, 71, 75, 80, 94, 104, 112, 115, 121, 126, 128, 155, 158, 160, 162, 169, 181, 192, 198, 200, 204, 212, 214, 224, 236, 239, 240, 241, 243, 244
Pilgrim (s) 6, 7, 14, 22, 56, 57, 120, 189, 235
Police 6, 7, 15, 22, 27, 35, 38, 47, 50, 51, 54, 57, 59, 65, 72, 73, 75, 76, 77, 78, 81, 104, 113, 114, 133, 137, 139, 144, 166, 172, 173, 176, 181, 183, 184, 185, 186, 187, 188, 189, 190, 191, 192, 194, 200, 209, 214, 217, 244
Post Offices 7, 8, 21
Protestant (s) 36, 38, 84, 92, 94, 112, 133, 137, 192, 200

Prüfer, Curt 75, 85, 86, 91, 98, 107, 110, 132, 135

R

Raphaël 34, 36, 48, 56, 62, 63, 64, 65, 66, 70, 71, 76, 85, 87, 97, 102, 110, 128, 157, 160, 165, 188
Rauf, Lorenzo 29, 32, 35, 39, 46, 48, 53, 54, 110, 133, 134, 138, 139, 166, 177, 178, 182, 192, 217
Roshan Bey 48, 74, 75, 82, 89, 105, 110, 116
Russia (Russian) 2, 3, 8, 9, 10, 11, 27, 28, 29, 31, 35, 36, 39, 43, 49, 52, 63, 72, 86, 91, 92, 117, 143, 153, 154, 156, 159, 163, 164, 168, 180, 188, 233, 242

S

Senni, Carlo 18, 27, 28, 35, 36, 51, 64, 69, 70
Spain 12, 13, 14, 16, 17, 18, 19, 20, 28, 30, 37, 58, 73, 79, 83, 90, 94, 98, 99, 102, 105, 109, 114, 124, 132, 133, 134, 137, 138, 142, 152, 153, 157, 158, 162 163, 165, 167, 170, 180, 185, 196, 197, 203, 206, 207, 210, 221, 229, 230, 233, 237, 242, 243, 245
Spanish (ambassador, clerics, consul, consulate, embassy, government, institutions) 1, 2, 12, 13, 14, 15, 16, 17, 18, 19, 20, 21, 22, 23, 27, 30, 31, 32, 33, 34, 36, 37, 40, 41, 43, 45, 47, 48, 53, 59, 60, 73, 101, 102, 116, 124, 127, 132, 139, 142, 146, 147, 148, 153, 155,

157, 158, 166, 167, 170, 176, 178, 180, 207, 242, 244
Status Quo (Holy Places) 14, 17, 40, 235
Storrs, Ronald xv, 194, 195, 202, 206, 209, 210, 217, 230, 232, 233, 235, 244
Syria 3, 5, 6, 10, 11, 21, 22, 71, 75, 77, 93, 94, 103, 126, 162, 200, 224, 240, 241

T

Tel Aviv 68, 164
Thon, Jacob 169, 179, 180, 181, 191
Trommer, Karl 56, 57, 62
Turk (s) 64, 92, 122, 162, 215, 223
Turkey 27, 31, 32, 36, 37, 39, 49, 51, 56, 57, 58, 59, 63, 64, 65, 69, 70, 72, 75, 77, 79, 85, 90, 91, 103, 110, 111, 124, 127, 132, 133, 151, 153, 158, 162, 165, 167, 180, 198, 210, 214, 218
Turkish (administration, army, government, institutions, paper money, prisoners) 6, 8, 29, 30, 35, 36, 38, 43, 44, 49, 51, 52, 53, 55, 58, 62, 63, 66, 70, 73, 74, 75, 76, 77, 78, 79, 80, 85, 86, 88, 89, 90, 93, 95, 96, 97, 99, 100, 101, 105, 106, 108, 109, 114, 115, 116, 117, 118, 119, 120, 122, 125, 126, 127, 130, 131, 133, 134, 139, 142, 144, 146, 151, 153, 156, 160, 164, 165, 169, 170, 173, 177, 178, 179, 181, 182, 183, 186, 188, 195, 197, 200, 201, 202, 203, 204, 209, 210, 211, 212, 214, 216, 218, 221, 222, 227

U

United States of America 13, 19, 28, 41, 109, 117, 136, 141, 153, 156, 196

V

Vatican 13, 14, 15, 17, 18, 19, 94, 204, 207
Vester Spafford, Bertha 23, 161
Von Falkenhayn, Erich 11, 157, 158, 167, 169, 171, 173, 175, 178, 180

W

Weizmann, Chaim 199

Y

Yellin, David 143, 220, 222, 223
Young Turks 6, 8, 9, 57

Z

Zaki Bey 22, 28, 31, 33, 35, 42, 66, 71, 78, 83, 92, 103, 105, 115, 131, 132, 155, 157, 190, 191, 192
Zionism (Zionist) 1, 5, 19, 111, 139, 145, 148, 179, 185, 199, 205, 213, 218, 228, 229, 233, 234, 235, 241, 242

1: Ballobar in his official uniform.

2: Young Ballobar.

3: Mayor of Jerusalem and Turkish Official, 1914-1917.

4: Enver Paşa visiting the Dome of the Rock, 1916.

5: Ballobar in the Gethsemane, 1913.

6: Mosque of Omar, northeast side.

7: Ceremony of the Holy Fire at the Holy Sepulchre.

8: Ballobar at the site of the Good Samaritan.

9: Ballobar amongst local clergy.

10: Ballobar and Casares.

11: Jamal Pasha (Kutchuk) with Zaki Bey, former Military Governor of Jerusalem, St George's Cathedral 1917.

12: Ballobar with Durieux, French Military Officer.

13: Franciscan monk reading the proclamation in Italian, 11 December 1917.

www.ingramcontent.com/pod-product-compliance
Ingram Content Group UK Ltd.
Pitfield, Milton Keynes, MK11 3LW, UK
UKHW022233250326
469359UK00007B/102